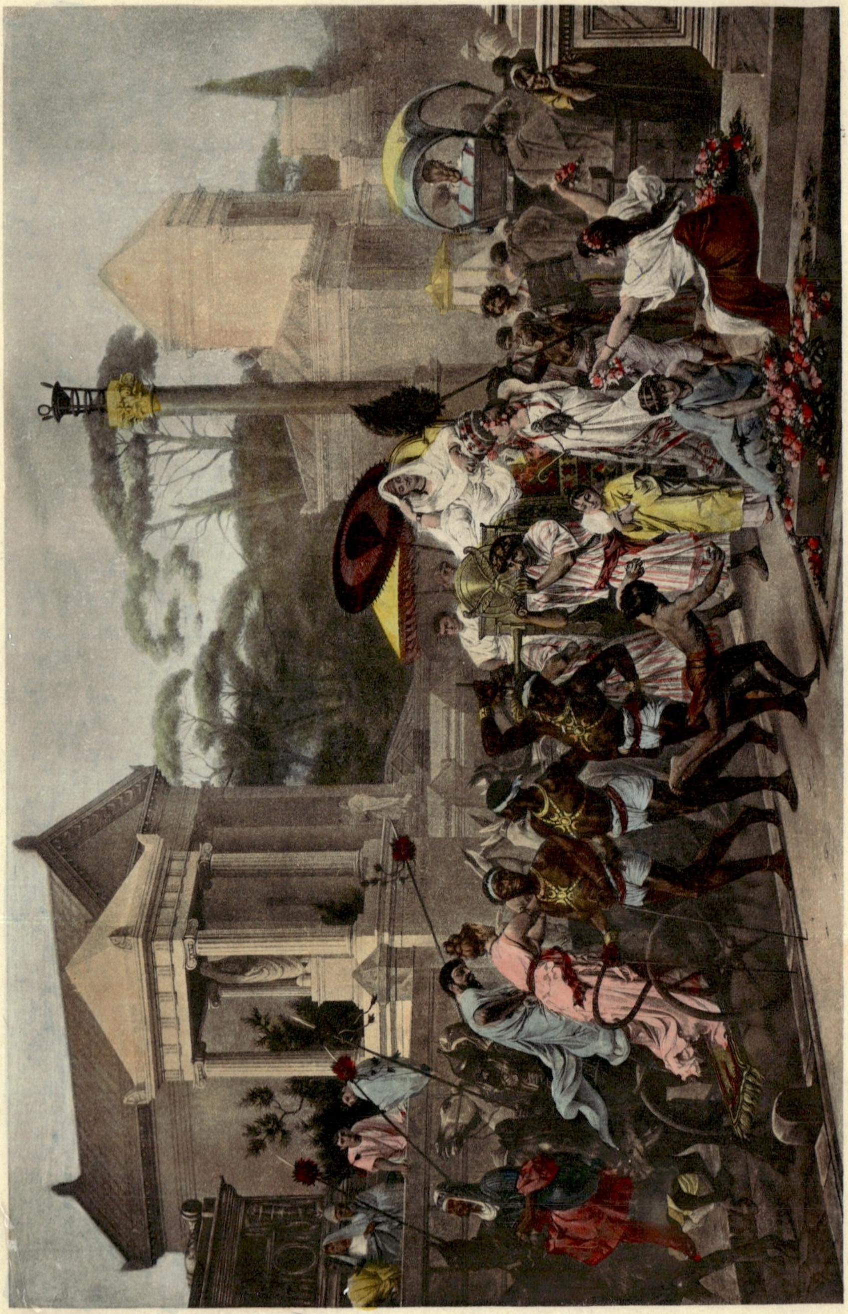

Appian Way.
In the time of the Emperor Augustus.
Hand-painted Photogravure from the Painting by E. Boulanger.
[Vol. IX.]

Appian Way.
In the time of the Emperor Augustus.
Hand-painted Photogravure from the Painting by E. Boulanger
Vol. IX.

MEMBER'S EDITION DE LUXE.

THE
BIBLIOPHILE·LIBRARY·OF LITERATURE·ART·AND RARE·MANUSCRIPTS

History, Biography, Science, Poetry, Drama, Travel, Adventure, Fiction, and Rare and Little-known Literature from the Archives of the Great Libraries of the World.

A Record of the Great Things that have been Said and Thought and Done from the Beginning of History.

WITH PRONOUNCING AND BIOGRAPHICAL DICTIONARY AND EXPLANATORY NOTES.

INTRODUCTIONS BY ANDREW LANG AND DONALD G. MITCHELL (IK MARVEL)

COMPILED AND ARRANGED BY NATHAN HASKELL DOLE, FORREST MORGAN, AND CAROLINE TICKNOR

Thirty · · · Volume 9 · · · Volumes

PUBLISHED BY THE INTERNATIONAL BIBLIOPHILE SOCIETY, NEW YORK-LONDON.

Member's Edition de Luxe.

Limited to 1000 Copies

By The International Bibliophile Society
Copyright, 1904.

This Member's Edition de Luxe of The Bibliophile Library of Literature, Art and Rare Manuscripts is limited to 1000 sets, of which this is copy No._____

THE BIBLIOPHILE LIBRARY

OF

LITERATURE, ART, AND RARE MANUSCRIPTS.

TABLE OF CONTENTS.

VOLUME IX.

		PAGE
The Plague of London	Daniel Defoe	2803
The Masque of the Red Death	Edgar A. Poe	2813
The Progress of the Pestilence	W. Harrison Ainsworth	2819
Valediction, Forbidding Mourning (poem)	John Donne	2830
The Undertaking (poem)	John Donne	2830
Scenes and Portraits from Clarendon's "History of the Rebellion and Civil Wars in England"	Clarendon	2831
An Horatian Ode	Andrew Marvell	2850
Oliver Cromwell	Thomas Carlyle	2853
L'Allegro (poem)	John Milton	2874
Il Penseroso (poem)	John Milton	2878
Sonnet to Cyriac Skinner	John Milton	2882
Religio Medici	Sir Thomas Browne	2883
A Happy Life (poem)	Sir Henry Wotton	2889
Walton's Angler	Izaak Walton	2890
Prithee, Send me back my Heart (poem)	Sir John Suckling	2905
Red and White Roses (sonnet)	Thomas Carew	2906
Angling	Leigh Hunt	2906
The Two Brothers	Sir John Vanbrugh	2910
Origin and Development of the Bank of England	Walter Bagehot	2918
Athos, Porthos, and Aramis	Alexandre Dumas	2921
The Fate of Mordaunt	Alexandre Dumas	2944
The Man in the Iron Mask	Alexandre Dumas	2964
Scenes from drama of "Athaliah"	Jean Baptiste Racine	2989
Sigismund (drama)	Pedro Calderon de La Barca	2998
Justina's Temptation (poem)	Pedro Calderon de La Barca	3003
The Mighty Magician (drama)	Pedro Calderon de La Barca	3005
The Times of Gustavus Adolphus	Zachris Topelius	3024
From the Kalevala (epic poem)	Tr. by John M. Crawford	3051
The Cid	Pierre Corneille	3065
The Story of Ali-Bey, the Persian	LaMothe-Fénelon	3074
Sonnets	Lope de Vega	3078

TABLE OF CONTENTS.

		PAGE
Funeral Oration on Henrietta, Duchess of Orleans	*Jacques Bénigne Bossuet*	3079
The Affected Ladies	*Molière*	3085
Fables	*Jean de La Fontaine*	3106
Madame de Sévigné's Letters	*Marquise de Sévigné*	3109
Memoirs of the Duke of Saint-Simon on the Reign of Louis XIV. and the Regency	*Duc de Saint-Simon*	3120
Boileau's Art of Poetry (poem)	*Nicholas Boileau-Despréaux*	3144

LIST OF ILLUSTRATIONS.

VOLUME IX.

The Appian Way in the Time of Augustus	*Hand-painted Photogravure of a Painting by E. Boulanger*	FRONTISPIECE
		PAGE
Daniel Defoe	*From an Engraving*	2804
Burying Dead Bodies During the Plague in London in 1665	*From a Rare Old Print*	2808
The Thames Embankment, London	*From a Photograph*	2812
Choir and South Aisle, St. Paul's Cathedral, London	*From a Photograph*	2828
MS. of Charles I.	*Fac-simile of Instructions to Sir E. Herbert, Attorney General, dated 1641*	2840
Cromwell at Marston Moor	*From a Painting by Ernest Crofts, A. R. A.*	2852
Milton Dictating to His Daughter	*From a Painting by M. Munkacsy*	2874
MS. of John Milton	*Fac-simile of Family Memoranda on Fly-leaf of Bible, dated 1646–1652*	2878
Izaak Walton and His Pupil	*From a Painting by Sadler W. Dendy*	2890
Leigh Hunt	*From a Portrait*	2906
Charles II.	*From a Portrait*	2918
Cardinal Richelieu	*From a Tripartite Engraving*	2932
The Three Musketeers	*From a Painting*	2940
The Man in the Iron Mask	*From an Engraving*	2964
Jean Baptiste Racine	*From a Portrait*	2988
Escort of the Corpse of Gustavus Adolphus	*From a Painting by Werner Schuch*	3024
Pierre Corneille	*From a Portrait*	3065
Archbishop Fénelon	*From a Portrait*	3074
Molière and His Troop of Players	*From a Painting by G. Melingen*	3085
The Peacock Complaining to Juno	*From an Etching*	3106

THE BIBLIOPHILE LIBRARY

OF

LITERATURE, ART, AND RARE MANUSCRIPTS.

THE PLAGUE OF LONDON.

By DANIEL DEFOE.

[DANIEL DEFOE, English journalist and man of letters, was born in London, about 1660; died in 1731. He wrote every sort of imaginable work in prose and verse, history, biography, and fiction, political and religious controversy, social and political pamphlets, satires, and other poems. His most famous work is "Robinson Crusoe" (1719); among his other novels are: "The Apparition of Mrs. Veal" (1706), "Memoirs of a Cavalier" (1720), "Captain Singleton" (1720), "Moll Flanders," "Cartouche," and "Colonial Jacque" (1722), "John Sheppard" (1724); and the "Journal of the Plague Year" (1722) and "Account of Jonathan Wild" (1725) are really such. Among his pamphlets are, "The Shortest Way with Dissenters" (1702) and "Political History of the Devil" (1726).]

I DESIRE to make a few Observations regarding the Great Plague of London, which may be of use hereafter to those into whose Hands this may come, if they should ever see the like dreadful Visitation. (1.) The Infection generally came into the Houses of the Citizens, by the Means of their Servants, who they were obliged to send up and down the Streets for Necessaries, that is to say, for Food, or Physick, to Bake-houses, Brew-houses, Shops, Markets, and the like, it was impossible, but that they should one way or other meet with distempered people, who conveyed the fatal Breath into them, and they brought it Home to the Families, to which they belonged. (2.) It was a great Mistake, that such a great City as this had but one Pest-House; for had there been, instead of one Pest-House, viz., beyond Bunhil-Fields, where, at most, they could receive, perhaps, 200 or 300 People; I say, had there instead of that one been several Pest-houses, every one able to contain a thousand People without lying two in a Bed, or two Beds in a Room; and had every Master of a Family, as soon as any Servant especially, had been taken sick in his House, been obliged to send them to the next Pest-House, if they were willing, as many were, and had the Examiners done the like among the poor People, when any had been stricken with the Infection; I say, had this been done where the People were willing (not otherwise), and the Houses not been shut, I am perswaded, and was all the While of that Opinion, that not so many, by several Thousands, had died; for it was observed, and I could give several Instances within the Compass of my own Knowledge, where a Servant had been taken sick, and the Family had either Time to send them out, or retire from the House, and leave the sick Person, as I have said above, they had all been preserved; whereas, when upon one, or more, sick'ning in a Family, the House has been shut up, the whole Family have perished, and the Bearers been oblig'd to go in to fetch out the Dead Bodies, none being able to bring them to the Door; and at last none left to do it.

(2.) This put it out of Question to me, that the Calamity was spread by Infection, that is to say, by some certain Steams, or Fumes, which the Physicians call Effluvia, by the Breath, or by the Sweat, or by the Stench of the Sores of the sick Persons, or some other way, perhaps, beyond even the Reach of the Physicians themselves, which Effluvia affected the Sound, who come within certain Distances of the Sick, immediately penetrating the Vital Parts of the said sound Persons, putting their Blood into an immediate ferment, and agitating their Spirits to that Degree which it was found they were agitated; and so those newly infected Persons communicated it in the same Manner to others; and this I shall give some Instances of, that cannot but convince those who seriously consider it; and I cannot but with some Wonder, find some People, now the Contagion is over, talk of its being an immediate Stroke from Heaven, without the Agency of Means, having Commission to strike this and that particular Person, and none other; which I look upon with Contempt, as the Effect of manifest Ignorance and Enthusiasm; likewise the Opinion of others, who talk of infection being carried on by the Air only, by carrying with it vast Numbers of Insects, and invisible Creatures, who enter into the Body with the Breath, or even at the Pores with the Air, and there generate, or emit most accute Poisons, or poisonous Ovæ, or Eggs, which mingle themselves with the Blood, and so infect the Body; a Discourse full of learned Simplicity,

DANIEL DE FOE

and manifested to be so by universal Experience; but I shall say more to this Case in its Order.

I must here take farther Notice that Nothing was more fatal to the Inhabitants of this City, than the Supine Negligence of the People themselves, who during the long Notice, or Warning they had of the Visitation, yet made no Provision for it, by laying in Store of Provisions, or of other Necessaries; by which they might have liv'd retir'd, and within their own Houses, as I have observed, others did, and who were in a great Measure preserv'd by that Caution; nor were they, after they were a little hardened to it, so shye of conversing with one another, when actually infected, as they were at first, no tho' they knew it.

I acknowledge I was one of those thoughtless Ones, that had made so little Provision, that my Servants were obliged to go out of Doors to buy every Trifle by Penny and Halfpenny, just as before it begun, even till my Experience shewing me the Folly, I began to be wiser so late, that I had scarce Time to store my self sufficient for our common Subsistence for a Month.

I had in Family only an antient Woman, that managed the House, a Maid-Servant, two Apprentices, and my self; and the Plague beginning to encrease about us, I had many sad Thoughts about what Course I should take, and how I should act; the many dismal Objects, which happened everywhere as I went about the Streets, had fill'd my Mind with a great deal of Horror, for fear of the Distemper it self, which was indeed very horrible in it self, and in some more than in others, the swellings which were generally in the Neck, or Groin, when they grew hard, and would not break, grew so painful, that it was equal to the most exquisite Torture; and some not able to bear the Torment threw themselves out at Windows, or shot themselves, or otherwise made themselves away, and I saw several dismal Objects of that Kind: Others unable to contain themselves, vented their Pain by incessant Roarings, and such loud and lamentable Cries were to be heard as we walk'd along the Streets, that would Pierce the very Heart to think of, especially when it was to be considered, that the same dreadful Scourge might be expected every Moment to seize upon our selves.

I cannot say but that now I began to faint in my Resolutions, my Heart fail'd me very much, and sorely I repented of my Rashness: When I had been out, and met with such terrible

Things as these I have talked of; I say, I repented my Rashness in venturing to abide in Town: I wish'd often, that I had not taken upon me to stay, but had gone away with my Brother and his Family.

Terrified by those frightful Objects, I would retire Home sometimes, and resolve to go out no more, and perhaps, I would keep those Resolutions for three or four Days, which Time I spent in the most serious Thankfulness for my Preservation, and the Preservation of my Family, and the constant Confession of my Sins, giving my self up to God every Day, and applying to him with Fasting, Humiliation, and Meditation: Such intervals as I had, I employed in reading Books, and in writing down my Memorandums of what occurred to me every Day, and out of which, afterwards. I formed most of this Work as it relates to my Observations without Doors: What I wrote of my private Meditations I reserve for private Use, and desire it may not be made publick on any Account whatever.

I also wrote other Meditations upon Divine Subjects, such as occurred to me at that Time, and were profitable to my self, but not fit for any other View, and therefore I say no more of that.

I had a very good Friend, a Physician, whose Name was Heath, who I frequently visited during this dismal Time, and to whose Advice I was very much oblig'd for many Things which he directed me to take, by way of preventing the Infection when I went out, as he found I frequently did, and to hold in my Mouth when I was in the Streets; he also came very often to see me, and as he was a good Christian, as well as a good Physician, his agreeable Conversation was a very great Support to me in the worst of this terrible Time.

It was now the Beginning of August, and the Plague grew very violent and terrible in the Place where I liv'd, and Dr. Heath coming to visit me, and finding that I ventured so often out in the Streets, earnestly perswaded me to lock my self up and my Family, and not to suffer any of us to go out of Doors; to keep all our Windows fast, Shutters and Curtains close, and never to open them; but first, to make a very strong Smoke in the Room, where the Window or Door was to be opened, with Rozen and Pitch, Brimstone, or Gunpowder, and the like; and we did this for some Time: But as I had not laid in a Store of Provision for such a retreat, it was impossible that we could keep within Doors entirely; however, I attempted, tho' it was so very late, to do something towards it; and first, as I had Convenience both for Brewing and Baking, I went and bought two Sacks of Meal, and for several Weeks, having an Oven, we baked all our own Bread; also I bought Malt, and brew'd as much Beer as all the Casks I had would hold, and which seem'd enough to serve my House for five or six Weeks; also I laid in a Quantity of Salt butter and Cheshire Cheese; but I had no Flesh-meat, and the Plague raged so violently among the Butchers, and Slaughter-Houses, on the other Side of our Street, where they are known to dwell in great Numbers, that it was not advisable, so much as to go over the Street among them.

And here I must observe again, that this Necessity of going out of our Houses to buy Provisions, was in a great Measure the Ruin of the whole City, for the People catch'd the Distemper, on those Occasions, one of another, and even the Provisions themselves were often tainted, at least I have great Reason to believe so; and therefore I cannot say with Satisfaction what I know is repeated with great Assurance, that the Market People, and such as brought Provisions to Town, were never infected: I am certain, the Butchers of White-Chapel where the greatest Part of the Flesh-meat was killed, were dreadfully visited, and that at last to such a Degree, that few of their Shops were kept open, and those that remain'd of them, kill'd their Meat at Mile-end, and that Way, and brought it to Market upon Horses.

However, the poor People cou'd not lay up Provisions, and there was a necessity, that they must go to Market to buy, and others to send Servants or their Children; and as this was a Necessity which renew'd it self daily; it brought abundance of unsound People to the Markets, and a great many that went thither Sound, brought Death Home with them.

It is true, People us'd all possible Precaution: when any one bought a Joint of Meat in the Market, they would not take it of the Butchers Hand, but take it off the Hooks themselves. On the other Hand, the Butcher would not touch the Money, but have it put into a Pot full of Vinegar which he kept for that purpose. The Buyer carry'd always small Money to make up any odd Sum, that they might take no Change. They carry'd Bottles for Scents, and Perfumes in their Hands, and all the Means that could be us'd, were us'd: But then the Poor cou'd not do even these things, and they went at all Hazards.

Innumerable dismal Stories we heard every Day on this very Account: Sometimes a Man or Woman dropt down Dead in the very Markets; for many People that had the Plague upon them, knew nothing of it; till the inward Gangreen had affected their Vitals and they dy'd in a few Moments; this caus'd, that many died frequently in that Manner in the Streets suddainly, without any warning: Others perhaps had Time to go to the next Bulk or Stall; or to any Door, Porch, and just sit down and die, as I have said before.

These Objects were so frequent in the Streets, that when the Plague came to be very raging, On one Side, there was scarce any passing by the Streets, but that several dead Bodies would be lying here and there upon the Ground; on the other hand it is observable, that tho' at first, the People would stop as they went along, and call to the Neighbors to come out on such an Occasion; yet, afterward, no Notice was taken of them; but that, if at any Time we found a Corps lying, go cross the Way, and not come near it; or if in a narrow Lane or Passage, go back again, and seek some other Way to go on the Business we were upon; and in those Cases, the Corps was always left, till the Officers had notice to come and take them away; or till Night, when the Bearers attending the Dead-Cart would take them up, and carry them away: Nor did those undaunted Creatures, who performed these Offices, fail to search their Pockets, and sometimes strip off their Cloths, if they were well drest, as sometimes they were, and carry off what they could get.

But to return to the Markets; the Butchers took that Care, that if any Person dy'd in the Market, they had the Officers always at Hand, to take them up upon Hand-barrows, and carry them to the next Church-Yard; and this was so frequent that such were not entred in the weekly Bill, found Dead in the Streets or Fields, as is the Case now; but they went into the general Articles of the great Distemper.

But now the Fury of the Distemper encreased to such a Degree, that even the Markets were but very thinly furnished with Provisions, or frequented with Buyers, compair'd to what they were before; and the Lord-Mayor caused the Country-People who brought Provisions, to be stop'd in the Streets leading into the Town, and to sit down there with their Goods, where they sold what they brought, and went immediately away; and this Encourag'd the Country People greatly to do

*View of the manner of burying the dead Bodies
At Holy-well mount during the dreadful* PLAGUE *in 1665*

From a rare old print

so, for they sold their Provisions at the very Entrances into the Town, and even in the Fields; as particularly in the Fields beyond White-Chappel, in Spittle-fields. Note, Those Streets now called Spittle-Fields, were then indeed open Fields: Also in St. George's-fields in Soutwork, in Bunhill Fields, and in a great Field, call'd Wood's-Close near Islington; thither the Lord Mayor, Aldermen, and Magistrates sent their Officers and Servants to buy for their Families, themselves keeping within Doors as much as possible; and the like did many other People; and after this Method was taken, the Country People came with great chearfulness, and brought Provisions of all Sorts, and very seldom got any harm; which I suppose, added also to that Report of their being Miraculously preserv'd.

As for my little Family, having thus, as I have said, laid in a Store of Bread, Butter, Cheese, and Beer, I took my Friend and Physician's Advice, and lock'd my self up, and my Family, and resolv'd to suffer the hardship of Living a few Months without Flesh-Meat, rather than to purchase it at the hazard of our Lives.

But tho' I confin'd my Family, I could not prevail upon my unsatisfy'd Curiosity to stay within entirely my self; and tho' I generally came frighted and terrified Home, yet I cou'd not restrain; only that indeed, I did not do it so frequently as at first.

I had some little Obligations indeed upon me, to go to my Brothers House, which was in Coleman's-street Parish, and which he had left to my Care, and I went at first every Day, but afterwards only once or twice a Week.

In these Walks I had many dismal Scenes before my Eyes, as particularly of Persons falling dead in the Streets, terrible Shrieks and Skreekings of Women, who in their Agonies would throw open their Chamber Windows, and cry out in a dismal Surprising Manner; it is impossible to describe the Variety of Postures, in which the Passions of the Poor People would Express themselves.

Passing thro' Token-House-Yard in Lothbury, of a sudden a Casement violently opened just over my Head, and a Woman gave three frightful Skreetches, and then cry'd, Oh! Death, Death, Death! in a most inimitable Tone, and which struck me with Horror, and a Chilness, in my very Blood. There was no Body to be seen in the whole Street, neither did any other Window open; for People had no Curiosity now in any Case;

nor could any Body help one another; so I went on to pass into Bell-Alley.

Just in Bell-Alley, on the right Hand of the Passage, there was a more terrible Cry than that, tho' it was not so directed out at the Window, but the whole Family was in a terrible Fright, and I could hear Women and Children run skreaming about the Rooms like distracted, when a Garret Window opened, and some body from a Window on the other Side the Alley, call'd and ask'd, What is the Matter? upon which, from the first Window it was answered, O Lord, my Old Master has hang'd himself! The other ask'd again, Is he quite dead? and the first answer'd, Ay, Ay, quite dead; quite dead and cold! This Person was a Merchant, and a Deputy Alderman and very rich. I care not to mention the Name, tho' I knew his Name too, but that would be an Hardship to the Family, which is now flourishing again.

But, this is but one; it is scarce credible what dreadful Cases happened in particular Families every Day; People in the Rage of the Distemper, or in the Torment of their Swellings, which was indeed intollerable, running out of their own Government, raving and distracted, and oftentimes laying violent Hands upon themselves, throwing themselves out at their Windows, shooting themselves, etc. Mothers murthering their own Children, in their Lunacy, some dying of mere Grief, as a Passion, some of mere Fright and Surprize, without any Infection at all; others frighted into Idiotism, and foolish Distractions, some into dispair and Lunacy; others into mellancholy Madness.

The Pain of the Swelling was in particular very violent, and to some intollerable; the Physicians and Surgeons may be said to have tortured many poor Creatures, even to Death. The Swellings in some grew hard, and they apply'd violent drawing Plasters, or Pultices, to break them; and if these did not do, they cut and scarified them in a terrible Manner: In some, those Swellings were made hard, partly by the Force of the Distemper, and partly by their being too violently drawn, and were so hard, that no Instrument could cut them, and then they burnt them with Causticks, so that many died raving mad with the Torment; and some in the very Operation. In these Distresses, some for want of Help to hold them down in their Beds, or to look to them, laid Hands upon themselves as above. Some broke out into the Streets, perhaps naked, and would run directly down to the River, if they were not stopt by the Watchmen, or other Officers, and plunge themselves into the Water, wherever they found it.

It often pierc'd my very Soul to hear the Groans and Crys of those who were thus tormented, but of the Two, this was counted the most promising Particular in the whole Infection; for, if these Swellings could be brought to a Head, and to break and run, or as the Surgeons call it, to digest, the Patient generally recover'd; whereas those who, like the Gentlewoman's Daughter, were struck with Death at the Beginning, and had the Tokens come out upon them, often went about indifferent easy, till a little before they died, and some till the Moment they dropt down, as in Appoplexies and Epelepsies, is often the Case; such would be taken suddenly very sick, and would run to a Bench or Bulk, or any convenient Place that offer'd it self, or to their own Houses, if possible, as I mentioned before, and there sit down, grow faint and die. This kind of dying was much the same, as it was with those who die of common Mortifications, who die swooning, and as it were go away in a Dream; such as die thus, had very little Notice of their being infected at all, till the Gangreen was spread thro' their whole Body; nor could Physicians themselves know certainly how it was with them, till they opened their Breasts, or other Parts of their Body, and saw the Tokens.

We had at this Time a great many frightful Stories told us of Nurses and Watchmen, who looked after the dying People, that is to say, hir'd Nurses, who attended infected People, using them barbarously, starving them, smothering them, or by other wicked Means hastening their End, that is to say, murthering of them: And Watchmen being set to guard Houses that were shut up, when there has been but one person left, and perhaps, that one lying sick, that they have broke in and murthered that Body, and immediately thrown them out into the Dead-Cart! and so they have gone scarce cold to the Grave.

I cannot say but that some such Murthers were committed, and I think two were sent to Prison for it, but died before they could be try'd; and I have heard that three others, at several Times, were excused for Murthers of that kind; but I must say I believe nothing of its being so common a Crime, as some have since been pleas'd to say, nor did it seem to be so rational, where the People were brought so low as not to be able to help themselves, for such seldom recovered, and there was no Temptation to commit a Murder, at least, none equal to the Fact where they were sure Persons would die in so short a Time; and could not live.

That there were a great many Robberies and wicked Practices committed even in this dreadful Time I do not deny; the Power of Avarice was so strong in some, that they would run any Hazard to steal and to plunder, and particularly in Houses where all the Families, or Inhabitants have been dead, and carried out, they would break in at all Hazards, and without Regard to the Danger of Infection, take even the Cloths off, of the dead Bodies, and the Bed-cloaths from others where they lay dead.

This, I suppose, must be the Case of a Family in Houndsditch, where a Man and his Daughter, the rest of the Family being, as I suppose, carried away before by the Dead-Cart, were found stark naked, one in one Chamber, and one in another, lying Dead on the Floor; and the Cloths of the Beds, from whence, 'tis supposed they were roll'd off by Thieves, stoln, and carried quite away.

It is indeed to be observ'd, that the Women were, in all this Calamity, the most rash, fearless, and desperate Creatures; and as there were vast Numbers that went about as Nurses, to tend those that were sick, they committed a great many petty Thieveries in the Houses where they were employed; and some of them were publickly whipt for it, when perhaps they ought rather to have been hanged for Examples; for Numbers of Houses were robbed on these Occasions, till at length the Parish Officers were sent to recommend Nurses to the Sick, and always took an Account who it was they sent, so as that they might call them to account, if the House had been abused where they were placed.

But these Robberies extended chiefly to Wearing-Cloths, Linen, and what Rings or Money they could come at, when the Person dyed who was under their Care, but not to a general Plunder of the Houses; and I could give an Account of one of these Nurses, who several Years after, being on her Death-bed, confest with the utmost Horror, the Robberries she had committed at the Time of her being a Nurse, and by which she had enriched herself to a great Degree: But as for murthers, I do not find that there was ever any Proof of the Facts, in the manner, as it has been reported, except as above.

They did tell me indeed of a Nurse in one place, that laid

THAMES EMBANKMENT, LONDON

a wet Cloth upon the Face of a dying Patient, who she tended, and so put an End to his Life, who was just expiring before: And another that smother'd a young Woman she was looking to, when she was in a fainting fit, and would have come to her self: Some that kill'd them by giving them one Thing, some another, and some starved them by giving them nothing at all: But these Stories had two Marks of Suspicion that always attended them, which caused me always to slight them, and to look on them as mere Stories, that People continually frighted one another with. (1.) That wherever it was that we heard it, they always placed the Scene at the farther End of the Town, opposite, or most remote from where you were to hear it: If you heard it in White-Chapel, it had happened at St. Giles's, or at Westminster, or Holborn, or that End of the Town; if you heard of it at that End of the Town, then it was done in White-Chapel, or the Minories, or about Cripplegate Parish: If you heard of it in the City, why, then it had happened in Southwark; and if you heard of it in Southwark, then it was done in the City, and the like.

In the next Place, of what Part soever you heard the Story, the Particulars were always the same, especially that of laying a wet double Clout on a dying Man's Face, and that of smothering a young Gentlewoman; so that it was apparent, at least to my Judgment, that there was more of Tale than of Truth in those Things.

THE MASQUE OF THE RED DEATH.

By EDGAR A. POE.

[EDGAR ALLAN POE: An American poet and author; born at Boston, Mass., 1809. Orphaned in his third year, he was adopted by John Allan, a wealthy merchant of Richmond, Va., by whom he was sent to school at Stoke-Newington, near London. He spent a year at the University of Virginia (1826); enlisted as a private in the United States army under an assumed name, becoming sergeant major (1829); and was admitted to West Point (1830), receiving his dismissal the next year. Thrown upon his own resources, he began writing for the papers. Subsequently he became editor of the *Southern Literary Messenger*, in Richmond; was on the staff of *The Gentleman's Magazine* and *Graham's Magazine*, in Philadelphia, and the *Broadway Journal* in New York. He died in a Baltimore hospital, October 7, 1849. "The Raven" and "The Bells" are his most popular poems. His fame as a prose writer rests on his tales of terror and mystery.]

The "Red Death" had long devastated the country. No pestilence had ever been so fatal or so hideous. Blood was its Avatar and its seal — the redness and the horror of blood. There were sharp pains, and sudden dizziness, and then profuse bleeding at the pores, with dissolution. The scarlet stains upon the body, and especially upon the face of the victim, were the pest ban which shut him out from the aid and from the sympathy of his fellow-men; and the whole seizure, progress, and termination of the disease were the incidents of half an hour.

But the Prince Prospero was happy and dauntless and sagacious. When his dominions were half-depopulated, he summoned to his presence a thousand hale and light-hearted friends from among the knights and dames of his court, and with these retired to the deep seclusion of one of his castellated abbeys. This was an extensive and magnificent structure, the creation of the prince's own eccentric yet august taste. A strong and lofty wall girdled it in. This wall had gates of iron. The courtiers, having entered, brought furnaces and massy hammers and welded the bolts. They resolved to leave means neither of ingress or egress to the sudden impulses of despair from without or of frenzy from within. The abbey was amply provisioned. With such precautions the courtiers might bid defiance to contagion. The external world could take care of itself. In the mean time it was folly to grieve or to think. The prince had provided all the appliances of pleasure. There were buffoons, there were improvisatori, there were ballet dancers, there were musicians, there was beauty, there was wine. All these and security were within. Without was the "Red Death."

It was toward the close of the fifth or sixth month of his seclusion, and while the pestilence raged most furiously abroad, that the Prince Prospero entertained his thousand friends at a masked ball of the most unusual magnificence.

It was a voluptuous scene, that masquerade. But first let me tell of the rooms in which it was held. There were seven — an imperial suite. In many palaces, however, such suites form a long and straight vista, while the folding doors slide back nearly to the walls on either hand, so that the view of the whole extent is scarcely impeded. Here the case was very different, as might have been expected from the prince's love of the *bizarre*. The apartments were so irregularly disposed that the vision embraced but little more than one at a time. There was a sharp turn at every twenty or thirty yards, and at each turn a novel effect. To the right and left, in the middle of each wall, a tall and narrow Gothic window looked out upon a closed corridor which pursued the windings of the suite. These windows were of stained glass, whose color varied in accordance with the prevailing hue of the decorations of the chamber into which it opened. That at the eastern extremity was hung, for example, in blue, and vividly blue were its windows. The second chamber was purple in its ornaments and tapestries, and here the panes were purple. The third was green throughout, and so were the casements. The fourth was furnished and lighted with orange, the fifth with white, the sixth with violet. The seventh apartment was closely shrouded in black velvet tapestries that hung all over the ceiling and down the walls, falling in heavy folds upon a carpet of the same material and hue. But in this chamber only the color of the windows failed to correspond with the decorations. The panes here were scarlet — a deep blood color. Now in no one of the seven apartments was there any lamp or candelabrum amid the profusion of golden ornaments that lay scattered to and fro or depended from the roof. There was no light of any kind emanating from lamp or candle within the suite of chambers; but in the corridors that followed the suite there stood opposite to each window a heavy tripod bearing a brasier of fire that projected its rays through the tinted glass, and so glaringly illumined the room. And thus were produced a multitude of gaudy and fantastic appearances. But in the western or black chamber, the effect of the firelight that streamed upon the dark hangings, through the blood-tinted panes, was ghastly in the extreme, and produced so wild a look upon the countenances of those who entered that there were few of the company bold enough to set foot within its precincts at all.

It was in this apartment also that there stood against the western wall a gigantic clock of ebony. Its pendulum swung to and fro with a dull, heavy, monotonous clang; and when the minute hand made the circuit of the face, and the hour was to be stricken, there came from the brazen lungs of the clock a sound which was clear and loud, and deep, and exceedingly musical, but of so peculiar a note and emphasis that, at each lapse of an hour, the musicians of the orchestra were constrained to pause momentarily in their performance to hearken to the sound; and thus the waltzers perforce ceased their evelutions, and there was a brief disconcert of the whole gay company, and while the chimes of the clock yet rang it was observed that the giddiest grew pale, and the more aged and sedate passed their hands over their brows as if in confused reverie or meditation; but when the echoes had fully ceased a light laughter at once pervaded the assembly; the musicians looked at each other and smiled as if at their own nervousness and folly, and made whispering vows each to the other that the next chiming of the clock should produce in them no similar emotion, and then, after the lapse of sixty minutes (which embrace three thousand and six hundred seconds of the time that flies), there came yet another chiming of the clock, and then were the same disconcert and tremulousness and meditation as before.

But in spite of these things it was a gay and magnificent revel. The tastes of the prince were peculiar. He had a fine eye for colors and effects. He disregarded the *decora* of mere fashion. His plans were bold and fiery, and his conceptions glowed with barbaric luster. There are some who would have thought him mad. His followers felt that he was not. It was necessary to hear, and see, and touch him to be *sure* that he was not.

He had directed, in great part, the movable embellishments of the seven chambers, upon occasion of this great *fête;* and it was his own guiding taste which had given character to the masqueraders. Be sure they were grotesque. There were much glare and glitter and piquancy and phantasm — much of what has been since seen in "Hernani." There were arabesque figures with unsuited limbs and appointments. There were delirious fancies such as the madman fashions. There were much of the beautiful, much of the wanton, much of the *bizarre*, something of the terrible, and not a little of that which might have excited disgust. To and fro in the seven chambers there stalked, in fact, a multitude of dreams. And these — the dreams — writhed in and about, taking hue from the rooms, and causing the wild music of the orchestra to seem as the echo of their steps. And, anon, there strikes the ebony clock which stands in the hall of the velvet and then, for a moment, all is still, and all is silent, save the voice of the clock. The dreams are stiff-frozen as they stand. But the echoes of the chime die away — they have endured but an instant — and a light, half-subdued laughter floats after them as they depart. And now again the music swells, and the dreams live, and writhe to and fro more merrily than ever, taking hue from the many-tinted windows through which stream the rays from the tripods. But to the chamber which lies more eastwardly of the seven there are now none of the maskers who venture; for the night is waning away; and there flows a ruddier light through the blood-colored panes; and the blackness of the sable drapery appalls; and to him whose foot falls upon the sable carpet there comes from the near clock of ebony a muffled peal more solemnly emphatic than any which reaches *their* ears who indulge in the more remote gayeties of the other apartments.

But these other apartments were densely crowded, and in them beat feverishly the heart of life. And the revel went whirlingly on, until at length there commenced the sounding of midnight upon the clock. And then the music ceased, as I have told; and the evolutions of the waltzers were quieted; and there was an uneasy cessation of all things as before. But now there were twelve strokes to be sounded by the bell of the clock; and thus it happened, perhaps, that more of thought crept, with more of time, into the meditations of the thoughtful among those who reveled. And thus, too, it happened, perhaps, that before the last echoes of the last chime had utterly sunk into silence, there were many individuals in the crowd who had found leisure to become aware of the presence of a masked figure which had arrested the attention of no single individual before. And the rumor of this new presence having spread itself whisperingly around, there arose at length from the whole company a buzz, or murmur, expressive of disapprobation and surprise — then, finally, of terror, of horror, and of disgust.

In an assembly of phantasms such as I have painted, it may well be supposed that no ordinary appearance could have excited such sensation. In truth, the masquerade license of the night was nearly unlimited; but the figure in question had out-Heroded Herod, and gone beyond the bounds of even the prince's indefinite decorum. There are chords in the hearts of the most reckless which cannot be touched without emotion. Even with the utterly lost, to whom life and death are equally jests, there are matters of which no jest can be made. The whole company indeed seemed now deeply to feel that in the costume and bearing of the stranger neither wit nor propriety existed. The figure was tall and gaunt, and shrouded from head to foot in the habiliments of the grave. The mask which concealed the visage was made so nearly to resemble the countenance of a stiffened corpse that the closest scrutiny must have had difficulty in detecting the cheat. And yet all this might have been endured, if not approved, by the mad revelers around. But the mummer had gone so far as to assume the type of the Red Death. His vesture was dabbled in *blood* — and his broad brow, with all the features of the face, was besprinkled with the scarlet horror.

When the eyes of Prince Prospero fell upon this spectral image (which with a slow and solemn movement, as if more fully to sustain its *rôle*, stalked to and fro among the waltzers), he was seen to be convulsed in the first moment with a strong shudder either of terror or distaste; but in the next his brow reddened with rage.

"Who dares," he demanded hoarsely of the courtiers who stood near him — "who dares insult us with this blasphemous mockery? Seize him and unmask him, that we may know whom we have to hang at sunrise from the battlements!"

It was in the eastern or blue chamber in which stood the Prince Prospero as he uttered these words. They rang throughout the seven rooms loudly and clearly — for the prince was a bold and robust man, and the music had become hushed at the waving of his hand.

It was in the blue room where stood the prince, with a group of pale courtiers by his side. At first, as he spoke, there was a slight rushing movement of this group in the direction of the intruder, who at the moment was also near at hand, and now, with deliberate and stately step, made closer approach to the speaker. But, from a certain nameless awe with which the mad assumption of the mummer had inspired the whole party, there were found none who put forth hand to seize him; so that unimpeded he passed within a yard of the prince's person; and while the vast assembly, as if with one impulse, shrank from the centers of the rooms to the walls, he made his way uninterruptedly, but with the same solemn and measured step which had distinguished him from the first, through the blue chamber to the purple — through the purple to the green — through the green to the orange — through this again to the white — and even thence to the violet, ere a decided movement had been made to arrest him. It was then, however, that the Prince Prospero, maddening with rage and the shame of his own momentary cowardice, rushed hurriedly through the six chambers, while none followed him on account of a deadly terror that had seized upon them all. He bore aloft a drawn dagger, and had approached in rapid impetuosity to within three or four feet of the retreating figure, when the latter, having attained the extremity of the velvet apartment, turned suddenly and confronted his pursuer. There was a sharp cry — and the dagger dropped gleaming upon the sable carpet, upon which, instantly afterwards, fell prostrate in death the Prince Prospero. Then, summoning the wild courage of despair, a throng of revelers at once threw themselves into the black apartment, and, seizing the mummer, whose tall figure stood erect and motionless within the shadow of the ebony clock, gasped in unutterable horror at finding the grave cerements and corpselike mask which they handled with so violent a rudeness untenanted by any tangible form.

And now was acknowledged the presence of the Red Death. He had come like a thief in the night; and one by one dropped the revelers in the blood-bedewed halls of their revel, and died each in the despairing posture of his fall; and the life of the ebony clock went out with that of the last of the gay; and the flames of the tripods expired; and darkness and decay and the Red Death held illimitable dominion over all.

THE PROGRESS OF THE PESTILENCE.

By W. HARRISON AINSWORTH.

(From "Old St. Paul's.")

[For biographical sketch, see page 2474.]

TOWARDS the middle of May, the bills of mortality began to swell greatly in amount, and though but few were put down to the plague, and a large number to the spotted fever (another frightful disorder raging at the period), it is well known that the bulk had died of the former disease. The rigorous measures adopted by the authorities (whether salutary or not has been questioned), in shutting up houses and confining the sick and sound within them for forty days, were found so intolerable, that most persons were disposed to run any risk rather than be subjected to such a grievance, and every artifice was resorted to for concealing a case when it occurred. Hence, it seldom happened, unless by accident, that a discovery was made. Quack doctors were secretly consulted, instead of the regular practitioners; the searchers were bribed to silence; and large fees were given to the undertakers and buriers to lay the deaths to the account of some other disorder. All this, however, did not blind the eyes of the officers to the real state of things. Redoubling their vigilance, they entered houses on mere suspicion; inflicted punishments where they found their orders disobeyed or neglected; sent the sound to prison,—the sick to the pesthouse; and replaced the faithless searchers by others upon whom they could place reliance. Many cases were thus detected; but in spite of every precaution, the majority escaped; and the vent was no sooner stopped in one quarter than it broke out with additional violence in another.

By this time the alarm had become general. All whose business or pursuits permitted it prepared to leave London, which they regarded as a devoted city, without delay. As many houses were, therefore, closed from the absence of the inhabitants as from the presence of the plague, and this added to the forlorn appearance of the streets, which in some quarters were almost deserted. For a while, nothing was seen at the great outlets of the city but carts, carriages, and other vehicles, filled with goods and movables, on their way to the country; and, as may be supposed, the departure of their friends did not tend to abate the dejection of those whose affairs compelled them to remain behind.

One circumstance must not be passed unnoticed, namely, the continued fineness and beauty of the weather. No rain had fallen for upwards of three weeks. The sky was bright and cloudless; the atmosphere, apparently, pure and innoxious; while the heat was as great as is generally experienced in the middle of summer. But instead of producing its usual enlivening effect on the spirits, the fine weather added to the general gloom and apprehension, inasmuch as it led to the belief (afterwards fully confirmed) that if the present warmth was so pernicious, the more sultry seasons which were near at hand would aggravate the fury of the pestilence. Sometimes, indeed, when the deaths were less numerous, a hope began to be entertained that the distemper was abating, and confidence was for a moment restored; but these anticipations were speedily checked by the reappearance of the scourge, which seemed to baffle and deride all human skill and foresight.

London now presented a lamentable spectacle. Not a street but had a house in it marked with a red cross — some streets had many such. The bells were continually tolling for burials, and the dead carts went their melancholy rounds at night and were constantly loaded. Fresh directions were issued by the authorities; and as domestic animals were considered to be a medium of conveying the infection, an order, which was immediately carried into effect, was given to destroy all dogs and cats. But this plan proved prejudicial rather than the reverse, as the bodies of the poor animals, most of which were drowned in the Thames, being washed ashore, produced a horrible and noxious effluvium, supposed to contribute materially to the propagation of the distemper.

No precautionary measure was neglected; but it may be doubted whether any human interference could have averted the severity of the scourge, which, though its progress might be checked for a few days by attention, or increased in the same ratio by neglect, would in the end have unquestionably fulfilled its mission. The College of Physicians, by the King's command, issued simple and intelligible directions in the mother tongue, for the sick. Certain of their number, amongst whom was the reader's acquaintance, Doctor Hodges, were appointed to attend the infected; and two out of the Court of Aldermen were required to see that they duly executed their dangerous office. Public prayers and a genuine fast were likewise enjoined. But Heaven seemed deaf to the supplications of the doomed inhabitants — their prayers being followed by a fearful increase of deaths. A vast crowd was collected within Saint Paul's to hear a sermon preached by Doctor Sheldon, Archbishop of Canterbury, — a prelate greatly distinguished during the whole course of the visitation, by his unremitting charity and attention to the sick; and before the discourse was concluded, several fell down within the sacred walls, and, on being conveyed to their own homes, were found to be infected. On the following day, too, many others who had been present were seized with the disorder.

A fresh impulse was given to the pestilence from an unlooked-for cause. It has been mentioned that the shutting up of houses and the seclusion of the sick were regarded as an intolerable grievance, and though most were compelled to submit to it, some few resisted, and tumults and disturbances ensued. As the plague increased, these disturbances became more frequent, and the mob always taking part against the officers, they were frequently interrupted in the execution of their duty.

About this time a more serious affray than usual occurred, attended with loss of life and other unfortunate consequences, which it may be worth while to relate, as illustrative of the peculiar state of the times. The wife of a merchant, named Barcroft, residing in Lothbury, being attacked by the plague, the husband, fearing his house would be shut up, withheld all information from the examiners and searchers. His wife died, and immediately afterwards one of his children was attacked. Still he refused to give notice. The matter, however, got wind. The searchers arrived at night, and being refused admittance, they broke into the house. Finding undoubted evidence of infection, they ordered it to be closed, stationed a watchman at the door, and marked it with the fatal sign. Barcroft remonstrated against their proceedings, but in vain. They told him he might think himself well off that he was not carried before the Lord Mayor, who would undoubtedly send him to Ludgate; and with other threats to the like effect, they departed.

The unfortunate man's wife and child were removed the following night in the dead-cart, and, driven half-mad by grief and terror, he broke open the door of his dwelling, and plunging a sword in the watchman's breast, who opposed his flight, gained the street. A party of the watch happened to be passing at the time, and the fugitive was instantly secured. He made a great clamor, however,—calling to his neighbors and the bystanders to rescue him, and in another moment the watch was beaten off, and Barcroft placed on a post, whence he harangued his preservers on the severe restraints imposed upon the citizens, urging them to assist in throwing open the doors of all infected houses, and allowing free egress to their inmates.

Greedily listening to this insane counsel, the mob resolved to act upon it. Headed by the merchant, they ran down Threadneedle Street, and, crossing Stock's Market, burst open several houses in Bearbinder Lane, and drove away the watchmen. One man, more courageous than the others, tried to maintain his post, and was so severely handled by his assailants, that he died a few days afterwards of the injuries he had received. Most of those who had been imprisoned within their dwellings immediately issued forth, and joining the mob, which received fresh recruits each moment, started on the same errand.

Loud shouts were now raised of — "Open the doors! No plague prisoners! No plague prisoners!" and the mob set off along the Poultry. They halted, however, before the Great Conduit, near the end of Bucklersbury, and opposite Mercer's Hall, because they perceived a company of the Trainbands advancing to meet them. A council of war was held, and many of the rabble were disposed to fly; but Barcroft again urged them to proceed, and they were unexpectedly aided by Solomon Eagle, who, bursting through their ranks, with his brasier on his head, crying, "Awake! sleepers, awake! the plague is at your doors! awake!" speeded toward the Trainbands, scattering sparks of fire as he pursued his swift career. The mob instantly followed, and, adding their shouts to his outcries, dashed on with such fury that the Trainbands did not dare to oppose them, and, after a slight and ineffectual resistance, were put to rout.

Barcroft, who acted as leader, informed them that there was a house in Wood Street shut up, and the crowd accompanied him thither. In a few minutes they had reached Bloundel's shop, but finding no one on guard — for the watchman, guessing their errand, had taken to his heels — they smeared over the fatal cross and inscription with a pail of mud gathered from the neighboring kennel, and then broke open the door. The grocer and his apprentice hearing the disturbance, and being greatly alarmed at it, hurried to the shop, and found it full of people.

"You are at liberty, Mr. Bloundel," cried the merchant, who was acquainted with the grocer. "We are determined no longer to let our families be imprisoned at the pleasure of the Lord Mayor and aldermen. We mean to break open all the plague houses, and set free their inmates."

"For Heaven's sake, consider what you are about, Mr. Barcroft," cried the grocer. "My house has been closed for nearly a month. Nay, as my son has entirely recovered, and received his certificate of health from Doctor Hodges, it would have been opened in three days hence by the officers; so that I have suffered all the inconvenience of the confinement, and can speak to it. It is no doubt very irksome, and may be almost intolerable to persons of an impatient temperament: but I firmly believe it is the only means to check the progress of contagion. Listen to me, Mr. Barcroft — listen to me, good friends, and hesitate before you violate laws which have been made expressly to meet this terrible emergency."

Here he was checked by loud groans and upbraidings from the bystanders.

"He tells you himself that the period of his confinement is just over," cried Barcroft. "It is plain he has no interest in the matter, except that he would have others suffer as he has done. Heed him not, my friends; but proceed with the good work. Liberate the poor plague prisoners. Liberate them. On! on!"

"Forbear, rash men!" cried Bloundel, in an authoritative voice. "In the name of those you are bound to obey, I command you to desist."

"Command us!" cried one of the bystanders, raising his staff in a menacing manner. "Is this your gratitude for the favor we have just conferred upon you? Command us, forsooth! You had better repeat the order, and see how it will be obeyed."

"I *do* repeat it," rejoined the grocer, firmly. "In the Lord Mayor's name, I command you to desist, and return to your homes."

The man would have struck him with his staff, if he had not been himself felled to the ground by Leonard. This was the signal for greater outrage. The grocer and his apprentice were instantly assailed by several others of the mob, who, leaving them both on the floor covered with bruises, helped themselves to all they could lay hands on in the shop, and then quitted the premises.

It is scarcely necessary to track their course further; and it may be sufficient to state that they broke open upwards of fifty houses in different streets. Many of the plague-stricken joined them, and several half-naked creatures were found dead in the streets on the following morning. Two houses in Blackfriars Lane were set on fire, and the conflagration was with difficulty checked; nor was it until late on the following day that the mob could be entirely dispersed. The originator of the disturbance, Barcroft, after a desperate resistance, was shot through the head by a constable.

The result of this riot, as will be easily foreseen, was greatly to increase the pestilence; and many of those who had been

THE PROGRESS OF THE PESTILENCE.

most active in it perished in prison of the distemper. Far from being discouraged by the opposition offered to their decrees, the city authorities enforced them with greater rigor than ever, and, doubling the number of the watch, again shut up all those houses which had been broken open during the late tumult. . . .

In this way, a month passed on. And now every other consideration was merged in the alarm occasioned by the daily increasing fury of the pestilence. Throughout July the excessive heat of the weather underwent no abatement, but in place of the clear atmosphere that had prevailed during the preceding month, unwholesome blights filled the air, and, confining the pestilential effluvia, spread the contagion far and wide with extraordinary rapidity. Not only was the city suffocated with heat, but filled with noisome smells, arising from the carcasses with which the close alleys and other out-of-the-way places were crowded, and which were so far decomposed as not to be capable of removal. The aspect of the river was as much changed as that of the city. Numbers of bodies were thrown into it, and, floating up with the tide, were left to taint the air on its banks, while strange, ill-omened fowl, attracted thither by their instinct, preyed upon them. Below the bridge, all captains of ships moored in the Pool, or off Wapping, held as little communication as possible with those on shore, and only received fresh provisions with the greatest precaution. As the plague increased, most of these removed lower down the river, and many of them put out entirely to sea. Above the bridge, most of the wherries and other smaller craft had disappeared, their owners having taken them up the river, and moored them against its banks at different spots, where they lived in them under tilts. Many hundreds of persons remained upon the river in this way during the whole continuance of the visitation.

August had now arrived, but the distemper knew no cessation. On the contrary, it manifestly increased in violence and malignity. The deaths rose a thousand in each week, and in the last week in this fatal month amounted to upwards of sixty thousand!

But, terrible as this was, the pestilence had not yet reached its height. Hopes were entertained that when the weather became cooler, its fury would abate; but these anticipations were fearfully disappointed. The bills of mortality rose the first week in September to seven thousand, and though they slightly decreased during the second week — awakening a momentary hope — on the third they advanced to twelve thousand! In less than ten days, upwards of two thousand persons perished in the parish of Aldgate alone; while Whitechapel suffered equally severely. Out of the hundred parishes in and about the city, one only, that of Saint John the Evangelist in Watling Street, remained uninfected, and this merely because there was scarcely a soul left within it, the greater part of the inhabitants having quitted their houses, and fled into the country.

The deepest despair now seized upon all the survivors. Scarcely a family but had lost half of its number — many, more than half — while those who were left felt assured that their turn would speedily arrive. Even the reckless were appalled, and abandoned their evil courses. Not only were the dead lying in the passages and alleys, but even in the main thoroughfares, and none would remove them. The awful prediction of Solomon Eagle that "grass would grow in the streets, and that the living should not be able to bury the dead," had come to pass. London had become one vast lazar house, and seemed in a fair way of becoming a mighty sepulcher.

During all this time, Saint Paul's continued to be used as a pesthouse, but it was not so crowded as heretofore, because, as not one in fifty of the infected recovered when placed under medical care, it was not thought worth while to remove them from their own abodes. The number of attendants, too, had diminished. Some had died, but the greater part had abandoned their offices from a fear of sharing the fate of their patients. . . .

On the tenth of September, which was afterwards accounted the most fatal day of this fatal month, a young man of a very dejected appearance, and wearing the traces of severe suffering in his countenance, entered the west end of London, and took his way slowly towards the city. He had passed Saint Giles' without seeing a single living creature, or the sign of one in any of the houses. The broad thoroughfare was completely grown over with grass, and the habitations had the most melancholy and deserted air imaginable. Some doors and windows were wide open, discovering rooms with goods and furniture scattered about, having been left in this state by their inmates; but most part of them were closely fastened up.

As he proceeded along Holborn, the ravages of the scourge were yet more apparent. Every house, on either side of the way, had a red cross, with the fatal inscription above it, upon

THE PROGRESS OF THE PESTILENCE.

the door. Here and there, a watchman might be seen, looking more like a phantom than a living thing. Formerly, the dead were conveyed away at night, but now the carts went about in the daytime. On reaching Saint Andrew's, Holborn, several persons were seen wheeling hand barrows filled with corpses, scarcely covered with clothing, and revealing the blue and white stripes of the pestilence, towards a cart which was standing near the church gates. The driver of the vehicle, a tall, cadaverous-looking man, was ringing his bell, and jesting with another person, whom the young man recognized, with a shudder, as Chowles. The coffin-maker also recognized him at the same moment, and called to him, but the other paid no attention to the summons and passed on.

Crossing Holborn Bridge, he toiled faintly up the opposite hill, for he was evidently suffering from extreme debility, and on gaining the summit was obliged to support himself against a wall for a few minutes, before he could proceed. The same frightful evidences of the ravages of the pestilence were observable here, as elsewhere. The houses were all marked with the fatal cross, and shut up. Another dead cart was heard rumbling along, accompanied by the harsh cries of the driver and the doleful ringing of the bell. The next moment the loathly vehicle was seen coming along the Old Bailey. It paused before a house, from which four bodies were brought, and then passed on towards Smithfield. Watching its progress with fearful curiosity, the young man noted how often it paused to increase its load. His thoughts, colored by the scene, were of the saddest and dreariest complexion. All around wore the aspect of death. The few figures in sight seemed staggering towards the grave, and the houses appeared to be plague-stricken like the inhabitants. The heat was intolerably oppressive, and the air tainted with noisome exhalations. Ever and anon, a window would be opened, and a ghastly face thrust from it, while a piercing shriek, or lamentable cry, was uttered. No business seemed going on — there were no passengers — no vehicles in the streets. The mighty city was completely laid prostrate.

Arrived in Great Knightrider Street, he was greatly shocked at finding the door of the doctor's habitation fastened, nor could he make any one hear, though he knocked loudly and repeatedly against it. The shutters of the lower windows were closed, and the place looked completely deserted. All the adjoining houses were shut up, and not a living being could be discerned in the street from whom information could be obtained relative to the physician. Here, as elsewhere, the pavement was overgrown with grass, and the very houses had a strange and melancholy look, as if sharing in the general desolation. On looking down a narrow street leading to the river, Leonard perceived a flock of poultry scratching among the staves in search of food, and instinctively calling them, they flew towards him, as if delighted at the unwonted sound of a human voice. These, and a half-starved cat, were the only things living that he could perceive. At the further end of the street he caught sight of the river, speeding in its course towards the bridge, and scarcely knowing whither he was going, sauntered to its edge. The tide had just turned, and the stream was sparkling in the sunshine, but no craft could be discovered upon its bosom; and except a few barges moored to its sides, all vestiges of the numberless vessels with which it was once crowded were gone. Its quays were completely deserted. Boxes and bales of goods lay untouched on the wharves; the cheering cries with which the workmen formerly animated their labor were hushed. There was no sound of creaking cords, no rattle of heavy chains — none of the busy hum ordinarily attending the discharge of freight from a vessel, or the packing of goods and stores on board. All traffic was at an end; and this scene, usually one of the liveliest possible, was now forlorn and desolate. On the opposite shore of the river it appeared to be the same — indeed, the borough of Southwark was now suffering the utmost rigor of the scourge, and except for the rows of houses on its banks, and the noble bridge by which it was spanned, the Thames appeared as undisturbed as it must have been before the great city was built upon its banks.

The apprentice viewed this scene with a singular kind of interest. He had become so accustomed to melancholy sights, that his feelings had lost their acuteness, and the contemplation of the deserted buildings and neglected wharves around him harmonized with his own gloomy thoughts. Pursuing his walk along the side of the river, he was checked by a horrible smell, and looking downward, he perceived a carcass in the last stage of decomposition lying in the mud. It had been washed ashore by the tide, and a large bird of prey was contending for the possession of it with a legion of water rats. Sickened by the sight, he turned up a narrow thoroughfare near Baynard's

CHOIR AND SOUTH AISLE, ST. PAUL'S CATHEDRAL

From a photo by G. W. Wilson & Co., Ltd., Aberdeen

Castle, and crossing Thames Street, was about to ascend Addle Hill, when he perceived a man wheeling a hand barrow, containing a couple of corpses, in the direction of the river, with the intention, doubtless, of throwing them into it, as the readiest means of disposing of them. Both bodies were stripped of their clothing, and the blue tint of the nails, as well as the blotches with which they were covered, left no doubt as to the disease of which they had died. Averting his gaze from the spectacle, Leonard turned off on the right along Carter Lane, and threading a short passage, approached the southern boundary of the cathedral; and proceeding towards the great door opposite him, passed through it. The mighty lazar house was less crowded than he expected to find it, but its terrible condition far exceeded his worst conceptions. Not more than half the pallets were occupied; but as the sick were in a great measure left to themselves, the utmost disorder prevailed. A troop of lazars, with sheets folded around them, glided, like phantoms, along Paul's Walk, and mimicked in a ghastly manner the air and deportment of the gallants who had formerly thronged the place. No attempt being made to maintain silence, the noise was perfectly stunning; some of the sick were shrieking — some laughing in a wild unearthly manner — some praying — some uttering loud execrations — others groaning and lamenting. The holy building seemed to have become the abode of evil and tormented spirits. Many dead were lying in the beds — the few attendants who were present not caring to remove them; and Leonard had little doubt that before another sun went down the whole of the ghastly assemblage before him would share their fate. If the habitations he had recently gazed upon had appeared plague-stricken, the sacred structure in which he was now standing seemed yet more horribly contaminated. Ill-kept and ill-ventilated, the air was loaded with noxious effluvia, while the various abominations that met the eye at every turn would have been sufficient to produce the distemper in any one who had come in contact with them. They were, however, utterly disregarded by the miserable sufferers and their attendants. The magnificent painted windows were dimmed by a thick clammy steam, which could scarcely be washed off — while the carved oak screens, the sculptured tombs, the pillars, the walls, and the flagged floors were covered with impurities.

POEMS OF JOHN DONNE.

[1573-1631.]

Valediction, forbidding Mourning.

As virtuous men pass mildly away,
   And whisper to their souls to go,
Whilst some of their sad friends do say,
   "The breath goes now," and some say, "No";

So let us melt and make no noise,
   No tear floods nor sigh tempests move,
'Twere profanation of our joys,
   To tell the laity our love.

Moving of th' earth brings harms and fears;
   Men reckon what it did and meant;
But trepidation of the spheres,
   Though greater far, is innocent.

Dull sublunary lover's love
   (Whose soul is sense) cannot admit
Absence, because it doth remove
   Those things which elemented it.

But we by a love so far refined
   That ourselves know not what it is,
Inter-assurèd of the mind,
   Care less, eyes, lips, and hands to miss.

Our two souls, therefore, which are one,
   Though I must go, endure not yet
A breach, but an expansion,
   Like gold to airy thinness beat.

The Undertaking.

I have done one braver thing
Than all the Worthies did;
And yet a braver thence doth spring,
Which is, to keep that hid.

It were but madness now t' impart
The skill of specular stone,
When he, which can have learned the art
To cut it, can find none.

So, if I now should utter this,
Others (because no more
Such stuff to work upon there is)
Would love but as before:

But he who loveliness within
Hath found, all outward loathes;
For he who color loves, and skin,
Loves but their oldest clothes.

If, as I have, you also do
Virtue [attired] in woman see,
And dare love that, and say so too,
And forget the He and She;

And if this love, though placèd so,
From profane men you hide,
Which will no faith on this bestow,
Or, if they do, deride;

Then you have done a braver thing
Than all the Worthies did,
And a braver thence will spring,
Which is, to keep that hid.

SCENES AND PORTRAITS FROM CLARENDON'S "HISTORY OF THE REBELLION AND CIVIL WARS IN ENGLAND."

[EDWARD HYDE, first EARL OF CLARENDON, the eminent English historian and statesman, was born at Dinton, Wiltshire, in 1609, the third son of Henry Hyde of that place. After a course of law under his uncle, Sir Nicholas Hyde, he entered the Long Parliament. At first he acted with the popular party in their efforts for reform, but about 1642 espoused the royalist cause and was the chief adviser of Charles I. during the civil war, and of Prince Charles during his exile. On the Restoration he became lord chancellor of England, and was prominent in state affairs until 1667, when, on account of his great unpopularity with all classes, he was deprived of the great seal, impeached, and banished. He died at Rouen, France, December 9, 1674. His daughter, Anne Hyde, married the Duke of York, afterwards James II., and was the mother of Mary and Anne, both queens of England. Hyde's notable contribution to literature is the "History of the Rebellion in England" (1704-1707).]

WESTON, EARL OF PORTLAND.

HE was a gentleman of a very good and ancient extraction by father and mother. His education had been very good amongst books and men. After some years' study of the law in the Middle Temple, and at an age fit to make observations and reflections, out of which that which is commonly called experience is constituted, he traveled into foreign parts, and was acquainted in foreign parts. (After this) he betook himself to the Court, and lived there some years, at that distance, and with that awe, as was agreeable to the modesty of that age, when men were seen some time before they were known, and well known before they were preferred, or durst pretend to be preferred.

He spent the best part of his fortune (a fair one, that he inherited from his father) in his attendance at Court, and involved his friends in securities with him, who were willing to run his hopeful fortune, before he received the least fruit from it but the countenance of great men and those in authority, the most natural and most certain stairs to ascend by.

He was then sent ambassador to the archdukes Albert and Isabella, into Flanders; and to the Diet in Germany, to treat about the restitution of the palatinate; in which negotiation he behaved himself with great prudence, and with the concurrent testimony of a wise man from all those with whom he treated, princes and ambassadors, and upon his return was made a Privy Councilor, and Chancellor of the Exchequer in the place of the Lord Brooke, who was either persuaded, or put out of the place; which, being an office of honor and trust, is likewise an excellent stage for men of parts to tread and expose themselves upon, and where they have occasion of all natures to lay out and spread all their faculties and qualifications most for their advantage. He behaved himself very well in this function, and appeared equal to it; and carried himself so luckily in Parliament that he did his master much service, and preserved himself in the good opinion and acceptation of the House; which is a blessing not indulged to many by those high powers. He did swim in those troubled and boisterous waters in which the duke of Buckingham rode as admiral with a good grace, when very many who were about him were drowned, or forced on shore with shrewd hurts and bruises: which showed he knew well how and when to use his limbs and strength to the best advantage, sometimes only to avoid sinking, and sometimes to advance and get ground. And by this dexterity he kept his credit with those who could do him good, and lost it not with others who desired the destruction of those upon whom he most depended.

He was made Lord Treasurer in the manner and at the time mentioned before, upon the removal of the earl of Marlborough, and few months before the death of the duke. The former circumstance, which is often attended by compassion towards the degraded and prejudice towards the promoted, brought him no disadvantage: for, besides the delight that season had in changes, there was little reverence towards the person removed; and the extreme visible poverty of the Exchequer sheltered that province from the envy it had frequently created, and opened a door for much applause to be the portion of a wise and provident minister. For the other, of the duke's death, though some who knew the duke's passions and prejudice (which often produced rather sudden indisposition than obstinate resolution) believed he would have been shortly cashiered, as so many had lately been; and so that the death of his founder was a greater confirmation of him in the office than the delivery of the white staff had been: many other wise men, who knew the Treasurer's talent in removing prejudice and reconciling himself to wavering and doubtful affections, believed that the loss of the duke was very unseasonable, and that the awe or apprehension of his power and displeasure was a very necessary allay for the impetuosity of the new officer's nature, which needed some restraint and check, for some time, to his immoderate pretenses and appetite of power.

He did indeed appear on the sudden wonderfully elated, and so far threw off his old affectation to please some very much and to displease none, in which art he excelled, that in few months after the duke's death he found himself to succeed him in the public displeasure and in the malice of his enemies, without succeeding him in his credit at Court or in the affection of any considerable dependents. And yet, though he was not superior to all other men in the affection, or rather resignation, of the King, so that he might dispense favors and disfavors according to his own election, he had a full share in his master's esteem, who looked upon him as a wise and able servant and worthy of the trust he reposed in him, and received no other advice in the large business of his revenue; nor was any man so much his superior as to be able to lessen him in the King's affection by his power. So that he was in a post in which he might have found much ease and delight if he could have contained himself within the verge of his own province, which was large enough, and of such an extent that he might, at the same time, have drawn a great dependence upon him of very considerable men, and appeared a very useful and profitable minister to the King, whose revenue had been very loosely managed during the late years, and might by industry and order have been easily improved; and no man better understood what method was necessary towards that good husbandry than he.

But I know not by what frowardness in his stars he took more pains in examining and inquiring into other men's offices than in the discharge of his own; and not so much joy in what he had as trouble and agony for what he had not. The truth is, he had so vehement a desire to be the sole favorite, that he had no relish of the power he had: and in that contention he had many rivals, who had credit enough to do him ill offices, though not enough to satisfy their own ambition; the King himself being resolved to hold the reins in his own hands, and to put no further trust in others than was necessary for the capacity they served in. Which resolution in his majesty was no sooner believed, and the Treasurer's pretense taken notice (of), than he found the number of his enemies exceedingly increased, and others to be less eager in the pursuit of his friendship. And every day discovered some infirmities in him, which, being before known to few and not taken notice of, did now expose him both to public reproach and to private animosities; and even his vices admitted those contradictions in them that he could hardly enjoy the pleasant fruit of any of them. That which first exposed him to the public jealousy, which is always attended with public reproach, was the concurrent suspicion of his religion. His wife and all his daughters were declared of the Roman religion; and though himself and his sons sometimes went to church, he was never thought to have zeal for it; and his domestic conversation and dependents, with whom only he used entire freedom, were all known Catholics, and were believed to be agents for the rest. And yet, with all this disadvantage to himself, he never had reputation and credit with that party, who were the only people of the kingdom who did not believe him to be of their profession. For the penal laws (those only excepted which were sanguinary, and even those sometimes let loose) were never more rigidly executed, nor had the Crown ever so great a revenue from them, as in his time; nor did they ever pay so dear for the favors and indulgences of his office towards them.

No man had greater ambition to make his family great, or stronger designs to leave a great fortune to it. Yet his expenses were so prodigiously great, especially in his house, that all the ways he used for supply, which were all that occurred, could not serve his turn; insomuch that he contracted so great debts (the anxiety whereof, he pretended, broke his mind, and restrained that intentness and industry which was necessary for the due execution of his office), that the King was pleased twice to pay his debts; at least, towards it, to disburse forty thousand pounds in ready money out of his Exchequer. Besides, his majesty gave him a whole forest, Chute forest in Hampshire, and much other land belonging to the Crown; which was the more taken notice of and murmured against, because, being the chief minister of the revenue, he was particularly obliged, as much as in him lay, to prevent and even oppose such disinherison, and because, under that obligation, he had, avowedly and sourly, crossed the pretenses of other men, and restrained the King's bounty from being exercised almost to any. And he had that advantage (if he had made the right use of it), that his credit was ample enough (seconded by the King's own experience and observation and inclination) to retrench very much of the late unlimited expenses, and especially those of bounties, which from the death of the duke ran in narrow channels, which never so much overflowed as towards himself who stopped the current to other men.

He was of an imperious nature, and nothing wary in disobliging and provoking other men, and had too much courage in offending and incensing them; but, after having offended and incensed them, he was of so unhappy a feminine temper that he was always in a terrible fright and apprehension of them.

He had not that application and submission and reverence

for the Queen as might have been expected from his wisdom and breeding, and often crossed her pretenses and desires with more rudeness than was natural to him. Yet he was impertinently solicitous to know what her majesty said of him in private, and what resentments she had towards him. And when by some confidants (who had their ends upon him from those offices) he was informed of some bitter expressions fallen from her majesty, he was so exceedingly afflicted and tormented with the sense of it that, sometimes by passionate complaints and representations to the King, sometimes by more dutiful addresses and expostulations with the Queen in bewailing his misfortunes, he frequently exposed himself, and left his condition worse than it was before: and the *éclaircissement* commonly ended in the discovery of the persons from whom he had received his most secret intelligence.

He quickly lost the character of a bold, stout, and magnanimous man, which he had been long reputed to be in worse times; and, in his most prosperous season, fell under the reproach of being a man of big looks and of a mean and abject spirit.

ARCHBISHOP WILLIAMS.

The bishops, who were in this manner driven and kept from the House of Peers and not very secure in their own, could not have the patience to attend the dissolution of this storm, which in wisdom they ought to have done; but considering right and reason too abstractly, and what in justice was due, not what in prudence was to be expected, suffered themselves implicitly to be guided by the archbishop of York (who was of a proud, restless, overweening spirit) to such an act of indiscretion and disadvantage to themselves, that all their enemies could not have brought upon them. This bishop, as is said, was a man of very imperious and fiery temper, Dr. Williams, who had been Keeper of the Great Seal of England in the time of King James, and bishop of Lincoln. After his removal from that church he had lived splendidly in his diocese, and made himself very popular amongst those who had no reverence for the Court, of which he would frequently, and in the presence of many, speak with too much freedom, and tell many stories of things and persons upon his own former experience; in which being a man of great pride and vanity, he did not always confine himself to a precise veracity, and did often presume in those unwary discourses to mention the person of the King with too little reverence. He did affect to be thought an enemy to the archbishop of Canterbury, whose person he seemed exceedingly to contemn; and to be much displeased with those ceremonies and innovations, as they were then called, which were countenanced by the other; and had himself written and published in his own name, and by his own authority, a book against the using those ceremonies, in which there was much good learning and too little gravity for a bishop. His passion and his levity gave every day great advantages to those who did not love him; and he provoked too many, not to have those advantages made use of: so that, after several informations against him in the Star Chamber, he was sentenced for no less crimes than for perjury and subordination of perjury, and fined in a great sum of money to the King, and committed prisoner to the Tower, without the pity or compassion of any but those who, out of hatred to the government, were sorry that they were without so useful a champion; for he appeared to be a man of a very corrupt nature, whose passions could have transported him into the most unjustifiable actions.

He had a faculty of making relations of things done in his own presence, and discourses made to himself or in his own hearing, with all the circumstances of answers and replies, and upon arguments of great moment; all which upon examination were still found to have nothing in them that was real, but to be the pure effect of his own invention. After he was sentenced in the Star Chamber, some of his friends resorted to him to lament and condole with him for his misfortune; and some of them seemed to wonder that, in an affair of such a nature, he had not found means to have made some submission and composition that might have prevented the public hearing, which proved so much to his prejudice in point of reputation as well as profit. He answered them, with all the formality imaginable, that "they had reason indeed to wonder at him upon the event; but when they should know how he had governed himself he believed they would cease to think him worthy of blame." And then related to them that "as soon as publication had passed in his cause, and the books were taken out, he had desired his counsel (who were all able men, and some of them very eminent) in the vacation time, and they at most leisure, to meet together, and carefully to look over and peruse all the evidence that was taken on both sides; and that then they would all attend him such a morning, which he appointed upon their consent, at his own house at Westminster: that they came at the time appointed, and, being then shut up in a room together, he asked them whether they had sufficiently perused all the books, and were thoroughly informed of his case? To which they all answered that they had not only read them all over together, but had severally, every man by himself, perused (them) again, and they believed they were all well informed of the whole. That he then told them, he had desired this conference with them not only as his counsel, by whose opinion he meant to govern himself, but as his particular friends, who, he was sure, would give him their best advice, and persuade him to do everything as they would do themselves if they were in his condition. That he was now offered to make his peace at Court, by such an humble submission to the King as he was most inclined and ready to make, and which he would make the next day after his cause was heard, though he should be declared to be innocent, of which he could make no doubt; but that which troubled him for the present was that the infamousness of the charge against him, which had been often exposed and enlarged upon in several motions, had been so much taken notice of through the kingdom that it could not consist with his honor to divert the hearing, which would be imputed to his want of confidence in his innocence, since men did not suspect his courage if he durst rely upon the other; but that he was resolved, as he said before, the next day after he should be vindicated from those odious aspersions, he would cast himself at the King's feet, with all the humility and submission which the most guilty man could make profession of. It was in this point he desired their advice, to which he would, without adhering to his own inclination, entirely conform himself; and therefore desired them, singly in order, to give him their advice." He repeated the several and distinct discourse every man had made, in which he was so punctual that he applied those phrases and expressions and manner of speech to the several men which they were all taken notice of frequently to use; as many men have some peculiar words in discourse, which they are most delighted with or by custom most addicted to; and in conclusion, that "they were unanimous in their judgments, that he could not, with the preservation of his honor and the opinion of his integrity, decline the public hearing; where he must be unquestionably declared innocent, there being no crime or misdemeanor proved against him in such a manner as could make him liable to censure : they all commended his resolution of submitting to the King as soon as he had made his innocence to appear, and they all advised him to pursue that method. This," he said, " had swayed him, and made him decline the other expedient that had been proposed to him."

This relation wrought upon those to whom it was made, to raise a prejudice in them against the justice of the cause, or the reputation of the counsel, as they were most inclined; whereas there was not indeed the least shadow of truth in the whole relation, except that there was such a meeting and conference as was mentioned, and which had been consented to by the bishop upon the joint desire and importunity of all the counsel; who at that conference unanimously advised and desired him "to use all the means and friends he could that the cause might not be brought to hearing; but that he should purchase his peace at any price, for that, if it were heard, he would be sentenced very grievously, and that there were many things proved against him which would so much reflect upon his honor and reputation, and the more for being a bishop, that all his friends would abandon him, and be ever after ashamed to appear on his behalf." Which advice, with great passion and reproaches upon the several persons for their presumption and ignorance in matters so much above them, he utterly and scornfully rejected. Nor indeed was it possible at that time for him to have made his peace; for though upon some former addresses and importunity on his behalf by some persons of power and place in the Court, in which the Queen herself had endeavored to have done him good offices, the King was inclined to have saved him, being a bishop, from the infamy he must undergo by a public trial, yet the bishop's vanity had, in those conjunctures, so far transported him that he had done all he could to have it insinuated that the Court was ashamed of what they had done, and had prevailed with some of his powerful friends to persuade him to that composition: upon which the King would never hear more any person who moved on his behalf.

It had been once mentioned to him, whether by authority or no was not known, that his peace should be made if he would resign his bishopric and deanery of Westminster (for he held that *in commendum*) and take a good bishopric in Ireland; which he positively refused, and said, "he had much to do to defend himself against the archbishop here : but if he were in Ireland, there was a man " (meaning the earl of Strafford) " who would cut off his head within one month."

This bishop had been for some years in the Tower, by the sentence of the Star Chamber, before this Parliament met, when the lords who were the most active and powerful presently resolved to have him at liberty. Some had much kindness for him, not only as a known enemy to the archbishop of Canterbury, but as a supporter of those opinions and those persons which were against the Church itself. And he was no sooner at liberty and brought in (to) the House, but he defended and seconded the Lord Say when he made an invective, with all the malice and bitterness imaginable, against the archbishop, then in prison ; and when he had concluded, that bishop said that "he had long known that noble lord, and had always believed him to be as well affected to the Church as himself ; " and so he continued to make all his address to that lord and those of the same party. Being now in full liberty, and in some credit and reputation, he applied himself to the King, and made all possible professions of duty to his majesty and zeal to the Church, protesting to have a perfect detestation of those persons who appeared to have no affection or duty towards his majesty and all evil intentions against the religion established ; and that the civilities he had expressed towards them was only out of gratitude for the good will they had shown to him, and especially that he might the better promote his majesty's service. And it being his turn shortly after, as dean of Westminster, to preach before the King, he took occasion to speak of the factions in religion; and mentioning the Presbyterian, he said, "it was a government only fit for tailors and shoemakers and the like, and not for noblemen and gentlemen ; " which gave great scandal and offense to his great patrons, to whom he easily reconciled himself, by making them as merry with some sharp sayings of the Court, and by performing more substantial offices for them.

The Attempt on the Five Members.

In the afternoon of a day when the two Houses sat, Harbert, the King's Attorney, informed the House of Peers that he had somewhat to say to them from the King; and thereupon, having a paper in his hand, he said that the King commanded

Manuscript of Charles I.

(a) Instructions to Sir Edward Herbert, Attorney General, relative to the impeachment of Viscount Mandeville [Lord Kimbolton] and the Five Members, the erasures showing that it was at first intended merely to call Mandeville as a witness. Jan. 3, 1641.

(b) Warrant to Sir E. Herbert to desist from further proceedings on the above impeachment. Done at Theobald's, Mar. 3, 1641.

1. You ar to accuse those six jointlie and seuerallie.
2. You ar to reserue the power of making additionalls.
3. When the Committie for examination is naming (which you must press to be close and under key of secresie) if eather Essex, Warwick, Holland, Say, Wharton, or Brooke, be named you must desyre that they be spared, because you ar to examine them as witnesses for me.

CHARLES R.

Trusty and welbiloued, wee greet you well. Whereas on ye third of January last Wee did command you to arrest six persons in ye House of Peeres in Parliament and deliuired you notices to be by you presented to that House against them. We do now hereby command you that you proceed noe further therein, nor produce nor discover any proofs concerning ye same, Wee being minded fully to desist from any further proceeding that matter. And for not doing this shall be your warrant. Given at Our Court at Theobalds this Third day of March 1641.

To Our trusty and welbiloued
Sr. Edward Herbert Kn. Our
Attorney Generall.

him to accuse the Lord Kimbolton, a member of that House, and five gentlemen who were all members of the House of Commons, of high treason, and that his majesty had himself delivered him in writing several articles upon which he accused them; and thereupon he read in a paper the ensuing articles, by which the Lord Mandevill, Denzil Hollis, Sir Arthur Haslerigg, Mr. Pimm, Mr. Hambden, and Mr. Strowde stood accused of high treason for conspiring against the King and the Parliament.

Articles of high treason, and other misdemeanors, against the Lord Kimbolton, Mr. Pymm, John Hampden, Denzil Hollis, Sir Arthur Haslerigg, and William Strode, members of the House of Commons.

1. "That they have traitorously endeavored to subvert the fundamental laws and government of this kingdom, and deprive the King of his regal power, and to place on his subjects an arbitrary and tyrannical power.

2. "That they have endeavored by many foul aspersions upon his majesty and his government to alienate the affections of his people, and to make his majesty odious unto them.

3. "That they have endeavored to draw his majesty's late army to disobedience to his majesty's command, and to side with them in their traitorous design.

4. "That they have traitorously invited and encouraged a foreign power to invade his majesty's kingdom of England.

5. "That they have traitorously endeavored to subvert the very rights and beings of parliaments.

6. "That, for the completing of their traitorous designs, they have endeavored, as far as in them lay, by force and terror to compel the Parliament to join with them in their traitorous designs, and to that end have actually raised and countenanced tumults against the King and Parliament.

7. "That they have traitorously conspired to levy, and actually have levied, war against the King."

The House of Peers was somewhat appalled at this alarum, but took time to consider of it till the next day, that they might see how their masters the Commons would behave themselves; the Lord Kimbolton being present in the House and making great professions of his innocence, and no lord being so hardy (as) to press for his commitment on the behalf of the King.

At the same time, a sergeant at arms demanded to be heard at the House of Commons from the King, and, being sent for to the bar, demanded the persons of the five members to be delivered to him in his majesty's name, his majesty having accused them of high treason. But the Commons were not so much surprised with the accident; for, besides that they quickly knew what had passed with the Lords, some servants of the King's, by special warrant, had visited the lodgings of some of the accused members, and sealed up their studies and trunks; upon information whereof, before the sergeant came to the House, or public notice was taken of the accusation, an order was made by the Commons, "That if any person whatsoever should come to the lodgings of any member of that House, and there offer to seal the doors, trunks, or papers of such member, or to seize upon their persons, that then such member should require the aid of the next constable to keep such persons in safe custody till the House should give further order; that if any person whatsoever should offer to arrest or detain any member of that House, without first acquainting that House therewith and receiving further order from thence, that it should be lawful for such member to stand upon his guard and make resistance, and (for) any person to assist him, according to the protestation taken to defend the privileges of Parliament." And so, when the sergeant had delivered his message, he was no more called in, but a message sent to the King that "the members should be forthcoming as soon as a legal charge should be preferred against them;" and so the House adjourned till the next day, every one of the accused persons taking a copy of that order which was made for their security.

The next day, in the afternoon, the King, attended only by his own guard, and some few gentlemen who put themselves into their company in the way, came to the House of Commons, and, commanding all his attendants to wait at the door and to give offense to no man, himself, with his nephew, the Prince Elector, went into the House, to the great amazement of all; and the Speaker leaving the chair, the King went into it, and told the House, "he was sorry for that occasion of coming to them; that yesterday he had sent a sergeant at arms to apprehend some that by his command were accused of high treason, whereunto he expected obedience, but instead thereof he had received a message." He declared to them that "no King of

England had been ever, or should be, more careful to maintain their privileges than he would be; but that in cases of treason no man had privileges, and therefore he came to see if any of those persons whom he had accused were there; for he was resolved to have them, wheresoever he should find them." And looking then about, and asking the Speaker whether they were in the House, and he making no answer, he said, "he perceived the birds were all flown, but expected they should be sent to him as soon as they returned thither;" and assured them, in the word of a king, that he never intended any force, but would proceed against them in a fair and legal way, and so returned to Whitehall; the accused persons, upon information and intelligence of what his majesty intended to do, how secretly soever it was carried at Court, having withdrawn from the House about half an hour before the King came thither.

The House, in great disorder, as soon as the King was gone adjourned till the next day in the afternoon; the Lords being in so great apprehension upon notice of the King's being at the House of Commons that the earl of Essex expressed a tender sense he had of the inconveniences which were like to ensue those divisions, and moved, "that the House of Peers, as a work very proper for them, would interpose between the King and his people, and mediate to his majesty on the behalf of the persons accused;" for which he was reprehended by his friends, and afterwards laughed at himself when he found how much a stronger defense they had than the best mediation could prove on their behalf.

How secretly soever this affair was carried, it was evident that the coming of the King to the House was discovered by the members withdrawing themselves, and by a composedness which appeared in the countenances of many who used to be disturbed at less surprising occurrences; and though the purpose of accusing the members was only consulted between the King and the Lord Digby, yet it was generally believed that the King's purpose of going to the House was communicated with William Murry, of the bedchamber, with whom the Lord Digby had great friendship, and that it was betrayed by him. And that lord who had promised the King to move the House for commitment of the Lord Kimbolton as soon as the Attorney General should have accused him (which if he had done would probably have raised a very hot dispute in the House, where many would have joined with him) never spake the least word, but, on the contrary, seemed the most surprised and perplexed with the Attorney's impeachment; and sitting at that time next to the Lord Mandevill, with whom he pretended to live with much friendship, he whispered him in the ear with some commotion (as he had a rare talent in dissimulation), "that the King was very mischievously advised, and that it should go very hard but he would know whence that counsel proceeded; in order to which, and to prevent further mischief, he would go immediately to his majesty," and so went out of the House; whereas he was the only person who gave the counsel, named the persons, and particularly named the Lord Mandevill (against whom less could be said than against many others, and who was more generally beloved), and undertook to prove that he bade the rabble, when they were about the Parliament House, that they should go to Whitehall.

And when he found the ill success of the impeachment in both Houses, and how unsatisfied all were with the proceeding, he advised the King the next morning to go to the Guildhall and to inform the mayor and aldermen of the grounds of his proceeding, which will be mentioned anon. And, that people might not believe that there was any dejection of mind or sorrow for what was done, the same night the same counsel caused a proclamation to be prepared for the stopping the ports, that the accused persons might not escape out of the kingdom, and to forbid all persons to receive and harbor them, when it was well known that they were all together in a house in the city, without any fear of their security. And all this was done without the least communication with anybody but the Lord Digby, who advised it, and, it is very true, was so willing to take the utmost hazard upon himself, that he did offer the King, when he knew in what house they were together, with a select company of gentlemen who would accompany him, whereof Sir Thomas Lunsford was one, to seize upon them, and bring them away alive or leave them dead in the place; but the King liked not such enterprises.

That night the persons accused removed themselves into their stronghold, the city: not that they durst not venture themselves at their old lodgings, for no man would have presumed to trouble them, but that the city might see that they relied upon that place for a sanctuary of their privileges against violence and oppression, and so might put on an early concernment for them. And they were not disappointed; for, in spite of all the lord mayor could do to compose their distempers (who like a very wise and stout magistrate bestirred himself), the city was that whole night in arms; some people, designed to that purpose, running from one gate to another, and crying out that "the *Cavaliers* were coming to fire the city," and some saying that "the King himself was in the head of them."

The next morning, the King, being informed of much that had passed that night, according to the advice he had received, sent to the lord mayor to call a Common Council immediately; and about ten of the clock, himself, attended only by three or four Lords, went to the Guildhall, and in the room where the people were assembled told them, "he was very sorry to hear of the apprehensions they had entertained of danger; that he was come to them to show how much he relied upon their affections for his security and guard, having brought no other with him; that he had accused certain men of high treason, against whom he would proceed in a legal way, and therefore he presumed they would not shelter them in the city." And using many other very gracious expressions of his value of them, and telling one of the shrieves (who was of the two thought less inclined to his service) that he would dine with him, he departed, without that applause and cheerfulness which he might have expected from the extraordinary grace he vouchsafed to them, and, in his passage through the city, the rude people flocking together, and crying out, "*Privilege of Parliament, privilege of Parliament,*" some of them pressing very near his own coach, and amongst the rest one calling out with a very loud voice, "*To your tents, O Israel.*" However, the King, though much mortified, continued his resolution, taking little notice of the distempers; and, having dined at the shrief's, returned in the afternoon to Whitehall; and published, the next day, a proclamation for the apprehension of all those whom he accused of high treason, forbidding any person to harbor them, the articles of their charge being likewise printed and dispersed.

When the House of Commons next met, none of the accused members appearing, they had friends enough, who (were) well enough instructed, to aggravate the late proceedings and to put the House into a thousand jealousies and apprehensions; and every slight circumstance carried weight enough in it to disturb their minds. They took very little notice of the accusing the members; but the King's coming to the House, which had been never known before, and declaring that "he would take them where he found them," was an evidence that he meant himself to have brought a force into the House to apprehend them, if they had been there, (and) was looked upon as the highest breach of privilege that could possibly be imagined. They who spake most passionately, and probably meant as maliciously, behaved themselves with modesty, and seemed only concerned in what concerned them all; and concluded, after many lamentations, "that they did not think themselves safe in that House till the minds of men were better composed; that the city was full of apprehensions, and was very zealous for their security;" and therefore wished that they might adjourn the Parliament to meet in some place in the city. But that was found not practicable, since it was not in their own power to do it without the consent of the Peers and the concurrence of the King, who were both like rather to choose a place more distant from the city. And, with more reason, in the end they concluded, "that the House should adjourn itself for two or three days, and name a committee, which should sit both morning and afternoon in the city, and all who came to have voices;" and Merchant Tailors' Hall was appointed for the place of their meeting, they who served for London undertaking that it should be ready against the next morning: no man opposing or contradicting anything that was said, they who formerly used to appear for all the rights and authority which belonged to the King not knowing what to say, between grief and anger that the violent party had by these late unskillful actions of the Court gotten great advantage and recovered new spirits; and the three persons before named, without whose privity the King had promised that he would enter upon no new counsel, were so much displeased and dejected that they were inclined never more to take upon them the care of anything to be transacted in the House, finding already that they could not avoid being looked upon as the authors of those counsels to which they were so absolute strangers, and which they so perfectly detested.

And, in truth, they had then withdrawn themselves from appearing often in the House, but upon the abstracted consideration of their duty and conscience, and of the present ill condition the King was in, who likewise felt within himself the trouble and agony which usually attends generous and magnanimous minds, upon their having committed errors which expose them to censure and to damage. In fine, the House of

Commons adjourned for some days to consult with their friends in the city; and the House of Lords held so good correspondence with them that they likewise adjourned to the same days they knew, by some intelligence, they intended to meet again. But the Lords made no committee to sit in the city.

When the committee met next morning at Merchant Tailors' Hall, where all who came were to have voices, and whither all did come at first (out of curiosity to observe what method they meant to proceed in rather than expectation that they should be able to do any good there), they found a guard ready to attend them of substantial citizens in arms, and a committee from the Common Council to bid them welcome into the city, and to assure them that "the city would take care that they and all their members should be secured from violence; and to that purpose had appointed that guard to attend them, which should be always relieved twice a day, if they resolved to sit morning and afternoon;" and acquainted them further, that "the Common Council, in contemplation that they might stand in want of anything, had likewise appointed a committee of so many aldermen and such a number of the Common Council, which should always meet, at a place named, at those hours which that committee should appoint to meet at; to the end that, if any things were to be required of the city, they might still know their pleasure and take care that it should be obeyed." And thus they had provided for such a mutual communication and confederacy that they might be sure always to be of one mind, and the one to help the other in the prosecution of those designs and expedients which they should find necessary to their common end: the committee of the city consisting of the most eminent persons, aldermen and others, for their disaffection to the government of Church and State.

At their first sitting, the committee began with the stating the manner of the King's coming to the House, and all he did there; the several members mentioning all that they would take upon them to remember of his majesty's doing or speaking, both as he came to the House and after he was there; some of them being walking in Westminster Hall when the King walked through, and so came to the House with him or near him; others reporting what they had heard some of the gentlemen who attended his majesty say, as they passed by, every idle word having its commentary; and the persons, whoever were named, being appointed to attend, they having power given them to send for all persons and to examine them touching that affair. Nor had any man the courage to refuse to obey their summons; so that all those of the King's servants who were sent for appeared punctually at the hour that was assigned them, and were examined upon all questions which any one of the committee would propose to them, whereof many were very impertinent, and of little respect to the King.

It was very well known where the accused persons were, all together in one house in Coleman Street, near the place where the committee sat, and whither persons trusted passed to and fro to communicate and receive directions; but it was not time for them yet to appear in public and to come and sit with the committee, or to own the believing that they thought themselves safe from the violence and assaults of the Court, the power whereof they exceedingly contemned whilst they seemed to apprehend it: nor was it yet time to model in what manner their friends in the city and the country should appear concerned for them, in preparing whereof no time was lost.

* * * * * * *

The truth is, it cannot be expressed how great a change there appeared to be in the countenance and minds of all sorts of people, in town and country, upon these late proceedings of the King. They who had before even lost their spirits, having lost their credit and reputation, except amongst the meanest people, who could never have been made use of by them when the greater should forsake them, and so, despairing of ever being able to compass their designs of malice or ambition, some of them were resuming their old resolutions of leaving the kingdom, now again recovered greater courage than ever, and quickly found that their credit and reputation was as great as ever it had been; the Court being reduced to a lower condition, and to more disesteem and neglect, than ever it had undergone. All that they had formerly said of plots and conspiracies against the Parliament, which had before been laughed at, (was) now thought true and real, and all their fears and jealousies looked upon as the effects of their great wisdom and foresight. All that had been whispered of Ireland was now talked aloud and printed, as all other seditious pamphlets and libels were. The shops of the city generally shut up, as if an enemy were at their gates ready to enter and to plunder them; and the people in all places at a gaze, as if they looked only for directions, and were then disposed to any undertaking.

On the other side, they who had, with the greatest courage and alacrity, opposed all their seditious practices, between grief and anger were confounded with the consideration of what had been done and what was like to follow. They were far from thinking that the accused members had received much wrong, yet they thought it an unseasonable time to call them to account for it; that if anything had been to be done of that kind, there should have been a better choice of the persons, there being many of the House of more mischievous inclinations and designs against the King's person and the government, and were more exposed to the public prejudice, than the Lord Kimbolton was, who was a civil and well-natured man, and had rather kept ill company than drunk deep of that infection and poison that had wrought upon many others. Then Sir Arthur Haslerigge and Strowde were persons of too low an account and esteem; and though their virulence and malice was as conspicuous and transcendent as any men's, yet their reputation and interest to do any mischief, otherwise than in concurring in it, was so small that they gained credit and authority by being joined with the rest, who had indeed a great influence. However, if there was a resolution to proceed against those men, it would have been much better to have caused them to have been all severally arrested and sent to the Tower or to other prisons, which might have been very easily done before suspected, than to send in that manner to the Houses with that formality which would be liable to so many exceptions. At least, they ought so far to have imparted it to members in both Houses who might have been trusted, that, in the instant of the accusation, when both Houses were in that consternation (as in a great consternation they were), somewhat might have been pressed confidently towards the King's satisfaction, which would have produced some opposition and contradiction, which would have prevented that universal concurrence and dejection of spirit which seized upon and possessed both Houses.

But, above all, the anger and indignation was very great and general that to all the other oversights and presumptions (was added) the exposing the dignity and majesty and safety of the King, in his coming in person in that manner to the House of Commons, and in going the next day, as he did, to the Guildhall and to the lord mayor's, which drew such reproaches upon him to his face. All which was justly imputed to the Lord Digby, who had before fewer true friends than he deserved, and had now almost the whole nation his enemies, being the most universally odious of any man in it.

AN HORATIAN ODE.

Upon Oliver Cromwell's Return from Ireland in 1650.

By ANDREW MARVELL.

[1620–1678.]

THE forward youth that would appear,
Must now forsake his Muses dear;
    Nor in the shadows sing
    His numbers languishing.

'Tis time to leave the books in dust,
And oil the unusèd armor's rust;
    Removing from the wall
    The corselet of the hall.

So restless Cromwell could not cease
In the inglorious arts of peace,
    But through adventurous war
    Urgèd his active star;

And like the three-forked lightning, first
Breaking the clouds where it was nurst,
    Did thorough his own side
    His fiery way divide.

For 'tis all one to courage high,
The emulous, or enemy;
    And, with such, to inclose,
    Is more than to oppose.

Then burning through the air he went,
And palaces and temples rent;
    And Cæsar's head at last
    Did through his laurels blast.

'Tis madness to resist or blame
The face of angry heaven's flame;
    And, if we would speak true,
    Much to the man is due,

Who, from his private gardens, where
He lived reservèd and austere,
    (As if his highest plot
    To plant the bergamot,)

Could by industrious valor climb
To ruin the great work of time,
    And cast the kingdoms old
    Into another mold!

Though justice against fate complain,
And plead the ancient rights in vain —
    But those do hold or break,
    As men are strong or weak.

Nature, that hateth emptiness,
Allows of penetration less,
    And therefore must make room
    Where greater spirits come.

What field of all the civil war,
Where his were not the deepest scar?
    And Hampton shows what part
    He had of wiser art:

Where, twining subtle fears with hope,
He wove a net of such a scope
    That Charles himself might chase
    To Carisbrook's narrow case;

That thence the royal actor borne,
The tragic scaffold might adorn.
    While around the armed bands
    Did clap their bloody hands,

He nothing common did or mean
Upon that memorable scene;
    But with his keener eye
    The axe's edge did try:

Nor called the gods, with vulgar spite,
To vindicate his helpless right;
    But bowed his comely head
    Down, as upon a bed.

This was that memorable hour,
Which first assured the forcèd power;
    So, when they did design
    The capitol's first line,

A bleeding head, where they begun,
Did fright the architects to run;
    And yet in that the state
    Foresaw its happy fate.

And now the Irish are ashamed
To see themselves in one year tamed;
    So much one man can do,
    That does both act and know.

They can affirm his praises best,
And have, though overcome, confest
    How good he is, how just,
    And fit for highest trust:

Nor yet grown stiffer with command,
But still in the republic's hand,
    How fit he is to sway
    That can so well obey.

He to the commons' feet presents
A kingdom for his first year's rents,
    And (what he may) forbears
    His fame to make it theirs:

And has his sword and spoils ungirt,
To lay them at the public's skirt:
    So when the falcon high
    Falls heavy from the sky,

She, having killed, no more doth search
But on the next green bough to perch,
    Where, when he first does lure,
    The falconer has her sure.

CROMWELL AT MARSTON MOOR

From a painting by Ernest Crofts, R.A.

What may not then our isle presume,
While victory his crest does plume?
    What may not others fear
    If thus he crowns each year?

As Cæsar, he, ere long, to Gaul;
To Italy an Hannibal;
    And to all states not free
    Shall climacteric be.

The Pict no shelter now shall find
Within his party-colored mind;
    But, from this valor sad,
    Shrink underneath the plaid—

Happy, if in the tufted brake
The English hunter him mistake,
    Nor lay his hounds in near
    The Caledonian deer.

But thou, the war's and fortune's son,
March indefatigably on;
    And, for the last effect,
    Still keep the sword erect!

Besides the force it has to fright
The spirits of the shady night,
    The same arts that did gain
    A power, must it maintain.

OLIVER CROMWELL.

By THOMAS CARLYLE.

[THOMAS CARLYLE, Scotch moralist, essayist, and historian, was born at Ecclefechan, December 4, 1795. He studied for the ministry at Edinburgh University, taught school, studied law, became a hack writer and tutor; in 1826 married Jane Welsh, and in 1828 removed to a farm at Craigenputtoch, where he wrote essays and "Sartor Resartus"; in 1834 removed to his final home in Cheyne Row, Chelsea. His "French Revolution" was issued in 1837. He lectured for three years, "Heroes and Hero Worship" gathering up one course. His chief succeeding works were "Chartism Past and Present," "Cromwell's Letters," "Latter-day Pamphlets," "Life of Sterling," and "Frederick the Great." He died February 4, 1881.]

THE young Oliver is sent to study Law; falls, or is said to have fallen, for a little period, into some of the dissipations of youth; but if so, speedily repents, abandons all this: not much above twenty, he is married, settled as an altogether grave and quiet man. "He pays back what money he had won at gambling," says the story; he does not think any gain of that kind could be really *his*. It is very interesting, very natural, this "conversion" as they well name it; this awakening of a great true soul from the worldly slough, to see into the awful *truth* of things; to see that Time and its shows all rested on Eternity, and this poor Earth of ours was the threshold either of Heaven or of Hell! Oliver's life at St. Ives and Ely, as a sober industrious Farmer, is it not altogether as that of a true and devout man? He has renounced the world and its ways: *its* prizes are not the thing that can enrich him. He tills the earth; he reads his Bible; daily assembles his servants round him to worship God. He comforts persecuted ministers, is fond of preachers; nay, can himself preach, — exhorts his neighbors to be wise, to redeem the time. In all this what "hypocrisy," "ambition," "cant," or other falsity? The man's hopes, I do believe, were fixed on the other Higher World; his aim to get well *thither*, by walking well through his humble course in *this* world. He courts no notice: what would notice here do for him? "Ever in his great Taskmaster's eye."

It is striking, too, how he comes out once into public view; he, since no other is willing to come: in resistance to a public grievance. I mean, in that matter of the Bedford Fens. No one else will go to law with Authority; therefore he will. That matter once settled, he returns back into obscurity, to his Bible and his Plow. "Gain influence?" His influence is the most legitimate; derived from personal knowledge of him, as a just, religious, reasonable, and determined man. In this way he has lived till past forty; old age is now in view of him, and the earnest portal of Death and Eternity; it was at this point that he suddenly became "ambitious"! I do not interpret his Parliamentary mission in that way!

His successes in Parliament, his successes through the war, are honest successes of a brave man; who has more resolution in the heart of him, more light in the head of him, than other men. His prayers to God; his spoken thanks to the God of Victory, who had preserved him safe, and carried him forward so far, through the furious clash of a world all set in conflict, through desperate-looking envelopments at Dunbar; through the death hail of so many battles; mercy after mercy; to the "crowning mercy" of Worcester Fight: all this is good and genuine for a deep-hearted Calvinistic Cromwell. Only to vain unbelieving Cavaliers, worshiping not God but their own "lovelocks" frivolities, and formalities, living quite apart from contemplations of God, living *without* God in the world, need it seem hypocritical.

Nor will his participation in the King's death involve him in condemnation with us. It is a stern business killing of a King! But if you once go to war with him, it lies *there;* this and all else lies there. Once at war, you have made wager of battle with him: it is he to die, or else you. Reconciliation is problematic; may be possible, or, far more likely, is impossible. It is now pretty generally admitted that the Parliament, having vanquished Charles First, had no way of making any tenable arrangement with him. The large Presbyterian party, apprehensive now of the Independents, were most anxious to do so; anxious indeed as for their own existence; but it could not be. The unhappy Charles, in those final Hampton-Court negotiations, shows himself as a man fatally incapable of being dealt with. A man who, once for all, could not and would not *understand:* whose thought did not in any measure represent to him the real fact of the matter; nay worse, whose *word* did not at all represent his thought. We may say this of him without cruelty, with deep pity rather; but it is true and undeniable. Forsaken there of all but the *name* of Kingship, he still, finding himself treated with outward respect as a King, fancied that he might play off party against party, and smuggle himself into his old power by deceiving both. Alas, they both *discovered* that he was deceiving them. A man whose *word* will not inform you at all what he means or will do, is not a man you can bargain with. You must get out of that man's way, or put him out of yours! The Presbyterians, in their despair, were still for believing Charles, though found false, unbelievable, again and again. Not so Cromwell: "For all our fighting," says he, "we are to have a little bit of paper?" No!—

In fact, everywhere we have to note the decisive practical *eye* of this man; how he drives towards the practical and practicable; has a genuine insight into what *is* fact. Such an intellect, I maintain, does not belong to a false man: the false man sees false shows, plausibilities, expediences: the true man is needed to discern even practical truth. Cromwell's advice about the Parliament's Army, early in the contest, How they were to dismiss their city tapsters, flimsy riotous persons, and choose substantial yeomen, whose hearts were in the work, to be soldiers for them: this is advice by a man who *saw*. Fact answers, if you see into Fact! Cromwell's *Ironsides* were the embodiment of this insight of his; men fearing God, and without any other fear. No more conclusively genuine set of fighters ever trod the soil of England, or of any other land.

Neither will we blame greatly that word of Cromwell's to them; which was so blamed: "If the King should meet me in battle, I would kill the King." Why not? These words were spoken to men who stood as before a Higher than Kings. They had set more than their own lives on the cast. The Parliament may call it, in official language, a fighting "*for* the King"; but we, for our share, cannot understand that. To us it is no dilettante work, no sleek officiality; it is sheer rough death and earnest. They have brought it to the calling forth of *War;* horrid internecine fight, man grappling with man in fire-eyed rage, — the *infernal* element in man called forth, to try it by that? *Do* that therefore; since that is the thing to be done. — The successes of Cromwell seem to me a very natural thing! Since he was not shot in battle, they were an inevitable thing. That such a man, with the eye to see, with the heart to dare, should advance, from post to post, from victory to victory, till the Huntingdon Farmer became, by whatever name you might call him, the acknowledged Strongest Man in England, virtually the King of England, requires no magic to explain it! —

Truly it is a sad thing for a people, as for a man, to fall into Skepticism, into dilettanteism, insincerity; not to know a Sincerity when they see it. For this world, and for all worlds, what curse is so fatal? The heart lying dead, the eye cannot see. What intellect remains is merely the *vulpine* intellect. That a true *King* be sent them is of small use; they do not know him when sent. They say scornfully, Is this your King? The Hero wastes his heroic faculty in bootless contradiction from the unworthy; and can accomplish little. For himself he does accomplish a heroic life, which is much, which is all; but for the world he accomplishes comparatively nothing. The wild rude Sincerity, direct from Nature, is not glib in answering from the witness box: in your small-debt *pie-powder* court, he is scouted as a counterfeit. The vulpine intellect "detects" him. For being a man worth any thousand men, the response your Knox, your Cromwell, gets is an argument for two centuries whether he was a man at all. God's greatest gift to this Earth is sneeringly flung away. The miraculous talisman is a paltry plated coin, not fit to pass in the shops as a common guinea.

Lamentable this! I say, this must be remedied. Till this be remedied in some measure, there is nothing remedied. "Detect quacks?" Yes do, for Heaven's sake; but know withal the men that are to be trusted! Till we know that, what is all our knowledge; how shall we even so much as "detect"? For the vulpine sharpness, which considers itself to be knowledge, and "detects" in that fashion, is far mistaken. Dupes indeed are many; but, of all *dupes*, there is none so fatally situated as he who lives in undue terror of being duped. The world does exist; the world has truth in it, or it would not exist! First recognize what is true, we shall *then* discern what is false; and properly never till then.

"Know the men that are to be trusted:" alas, this is yet, in these days, very far from us. The sincere alone can recognize sincerity. Not a Hero only is needed, but a world fit for him; a world not of *Valets*,—the Hero comes almost in vain to it otherwise! Yes, it is far from us: but it must come; thank God, it is visibly coming. Till it do come, what have we? Ballot boxes, suffrages, French Revolutions: if we are as Valets, and do not know the Hero when we see him, what good are all these? A heroic Cromwell comes; and for a hundred and fifty years he cannot have a vote from us. Why, the insincere, unbelieving word is the *natural property* of the Quack, and of the Father of quacks and quackeries! Misery, confusion, unveracity, are alone possible there. By ballot boxes we alter the *figure* of our Quack; but the substance of him continues. The Valet World *has* to be governed by the Sham Hero, by the king merely *dressed* in King gear. It is his; he is its! In brief, one of two things: We shall either learn to know a Hero, a true Governor and Captain, somewhat better, when we see him; or else go on to be forever governed by the Unheroic; had we ballot boxes clattering at every street corner, there were no remedy in these.

Poor Cromwell,—great Cromwell! The inarticulate Prophet; Prophet who could not *speak*. Rude, confused, struggling to utter himself, with his savage depth, with his wild sincerity; and he looked so strange, among the elegant Euphemisms, dainty little Falklands, didactic Chillingworths, diplomatic Clarendons! Consider him. An outer hull of chaotic confusion, visions of the Devil, nervous dreams, almost semimadness; and yet such a clear determinate man's energy working in the heart of that. A kind of chaotic man. The ray as of pure starlight and fire, working in such an element of boundless hypochondria, *un*formed black of darkness! And yet withal this hypochondria, what was it but the very greatness of the man? The depth and tenderness of his wild affections: the quantity of *sympathy* he had with things,— the quantity of insight he would yet get into the heart of things, the mastery he would yet get over things: this was his hypochondria. The man's misery as man's misery always does, came of his greatness. Samuel Johnson too is that kind of man. Sorrow-stricken, half-distracted; the wide element of mournful *black* enveloping him,—wide as the world. It is the character of a prophetic man; a man with his whole soul *seeing*, and struggling to see.

On this ground, too, I explain to myself Cromwell's reputed confusion of speech. To himself the internal meaning was sun-clear; but the material with which he was to clothe it in utterance was not there. He had *lived* silent; a great unnamed sea of Thought round him all his days; and in his way of life little call to attempt *naming* or uttering that. With his sharp power of vision, resolute power of action, I doubt not he could have learned to write Books withal, and speak fluently enough; he did harder things than writing of Books. This kind of man is precisely he who is fit for doing manfully all things you will set him on doing. Intellect is not speaking and logicizing; it is seeing and ascertaining. Virtue, *Vir-tus*, manhood, *hero*hood, is not fair-spoken, immaculate regularity; it is first of all what the Germans well name it, *Tugend* (*Taugend*, dowing or *Dough*-tiness), Courage and the Faculty to *do*. This basis of the matter Cromwell had in him.

One understands moreover how, though he could not speak in Parliament, he might *preach*, rhapsodic preaching; above all, how he might be great in extempore prayer. These are the free outpouring utterances of what is in the heart; method is not required in them; warmth, depth, sincerity, are all that is required. Cromwell's habit of prayer is a notable feature of him. All his great enterprises were commenced with prayer. In dark, inextricable-looking difficulties, his Officers and he used to assemble, and pray alternately, for hours, for days, till some definite resolution rose among them, some "door of hope," as they would name it, disclosed itself. Consider that. In tears, in fervent prayers, and cries to the great God, to have pity on them, to make His light shine before them. They, armed Soldiers of Christ, as they felt themselves to be; a little band of Christian Brothers, who had drawn the sword against a great black devouring world not Christian, but Mammonish, Devilish, — they cried to God in their straits, in their extreme need, not to forsake the Cause that was His. The light which now rose upon them, — how could a human soul, by any means at all, get better light? Was not the purpose so formed like to be precisely the best, wisest, the one to be followed without hesitation any more? To them it was as the shining of Heaven's own Splendor in the waste-howling darkness; the Pillar of Fire by night, that was to guide them on their desolate, perilous way. *Was* it not such? Can a man's soul, to this hour, get guidance by any other method than intrinsically by that same, — devout prostration of the earnest struggling soul before the Highest, the Giver of all Light; be such *prayer* a spoken, articulate, or be it a voiceless, inarticulate one? There is no other method. "Hypocrisy"? One begins to be weary of all that. They who call it so have no right to speak on such matters. They never formed a purpose, what one can call a purpose. They went about balancing expediences, plausibilities; gathering votes, advices; they never were alone with the *truth* of a thing at all. — Cromwell's prayers were likely to be "eloquent," and much more than that. His was the heart of a man who *could* pray.

But indeed his actual Speeches, I apprehend, were not nearly so ineloquent, incondite, as they look. We find he was, what all speakers aim to be, an impressive speaker, even in Parliament; one who, from the first, had weight. With that rude, passionate voice of his, he was always understood to *mean* something, and men wished to know what. He disregarded eloquence, — nay, despised and disliked it; spoke always without premeditation of the words he was to use. The Reporters, too, in those days seem to have been singularly candid; and to have given the Printer precisely what they found on their own note paper. And withal, what a strange proof is it of Cromwell's being the premeditative, ever-calculating hypocrite, acting a play before the world, That to the last he took no more charge of his Speeches! How came he not to study his words a little, before flinging them out to the public? If the words were true words, they could be left to shift for themselves.

But with regard to Cromwell's "lying," we will make one remark. This, I suppose, or something like this, to have been the nature of it. All parties found themselves deceived in him; each party understood him to be meaning *this*, heard him even say so, and behold he turns out to have been meaning *that!* He was, cry they, the chief of liars. But now, intrinsically, is not all this the inevitable fortune, not of a false man in such times, but simply of a superior man? Such a man must have *reticences* in him. If he walk wearing his heart upon his sleeve for daws to peck at, his journey will not extend far! There is no use for any man's taking up his abode in a house built of glass. A man always is to be himself the judge how much of his mind he will show to other men; even to those he would have work along with him. There are impertinent inquiries made: your rule is, to leave the inquirer *un*informed on that matter; not, if you can help it, *mis*informed, but precisely as dark as he was!

This, could one hit the right phrase of response, is what the wise and faithful man would aim to answer in such a case.

Cromwell, no doubt of it, spoke often in the dialect of small subaltern parties; uttered to them a *part* of his mind. Each little party thought him all its own. Hence their rage, one and all, to find him not of their party, but of his own party! Was it his blame? At all seasons of his history he must have felt, among such people, how, if he explained to them the deeper insight he had, they must either have shuddered aghast at it, or believing it, their own little compact hypothesis must have gone wholly to wreck. They could not have worked in his province any more; nay, perhaps they could not now have worked in their own province. It is the inevitable position of a great man among small men. Small men, most active, useful, are to be seen everywhere, whose whole activity depends on some conviction which to you is palpably a limited one; imperfect, what we call an *error*. But would it be a kindness always, is it a duty always or often, to disturb them in that? Many a man, doing loud work in the world, stands only on some thin traditionality, conventionality, to him indubitable, to you incredible: break that beneath him, he sinks to endless depths! "I might have my hand full of truth," said Fontenelle, "and open only my little finger."

And if this be the fact even in matters of doctrine, how much more in all departments of practice! He that cannot withal *keep his mind to himself* cannot practice any considerable thing whatever. And we call it "dissimulation," all this? What would you think of calling the general of an army a dissembler because he did not tell every corporal and private soldier, who pleased to put the question, what his thoughts were about everything?— Cromwell, I should rather say, managed all this in a manner we must admire for its perfection. An endless vortex of such questioning "corporals" rolled confusedly round him through his whole course; whom he did answer. It must have been as a great true-seeing man that he managed this too. Not one proved falsehood, as I said; not one! Of what man that ever wound himself through such a coil of things will you say so much?—

But in fact there are two errors, widely prevalent, which pervert to the very basis our judgments formed about such men as Cromwell; about their "ambition," "falsity," and suchlike. The first is what I might call substituting the *goal* of their career for the course and starting point of it. The vulgar Historian of a Cromwell fancies that he had determined on being Protector of England, at the time when he was plowing the marsh lands of Cambridgeshire. His career lay all mapped out: a programme of the whole drama; which he then step by step dramatically unfolded with all manner of cunning, deceptive dramaturgy, as he went on,— the hollow scheming Ὑποκριτής, or Play-actor, that he was! This is a radical perversion; all but universal in such cases. And think for an instant how different the fact is! How much does one of *us* foresee of his own life? Short way ahead of us it is all dim; an *un*wound skein of possibilities, of apprehensions, attemptabilities, vague-looming hopes. This Cromwell had *not* his life lying all in that fashion of Programme, which he needed then, with that unfathomable cunning of his, only to enact dramatically, scene after scene! Not so. We see it so; but to him it was in no measure so. What absurdities would fall away of themselves, were this one undeniable fact kept honestly in view by History! Historians indeed will tell you that they do keep it in view; but look whether such is practically the fact! Vulgar History, as in this Cromwell's case, omits it altogether; even the best kinds of History only remember it now and then. To remember it duly with rigorous perfection, as in the fact it *stood*, requires indeed a rare faculty; rare, nay impossible. A very Shakespeare for faculty; or more than Shakespeare; who could *enact* a brother man's biography, see with the brother man's eyes at all points of his course what things *he* saw; in short, *know* his course and him, as few "Historians" are like to do. Half or more of all the thick-plied perversions which distort our image of Cromwell will disappear, if we honestly so much as try to represent them so; in sequence, as they *were;* not in the lump, as they are thrown down before us.

But a second error, which I think the generality commit, refers to this same "ambition" itself. We exaggerate the ambition of Great Men; we mistake what the nature of it is. Great men are not ambitious in that sense; he is a small, poor man that is ambitious so. Examine the man who lives in misery because he does not shine above other men; who goes about producing himself, pruriently anxious about his gifts and claims; struggling to force everybody, as it were begging everybody for God's sake, to acknowledge him a great man, and set him over the heads of men! Such a creature is among the wretchedest sights seen under the sun. A *great* man? A poor morbid prurient empty man; fitter for the ward of a hospital, than for a throne among men. I advise you to keep out of his way. He cannot walk on quiet paths; unless you will look at him, wonder at him, write paragraphs about him, he cannot live. It is the *emptiness* of the man, not his greatness. Because there is nothing in himself, he hungers and thirsts that you would find something in him. In good truth, I believe no great man, not so much as a genuine man who had health and real substance in him of whatever magnitude, was ever much tormented in this way.

Your Cromwell, what good could it do him to be "noticed" by noisy crowds of people? God his Maker already noticed him. He, Cromwell, was already there; no notice would make *him* other than he already was. Till his hair was grown gray, and Life from the downhill slope was all seen to be limited, not infinite but finite, and all a measurable matter *how* it went, — he had been content to plow the ground, and read his Bible. He in his old days could not support it any longer, without selling himself to Falsehood, that he might ride in gilt carriages to Whitehall, and have clerks with bundles of papers haunting him, "Decide this, decide that," which in utmost sorrow of heart no man can perfectly decide! What could gilt carriages do for this man? From of old, was there not in his life a weight of meaning, a terror and a splendor as of Heaven itself? His existence there as man set him beyond the need of gilding. Death, Judgment, and Eternity: these already lay as the background of whatsoever he thought or did. All his life lay begirt as in a sea of nameless Thoughts, which no speech of a mortal could name. God's Word, as the Puritan prophets of that time had read it; this was great, and all else was little to him. To call such a man "ambitious," to figure him as the prurient windbag described above, seems to me the poorest solecism. Such a man will say: "Keep your gilt carriages and huzzaing mob; keep your red-tape clerks, your influentialities, your important businesses. Leave me alone, leave me alone; there is *too much of life* in me already!" Old Samuel Johnson, the greatest soul in England in his day, was not ambitious. "Corsica Boswell" flaunted at public shows with printed ribbons round his hat; but the great old Samuel stayed at home. The world-wide soul wrapt up in its thoughts, in its sorrows; what could paradings, and ribbons in the hat, do for it?

Ah yes, I will say again: The great *silent* men! Looking round on the noisy inanity of the world, words with little meaning, actions with little worth, one loves to reflect on the great Empire of *Silence*. The noble silent men, scattered here and there, each in his department; silently thinking, silently working; whom no Morning Newspaper makes mention of! They are the salt of the Earth. A country that has none or few of these is in a bad way. Like a forest which had no *roots;* which had all turned into leaves and boughs; which must soon wither and be no forest. Woe for us if we had nothing but what we can *show*, or speak. Silence, the great Empire of Silence: higher than the stars; deeper than the Kingdoms of Death! It alone is great; all else is small. — I hope we English will long maintain our *grand talent pour le silence.* Let others that cannot do without standing on barrel heads, to spout, and be seen of all the market place, cultivate speech exclusively, — become a most green forest without roots! Solomon says, There is a time to speak; but also a time to keep silence. Of some great silent Samuel, not urged to writing, as old Samuel Johnson says he was, by *want of money,* and nothing other, one might ask, "Why do not you too get up and speak; promulgate your system, found your sect?" "Truly,' he will answer, "I am *continent* of my thought hitherto; happily I have yet had the ability to keep it in me, no compulsion strong enough to speak it. My 'system' is not for promulgation first of all; it is for serving myself to live by. That is the great purpose of it to me. And then the 'honor? Alas, yes; but as Cato said of the statue: So many statues in that Forum of yours, may it not be better if they ask, Where is Cato's statue?——"

But now, by way of counterpoise to this of Silence, let me say that there are two kinds of ambition: one wholly blamable, the other laudable and inevitable. Nature has provided that the great silent Samuel shall not be silent too long. The selfish wish to shine over others, let it be accounted altogether poor and miserable. "Seekest thou great things, seek them not:" this is most true. And yet, I say, there is an irrepressible tendency in every man to develop himself according to the magnitude which Nature has made him of; to speak out, to act out, what Nature has laid in him. This is proper, fit, inevitable; nay, it is a duty, and even the summary of duties for a man. The meaning of life here on earth might be defined as consisting in this: To unfold your *self*, to work what thing you have the faculty for. It is a necessity for the human being, the first law of our existence. Coleridge beautifully remarks that the infant learns to *speak* by this necessity it feels. — We will say therefore: To decide about ambition, whether it is bad or not, you have two things to take into view. Not the coveting of the place alone, but the fitness for the man of the place withal: that is the question. Perhaps the place was *his;* perhaps he had a natural right, and even obligation, to seek the place! Mirabeau's ambition to be Prime Minister, how shall we blame it, if he were "the only man in France that could have done any good there"? Hopefuler perhaps had he not so clearly *felt* how much good he could do! But a poor Necker, who could do no good, and had even felt that he could do none, yet sitting broken-hearted because they had flung him out, and he was now quit of it, well might Gibbon mourn over him. — Nature, I say, has provided amply, that the silent great man shall strive to speak withal; *too* amply, rather!

Fancy, for example, you had revealed to the brave old Samuel Johnson, in his shrouded-up existence, that it was possible for him to do priceless divine work for his country and the whole world. That the perfect Heavenly Law might be made Law on this Earth; that the prayer he prayed daily, "Thy kingdom come," was at length to be fulfilled! If you had convinced his judgment of this; that it was possible, practicable; that he, the mournful, silent Samuel, was called to take a part in it! Would not the whole soul of the man have flamed up into a divine clearness, into noble utterance and determination to act; casting all sorrows and misgivings under his feet, counting all affliction and contradiction small, — the whole dark element of his existence blazing into articulate radiance of light and lightning? It were a true ambition this! And think now how it actually was with Cromwell. From of old, the sufferings of God's Church, true zealous Preachers of the truth flung into dungeons, whipt, set on pillories, their ears cropt off, God's Gospel cause trodden under foot of the unworthy: all this had lain heavy on his soul. Long years he had looked upon it, in silence, in prayer; seeing no remedy on Earth; trusting well that a remedy in Heaven's goodness would come, — that such a course was false, unjust, and could not last forever. And now behold the dawn of it; after twelve years' silent waiting, all England stirs itself; there is to be once more a Parliament, the Right will get a voice for itself: inexpressible, well-grounded hope has come again into the Earth. Was not such a Parliament worth being a member of? Cromwell threw down his plows, and hastened thither.

He spoke there, — rugged bursts of earnestness, of a self-seen truth, where we get a glimpse of them. He worked there; he fought and strove, like a strong true giant of a man, through cannon tumult and all else, — on and on, till the Cause *triumphed*, its once so formidable enemies all swept from before it, and the dawn of hope had become clear light of victory and certainty. That *he* stood there as the strongest soul of England, the undisputed Hero of all England, — what of this? It was possible that the Law of Christ's Gospel could now establish itself in the world! The Theocracy which John Knox in his pulpit might dream of as a "devout imagination," this practical man, experienced in the whole chaos of most rough practice, dared to consider as capable of being *realized*. Those that were highest in Christ's Church, the devoutest, wisest men, were to rule the land: in some considerable degree, it might be so and should be so. Was it not *true*, God's truth? And if *true*, was it not then the very thing to do? The strongest practical intellect in England dared to answer, Yes! This I call a noble true purpose; is it not, in its own dialect, the noblest that could enter into the heart of Statesman or man? For a Knox to take it up was something; but for a Cromwell, with his great sound sense and experience of what our world *was*,— History, I think, shows it only this once in such a degree. I account it the culminating point of Protestantism; the most heroic phasis that "Faith in the Bible" was appointed to exhibit here below. Fancy it: that it were made manifest to one of us, how we could make the Right supremely victorious over Wrong, and all that we had longed and prayed for, as the highest good to England and all lands, an attainable fact!

Well, I must say, the *vulpine* intellect, with its knowingness, its alertness, and expertness in "detecting hypocrites," seems to me a rather sorry business. We have had but one such Statesman in England; one man, that I can get sight of, who ever had in the heart of him any such purpose at all. One man, in the course of fifteen hundred years; and this was his welcome. He had adherents by the hundred or the ten; opponents by the million. Had England rallied all round him,—why, then, England might have been a *Christian* land! As it is, vulpine knowingness sits yet at its hopeless problem, "Given a world of Knaves, to educe an Honesty from their united action;" how cumbrous a problem, you may see in Chancery Law Courts, and some other places! Till at length, by Heaven's just anger, but also by Heaven's great grace, the matter begins to stagnate; and this problem is becoming to all men a *palpably* hopeless one.

But with regard to Cromwell and his purposes: Hume, and a multitude following him, come upon me here with an admission that Cromwell *was* sincere at first; a sincere "Fanatic" at first, but gradually became a "Hypocrite" as things opened round him. This of the Fanatic Hypocrite is Hume's theory of it; extensively applied since,—to Mahomet and many others. Think of it seriously, you will find something in it;

not much, not all, very far from all. Sincere hero hearts do not sink in this miserable manner. The Sun flings forth impurities, gets balefully incrusted with spots; but it does not quench itself, and become no Sun at all, but a mass of Darkness! I will venture to say that such never befell a great deep Cromwell; I think, never. Nature's own lion-hearted Son; Antæuslike, his strength is got by *touching the Earth*, his Mother; lift him up from the Earth, lift him up into Hypocrisy, Inanity, his strength is gone. We will not assert that Cromwell was an immaculate man; that he fell into no faults, no insincerities, among the rest. He was no dilettante professor of "perfections," "immaculate conducts." He was a rugged Orson, rending his rough way through actual, true *work*, — doubtless with many a *fall* therein. Insincerities, faults, very many faults, daily and hourly: it was too well known to him; known to God and him! The Sun was dimmed many a time; but the Sun had not himself grown a Dimness. Cromwell's last words, as he lay waiting for death, are those of a Christian, heroic man. Broken prayers to God, that He would judge him and this Cause, He since man could not, in justice yet in pity. They are most touching words. He breathed out his wild, great soul, its toils and sins all ended now, into the presence of his Maker, in this manner.

I, for one, will not call the man a Hypocrite! Hypocrite, mummer, the life of him a mere theatricality; empty barren quack, hungry for the shouts of mobs? The man had made obscurity do very well for him till his head was gray; and now he *was*, there as he stood recognized unblamed, the virtual King of England. Cannot a man do without King's Coaches and Cloaks? Is it such a blessedness to have clerks forever pestering you with bundles of papers in red tape? A simple Diocletian prefers planting of cabbages; a George Washington, no very immeasurable man, does the like. One would say, it is what any genuine man could do; and would do. The instant his real work were out in the matter of Kingship, — away with it!

Let us remark, meanwhile, how indispensable everywhere a *King* is, in all movements of men. It is strikingly shown, in this very War, what becomes of men when they cannot find a Chief Man, and their enemies can. The Scotch Nation was all but unanimous in Puritanism; zealous and of one mind about it, as in this English end of the Island was always far from being the case. But there was no great Cromwell among them; poor, tremulous, hesitating, diplomatic Arygles and suchlike; none of them had a heart true enough for the truth, or durst commit himself to the truth. They had no leader; and the scattered Cavalier party in that country had one; Montrose, the noblest of all the Cavaliers; an accomplished, gallant-hearted, splendid man; what one may call the Hero Cavalier. Well, look at it; on the one hand subjects without a King; on the other a King without subjects! The subjects without King can do nothing; the subjectless King can do something. This Montrose, with a handful of Irish or Highland savages, few of them so much as guns in their hands, dashes at the drilled Puritan armies like a wild whirlwind; sweeps them, time after time, some five times over, from the field before him. He was at one period, for a short while, master of all Scotland. One man; but he was a man: a million zealous men, but *without* the one; they against him were powerless! Perhaps of all the persons in that Puritan struggle, from first to last, the single indispensable one was verily Cromwell. To see and dare, and decide; to be a fixed pillar in the welter of uncertainty; a King among them, whether they called him so or not.

Precisely here, however, lies the rub for Cromwell. His other proceedings have all found advocates, and stand generally justified; but this dismissal of the Rump Parliament and assumption of the Protectorship is what no one can pardon him. He had fairly grown to be King in England; Chief Man of the victorious party in England: but it seems he could not do without the King's Cloak, and sold himself to perdition in order to get it. Let us see a little how this was.

England, Scotland, Ireland, all lying now subdued at the feet of the Puritan Parliament, the practical question arose, What was to be done with it? How will you govern these Nations, which Providence in a wondrous way has given up to your disposal? Clearly those hundred surviving members of the Long Parliament, who sit there as supreme authority, cannot continue forever to sit. What *is* to be done?—It was a question which theoretical constitution builders may find easy to answer; but to Cromwell, looking there into the real practical facts of it, there could be none more complicated. He asked of the Parliament, What it was they would decide upon was for the Parliament to say. Yet the Soldiers too, however contrary to Formula, they who had purchased this victory with their blood, it seemed to them that they also should have something to say in it! We will not "For all our fighting have nothing but a little piece of paper." We understand that the Law of God's Gospel, to which He through us has given the victory, shall establish itself, or try to establish itself, in this land!

For three years, Cromwell says, this question had been sounded in the ears of the Parliament. They could make no answer; nothing but talk, talk. Perhaps it lies in the nature of parliamentary bodies; perhaps no Parliament could in such case make any answer but even that of talk, talk! Nevertheless the question must and shall be answered. You sixty men there, becoming fast odious, even despicable, to the whole nation, whom the nation already calls Rump Parliament, *you* cannot continue to sit there; who or what then is to follow? "Free Parliament," right of Election, Constitutional Formulas of one sort or the other, — the thing is a hungry Fact coming on us, which we must answer or be devoured by it! And who are you that prate of Constitutional Formulas, rights of Parliament? You have had to kill your King, to make Pride's Purges, to expel and banish by the law of the stronger whosoever would not let your Cause prosper: there are but fifty or three-score of you left there, debating, in these days. Tell us what we shall do; not in the way of Formula, but of practicable Fact!

How they did finally answer remains obscure to this day. The diligent Godwin himself admits that he cannot make it out. The likeliest is that this poor Parliament still would not, and indeed could not, dissolve and disperse; that when it came to the point of actually dispersing, they again, for the tenth or twentieth time, adjourned it, — and Cromwell's patience failed him. But we will take the favorablest hypothesis ever started for the Parliament; the favorablest, though I believe it is not the true one, but too favorable.

According to this version: At the uttermost crisis, when Cromwell and his Officers were met on the one hand, and the fifty or sixty Rump Members on the other, it was suddenly told Cromwell that the Rump in its despair *was* answering in a very singular way; that in their splenetic, envious despair, to keep out the Army at least, these men were hurrying through the

House a kind of Reform Bill,— Parliament to be chosen by the whole of England; equable electoral division into districts; free suffrage, and the rest of it! A very questionable, or indeed for *them* an unquestionable thing. Reform Bill, free suffrage of Englishmen? Why, the Royalists, themselves, silenced indeed but not exterminated, perhaps out*number* us; the great numerical majority of England was always indifferent to our Cause, merely looked at it and submitted to it. It is in weight and force, not by counting of heads, that we are the majority! And now with your Formulas and Reform Bills, the whole matter sorely won by our swords, shall again launch itself to sea; become a mere hope, and likelihood, *small* even as a likelihood? And it is not a likelihood; it is a certainty, which we have won, by God's strength and our own right hands, and do now hold *here*. Cromwell walked down to these refractory Members; interrupted them in that rapid speed of their Reform Bill; ordered them to begone, and talk there no more. — Can we not forgive him? Can we not understand him? John Milton, who looked on it all near at hand, could applaud him. The Reality had swept the Formulas away before it. I fancy, most men who were realities in England might see into the necessity of that.

The strong, daring man, therefore, has set all manner of Formulas and logical superficialities against him; has dared appeal to the genuine Fact of this England, Whether it will support him or not? It is curious to see how he struggles to govern in some constitutional way; find some Parliament to support him; but cannot. His first Parliament, the one they call Barebones' Parliament, is, so to speak, a *Convocation of the Notables*. From all quarters of England the leading Ministers and chief Puritan Officials nominate the men most distinguished by religious reputation, influence, and attachment to the true Cause: these are assembled to shape out a plan. They sanctioned what was past; shaped as they could what was to come. They were scornfully called *Barebones' Parliament*, the man's name, it seems, was not *Barebones*, but Barbone, — a good enough man. Nor was it a jest, their work; it was a most serious reality, — a trial on the part of these Puritan Notables how far the Law of Christ could become the Law of this England. There were men of sense among them, men of some quality; men of deep piety I suppose the most of them were. They failed, it seems, and broke down, endeavoring to reform the Court of Chancery! They dissolved themselves, as incompetent; delivered up their power again into the hands of the Lord General Cromwell, to do with it what he liked and could.

What *will* he do with it? The Lord General Cromwell, "Commander in chief of all the Forces raised and to be raised"; he hereby sees himself, at this unexampled juncture, as it were the one available Authority left in England, nothing between England and utter Anarchy but him alone. Such is the undeniable Fact of his position and England's, there and then. What will he do with it? After deliberation, he decides that he will *accept* it; will formally, with public solemnity, say and vow before God and men, "Yes, the Fact is so, and I will do the best I can with it!" Protectorship, Instrument of Government, — these are the external forms of the thing; worked out and sanctioned as they could in the circumstances be, by the Judges, by the leading Official people, "Council of Officers and Persons of interest in the Nation": and as for the thing itself, undeniably enough, at the pass matters had now come to, there was no alternative but Anarchy or that. Puritan England might accept it or not; but Puritan England was, in real truth, saved from suicide thereby! — I believe the Puritan People did, in an inarticulate, grumbling, yet on the whole grateful and real way, accept this anomalous act of Oliver's; at least, he and they together made it good, and always better to the last. But in their Parliamentary *articulate* way, they had their difficulties, and never knew fully what to say to it! —

Oliver's second Parliament, properly his *first* regular Parliament, chosen by the rule laid down in the Instrument of Government, did assemble, and worked; but got, before long, into bottomless questions as to the Protector's *right*, as to "usurpation," and so forth; and had at the earliest legal day to be dismissed. Cromwell's concluding Speech to these men is a remarkable one. So likewise to his third Parliament, in similar rebuke for their pedantries and obstinacies. Most rude, chaotic, all these Speeches are; but most earnest-looking. You would say, it was a sincere, helpless man; not used to *speak* the great inorganic thought of him, but to act it rather! A helplessness of utterance, in such bursting fullness of meaning. He talks much about "births of Providence." All these changes, so many victories and events, were not forethoughts, and theatrical contrivances of men, of *me* or of men; it is blind blasphemers that will persist in calling them so! He insists with a heavy sulphurous wrathful emphasis on this. As he well might. As if a Cromwell in that dark, huge game he had been playing, the world wholly thrown into chaos round him, had *foreseen* it all, and played it all off like a precontrived puppet show by wood and wire! These things were foreseen by no man, he says; no man could tell what a day would bring forth: they were "births of Providence," God's finger guided us on, and we came at last to clear height of victory, God's Cause triumphant in these Nations; and you as a Parliament could assemble together, and say in what manner all this could be *organized*, reduced into rational feasibility among the affairs of men. You were to help with your wise counsel in doing that. "You have had such an opportunity as no Parliament in England ever had." Christ's Law, the Right and True, was to be in some measure made the Law of this land. In place of that, you have got into your idle pedantries, constitutionalities, bottomless cavilings, and questionings about written laws for *my* coming here; and would send the whole matter in chaos again, because I have no Notary's parchment, but only God's voice from the battle whirlwind, for being President among you. That opportunity is gone; and we know not when it will return. You have had your constitutional Logic; and Mammon's Law, not Christ's Law, rules yet in this land. "God be judge between you and me!" These are his final words to them: Take you your constitution formulas in your hand; and I my *in*formal struggles, purposes, realities, and acts; and "God be judge between you and me!"

We said above what shapeless, involved chaotic things the printed Speeches of Cromwell are. *Willfully* ambiguous, unintelligible, say the most: a hypocrite shrouding himself in confused Jesuitic jargon! To me they do not seem so. I will say rather, they afforded the first glimpses I could ever get into the reality of this Cromwell, — nay, into the possibility of him. Try to believe that he means something, search lovingly what that may be: you will find a real *speech* lying imprisoned in these broken, rude, tortuous utterances; a meaning in the great heart of this inarticulate man! You will, for the first time, begin to see that he was a man; not an enigmatic chimera, unintelligible to you, incredible to you. The Histories and Biographies written of this Cromwell, written in shallow, skeptical generations that could not know or conceive of a deep believing man, are far more *obscure* than Cromwell's Speeches.

You look through them only into the infinite vague of Black and the Inane. "Heats and jealousies," says Lord Clarendon himself: "heats and jealousies," mere crabbed whims, theories and crotchets; these induced slow, sober, quiet Englishmen to lay down their plows and work; and fly into red fury of confused war against the best-conditioned of Kings! *Try* if you can find that true. Skepticism writing about Belief may have great gifts; but it is really *ultra vires* there. It is Blindness laying down the Laws of Optics. —

Cromwell's third Parliament split on the same rock as his second. Ever the constitutional Formula: How came *you* there? Show us some Notary parchment! Blind pedants: "Why, surely the same power which makes you a Parliament, that, and something more, made me a Protector!" If my Protectorship is nothing, what in the name of wonder is your Parliamenteership, a reflex and creation of that?—

Parliaments having failed, there remained nothing but the way of Despotism. Military Dictators, each with his district, to *coerce* the Royalist and other gainsayers, to govern them, if not by act of Parliament, then by the sword. Formula shall *not* carry it, while the Reality is here! I will go on, protecting oppressed Protestants abroad, appointing just judges, wise managers, at home cherishing true Gospel ministers; doing the best I can to make England a Christian England, greater than old Rome, the Queen of Protestant Christianity; I, since you will not help me; I, while God leaves me life! — Why did he not give it up; retire into obscurity again, since the Law would not acknowledge him? cry several. That is where they mistake. For him there was no giving of it up! Prime Ministers have governed countries, Pitt, Bombal, Choiseul; and their word was a law while it held: but this Prime Minister was one that *could not get resigned*. Let him once resign, Charles Stuart and the Cavaliers waited to kill him; to kill the Cause *and* him. Once embarked, there is no retreat, no return. This Prime Minister could *retire* no-whither except into his tomb.

One is sorry for Cromwell in his old days. His complaint is incessant of the heavy burden Providence has laid on him. Heavy; which he must bear till death. Old Colonel Hutchinson, as his wife relates it, Hutchinson, his old battle mate, coming to see him on some indispensable business, much against his will, — Cromwell "follows him to the door," in a most fraternal, domestic, conciliatory style; begs that he would be reconciled to him, his old brother in arms; says how much it grieves him to be misunderstood, deserted by true fellow-soldiers, dear to him from of old: the rigorous Hutchinson, cased in his Republican formula, sullenly goes his way. — And the man's head now white; his strong arm growing weary with its long work! I think always too of his poor Mother, now very old, living in that Palace of his; a right brave woman; as indeed they lived all an honest God-fearing Household there: if she heard a shot go off, she thought it was her son killed. He had to come to her at least once a day, that she might see with her own eyes that he was yet living. The poor old Mother!—What had this man gained; what had he gained? He had a life of sore strife and toil, to his last day. Fame, ambition, place in History? His dead body was hung in chains; his "place in History,"—place in History forsooth!—has been a place of ignominy, accusation, blackness, and disgrace; and here, this day, who knows if it is not rash in me to be among the first that ever ventured to pronounce him not a knave and liar, but a genuinely honest man! Peace to him. Did he not, in spite of all, accomplish much for us? *We* walk smoothly over his great rough heroic life; step over his body sunk in the ditch there. We need not *spurn* it, as we step on it! Let the Hero rest. It was not to *men's* judgment that he appealed: nor have men judged him very well.

L'ALLEGRO.

BY JOHN MILTON.

[JOHN MILTON: English poet; born in London, December 9, 1608; died in London, November 8, 1674. He was graduated from Cambridge, 1629; was Latin secretary, 1649–1660. He became totally blind in 1652. At the Restoration he was proscribed and his works were ordered burnt by the hangman; but after a time he was left unmolested and spent the last years of his life in quiet literary labors. "Paradise Lost" was issued in 1666, "Paradise Regained" in 1671, and "Samson Agonistes" in 1671. His masque of "Comus" was published in 1634, "Lycidas" in 1637, "L'Allegro" and "Penseroso" in 1645. Among his prose works the "Areopagitica" (1644), advocating the freedom of the press, his work on Divorce, and his "Defense of the English People" (1654) are most famous. His sonnets in the Italian manner are among the finest in the English language.]

    HENCE, loathed Melancholy,
      Of Cerberus and blackest Midnight born,
    In Stygian cave forlorn,

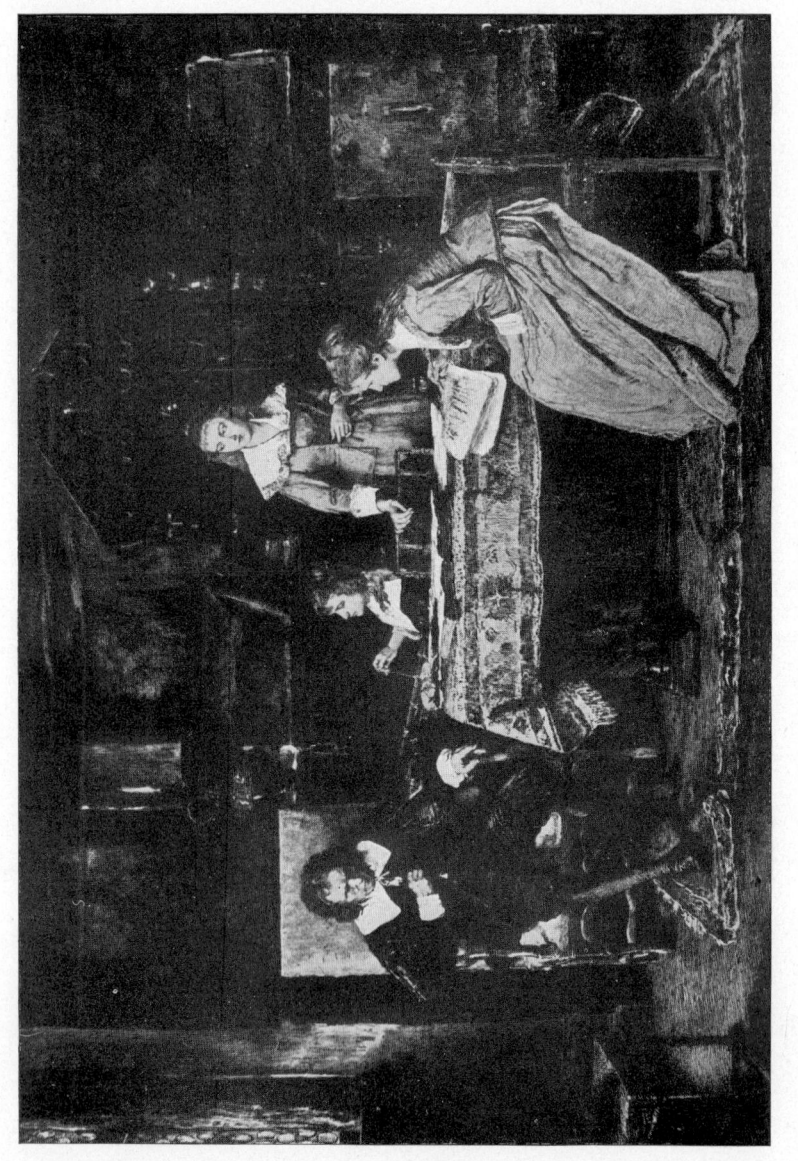

MILTON DICTATING TO HIS DAUGHTER
From a painting by M. Munkacsy

L'ALLEGRO.

'Mongst horrid shapes, and shrieks, and sights unholy!
    Find out some uncouth cell,
Where brooding Darkness spreads his jealous wings,
    And the night raven sings;
There, under ebon shades and low-browed rocks,
    As ragged as thy locks,
  In dark Cimmerian desert ever dwell.

    But come, thou goddess fair and free,
    In heaven yclept Euphrosyne,
    And by men heart-easing Mirth;
    Whom lovely Venus, at a birth,
    With two sister Graces more,
    To ivy-crownèd Bacchus bore:
    Or whether (as some sager sing)
    The frolic wind that breathes the spring,
    Zephyr, with Aurora playing,
    As he met her once a-Maying,
    There, on beds of violets blue,
    And fresh-blown roses washed in dew,
    Filled her with thee, a daughter fair,
    So buxom, blithe, and debonair.

      Haste thee, Nymph, and bring with thee
    Jest, and youthful Jollity,
    Quips and Cranks and wanton Wiles,
    Nods and Becks and wreathèd Smiles,
    Such as hang on Hebe's cheek,
    And love to live in dimple sleek;
    Sport, that wrinkled Care derides,
    And laughter holding both his sides.
    Come, and trip it, as you go,
    On the light fantastic toe;
    And in thy right hand lead with thee
    The mountain nymph, sweet Liberty;
    And, if I give thee honor due,
    Mirth, admit me of thy crew,
    To live with her, and live with thee,
    In unreprovèd pleasures free;
    To hear the lark begin his flight,
    And, singing, startle the dull night,
    From his watch tower in the skies,
    Till the dappled dawn doth rise;
    Then to come, in spite of sorrow,
    And at my window bid good morrow,

Through the sweetbrier or the vine,
Or the twisted eglantine;
While the cock, with lively din,
Scatters the rear of darkness thin,
And to the stack, or the barn door,
Stoutly struts his dames before;
Oft listening how the hounds and horn
Cheerily rouse the slumbering morn,
From the side of some hoar hill,
Through the high wood echoing shrill:
Sometime walking, not unseen,
By hedgerow elms, on hillocks green,
Right against the eastern gate
Where the great Sun begins his state,
Robed in flames and amber light,
The clouds in thousand liveries dight;
While the plowman, near at hand,
Whistles o'er the furrowed land,
And the milkmaid singeth blithe,
And the mower whets his scythe,
And every shepherd tells his tale
Under the hawthorn in the dale.

    Straight mine eye hath caught new pleasures,
Whilst the landscape round it measures:
Russet lawns, and fallows gray,
Where the nibbling flocks do stray;
Mountains on whose barren breast
The laboring clouds do often rest;
Meadows trim with daisies pied;
Shallow brooks, and rivers wide;
Towers and battlements it sees
Bosomed high in tufted trees,
Where perhaps some beauty lies,
The cynosure of neighboring eyes.
Hard by, a cottage chimney smokes
From betwixt two aged oaks,
Where Corydon and Thyrsis met,
Are at their savory dinner set
Of herbs and other country messes,
Which the neat-handed Phillis dresses;
And then in haste her bower she leaves,
With Thestylis to bind the sheaves;
Or, if the earlier season lead,
To the tanned haycock in the mead.

L'ALLEGRO.

Sometimes with secure delight
The upland hamlets will invite,
When the merry bells ring round,
And the jocund rebecs sound
To many a youth and many a maid
Dancing in the checkered shade,
And young and old come forth to play
On a sunshine holiday,
Till the livelong daylight fail:
Then to the spicy nut-brown ale,
With stories told of many a feat,
How Faery Mab the junkets eat.
She was pinched and pulled, she said;
And he, by Friar's lantern led,
Tells how the drudging goblin sweat,
To earn his cream bowl duly set,
When in one night, ere glimpse of morn,
His shadowy flail hath threshed the corn
That ten day-laborers could not end;
Then lies him down, the lubber fiend,
And, stretched out all the chimney's length,
Basks at the fire his hairy strength,
And crop-full out of doors he flings,
Ere the first cock his matin rings.
Thus done the tales, to bed they creep,
By whispering winds soon lulled asleep.

Towered cities please us then,
And the busy hum of men,
Where throngs of knights and barons bold,
In weeds of peace, high triumphs hold,
With store of ladies, whose bright eyes
Rain influence, and judge the prize
Of wit or arms, while both contend
To win her grace whom all commend.
There let Hymen oft appear
In saffron robe, with taper clear,
And pomp and feast and revelry,
With mask and antique pageantry;
Such sights as youthful poets dream
On summer eves by haunted stream.
Then to the well-trod stage anon,
If Jonson's learned sock be on,
Or sweetest Shakespeare, Fancy's child,
Warble his native wood notes wild.

And ever, against eating cares,
Lap me in soft Lydian airs,
Married to immortal verse,
Such as the meeting soul may pierce,
In notes with many a winding bout
Of linkèd sweetness long drawn out
With wanton heed and giddy cunning,
The melting voice through mazes running,
Untwisting all the chains that tie
The hidden soul of harmony;
That Orpheus' self may heave his head
From golden slumber on a bed
Of heaped Elysian flowers, and hear
Such strains as would have won the ear
Of Pluto, to have quite set free
His half-regained Eurydice.

These delights if thou canst give,
Mirth, with thee I mean to live.

IL PENSEROSO.

By JOHN MILTON.

HENCE, vain deluding Joys,
The brood of Folly without father bred!
How little you bestead,
    Or filled the fixèd mind with all your toys.
  Dwell in some idle brain,
And fancies fond with gaudy shapes possess,
  As thick and numberless
As the gay motes that people the sunbeams,
Or likest hovering dreams,
    The fickle pensioners of Morpheus' train.

But, hail! thou Goddess sage and holy!
Hail, divinest melancholy!
Whose saintly visage is too bright
To hit the sense of human sight,
And therefore to our weaker view
O'erlaid with black, staid Wisdom's hue;
Black, but such as in esteem
Prince Memnon's sister might beseem,

Manuscript of John Milton.

The Holy Bible, printed by Robert Barker, London, 1612, a copy of which belonged to John Milton, who, on the page here reproduced, facing the beginning of Genesis, entered memoranda of the dates of the births, etc., of himself and members of his family, including his brother, Christopher Milton, and his nephews, Edward and John Phillips. The first five entries appear to have been made together in 1646; the last two, written in 1657–58, after Milton had become totally blind, were added under his direction by another hand.

John Milton was born the 9th of December 1608, die Veneris half an hour after 6 in the morning.

Christofer Milton was born on Friday about a month before Christmas at five in the morning, 1615.

Edward Phillips was 10 years old August, 1640.

John Phillips is a year younger about Octob.

My daughter Anne was born July 29th on the fast at evening about half an howre after six, 1646.

My daughter Mary, was born on Wednesday October, 25th on the fast day in the morning about 6 a clock, 1648.

My son John was born on Sunday March, the 16th about half an hower past nine at night, 1650.

My daughter Deborah was born the 2nd of May, being Sunday, somewhat before 3 of the clock in the morning, 1652.

My wife hir mother dyed about 3 days after. And my son about 6 weeks after his mother. Katherin my daughter, by Katherin my second wife, was borne ye 19th of October, between 5 and 6 in ye morning and dyed ye 17th of March following, 6 weeks after hir mother, who dyed ye 3rd of Feb. 1657.

Manuscript of John Milton.

The Holy Bible, printed by Robert Barker, London, 1612, a copy of which belonged to John Milton, who, on the page here reproduced, facing the beginning of Genesis, entered memoranda of the dates of the births, etc., of himself and members of his family, including his brother, Christopher Milton, and his nephews, Edward and John Phillips. The first five entries appear to have been made together in 1646; the last two, written in 1657–58, after Milton had become totally blind, were added under his direction by another hand.

John Milton was born the 9th of December 1608, die Veneris half an howr after 6 in the morning.

Christofer Milton was born on Friday about a month before Christmass at five in the morning, 1615

Edward Phillips was 15 years old August, 1645

John Phillips is a year younger about Octob.

My daughter Anne was born July 29th on the fast at eevning about half an howre after six, 1646.

My daughter Mary, was born on Wednesday October, 25th on the fast day in the morning about 6 a clock, 1648.

My son John was born on Sunday March the 16th about half an hower past nine at night, 1650.

My daughter Deborah was born the 2nd of May, being Sunday, somewhat before 3 of the clock in the morning, 1652.

My wife hir mother dyed about 3 days after. And my son about 6 weeks after his mother. Katherin my daughter, by Katherin my second wife, was borne ye 19th of October, between 5 and 6 in ye morning and dyed ye 17th of March following, 6 weeks after hir mother, who dyed ye 3rd of Feb. 1657.

John Milton was born the 9th of December
1608 die Veneris half an howr after 6 in the
morning
Christofer Milton was born on Friday about
a month before Christmass at 5 in the morning.
1615
Edward Phillips was 15 year old August 1645
John Phillips is a year younger about Octob.

My daughter Anne was born July the 29th
on the fast at eebning about half an houre
after six 1646.
My daughter Mary was born on Wedensday
Octob. 25th on the fast day in the morning about
6 a clock 1648.
My son John was born on Sunday March the
16th about half an hower past nine at night 1650
My daughter Deborah was born the 2d of May
being Sunday somwhat before 3 of the clock in the
morning. 1652.
my wife hir mother dyed about 3 days after. And my
son about 6. weeks after his mothers
Katherin my daughter by Katherin my second wife, was
borne ye 19th of October between 5 and 6 in ye morning
and dyed ye 17th of March following 6 weeks after hir
mother, who dyed ye 3d of feb. 1657

JOHN MILTON, 1646–1652.

BRIT. MUS. ADD. MS. 32,310.

John Milton was born the 9th of December 1608 the Xeans half an hour after 6 in the morning

Christofer Milton was born on Friday about a month before Christmass at 5 in the morning 1615

Anna Milton was 15 year old August 1617
John Milton is a year younger about the

My daughter Anne was born July the 29th on the fast at evening about half an hour after the 6th 1646

My daughter Mary was born on Wednesday Octob 25th on the fast in the morning about 6 a clock 1648

My son John was born on Sunday Martch the 16th about half an hour past one at night 1650
My daughter Deborah was born the 2d of May being Sunday somwhat before 3 of the clock in the

My wife hir mother dyed about 3 days of her about the end of the same month

Katherin my daughter by Katherin my second wife was born the 19th of October between 5 and 6 in the morning and dyed the 17th of March following 6 weeks after hir mother who dyed the 3d Feb. 1657

JOHN MILTON, 1608–1674
From *Vita, Sua Manu*, p. 110

IL PENSEROSO.

Or that starred Ethiop queen that strove
To set her beauty's praise above
The Sea Nymphs, and their powers offended.
Yet thou art higher far descended:
Thee bright-haired Vesta long of yore
To solitary Saturn bore;
His daughter she; in Saturn's reign
Such mixture was not held a stain.
Oft in glimmering bowers and glades
He met her, and in secret shades
Of woody Ida's inmost grove,
Whilst yet there was no fear of Jove.

Come, pensive Nun, devout and pure,
Sober, steadfast, and demure,
All in a robe of darkest grain,
Flowing with majestic train,
And sable stole of cypress lawn
Over thy decent shoulders drawn.
Come; but keep thy wonted state,
With even step, and musing gait,
And looks commercing with the skies,
Thy rapt soul sitting in thine eyes:
There, held in holy passion still,
Forget thyself to marble, till
With a sad leaden downward cast
Thou fix them on the earth as fast.
And join with thee calm Peace, and Quiet,
Spare Fast, that oft with gods doth diet,
And hears the Muses in a ring
Aye round about Jove's altar sing;
And add to these retired Leisure,
That in trim gardens takes his pleasure;
But, first and chiefest, with thee bring
Him that yon soars on golden wing,
Guiding the fiery wheelèd throne,
The Cherub Contemplation;
And the mute Silence hist along,
'Less Philomel will deign a song
In her sweetest saddest plight,
Smoothing the rugged brow of Night,
While Cynthia checks her dragon yoke
Gently o'er the accustomed oak;
Sweet bird, that shunn'st the noise of folly,
Most musical, most melancholy!

Thee, chantress, oft the woods among
I woo, to hear thy evensong;
And, missing thee, I walk unseen
On the dry smooth-shaven green,
To behold the wandering moon,
Riding near her highest noon,
Like one that had been led astray
Through the heaven's wide pathless way,
And oft, as if her head she bowed,
Stooping through a fleecy cloud.
Oft, on a plat of rising ground,
I hear the far-off curfew sound,
Over some wide-watered shore,
Swinging slow with sullen roar;
Or, if the air will not permit,
Some still removèd place will fit,
Where glowing embers through the room
Teach light to counterfeit a gloom,
Far from all resort of mirth,
Save the cricket on the hearth,
Or the bellman's drowsy charm
To bless the doors from nightly harm.
Or let my lamp, at midnight hour,
Be seen in some high lonely tower,
Where I may oft outwatch the Bear
With thrice great Hermes, or unsphere
The spirit of Plato, to unfold
What worlds or what vast regions hold
The immortal mind that hath forsook
Her mansion in this fleshly nook;
And of those demons that are found
In fire, air, flood, or underground,
Whose power hath a true consent
With planet or with element.
Sometime let gorgeous Tragedy
In sceptered pall come sweeping by
Presenting Thebes or Pelops' line,
Or the tale of Troy divine,
Or what (though rare) of later age
Ennobled hath the buskined stage.

But, O sad Virgin! that thy power
Might raise Musæus from his bower;
Or bid the soul of Orpheus sing
Such notes as, warbled to the string,

Drew iron tears down Pluto's cheek,
And made Hell grant what love did seek;
Or call up him that left half-told
The story of Cambuscan bold,
Of Camball, and of Algarsife,
And who had Canace to wife,
That owned the virtuous ring and glass,
And of the wondrous horse of brass
On which the Tartar king did ride!
And if aught else great bards beside
In sage and solemn tunes have sung,
Of tourneys and of trophies hung,
Of forests, and enchantments drear,
Where more is meant than meets the ear.

Thus, Night, oft see me in thy pale career,
Till civil-suited Morn appear,
Not tricked and frounced, as she was wont
With the Attic boy to hunt,
But kerchieft in a comely cloud,
While rocking winds are piping loud,
Or ushered with a shower still,
When the gust hath blown his fill,
Ending on the rustling leaves,
With minute drops from off the eaves.
And, when the sun begins to fling
His flaring beams, me, Goddess, bring
To archèd walks of twilight groves,
And shadows brown, that Sylvan loves,
Of pine, or monumental oak,
Where the rude ax with heavèd stroke
Was never heard the nymphs to daunt,
Or fright them from their hallowed haunt.
There, in close covert, by some brook,
Where no profaner eye may look,
Hide me from day's garish eye,
While the bee with honeyed thigh,
That at her flowery work doth sing,
And the waters murmuring,
With such consort as they keep,
Entice the dewy-feathered Sleep.
And let some strange mysterious dream
Wave at his wings, in airy stream
Of lively portraiture displayed,
Softly on my eyelids laid;

And, as I wake, sweet music breathe
Above, about, or underneath,
Sent by some Spirit to mortals good,
Or the unseen Genius of the wood.

But let my due feet never fail
To walk the studious cloisters pale,
And love the high embowèd roof,
With antique pillars massy-proof,
And storied windows richly dight,
Casting a dim religious light.
There let the pealing organ blow,
To the full-voiced choir below,
In service high and anthems clear,
As may with sweetness, through mine ear,
Dissolve me into ecstasies,
And bring all Heaven before mine eyes.

And may at last my weary age
Find out the peaceful hermitage,
The hairy gown and mossy cell,
Where I may sit and rightly spell
Of every star that heaven doth show,
And every herb that sips the dew,
Till old experience do attain
To something like prophetic strain.

These pleasures, Melancholy, give;
And I with thee will choose to live.

SONNET TO CYRIAC SKINNER.

By JOHN MILTON.

CYRIAC, this three years' day these eyes, though clear,
   To outward view, of blemish or of spot,
   Bereft of light, their seeing have forgot;
   Nor to their idle orbs doth sight appear
Of sun, or moon, or star, throughout the year,
   Or man, or woman. Yet I argue not
   Against Heaven's hand or will, nor bate a jot
   Of heart or hope, but still bear up and steer
Right onward. What supports me, dost thou ask?

The conscience, friend, to have lost them overplied
In Liberty's defense, my noble task,
Of which all Europe rings from side to side.
This thought might lead me through the world's vain mask
Content, though blind, had I no better guide.

RELIGIO MEDICI.

By Sir THOMAS BROWNE.

[SIR THOMAS BROWNE: English physician and antiquary; born in London, 1605; died at Norwich, 1682. He studied at Oxford, Montpellier, Padua, and Leyden (where he received the degree of M.D.), and in 1637 settled in practice at Norwich. He received the honor of knighthood from Charles II. (1671). His masterpiece, "Religio Medici" (1643), is one of the classics of English literature, and has been translated into the principal European languages. Other works are: " Inquiries into Vulgar and Common Errors"; " Hydriotaphia, or Urn Burial"; " Christian Morals," a collection of aphorisms.]

As all that die in the war are not termed soldiers, so neither can I properly term all those that suffer in matters of religion, martyrs. The council of Constance condemns John Huss for a heretic; the stories of his own party style him a martyr. He must needs offend the divinity of both, that says he was neither the one nor the other. There are many (questionless) canonized on earth, that shall never be saints in heaven, and have their names in histories and martyrologies, who, in the eyes of God, are not so perfect martyrs as was that wise heathen Socrates, that suffered on a fundamental point of religion,— the unity of God. I have often pitied the miserable bishop that suffered in the cause of antipodes, yet cannot choose but accuse him of as much madness, for exposing his living on such a trifle, as those of ignorance and folly, that condemned him. I think my conscience will not give me the lie, if I say there are not many extant, that, in a noble way, fear the face of death less than myself; yet, from the moral duty I owe to the commandment of God, and the natural respect that I tender unto the conservation of my essence and being, I would not perish upon a ceremony, politic points, or indifferency: nor is my belief of that untractable temper as not to bow at their obstacles, or connive at matters wherein there are not manifest impieties. The leaven, therefore, and ferment of all, not only civil, but religious, actions, is wisdom; without which, to commit ourselves to the flames is homicide, and (I fear) but to pass through one fire into another.

I am naturally bashful; nor hath conversation, age, or travel been able to effront or enharden me; yet I have one part of modesty, which I have seldom discovered in another, that is (to speak truly), I am not so much afraid of death as ashamed thereof; 'tis the very disgrace and ignominy of our natures, that in a moment can so disfigure us, that our nearest friends, wife, and children stand afraid, and start at us. The birds and beasts of the field, that before, in a natural fear, obeyed us, forgetting all allegiance, begin to prey upon us. This very conceit hath, in a tempest, disposed and left me willing to be swallowed up in the abyss of waters, wherein I had perished unseen, unpitied, without wondering eyes, tears of pity, lectures of morality, and none had said, *Quantum mutatus ab illo!*

Some, upon the courage of a fruitful issue, wherein, as in the truest chronicle, they seem to outlive themselves, can with greater patience away with death. This conceit and counterfeit subsisting in our progenies seems to me a mere fallacy, unworthy the desires of a man, that can but conceive a thought of the next world; who, in a nobler ambition, should desire to live in his substance in heaven, rather than his name and shadow in the earth. And therefore, at my death, I mean to take a total adieu of the world, not caring for a monument, history, or epitaph; not so much as the bare memory of my name to be found anywhere, but in the universal register of God. I am not yet so cynical as to approve the testament of Diogenes, nor do I altogether allow that rodomontado of Lucan:—

—— *Cœlo tegitur, qui non habet urnam.*——

He that unburied lies wants not his hearse;
For unto him a tomb's the universe;

but commend, in my calmer judgment, those ingenuous intentions that desire to sleep by the urns of their fathers, and strive to go the neatest way unto corruption. I do not envy the temper of crows and daws, nor the numerous and weary days of our fathers before the flood. If there be any truth in astrology, I may outlive a jubilee; as yet I have not seen one revolution of Saturn, nor hath my pulse beat thirty years, and yet, **excepting** one, have seen the ashes of, and left underground, all the kings of Europe; have been contemporary to three emperors, four grand signiors, and as many popes: methinks I have outlived myself, and begin to be weary of the sun; I have shaken hands with delight in my warm blood and canicular days; I perceive I do anticipate the vices of age; the world to me is but a dream or mock show, and we all therein but pantaloons and antics, to my severer contemplations.

It is not, I confess, an unlawful prayer to desire to surpass the days of our Savior, or wish to outlive that age wherein he thought fittest to die; yet, if (as divinity affirms) there shall be no gray hairs in heaven, but all shall rise in the perfect state of men, we do but outlive those perfections in this world, to be recalled unto them by a greater miracle in the next, and run on here but to be retrograde hereafter. Were there any hopes to outlive vice, or a point to be superannuated from sin, it were worthy our knees to implore the days of Methuselah. But age doth not rectify, but incurvate our natures, turning bad dispositions into worse habits, and (like diseases) brings on incurable vices; for every day, as we grow weaker in age, we grow stronger in sin, and the number of our days doth but make our sins innumerable. The same vice, committed at sixteen, is not the same, though it agrees in all other circumstances, at forty; but swells and doubles from the circumstance of our ages, wherein, besides the constant and inexcusable habit of transgressing, the maturity of our judgment cuts off pretense unto excuse or pardon. Every sin, the oftener it is committed, the more it acquireth in the quality of evil; as it succeeds in time, so it proceeds in degrees of badness; for as they proceed they ever multiply, and, like figures in arithmetic, the last stands for more than all that went before it. And, though I think no man can live well once, but he that could live twice, yet, for my own part, I would not live over my hours past, or begin again the thread of my days; not upon Cicero's ground, because I have lived them well, but for fear I should live them worse. I find my growing judgment daily instruct me how to be better, but my untamed affections and confirmed vitiosity make me daily do worse. I find in my confirmed age the same sins I discovered in my youth; I committed many then because I was a child; and, because I commit them still, I am yet an infant. Therefore I perceive a man may be twice a child before the days of dotage, and stand in need of Æson's bath before threescore.

And truly there goes a deal of providence to produce a man's life unto three-score; there is more required than an able temper for those years: though the radical humor contain in it sufficient oil for seventy, yet I perceive in some it gives no light past thirty: men assign not all the causes of long life, that write whole books thereof. They that found themselves on the radical balsam, or vital sulphur of the parts, determine not why Abel lived not so long as Adam. There is therefore a secret gloom or bottom of our days: 'twas his wisdom to determine them: but his perpetual and waking providence that fulfills and accomplisheth them; wherein the spirits, ourselves, and all the creatures of God, in a secret and disputed way, do execute his will. Let them not therefore complain of immaturity that die about thirty: they fall but like the whole world, whose solid and well-composed substance must not expect the duration and period of its constitution: when all things are completed in it, its age is accomplished; and the last and general fever may as naturally destroy it before six thousand, as me before forty. There is therefore some other hand that twines the thread of life than that of nature: we are not only ignorant in antipathies and occult qualities; our ends are as obscure as our beginnings; the line of our days is drawn by night, and the various effects therein by a pencil that is invisible; wherein, though we confess our ignorance, I am sure we do not err if we say it is the hand of God.

I am much taken with two verses of Lucan, since I have been able not only, as we do at school, to construe, but understand:—

>   *Victurosque Dei celant ut vivere durent,*
>   *Felix esse mori.*

>   We're all deluded, vainly searching ways
>   To make us happy by the length of days;
>   For cunningly, to make 's protract this breath,
>   The gods conceal the happiness of death.

There be many excellent strains in that poet, wherewith his stoical genius hath liberally supplied him: and truly there are singular pieces in the philosophy of Zeno, and doctrine of the stoics, which I perceive, delivered in a pulpit, pass for current divinity: yet herein are they in extremes, that can allow a man to be his own assassin, and so highly extol the end and suicide of Cato. This is indeed not to fear death, but yet to be afraid of life. It is a brave act of valor to contemn death; but, where life is more terrible than death, it is then the truest valor to dare to live: and herein religion hath taught us a noble example; for all the valiant acts of Curtius, Scævola, or Codrus, do not parallel, or match, that one of Job; and sure there is no torture to the rack of a disease, nor any poniards in death itself, like those in the way or prologue unto it. *Emori nolo, sed me esse mortuum nihil curo;* I would not die, but care not to be dead. Were I of Cæsar's religion, I should be of his desires, and wish rather to go off at one blow, than to be sawed in pieces by the grating torture of a disease. Men that look no further than their outsides, think health an appurtenance unto life, and quarrel with their constitutions for being sick; but I, that have examined the parts of man, and know upon what tender filaments that fabric hangs, do wonder that we are not always so; and, considering the thousand doors that lead to death, do thank my God that we can die but once. 'Tis not only the mischief of diseases, and the villainy of poisons, that make an end of us; we vainly accuse the fury of guns, and the new inventions of death:—it is in the power of every hand to destroy us, and we are beholden unto every one we meet, he doth not kill us. There is therefore but one comfort left, that though it be in the power of the weakest arm to take away life, it is not in the strongest to deprive us of death. God would not exempt himself from that; the misery of immortality in the flesh he undertook not, that was in it, immortal. Certainly there is no happiness within this circle of flesh; nor is it in the optics of these eyes to behold felicity. The first day of our jubilee is death; the devil hath therefore failed of his desires; we are happier with death than we should have been without it: there is no misery but in himself, where there is no end of misery; and so indeed, in his own sense, the stoic is in the right. He forgets that he can die, who complains of misery: we are in the power of no calamity while death is in our own.

Men commonly set forth the torments of hell by fire, and the extremity of corporal afflictions, and describe hell in the same method that Mahomet doth heaven. This indeed makes a noise, and drums in popular ears: but if this be the terrible piece thereof, it is not worthy to stand in diameter with heaven, whose happiness consists in that part that is best able to comprehend it, that immortal essence, that translated divinity and colony of God, the soul. Surely, though we place hell under earth, the devil's walk and purlieu is about it. Men speak too popularly who place it in those flaming mountains, which to grosser apprehensions represent hell. The heart of man is the place the devils dwell in; I feel sometimes a hell within myself; Lucifer keeps his court in my breast; Legion is revived in me.

I have so fixed my contemplations on heaven, that I have almost forgot the idea of hell; and am afraid rather to lose the joys of the one, than endure the misery of the other: to be deprived of them is a perfect hell, and needs methinks no addition to complete our afflictions. That terrible term hath never detained me from sin, nor do I owe any good action to the name thereof. I fear God, yet am not afraid of him; his mercies make me ashamed of my sins, before his judgments afraid thereof: these are the forced and secondary method of his wisdom, which he useth but as the last remedy, and upon provocation;—a course rather to deter the wicked, than incite the virtuous to his worship. I can hardly think there was ever any scared into heaven: they go the fairest way to heaven that would serve God without a hell: other mercenaries, that crouch unto him in fear of hell, though they term themselves the servants, are indeed but the slaves of the Almighty.

The skeptics, that affirmed they knew nothing, even in that opinion confuted themselves, and thought they knew more than all the world beside. Diogenes I hold to be the most vainglorious man of his time, and more ambitious in refusing all honors, than Alexander in rejecting none. Vice and the devil put a fallacy upon our reasons; and, provoking us too hastily to run from it, entangle and profound us deeper in it. The duke of Venice, that [yearly] weds himself unto the sea, by [casting thereinto] a ring of gold, I will not accuse of prodigality, because it is a solemnity of good use and consequence in the state: but the philosopher, that threw his money into the sea to avoid avarice, was a notorious prodigal. There is no road or ready way to virtue; it is not an easy point of art to disentangle ourselves from this riddle or web of sin. To perfect virtue, as to religion, there is required a *panoplia*, or complete armor; that whilst we lie at close ward against one vice, we lie not open to the veney of another. And indeed wiser discretions, that have the thread of reason to conduct them, offend without a pardon; whereas under heads may stumble without dishonor. There go so many circumstances to piece up one good action, that it is a lesson to be good, and we are forced to be virtuous by the book. Again, the practice of men holds not an equal pace, yea and often runs counter to their theory; we naturally know what is good, but naturally pursue what is evil: the rhetoric wherewith I persuade another cannot persuade myself. There is a depraved appetite in us, that will with patience hear the learned instructions of reason, but yet perform no further than agrees to its own irregular humor. In brief, we all are monsters; that is, a composition of man and beast: wherein we must endeavor to be as the poets fancy that wise man, Chiron; that is, to have the region of man above that of beast, and sense to sit but at the feet of reason. Lastly, I do desire with God that all, but yet affirm with men that few, shall know salvation, — that the bridge is narrow, the passage strait unto life: yet those who do confine the church of God either to particular nations, churches, or families have made it far narrower than our Savior ever meant it.

No man can justly censure or condemn another; because, indeed, no man truly knows another. This I perceive in myself; for I am in the dark to all the world, and my nearest friends behold me but in a cloud. Those that know me but superficially think less of me than I do of myself; those of my near acquaintance think more; God, who truly knows me, knows that I am nothing.

A HAPPY LIFE.

By Sir HENRY WOTTON.

[1568–1639.]

How happy is he born and taught,
    That serveth not another's will;
Whose armor is his honest thought,
    And simple truth his utmost skill!

Whose passions not his master are,
    Whose soul is still prepared for death,
Untied unto the worldly care
    Of public fame or private breath:

Who envies none that chance doth raise,
   Or vice; who never understood
How deepest wounds are given by praise;
   Nor rules of state, but rules of good:

Who hath his life from rumors freed,
   Whose conscience is his strong retreat,
Whose state can neither flatterers feed,
   Nor ruin make oppressors great:

Who God doth late and early pray,
   More of his grace than gifts to lend,
And entertains the harmless day
   With a religious book or friend.

This man is freed from servile bands
   Of hope to rise, or fear to fall;
Lord of himself, though not of lands,
   And, having nothing, yet hath all.

WALTON'S ANGLER.

[IZAAK WALTON, the "Father of Angling," was born at Stafford, August 9, 1593, and for twenty years kept a linen draper's shop in Fleet Street, London. In 1644 he retired on a competency and passed a large part of the remainder of his life at Winchester, where he died in 1683, in the house of his son-in-law, a prebendary of Winchester cathedral. His masterpiece is "The Compleat Angler, or the Contemplative Man's Recreation" (1653), a discourse on angling interspersed with reflections, dialogue, verses, etc. He also wrote lives of Donne, Wotton, Hooker, Sanderson, and other friends and contemporaries.]

Piscator — The water is the eldest daughter of the creation, the element upon which the Spirit of God did first move, the element which God commanded to bring forth living creatures abundantly; and without which those that inhabit the land, even all creatures that have breath in their nostrils, must suddenly return to putrefaction. Moses, the great lawgiver, and chief philosopher, skilled in all the learning of the Egyptians, who was called the friend of God, and knew the mind of the Almighty, names this element the first in the creation; this is the element upon which the Spirit of God did first move, and is the chief ingredient in the creation: many philosophers have

IZAAK WALTON AND HIS PUPIL
From a painting by Sadler W. Dendy

made it to comprehend all the other elements, and most allow it the chiefest in the mixtion of all living creatures.

There be that profess to believe that all bodies are made of water, and may be reduced back again to water only: they endeavor to demonstrate it thus: —

Take a willow, or any like speedy growing plant, newly rooted in a box or barrel full of earth, weigh them all together exactly when the tree begins to grow, and then weigh all together after the tree is increased from its first rooting, to weigh a hundred pound weight more than when it was first rooted and weighed; and you shall find this augment of the tree to be without the diminution of one drachm weight of the earth. Hence they infer this increase of wood to be from water of rain, or from dew, and not to be from any other element. And they affirm they can reduce this wood back again to water; and they affirm also the same may be done in any animal or vegetable. And this I take to be a fair testimony of the excellency of my element of water.

The water is more productive than the earth. Nay, the earth hath no fruitfulness without showers or dews; for all the herbs and flowers and fruit are produced, and thrive by the water; and the very minerals are fed by streams that run underground, whose natural course carries them to the tops of many high mountains, as we see by several springs breaking forth on the tops of the highest hills; and this is also witnessed by the daily trial and testimony of several miners.

Nay, the increase of those creatures that are bred and fed in the water is not only more and more miraculous, but more advantageous to man, not only for the lengthening of his life, but for preventing of sickness, for it is observed by the most learned physicians, that the casting off of Lent and other fish days, which hath not only given the lie to so many learned, pious, wise founders of colleges, for which we should be ashamed, hath doubtless been the chief cause of those many putrid, shaking, intermitting agues, unto which this nation of ours is now more subject than those wiser countries that feed on herbs, salads, and plenty of fish; of which it is observed in story, that the greatest part of the world now do. And it may be fit to remember that Moses appointed fish to be the chief diet for the best commonwealth that ever yet was.

And it is observable, not only that there are fish, as, namely, the whale, three times as big as the mighty elephant, that is so fierce in battle, but that the mightiest feasts have been of fish. The Romans in the height of their glory have made fish the mistress of all their entertainments; they have had music to usher in their sturgeons, lampreys, and mullets, which they would purchase at rates rather to be wondered at than believed. He that shall view the writings of Macrobius or Varro may be confirmed and informed of this, and of the incredible value of their fish and fish ponds.

But, gentlemen, I have almost lost myself, which I confess I may easily do in this philosophical discourse; I met with most of it very lately, and I hope happily, in a conference with a most learned physician, Dr. Wharton, a dear friend, that loves both me and my art of angling. But, however, I will wade no deeper in these mysterious arguments, but pass to such observations as I can manage with more pleasure, and less fear of running into error. But I must not yet forsake the waters, by whose help we have so many known advantages.

And first, to pass by the miraculous cures of our known baths, how advantageous is the sea for our daily traffic, without which we could not now subsist! How does it not only furnish us with food and physic for the bodies, but with such observations for the mind as ingenious persons would not want!

How ignorant had we been of the beauty of Florence, of the monuments, urns, and rarities that yet remain in and near unto old and new Rome, so many as it is said will take up a year's time to view, and afford to each of them but a convenient consideration! And therefore it is not to be wondered at that so learned and devout a father as St. Jerome, after his wish to have seen Christ in the flesh, and to have heard St. Paul preach, makes his third wish, to have seen Rome in her glory; and that glory is not yet all lost, for what pleasure is it to see the monuments of Livy, the choicest of the historians; of Tully, the best of orators; and to see the bay trees that now grow out of the very tomb of Virgil! These, to any that love learning, must be pleasing. But what pleasure is it to a devout Christian to see there the humble house in which St. Paul was content to dwell, and to view them any rich statues that are made in honor of his memory! nay, to see the very place in which St. Peter and he lie buried together! These are in and near to Rome. And how much more doth it please the pious curiosity of a Christian to see that place on which the blessed Savior of the world was pleased to humble himself, and to take our nature upon him, and to converse with men : to see Mount Zion, Jerusalem, and the very sepulcher of our Lord Jesus? How may it beget and heighten the zeal of a Christian to see the devotions that are daily paid to him at that place! Gentlemen, lest I forget myself I will stop here, and remember you, that but for my element of water, the inhabitants of this poor island must remain ignorant that such things ever were, or that any of them have yet a being.

Gentlemen, I might both enlarge and lose myself in such like arguments; I might tell you that Almighty God is said to have spoken to a fish but never to a beast; that he hath made a whale a ship to carry, and set his prophet Jonah safe on the appointed shore. Of these I might speak, but I must in manners break off, for I see Theobald's house. I cry your mercy for being so long, and thank you for your patience.

Auceps — Sirs, my pardon is easily granted you: I except against nothing that you have said; nevertheless I must part with you at this park wall, for which I am very sorry; but I assure you, Mr. Piscator, I now part with you full of good thoughts, not only of yourself, but your recreation. And so, gentlemen, God keep you both.

Piscator — Well, now, Mr. Venator, you shall neither want time nor my attention to hear you enlarge your discourse concerning hunting.

Venator — Not I, sir: I remember you said that angling itself was of great antiquity and a perfect art, and an art not easily attained to; and you have so won upon me in your former discourse, that I am very desirous to hear what you can say farther concerning those particulars.

Piscator — Sir, I did say so: and I doubt not but if you and I did converse together but a few hours, to leave you possessed with the same high and happy thoughts that now possess me of it; not only of the antiquity of angling, but that it deserves commendations; and that it is an art, and an art worthy the knowledge and practice of a wise man.

Venator — Pray, sir, speak of them what you think fit, for we have yet five miles to the Thatched House; during which walk I dare promise you my patience and diligent attention shall not be wanting. And if you shall make that to appear which you have undertaken — first that it is an art, and an art worth the learning, I shall beg that I may attend you a day or two a fishing, and that I may become your scholar and be instructed in the art itself which you so much magnify.

Piscator — O sir, doubt not that angling is an art. Is it not an art to deceive a trout with an artificial fly? a trout! that is more sharp-sighted than any hawk you have named, and more watchful and timorous than your high-mettled merlin is bold; and yet I doubt not to catch a brace or two to-morrow for a friend's breakfast; — doubt not, therefore, sir, but that angling is an art, and an art worth your learning. The question is rather, whether you be capable of learning it? for angling is somewhat like poetry, men are to be born so: I mean, with inclinations to it, though both may be heightened by discourse and practice: but he that hopes to be a good angler must not only bring an inquiring, searching, observing wit, but he must bring a large measure of hope and patience, and a love and propensity to the art itself; but having once got and practiced it, then doubt not but angling will prove to be so pleasant that it will prove to be like virtue, a reward to itself.

Venator — Sir, I am now become so full of expectation, that I long much to have you proceed; and in the order you propose.

Piscator — Then first, for the antiquity of angling, of which I shall not say much, but only this: some say it is as ancient as Deucalion's flood; others, that Belus, who was the first inventor of godly and virtuous recreations, was the first inventor of angling; and some others say, for former times have had their disquisitions about the antiquity of it, that Seth, one of the sons of Adam, taught it to his sons, and that by them it was derived to posterity: others say that he left it engraven on those pillars which he erected, and trusted to preserve the knowledge of the mathematics, music, and the rest of that precious knowledge and those useful arts which by God's appointment or allowance and his noble industry were thereby preserved from perishing in Noah's flood.

These, sir, have been the opinions of several men that have possibly endeavored to make angling more ancient than is needful, or may well be warranted; but for my part, I shall content myself in telling you that angling is much more ancient than the Incarnation of our Savior; for in the prophet Amos mention is made of fishhooks; and in the book of Job, which was long before the days of Amos, for that book is said to be writ by Moses, mention is made also of fishhooks, which must imply anglers in those times.

But, my worthy friend, as I would rather prove myself a gentleman, by being learned and humble, valiant and inoffensive, virtuous and communicable, than by any fond ostentation of riches; or wanting those virtues myself, boast that these were in my ancestors (and yet I grant that where a noble and ancient descent, and such merit meet in any man, it is a double dignification of that person); so, if this antiquity of angling, which for my part I have not forced, shall, like an ancient family, be either an honor or an ornament to this virtuous art which I profess to love and practice, I shall be the gladder that I made an accidental mention of the antiquity of it, of which I shall say no more, but proceed to that just commendation which I think it deserves.

And for that, I shall tell you that in ancient times a debate hath arisen, and it remains yet unresolved; whether the happiness of man in this world doth consist more in contemplation or action?

Concerning which some have endeavored to maintain their opinion of the first, by saying that the nearer we mortals come to God by way of imitation, the more happy we are. And they say that God enjoys himself only, by a contemplation of his own infiniteness, eternity, power, and goodness, and the like. And upon this ground, many cloisteral men of great learning and devotion prefer contemplation before action. And many of the fathers seem to approve this opinion, as may appear in their commentaries upon the words of our Savior to Martha (Luke x. 41, 42).

And on the contrary, there want not men of equal authority and credit, that prefer action to be the more excellent; as namely, experiments in physic, and the application of it both for the ease and prolongation of man's life; by which each man is enabled to act and do good to others, either to serve his country or do good to particular persons. And they say also that action is doctrinal, and teaches both art and virtue, and is a maintainer of human society; and for these, and other like reasons, to be preferred before contemplation.

Concerning which two opinions, I shall forbear to add a third, by declaring my own; and rest myself contented in telling you, my very worthy friend, that both these meet together, and do most properly belong to the most honest, ingenious, quiet, and harmless art of angling.

And first, I shall tell you what some have observed, and I have found it to be a real truth, that the very sitting by the river's side is not only the quietest and fittest place for contemplation, but will invite an angler to it: and this seems to be maintained by the learned Peter Du Moulin, who, in his discourse of the fulfilling of prophecies, observes that when God intended to reveal any future events or high notions to his prophets, he then carried them either to the deserts or the seashore, that having so separated them from amidst the press of people and business, and the cares of the world, he might settle their minds in a quiet repose, and there make them fit for revelation.

And this seems also to be intimated by the Children of Israel (Psal. cxxxvii.), who, having in a sad condition banished all mirth and music from their pensive hearts, and having hung up their then mute harps upon the willow trees growing by the rivers of Babylon, sat down upon these banks bemoaning the ruins of Sion, and contemplating their own sad condition.

And an ingenious Spaniard says that "rivers and the inhabitants of the watery element were made for wise men to contemplate and fools to pass by without consideration." And though I will not rank myself in the number of the first, yet give me leave to free myself from the last, by offering to you a short contemplation, first of rivers and then of fish; concerning which I doubt not but to give you many observations that will appear very considerable: I am sure they have appeared so to me, and made many an hour to pass away more pleasantly, as I have sat quietly on a flowery bank by a calm river, and contemplated what I shall now relate to you.

And first, concerning rivers: there be so many wonders reported and written of them, and of the several creatures that be bred and live in them; and those by authors of so good credit, that we need not to deny them an historical faith.

As namely of a river in Epirus, that puts out any lighted torch, and kindles any torch that was not lighted. Some waters being drunk cause madness, some drunkenness, and some laughter to death. The river Selarus in a few hours turns a rod or wand to stone; and our Camden mentions the like in England, and the like in Lochmere in Ireland. There is also a river in Arabia, of which all the sheep that drink thereof have their wool turned into a vermilion color. And one of no less credit than Aristotle tells us of a merry river, the river Elusina, that dances at the noise of music, for with music it bubbles, dances, and grows sandy, and so continues till the music ceases, but then it presently returns to its wonted calmness and clearness. And Camden tells us of a well near to Kirby in Westmoreland, that ebbs and flows several times every day: and he tells us of a river in Surrey, it is called Mole, that after it has run several miles, being opposed by hills, finds or makes itself a way underground, and breaks out again so far off, that the inhabitants thereabout boast, as the Spaniards do of their river Anus, that they feed divers flocks of sheep upon a bridge. And lastly, for I would not tire your patience, one of no less authority than Josephus, that learned Jew, tells us of a river in Judea that runs swiftly all the six days of the week, and stands still and rests all their sabbath.

But I will lay aside my discourse of rivers, and tell you some things of the monsters, or fish, call them what you will, that they breed and feed in them. Pliny, the philosopher, says, in the third chapter of his ninth book, that in the Indian Sea, the fish called *balæna*, or whirlpool, is so long and broad as to take up more in length and breadth than two acres of ground; and of other fish of two hundred cubits long; and that, in the river Ganges, there be eels of thirty feet long. He says there that these monsters appear in the sea only when tempestuous winds oppose the torrents of water falling from the rocks into it, and so turning what lay at the bottom to be seen on the water's top. And he says that the people of Cadara, an island near this place, make the timber for their houses of those fish bones. He there tells us that there are sometimes a thousand of these great eels found wrapt or interwoven together. He tells us there that it appears that dolphins love music, and will come when called for, by some men or boys that know, and used to feed them, and that they can swim as swift as an arrow can be shot out of a bow; and much of this is spoken concerning the dolphin, and other fish, as may be found also in the learned Dr. Casaubon's "Discourse of Credulity and Incredulity," printed by him about the year 1670.

I know that we islanders are averse to the belief of these wonders; but there be so many strange creatures to be now seen, many collected by John Tradescant, and others added by my friend Elias Ashmole, Esq., who now keeps them carefully and methodically at his house, near to Lambeth near London, as may get some belief of some of the other wonders I mentioned. I will tell you some of the wonders that you may now see, and not till then believe, unless you think fit.

You may see the hogfish, the dogfish, the dolphin, the coneyfish, the parrotfish, the shark, the poisonfish, the swordfish, and not only other incredible fish, but you may there see the salamander, several sorts of barnacles, and Solan geese, the bird of Paradise, such sorts of snakes, and such birds' nests, and of so various forms, and so wonderfully made, as may beget wonder and amusement in any beholder: and so many hundred of other rarities in that collection, as will make the other wonders I spake of the less incredible; for you may note that the waters are nature's storehouse, in which she locks up her wonders.

But, sir, lest this discourse may seem tedious, I shall give it a sweet conclusion out of that holy poet Mr. George Herbert his divine "Contemplation on God's Providence."

> Lord, who hath praise enough; nay, who hath any?
>   None can express thy works but he that knows them;
> And none can know thy works, they are so many,
>   And so complete, but only he that owes them.
>
> We all acknowledge both thy power and love
>   To be exact, transcendent, and divine;
> Who dost so strongly and so sweetly move,
>   Whilst all things have their end, yet none but **thine.**
>
> Therefore, most sacred Spirit, I here present,
>   For me, and all my fellows, praise to thee;
> And just it is that I should pay the rent,
>   Because the benefit accrues to me.

* * * * * * *

You shall read in Seneca, his "Natural Questions," Lib. 3, Cap. 17, that the ancients were so curious in the newness of their fish, that that seemed not new enough that was not put alive into the guest's hand; and he says that to that end they did usually keep them living in glass bottles in their dining rooms: and they did glory much in their entertaining of friends, to have that fish taken from under their table alive that was instantly to be fed upon. And he says, they took great pleasure to see their Mullets change to several colors, when they were dying.

But enough of this, for I doubt I have stayed too long from giving you some observations of the trout, and how to fish for him, which shall take up the next of my spare time.

The Trout is a fish highly valued both in this and foreign nations : he may be justly said, as the old poet said of wine, and we English say of venison, to be a generous fish : a fish that is so like the buck that he also has his seasons ; for it is observed that he comes in and goes out of season with the stag and buck; Gesner says, his name is of a German offspring, and says he is a fish that feeds clean and purely, in the swiftest streams and on the hardest gravel ; and that he may justly contend with all fresh-water fish, as the Mullet may with all sea fish, for precedency and daintiness of taste, and that being in right season, the most dainty palates have allowed precedency to him. . . .

But turn out of the way a little, good scholar! towards yonder high honeysuckle hedge ; there we'll sit and sing, whilst this shower falls so gently upon the teeming earth, and gives yet a sweeter smell to the lovely flowers that adorn these verdant meadows.

Look! under that broad beech tree I sat down when I was last this way a fishing. And the birds in the adjoining grove seemed to have a friendly contention with an echo, whose dead voice seemed to live in a hollow tree, near to the brow of that primrose hill. There I sat viewing the silver streams glide silently towards their center, the tempestuous sea ; yet sometimes opposed by rugged roots and pebblestones, which broke their waves and turned them into foam. And sometimes I beguiled time by viewing the harmless lambs; some leaping securely in the cool shade, whilst others sported themselves in the cheerful sun ; and saw others craving comfort from the swollen udders of their bleating dams. As I thus sat, these and other sights had so fully possessed my soul with content, that I thought, as the poet hath happily expressed it,

> I was for that time lifted above earth,
> And possessed joys not promised in my birth.

As I left this place, and entered into the next field, a second pleasure entertained me : 'twas a handsome milkmaid, that had not yet attained so much age and wisdom as to load her mind with any fears of many things that will never be, as too many men too often do : but she cast away all care, and sung like a nightingale; her voice was good, and the ditty fitted for it: it was that smooth song which was made by Kit Marlow, now at least fifty years ago; and the milkmaid's mother sung an answer to it, which was made by Sir Walter Raleigh in his younger days.

They were old-fashioned poetry, but choicely good, I think much better than the strong lines that are now in fashion in this critical age. Look yonder! on my word, yonder they both be a milking again. I will give her the chub, and persuade them to sing those two songs to us.

God speed you, good woman! I have been a fishing, and am going to Bleak Hall to my bed, and having caught more fish than will sup myself and my friend, I will bestow this upon you and your daughter, for I use to sell none.

Milk Woman — Marry, God requite you, sir, and we'll eat it cheerfully; and if you come this way a fishing two months hence, a grace of God, I'll give you a syllabub of new verjuice in a new-made haycock for it, and my Maudlin shall sing you one of her best ballads; for she and I both love all anglers, they be such honest, civil, quiet men; in the mean time will you drink a draught of red cow's milk? you shall have it freely.

Piscator — No, I thank you; but, I pray, do us a courtesy that shall stand you and your daughter in nothing, and yet we will think ourselves still something in your debt; it is but to sing us a song that was sung by your daughter when I last passed over this meadow about eight or nine days since.

Milk Woman — What song was it, I pray? Was it " Come Shepherds, deck your heads"? or, "As at noon Dulcina rested"? or, "Philida flouts me"? or, "Chevy Chace"? or, "Johnny Armstrong"? or, "Troy Town"?

Piscator — No, it is none of those; it is a song that your daughter sung the first part, and you sung the answer to it.

Milk Woman — Oh, I know it now. I learned the first part in my golden age, when I was about the age of my poor daughter; and the latter part, which indeed fits me best now, but two or three years ago, when the cares of the world began to take hold of me: but you shall, God willing, hear them both, and sung as well as we can, for we both love anglers. Come, Maudlin, sing the first part to the gentleman with a merry heart, and I'll sing the second, when you have done.

The Milkmaid's Song.

Come live with me, and be my love,
And we will all the pleasures prove
The valleys, groves, or hills, or field,
Or woods and steepy mountains yield;

Where we will sit upon the rocks,
And see the shepherds feed our flocks
By shallow rivers, to whose falls
Melodious birds sing madrigals.

And I will make thee beds of roses,
And then a thousand fragrant posies,
A cap of flowers, and a kirtle
Embroidered all with leaves of myrtle;

A gown made of the finest wool
Which from our pretty lambs we pull;
Slippers lined choicely for the cold,
With buckles of the purest gold;

A belt of straw and ivy buds,
With coral clasps and amber studs:
And if these pleasures may thee move,
Come live with me, and be my love.

Thy silver dishes for my meat,
As precious as the gods do eat,
Shall, on an ivory table, be
Prepared each day for thee and me.

The shepherd swains shall dance and sing,
For thy delight, each May morning.
If these delights thy mind may move,
Then live with me, and be my love.

Venator — Trust me, my master, it is a choice song, and sweetly sung by honest Maudlin. I now see it was not without cause that our good Queen Elizabeth did so often wish herself a milkmaid all the month of May, because they are not troubled with fears and cares, and sing sweetly all the day, and sleep securely all the night: and without doubt, honest, innocent, pretty Maudlin does so. I'll bestow Sir Thomas Overbury's milkmaid's wish upon her, "That she may die in the spring, and being dead, may have good store of flowers stuck round about her winding sheet."

The Milkmaid's Mother's Answer.

If all the world and love were young,
And truth in every shepherd's tongue,
These pretty pleasures might me move
To live with thee, and be thy love.

But Time drives flocks from field to fold,
When rivers rage and rocks grow cold;
Then Philomel becometh dumb,
And age complains of care to come.

The flowers do fade, and wanton fields
To wayward winter reckoning yields.
A honey tongue, a heart of gall,
Is fancy's spring, but sorrow's fall.

Thy gowns, thy shoes, thy beds of roses,
Thy cap, thy kirtle, and thy posies,
Soon break, soon wither, soon forgotten;
In folly ripe, in reason rotten.

Thy belt of straw and ivy buds,
Thy coral clasps and amber studs,
All these in me no means can move
To come to thee and be thy love.

What should we talk of dainties, then,
Of better meat than's fit for men?
These are but vain; that's only good
Which God hath blessed, and sent for food.

But could youth last and love still breed —
Had joys no date, or age no need —
Then those delights my mind might move
To live with thee, and be thy love.

Mother — Well! I have done my song. But stay, honest anglers; for I will make Maudlin to sing you one short song more. Maudlin! sing that song that you sung last night, when young Coridon the shepherd played so purely on his oaten pipe to you and your cousin Betty.

Maudlin — I will, mother.

"I married a wife of late,
　The more's my unhappy fate;
　I married her for love,
　As my fancy did me move,
And not for a worldly estate;

"But oh! the green sickness
Soon changed her likeness
　And all her beauty did fail.
　　But 'tis not so
　　With those that go
　Through frost and snow,
　　As all men know,
And carry the milking pail."

Piscator — Well sung, good woman; I thank you. I'll give you another dish of fish one of these days, and then beg another song of you. Come, scholar, let Maudlin alone; do not you offer to spoil her voice. Look, yonder comes mine hostess, to call us to supper. How now? Is my brother Peter come?

Hostess — Yes, and a friend with him; they are both glad to hear that you are in these parts, and long to see you, and long to be at supper, for they be very hungry.

　　＊　　＊　　＊　　＊　　＊　　＊　　＊

Piscator — What would a blind man give to see the pleasant rivers and meadows and flowers and fountains that we have met with since we met together? I have been told that if a man that was born blind could obtain to have his sight for but only one hour during his whole life, and should, at the first opening of his eyes, fix his sight upon the sun when it was in its full glory, either at the rising or setting of it, he would be so transported and amazed, and so admire the glory of it, that he would not willingly turn his eyes from that first ravishing object, to behold all the other various beauties this world could present to him. And this, and many other like blessings, we enjoy daily. And for most of them, because they be so common, most men forget to pay their praises; but let not us, because it is a sacrifice so pleasing to Him that made that sun and us, and still protects us, and gives us flowers and showers, and stomachs and meat, and content and leisure to go a fishing.

Well, scholar, I have almost tired myself, and, I fear, more than almost tired you; but I now see Tottenham High Cross, and our short walk thither shall put a period to my too long discourse, in which my meaning was and is to plant that in your mind with which I labor to possess my own soul : that is, a meek and thankful heart. And to that end I have showed you riches, without them, do not make any man happy. But let me tell you that riches, with them, remove many fears and cares ; and therefore my advice is that you endeavor to be honestly rich, or contentedly poor : but be sure that your riches be justly got, or you spoil all. For it is well said by Caussin, " He that loses his conscience, has nothing left that is worth keeping." Therefore be sure you look to that. And, in the next place, look to your health : and if you have it, praise God, and value it next to a good conscience ; for health is the second blessing that we mortals are capable of ; a blessing that money cannot buy, and therefore value it, and be thankful for it. As for money, which may be said to be the third blessing, neglect it not : but note, that there is no necessity of being rich ; for I told you there be as many miseries beyond riches, as on this side them : and if you have a competence, enjoy it with a meek, cheerful, thankful heart. I will tell you, scholar, I have heard a grave divine say that God has two dwellings, one in heaven, and the other in a meek and thankful heart. Which Almighty God grant to me, and to my honest scholar ; and so you are welcome to Tottenham High Cross.

Venator — Well, master, I thank you for all your good directions ; but for none more than this last, of thankfulness, which I hope I shall never forget. . . .

Here I must part with you, here in this now sad place where I was so happy as first to meet you : but I shall long for the ninth of May ; for then I hope again to enjoy your beloved company, at the appointed time and place. And now I wish for some somniferous potion, that might force me to sleep away the intermitted time, which will pass away with me as tediously as it does with men in sorrow ; nevertheless, I will make it as short as I can by my hopes and wishes. And, my good master, I will not forget the doctrine which you told me Socrates taught his scholars, that they should not think to be honored so much for being philosophers, as to honor philosophy by their virtuous lives. You advised me to the like concerning angling, and I will endeavor to do so ; and to live like those many worthy men of which you made mention in the former part of your discourse. This is my firm resolution ; and as a pious man advised his friend, that to beget mortification he should frequent churches, and view monuments, and charnel houses, and then and there consider how many dead bodies time had piled up at the gates of death: so when I would beget content, and increase confidence in the power, and wisdom, and providence of Almighty God, I will walk the meadows by some gliding stream, and there contemplate the lilies that take no care, and those very many other various little living creatures, that are not only created but fed, man knows not how, by the goodness of the God of nature, and therefore trust in him. This is my purpose; and so, let everything that hath breath praise the Lord: and let the blessing of St. Peter's master be with mine.

Piscator — And upon all that are lovers of virtue, and dare trust in his providence, and be quiet, and go a angling.

PRITHEE, SEND ME BACK MY HEART.

By Sir JOHN SUCKLING.

[1609-1641.]

I PRITHEE send me back my heart,
   Since I cannot have thine;
For if from yours you will not part,
   Why, then, shouldst thou have mine?

Yet now I think on't, let it lie,
   To find it were in vain;
For th' hast a thief in either eye
   Would steal it back again!

Why should two hearts in one breast lie,
   And yet not lodge together?
Oh, Love! where is thy sympathy,
   If thus our breasts thou sever?

But love is such a mystery,
   I cannot find it out;
For when I think I'm best resolved,
   I then am in most doubt.

Then farewell care, and farewell woe,
   I will no longer pine;
For I'll believe I have her heart
   As much as she hath mine.

RED AND WHITE ROSES.

By THOMAS CAREW.

[1589-1639.]

READ in these roses the sad story
Of my hard fate and your own glory;
In the white you may discover
The paleness of the fainting lover;
In the red the flames still feeding
On my heart with fresh wounds bleeding.
The white will tell you how I languish,
And the red express my anguish;
The white my innocence displaying,
The red my martyrdom betraying.
The frowns that on your brow resided
Have those roses thus divided.
Oh, let your smiles but clear the weather,
And then they both shall grow together!

ANGLING.

By LEIGH HUNT.

[JAMES HENRY LEIGH HUNT, English poet and man of letters, was born near London, October 19, 1784. After a clerkship in the War Office, he became editor of the *Examiner* on its foundation by his brother; made it a leading organ of literature and later of politics; was imprisoned two years with £1000 fine for portraying the Prince Regent (afterwards George IV.), and wrote "Rimini" during the time; as the friend of Byron and Shelley he was invited by them to Genoa to start a Liberal magazine, but Shelley was drowned and Byron went to Greece (1822), and the magazine stopped. Returning to England in 1825, he produced "Lord Byron and his Contemporaries" (1828); "Ralph Esher" and "Christianism" (1832); "The *Indicator* and the *Companion*," selected essays (1834); the *London Journal* (1834-1835); "Captain Sword and Captain Pen" (1835); "A Legend of Florence," a play (1840); "The Palfrey," based on an old French poem (1842); "Stories from the Italian Poets" (1846); and many other volumes of collected essays, poems, etc. He died August 28, 1859.]

THE anglers are a race of men who puzzle us. We do not mean for their patience, which is laudable, nor for the infinite non-success of some of them, which is desirable. Neither do we agree with the good old joke attributed to Swift, that angling is always to be considered as "a stick and a string, with a fly at one end and a fool at the other." Nay, if he had hooks with him, and a pleasant day, we can account for the joyousness

LEIGH HUNT

of that prince of punters, who, having been seen in the same spot one morning and evening, and asked whether he had had any success, said No, but in the course of the day he had had "a glorious nibble."

But the anglers boast of the innocence of their pastime; yet it puts fellow-creatures to the torture. They pique themselves on their meditative faculties; and yet their only excuse is a want of thought. It is this that puzzles us. Old Isaac Walton, their patriarch, speaking of his inquisitorial abstractions on the banks of a river, says: —

> Here we may
> Think and pray,
> Before death
> Stops our breath.
> Other joys
> Are but toys,
> And to be lamented.

So saying, he "stops the breath" of a trout, by plucking him up into an element too thin to respire, with a hook and a tortured worm in his jaws—

> Other joys
> Are but toys.

If you ride, walk, or skate, or play at cricket, or at rackets, or enjoy a ball or a concert, it is "to be lamented." To put pleasure into the faces of half a dozen agreeable women is a toy unworthy of the manliness of a worm sticker. But to put a hook into the gills of a carp—there you attain the end of a reasonable being; there you show yourself truly a lord of the creation. To plant your feet occasionally in the mud is also a pleasing step. So is cutting your ankles with weeds and stones—

> Other joys
> Are but toys.

The book of Isaac Walton upon angling is a delightful performance in some respects. It smells of the country air, and of the flowers in cottage windows. Its pictures of rural scenery, its simplicity, its snatches of old songs, are all good and refreshing; and his prodigious relish of a dressed fish would not be grudged him, if he had killed it a little more decently. He really seems to have a respect for a piece of salmon,— to approach it, like the grace, with his hat off. But what are we to think of a man who, in the midst of his tortures of other animals, is always valuing himself on his harmlessness; and who actually follows up one of his most complacent passages of this kind with an injunction to impale a certain worm twice upon the hook, because it is lively, and might get off! All that can be said of such an extraordinary inconsistency is that, having been bred up in an opinion of the innocence of his amusement, and possessing a healthy power of exercising voluntary thoughts (as far as he had any), he must have dozed over the opposite side of the question, so as to become almost, perhaps quite, insensible to it. And angling does indeed seem the next thing to dreaming. It dispenses with locomotion, reconciles contradictions, and renders the very countenance null and void. A friend of ours, who is an admirer of Walton, was struck, just as we were, with the likeness of the old angler's face to a fish. It is hard, angular, and of no expression. It seems to have been "subdued to what it worked in"; to have become native to the watery element. One might have said to Walton, "Oh flesh, how art thou fishified!" He looks like a pike, dressed in broadcloth instead of butter.

The face of his pupil and follower, or, as he fondly called himself, son, Charles Cotton, a poet and a man of wit, is more good-natured and uneasy. Cotton's pleasures had not been confined to fishing. His sympathies, indeed, had been a little superabundant, and left him, perhaps, not so great a power of thinking as he pleased. Accordingly, we find in his writings more symptoms of scrupulousness upon the subject than in those of his father.

Walton says that an angler does no hurt but to fish; and this he counts as nothing. Cotton argues that the slaughter of them is not to be "repented"; and he says to his father (which looks as if the old gentleman sometimes thought upon the subject too):—

"There whilst behind some bush we wait
  The scaly people to betray,
We'll *prove it just*, with treacherous bait,
  To make the preying trout our prey."

This argument, and another about fish's being made for "man's pleasure and diet," are all that anglers have to say for the innocence of their sport. But they are both as rank sophistications as can be; sheer beggings of the question. To kill fish outright is a different matter. Death is common to all; and a trout, speedily killed by a man, may suffer no worse fate than from the jaws of a pike. It is the mode, the lingering catlike cruelty of the angler's sport, that renders it unworthy. If fish were made to be so treated, then men were also made to be racked and throttled by inquisitors. Indeed, among other advantages of angling, Cotton reckons up a tame, fishlike acquiescence to whatever the powerful choose to inflict.

> We scratch not our pates,
> Nor repine at the rates
> Our superiors impose on our living;
> But do frankly submit,
> Knowing they have more wit
> In demanding, than we have in giving.
>
> Whilst quiet we sit,
> We conclude all things fit,
> Acquiescing with hearty submission, etc.

And this was no pastoral fiction. The anglers of those times, whose skill became famous from the celebrity of their names, chiefly in divinity, were great fallers-in with passive obedience. They seemed to think (whatever they found it necessary to say now and then upon that point) that the great had as much right to prey upon men, as the small had upon fishes; only the men, luckily, had not hooks put into their jaws, and the sides of their cheeks torn to pieces. The two most famous anglers in history are Antony and Cleopatra. These extremes of the angling character are very edifying.

We should like to know what these grave divines would have said to the heavenly maxim of "Do as you would be done by." Let us imagine ourselves, for instance, a sort of human fish. Air is but a rarer fluid; and at present, in this November weather, a supernatural being who should look down upon us from a higher atmosphere would have some reason to regard us as a kind of pedestrian carp. Now, fancy a Genius fishing for us. Fancy him baiting a great hook with pickled salmon, and twitching up old Isaac Walton from the banks of the river Lee, with the hook through his ear. How he would go up, roaring and screaming, and thinking the devil had got him!

> Other joys
> Are but toys.

We repeat that if fish were made to be so treated, then we were just as much made to be racked and suffocated; and a footpad might have argued that old Isaac was made to have his pocket picked, and be tumbled into the river. There is no end of these idle and selfish beggings of the question, which at last argue quite as much against us as for us. And granting them, for the sake of argument, it is still obvious, on the very same ground, that men were also made to be taught better. We do not say that all anglers are of a cruel nature; many of them, doubtless, are amiable men in other matters. They have only never thought, perhaps, on that side of the question, or been accustomed from childhood to blink it. But once thinking, their amiableness and their practice become incompatible; and if they should wish, on that account, never to have thought upon the subject, they would only show that they cared for their own exemption from suffering, and not for its diminution in general.

THE TWO BROTHERS.

By Sir JOHN VANBRUGH.

(From "The Relapse.")

[SIR JOHN VANBRUGH, English dramatist of the Restoration period, was born about 1666; died in London, March 26, 1726. His best-known comedies are "The Relapse" and "The Provoked Wife," both of date 1697. He wrote also, among others, "The False Friend" (1702), "The Confederacy" (1705), and the unfinished "Journey to London," completed by Colley Cibber.]

Scene: Whitehall.

Enter YOUNG FASHION, LORY, *and* Waterman.

Young Fashion — Come, pay the waterman, and take the portmanteau.

Lory — Faith, sir, I think the waterman had as good take the portmanteau, and pay himself.

Young Fashion — Why, sure there's something left in't.

Lory — But a solitary old waistcoat, upon my honor, sir.

Young Fashion — Why, what's become of the blue coat, sirrah?

Lory — Sir, 'twas eaten at Gravesend; the reckoning came to thirty shillings, and your privy purse was worth but two half-crowns.

Young Fashion — 'Tis very well.

Waterman — Pray, master, will you please to dispatch me?

Young Fashion — Ay, here a — Canst thou change me a guinea?

Lory [*aside*] — Good.

Waterman — Change a guinea, master! Ha, ha, your honor's pleas'd to compliment.

Young Fashion — I'gad I don't know how I shall pay thee then, for I have nothing but gold about me.

Lory [*aside*] — Hum, hum.

Young Fashion — What dost thou expect, friend?

Waterman — Why, master, so far against wind and tide, is richly worth half a piece.

Young Fashion — Why, faith, I think thou art a good conscionable fellow. I'gad, I begin to have so good an opinion of thy honesty, I care not if I leave my portmanteau with thee, till I send thee thy money.

Waterman — Ha! God bless your honor; I should be as willing to trust you, master, but that you are, as a man may say, a stranger to me, and these are nimble times; there are a great many sharpers stirring. [*Taking up the portmanteau.*] Well, master, when your worship sends the money, your portmanteau shall be forthcoming. My name's Tugg, my wife keeps a brandy shop in Drab Alley at Wapping.

Young Fashion — Very well; I'll send for't to-morrow.

[*Exit* Waterman.

Lory — So — Now, sir, I hope you'll own yourself a happy man, you have outliv'd all your cares.

Young Fashion — How so, sir?

Lory — Why you have nothing left to take care of.

Young Fashion — Yes, sirrah, I have myself and you to take care of still.

Lory — Sir, if you cou'd but prevail with somebody else to do that for you, I fancy we might both fare the better for't.

Young Fashion — Why, if thou canst tell me where to apply myself, I have at present so little money, and so much humility about me, I don't know but I may follow a fool's advice.

Lory— Why then, sir, your fool advises you to lay aside all animosity, and apply to Sir Novelty, your elder brother.

Young Fashion— D—— my elder brother.

Lory— With all my heart; but get him to redeem your annuity, however.

Young Fashion— My annuity! 'Sdeath, he's such a dog, he would not give his powder puff to redeem my soul.

Lory— Look you, sir, you must wheedle him, or you must starve.

Young Fashion— Look you, sir, I will neither wheedle him, nor starve.

Lory— Why? what will you do then?

Young Fashion— I'll go into the army.

Lory— You can't take the oaths; you are a Jacobite.

Young Fashion— Thou mayst as well say I can't take orders because I'm an atheist.

Lory— Sir, I ask your pardon; I find I did not know the strength of your conscience so well as I did the weakness of your purse.

Young Fashion— Methinks, sir, a person of your experience should have known that the strength of the conscience proceeds from the weakness of the purse.

Lory— Sir, I am very glad to find you have a conscience able to take care of us, let it proceed from what it will; but I desire you'll please to consider that the army alone will be but a scanty maintenance for a person of your generosity (at least as rents now are paid); I shall see you stand in damnable need of some auxiliary guineas for your *menus plaisirs;* I will therefore turn fool once more for your service, and advise you to go directly to your brother.

Young Fashion— Art thou then so impregnable a blockhead, to believe he'll help me with a farthing?

Lory— Not if you treat him *de haut en bas*, as you used to do.

Young Fashion— Why, how wouldst have me treat him?

Lory— Like a trout, tickle him.

Young Fashion— I can't flatter——

Lory— Can you starve?

Young Fashion— Yes——

Lory— I can't; Good-by t'ye, sir——　　　　[*Going.*

Young Fashion— Stay, thou wilt distract me. What wouldst thou have me to say to him?

Lory — Say nothing to him, apply yourself to his favorites; speak to his periwig, his cravat, his feather, his snuffbox, and when you are well with them — desire him to lend you a thousand pounds. I'll engage you prosper.

Young Fashion — 'Sdeath and Furies! Why was that coxcomb thrust into the world before me? O Fortune — Fortune — thou art a ——, by Gad ——   [*Exeunt.*

Scene: A Dressing Room.

Enter LORD FOPPINGTON *in his nightgown.*

Lord Foppington — Page ——

Enter Page.

Page — Sir.

Lord Foppington — Sir! Pray, sir, do me the favor to teach your tongue the title the king has thought fit to honor me with.

Page — I ask your lordship's pardon, my lord.

Lord Foppington — O, you can pronounce the word then — I thought it would have chok'd you — D'ye hear?

Page — My lord.

Lord Foppington — Call La Varole, I wou'd dress ——
    [*Exit* Page.

Solus.

Well, 'tis an unspeakable pleasure to be a man of quality — Strike me dumb — My lord — Your lordship — My Lord Foppington — *Ah! c'est quelque chose de beau, que la Diable m'emporte* — Why, the ladies were ready to puke at me, whilst I had nothing but Sir Navelty to recommend me to 'em — Sure whilst I was but a knight, I was a very nauseous fellow — Well, 'tis ten thousand pawnd well given — Stap my vitals ——

Enter LA VAROLE.

La Varole — Me Lord, de shoemaker, de tailor, de hosier, de sempstress, de peru, be all ready, if your lordship please to dress.

Lord Foppington — 'Tis well; admit 'em.

La Varole — Hey, messieurs, entrez.

Enter Tailor, etc.

Lord Foppington — So, gentlemen, I hope you have all taken pains to show yourselves masters in your professions.

Tailor — I think I may presume to say, sir ——

La Varole — My lord — you clawn you.

Tailor — Why, is he made a lord? — My lord, I ask your lordship's pardon; my lord, I hope, my lord, your lordship will please to own, I have brought your lordship as accomplish'd a suit of clothes, as ever peer of England trode the stage in, my lord. Will your lordship please to try 'em now?

Lord Foppington — Ay, but let my people dispose the glasses so that I may see myself before and behind; for I love to see myself all raund ——

[*Whilst he puts on his clothes, enter* YOUNG FASHION *and* LORY.

Young Fashion — Heydey, what the devil have we here? Sure my gentleman's grown a favorite at Court, he has got so many people at his levee.

Lory — Sir, these people come in order to make him a favorite at Court; they are to establish him with the ladies.

Young Fashion — Good God! to what an ebb of taste are women fallen, that it shou'd be in the power of a lac'd coat to recommend a gallant to 'em ——

Lory — Sir, tailors and periwig makers are now become the bawds of the nation; 'tis they debauch all the women.

Young Fashion — Thou sayest true; for there's that fop now, has not by nature wherewithal to move a cookmaid, and by that time these fellows have done with him, I'gad he shall melt down a countess — But now for my reception, I engage it shall be as cold a one as a courtier's to his friend who comes to put him in mind of his promise.

Lord Foppington [*to his tailor*] — Death and eternal tartures! Sir, I say the packet's too high by a foot.

Tailor — My lord, if it had been an inch lower, it would not have held your lordship's pocket handkerchief.

Lord Foppington — Rat my packet handkerchief! Have not I a page to carry it? You may make him a packet up to his chin a purpose for it; but I will not have mine come so near my face.

Tailor — 'Tis not for me to dispute your lordship's fancy.

Young Fashion [*to* LORY] — His lordship! Lory, did you observe that?

Lory — Yes, sir; I always thought 'twould end there. Now, I hope, you'll have a little more respect for him.

Young Fashion — Respect! D—— him for a coxcomb; now has he ruined his estate to buy a title, that he may be a fool of the first rate. But let's accost him. — [*To* LORD FOPPINGTON] Brother, I'm your humble servant.

Lord Foppington — O Lard, Tam; I did not expect you in England: Brother, I am glad to see you. — [*Turning to his tailor*] Look you, sir, I shall never be reconcil'd to this nauseous packet; therefore pray get me another suit with all manner of expedition, for this is my eternal aversion. Mrs. Callicoe, are not you of my mind?

Sempstress — O, directly, my lord, it can never be too low——

Lord Foppington — You are passitively in the right on't, for the packet becomes no part of the body but the knee.

Sempstress — I hope your lordship is pleas'd with your steenkirk [neckcloth].

Lord Foppington — In love with it, stap my vitals. Bring your bill, you shall be paid to-marrow ——

Sempstress — I humbly thank your honor ——

[*Exit* Sempstress.

Lord Foppington — Hark thee, shoemaker, these shoes a'n't ugly, but they don't fit me.

Shoemaker — My lord, my thinks they fit you very well.

Lord Foppington — They hurt me just below the instep.

Shoemaker [*feeling his foot*] — My lord, they don't hurt you there.

Lord Foppington — I tell thee, they pinch me execrably.

Shoemaker — My lord, if they pinch you, I'll be bound to be hanged, that's all.

Lord Foppington — Why, wilt thou undertake to persuade me I cannot feel?

Shoemaker — Your lordship may please to feel what you think fit; but that shoe does not hurt you — I think I understand my trade ——

Lord Foppington — Now by all that's great and powerful, thou art an incomprehensible coxcomb; but thou makest good shoes, and so I'll bear with thee.

Shoemaker — My lord, I have work'd for half the people of

quality in town these twenty years; and 'tis very hard I should not know when a shoe hurts, and when it don't.

Lord Foppington — Well, prithee, begone about thy business. [*Exit* Shoemaker.

[*To the* Hosier] Mr. Mend Legs, a word with you; the calves of the stockings are thicken'd a little too much. They make my legs look like a chairman's ——

Mend Legs — My lord, my thinks they look mighty well.

Lord Foppington — Ay, but you are not so good a judge of those things as I am, I have study'd them all my life; therefore pray let the next be the thickness of a crawnpiece less. [*Aside*] If the town takes notice my legs are fallen away, 'twill be attributed to the violence of some new intrigue. [*To the* Periwig Maker] Come, Mr. Foretop, let me see what you have done, and then the fatigue of the morning will be over.

Foretop — My lord, I have done what I defy any prince in Europe to outdo; I have made you a periwig so long, and so full of hair, it will serve you for a hat and cloak in all weathers.

Lord Foppington — Then thou hast made me thy friend to eternity. Come, comb it out.

Young Fashion — Well, Lory, what do'st think on't? A very friendly reception from a brother after three years' absence!

Lory — Why, sir, 'tis your own fault; we seldom care for those that don't love what we love: if you wou'd creep into his heart, you must enter into his pleasures. Here you have stood ever since you came in, and have not commended any one thing that belongs to him.

Young Fashion — Nor never shall, while they belong to a coxcomb.

Lory — Then, sir, you must be content to pick a hungry bone.

Young Fashion — No, sir, I'll crack it, and get to the marrow before I have done.

Lord Foppington — Gad's curse! Mr. Foretop, you don't intend to put this upon me for a full periwig?

Foretop — Not a full one, my lord! I don't know what your lordship may please to call a full one, but I have cramm'd twenty ounces of hair into it.

Lord Foppington — What it may be by weight, sir, I shall not dispute; but by tale, there are not nine hairs on a side.

Foretop—O Lord! O Lord! O Lord! Why, as God shall judge me, your honor's side face is reduc'd to the tip of your nose.

Lord Foppington—My side face may be in an eclipse for aught I know; but I'm sure my full face is like the full moon.

Foretop—Heaven bless my eyesight. [*Rubbing his eyes.*] Sure I look thro' the wrong end of the perspective; for by my faith, an't please your honor, the broadest place I see in your face does not seem to me to be two inches' diameter.

Lord Foppington—If it did, it would just be two inches too broad; for a periwig to a man should be like a mask to a woman, nothing should be seen but his eyes——

Foretop—My lord, I have done; if you please to have more hair in your wig, I'll put it in.

Lord Foppington—Passitively, yes.

Foretop—Shall I take it back now, my lord?

Lord Foppington—No: I'll wear it to-day, tho' it show such a manstrous pair of cheeks, stap my vitals, I shall be taken for a trumpeter. [*Exit* FORETOP.

Young Fashion—Now your people of business are gone, brother, I hope I may obtain a quarter of an hour's audience of you.

Lord Foppington—Faith, Tam, I must beg you'll excuse me at this time, for I must away to the House of Lards immediately; my Lady Teaser's case is to come on to-day, and I would not be absent for the salvation of mankind. Hey, page! is the coach at the door?

Page—Yes, my lord.

Lord Foppington—You'll excuse me, brother. [*Going.*

Young Fashion—Shall you be back at dinner?

Lord Foppington—As Gad shall jedge me, I can't tell; far 'tis passible I may dine with some of aur hause at Lacket's.

Young Fashion—Shall I meet you there? for I must needs talk with you.

Lord Foppington—That, I'm afraid, mayn't be so praper; far the lards I commonly eat with are a people of a nice conversation; and you know, Tam, your education has been a little at large: but if you'll stay here, you'll find a family dinner. Hey, fellow! What is there for dinner? There's beef: I suppose my brother will eat beef. Dear Tam, I'm glad to see thee in England, stap my vitals.

[*Exit, with his equipage.*

Young Fashion — Hell and Furies, is this to be borne?
Lory — Faith, sir, I cou'd almost have given him a knock o' th' pate myself.

ORIGIN AND DEVELOPMENT OF THE BANK OF ENGLAND.[1]

By WALTER BAGEHOT.

(From " Lombard Street.")

[WALTER BAGEHOT, English writer, was born in Somersetshire, February 3, 1826. He was graduated at London University; was in France at the time of Louis Napoleon's coup d'état of December 2, 1851, and wrote letters to the London *Inquirer* on it which are classic; took part in his father's banking and shipping business; in 1860 succeeded his father-in-law as editor of the *Economist*, which he raised from a purely business organ to a great political review. He wrote " Physics and Politics " (1863), edited the *National Review* 1864-1868, and wrote many literary and biographical essays for it; published "The English Constitution " (1867), " Lombard Street " (1873), and articles collected after his death as " Economic Studies." He died March 24, 1877.]

OF all institutions in the world, the Bank of England is now probably the most remote from party politics and from "financing"; but in its origin it was not only a finance company, but a Whig finance company, — it was founded by a Whig government because it was in desperate want of money, and supported by the " City " because the " City " was Whig. Very briefly, the story was this : —

The government of Charles II. (under the Cabal ministry) had brought the credit of the English state to the lowest possible point : it had perpetrated one of those monstrous frauds which are likewise gross blunders. The goldsmiths, who then carried on upon a trifling scale what we should now call " banking," used to deposit their reserve of treasure in the Exchequer, with the sanction and under the care of the government. In many European countries, the credit of the state had been so much better than any other credit that it had been used to strengthen the beginnings of banking. The credit of the state had been so used in England : though there had lately been a civil war and several revolutions, the honesty of the English government was trusted implicitly. But Charles II. showed that it was trusted undeservedly : he shut up the Exchequer, would pay no one, and so the goldsmiths were ruined.

[1] By permission of Kegan Paul, Trench, Trübner & Co. (Crown 8vo., price 3*s.* 6*d.*)

CHARLES II

The credit of the Stuart government never recovered from this monstrous robbery, and the government created by the revolution of 1688 could hardly expect to be more trusted with money than its predecessor. A government created by a revolution hardly ever is: there is a taint of violence which capitalists dread instinctively, and there is always a rational apprehension that the government which one revolution thought fit to set up, another revolution may think fit to pull down. In 1694 the credit of William III.'s government was so low in London that it was impossible for it to borrow any large sum; and the evil was the greater, because in consequence of the French war the financial straits of the government were extreme. At last a scheme was hit upon which would relieve their necessities. "The plan," says Macaulay, "was that twelve hundred thousand pounds should be borrowed by the government, on what was then considered as the moderate interest of 8 per cent. In order to induce capitalists to advance the money promptly on terms so favorable to the public, the subscribers were to be incorporated by the name of 'The Governor and Company of the Bank of England';" they were so incorporated, and the £1,200,000 was obtained.

On many succeeding occasions, their credit was of essential use to the government. Without their aid, our National Debt could not have been borrowed; and if we had not been able to raise that money we should have been conquered by France and compelled to take back James II. And for many years afterwards, the existence of that debt was a main reason why the industrial classes never would think of recalling the Pretender or of upsetting the Revolution settlement: the "fundholder" is always considered in the books of that time as opposed to his "legitimate" sovereign, because it was to be feared that this sovereign would repudiate the debt which was raised by those who dethroned him, and which was spent in resisting him and his allies. For a long time the Bank of England was the focus of London Liberalism, and in that capacity rendered to the state inestimable services; in return for these substantial benefits, the Bank of England received from the government, either at first or afterwards, three most important privileges: —

First. The Bank of England had the exclusive possession of the government balances. In its first period, as I have shown, the Bank gave credit to the government; but afterwards it derived credit from the government. There is a natural tendency in men to follow the example of the government under which they live: the government is the largest, most important, and most conspicuous entity with which the mass of any people are acquainted; its range of knowledge must always be infinitely greater than the average of their knowledge, and therefore, unless there is a conspicuous warning to the contrary, most men are inclined to think their government right, and when they can, to do what it does. Especially in money matters, a man might fairly reason, " If the government is right in trusting the Bank of England with the great balance of the nation, I cannot be wrong in trusting it with my little balance."

Second. The Bank of England had till lately the monopoly of limited liability in England. It was an exception of the greatest value to the Bank of England, because it induced many quiet merchants to be directors of the Bank, who certainly would not have joined any bank where *all* their fortunes were liable, and where the liability was not limited.

Third. The Bank of England had the privilege of being the sole *joint-stock company* permitted to issue bank notes in England. Private London bankers did indeed issue notes down to the middle of the last century, but no joint-stock company could do so. Its effect was very important: it in time gave the Bank of England the monopoly of the note issue of the metropolis. No company but the Bank of England could issue notes, and unincorporated individuals gradually gave way and ceased to do so. The Act of 1742 stipulated that no other bank shall be created, established, or allowed, by Parliament or a copartnership, exceeding the number of six persons, in England, to borrow, owe, or take up any sum, or sums, of money on their bills or notes, during the continuance of said privilege to said Governor and Company.

With so many advantages over all competitors, it is quite natural that the Bank of England should have far outstripped them all. Inevitably it became *the* bank in London; all the other bankers grouped themselves round it and lodged their reserve with it. Thus our *one*-reserve system of banking was not deliberately founded upon definite reasons: it was the gradual consequence of many singular events, and of an accumulation of legal privileges on a single bank which has now been altered, and which no one would now defend.

ATHOS, PORTHOS, AND ARAMIS.

By ALEXANDRE DUMAS, Père.

(From "The Three Musketeers.")

[ALEXANDRE DUMAS PÈRE, French novelist and dramatist, was born July 24, 1803; his grandmother was a Haytian negress. His youth was roving and dissipated; the few years after he became of age were spent in Paris experimenting in literary forms; at twenty-six he took the public by storm with his play "Henry III. and his Court." He was probably the most prolific great writer that ever lived, his works singly and in collaboration amounting to over two thousand volumes; he had some ninety collaborators, few of whom ever did successful independent work. A catalogue of his productions would fill many pages of this work. The most popular of his novels are: "The Three Musketeers" series (including "Twenty Years After" and "The Viscount de Bragelonne") and "The Count of Monte Christo." He died December 5, 1870.]

THE BASTION OF ST. GERVAIS.

D'ARTAGNAN rose early, and while attending to his toilet, gave vent to his opinion of his companions by reciting aloud a catalogue of their virtues.

"Athos, Porthos, and Aramis," said he, slapping his thigh by way of emphasis, "you are a magnificent trio. You fascinate me, you enthrall me with your simple-hearted good humor and your worthy exploits. What chevalier can command three better knights, whose watchwords are 'Honor, Chivalry, and Friendship'?"

The sound of a distant bugle interrupted D'Artagnan's reverie, warning him it was time for the business in hand.

On arriving at his friends' quarters, D'Artagnan found them assembled in the same room. Athos was thinking; Porthos was twisting his mustache; and Aramis was reading his prayers in a charming little book, bound in blue velvet.

"By my soul, gentlemen," said he, "I hope that what you have to tell me is worth the trouble, otherwise I should not forgive your depriving me of rest after a night passed in dismantling a bastion, entirely by myself. Ah! why were you not there, gentlemen? It was hot work!"

"We were in another place, where it was by no means cold either," said Porthos, giving his mustache a peculiar turn.

"Hush!" said Athos.

"Oh, oh!" said D'Artagnan, understanding the slight frown of the musketeer, "it seems something is stirring."

"Aramis," said Athos, "you breakfasted at the Parpaillot tavern the day before yesterday, I believe."

"Yes."

"How are things there?"

"Why, I fared but poorly myself; it was a fast day, and they had only eggs."

"What," said Athos, "in a seaport, and no fish?"

"They say that the dike which the cardinal is digging drives the fish out into the open sea," said Aramis, resuming his pious reading.

"But that is not what I wanted to know, Aramis," continued Athos. "Were you free, and did no one disturb you?"

"Why, I think that there were not many idlers," replied Aramis. "Yes, in fact, for what you want, Athos, I think we shall do well enough at the Parpaillot."

"Come, then, let us to the Parpaillot," said Athos, "for here the walls are like sheets of paper."

D'Artagnan, who was accustomed to his friend's manner, and understood by a word, a gesture, or a look from him that circumstances called for seriousness, took his arm and went out with him, without uttering a word. Porthos followed them, in conversation with Aramis.

On their way they met Grimaud, and Athos beckoned him to attend them. Grimaud, according to custom, obeyed in silence. The poor fellow had finished by almost forgetting how to speak.

When they arrived at the Parpaillot, it was seven in the morning, and the day was just beginning to dawn. The three friends ordered a good breakfast, and entered a room where the landlord assured them that they would not be disturbed.

The hour was, unfortunately, ill chosen for a consultation. The morning drum had just been beaten; every one was busy shaking off the sleepiness of night, and to drive away the dampness of the morning air, came to take a little dram at the tavern. Dragoons, Swiss guards, musketeers, and light cavalry succeeded one another with a rapidity very beneficial to the business of mine host, but very unfavorable to the designs of our four friends, who replied but sullenly to the salutations, toasts, and jests of their companions.

"Come," said Athos, "we shall invite some rousing quarrel on our hands presently, and we do not want that just now."

D'Artagnan, tell us about your night's work: we will tell you ours afterward."

"In fact," said one of the light cavalry, who, whilst rocking himself, held in his hand a glass of brandy, which he slowly sipped, "in fact, you were in the trenches, you gentlemen of the guards, and it seems to me that you had a squabble with the Rochellais."

D'Artagnan looked at Athos, to see whether he ought to answer this intruder who thrust himself into the conversation.

"Well," said Athos, "did you hear M. de Busigny, who did you the honor to address you? Tell us what took place in the night, since these gentlemen desire it."

"Did you not take a bastion?" asked a Swiss, who was drinking rum and beer mixed.

"Yes, sir," replied D'Artagnan, bowing, "we had that honor. And also, as you have heard, we introduced a barrel of powder under one of the angles, which, on exploding, made a very pretty breach, without reckoning that, as the bastion is very old, all the rest of the building is much shaken."

"And what bastion is it?" asked a dragoon who held, spitted on his saber, a goose which he had brought to be cooked.

"The bastion St. Gervais," replied D'Artagnan, "from behind which the Rochellais annoyed our workmen."

"And was it warm work?"

"Yes. We lost five men and the Rochellais some eight or ten."

"Balzampleu!" said the Swiss, who, in spite of the admirable collection of oaths which the German language possesses, had got a habit of swearing in French.

"But it is probable," said the light horseman, "that they will send pioneers to repair the bastion this morning."

"Yes, it is probable," said D'Artagnan.

"Gentlemen," said Athos, "a wager!"

"Ah! a wager," said the Swiss.

"What is it?" asked the light horseman.

"Stop," said the dragoon, laying his saber like a spit on the two great iron dogs which kept up the fire in the chimney, "I am busy. A dripping pan here, you noodle of a landlord, that I may not lose one drop of the fat of this celestial bird."

"He is right," said the Swiss, "the juice of a goose is very good with puddings."

"There!" said the dragoon; "and now for the wager. We are listening, M. Athos."

"Well, M. de Busigny," said Athos, "I bet you that my three comrades, Messieurs Porthos, Aramis, and D'Artagnan, and myself will go and breakfast in the bastion of St. Gervais, and that we will stay there for one hour by the clock, whatever the enemy may do to dislodge us."

Porthos and Aramis looked at each other, for they began to understand.

"Why," said D'Artagnan, stooping to Athos' ear, "you are going to get us all killed without mercy."

"We shall be more certainly killed if we do not go," replied Athos.

"Ah, faith, gentlemen," said Porthos, throwing himself back in his chair, and twisting his mustache, "that is a fine wager, I hope."

"And I accept it," said M. de Busigny. "Now we must fix the stakes."

"You are four, gentlemen," said Athos, "and we are four: a dinner for eight — will that suit you?"

"Just the thing!" replied M. de Busigny.

"The very thing!" added the dragoon.

"That will do!" exclaimed the Swiss. The fourth auditor, who had remained silent throughout the conversation, bowed his head, as a sign that he acquiesced in the proposition.

"The déjeuner of these gentlemen is ready," said the landlord.

"Well, then, bring it here," said Athos.

The landlord obeyed. Athos called Grimaud, showed him a large basket, which was lying in a corner, and made him a sign to wrap up in the napkins all the eatables that had been brought.

Grimaud, comprehending at once that they were going to breakfast on the grass, took the basket, packed up the eatables, put in the bottles, and took the basket up in his arms.

"But where are you going to eat this breakfast?" said the landlord.

"What does it signify to you," replied Athos, "provided you are paid for it?" And he threw two pistoles majestically on the table.

"Shall I get you change, sir?" said mine host.

"No; but add a couple of bottles of champagne, and the difference will pay for the napkins."

The landlord had not made quite such a good thing of it as he at first expected; but he recompensed himself for it by palming off, on his four guests, two bottles of Anjou wine, instead of the two bottles of champagne.

"M. de Busigny, will you regulate your watch by mine, or permit me to regulate mine by yours?" inquired Athos.

"Whichever you please," said the light dragoon, drawing from his fob a very beautiful watch encircled with diamonds. "Half-past seven," added he.

"Five and thirty minutes after seven," said Athos; "we shall remember that I am five minutes in advance, sir."

Then bowing to the astonished waiters, the four young men took the road toward the bastion of St. Gervais, followed by Grimaud, who carried the basket, not knowing where he was going, and, from the passive obedience that was habitual to him, not thinking even of inquiring.

Whilst they were within the precincts of the camp, the four friends did not exchange a word; they were, besides, followed by the curious, who, having heard of the wager, wished to know how they would extricate themselves from the affair. But when once they had got beyond the lines of fortification, and found themselves in the open country, D'Artagnan, who was entirely ignorant of what they were about, thought it high time to demand some explanation.

"And now, my dear Athos," said he, "have the kindness to tell me where you are going."

"You can see well enough," replied Athos, "we are going to the bastion."

"But what are we going to do there?"

"You know very well — we are going to breakfast there."

"But why do we not breakfast at the Parpaillot?"

"Because we have most important things to tell you, and it was impossible to converse for five minutes in that tavern with all those troublesome fellows, who come and go, and continually address us. Here, at least," continued Athos, pointing to the bastion, "no one will come to interrupt us."

"It appears to me," said D'Artagnan, with that prudence which was so intimately and so naturally connected with his superb courage — "it appears to me that we could have found some retired spot, somewhere in the sand hills, on the seashore."

"Where we should have been seen all four in council together, so that, in a quarter of an hour, the cardinal would have been informed by his spies that we were holding a consultation."

"Yes," said Aramis. "Athos is right; *animadvertuntur in desertis.*"

"A desert would not have been a bad place," remarked Porthos; "but the difficulty is to find it."

"There is no desert where a bird could not pass over one's head, or a fish jump from the water, or a rabbit run from her seat; and I believe that bird, fish, and rabbit, one and all, have become the cardinal's spies. It is much better, therefore, to pursue our enterprise. Besides, we cannot now recede without disgrace. We have made a bet — a bet which could not have been foreseen, and of which I defy any one to guess the true cause. To win it, we must remain an hour in the bastion. Either we shall, or shall not, be attacked. If we are not, we shall have time to talk, and no one will hear us: for I will answer for it that the walls of that bastion have no ears. If we are attacked, we will talk just the same, and shall, moreover, by defending ourselves, be covered with glory. So you see that everything is favorable to us."

"Yes," said D'Artagnan, "but we shall inevitably be shot."

"Yes," rejoined Athos, "but you know very well that the bullets most to be feared are not those of the enemy."

"Yet it seems to me," said Porthos, "that for such an expedition we should at least have brought our muskets."

"You are a simpleton, friend Porthos; why should we encumber ourselves with a useless burden?"

"I do not find a good regulation musket, with a dozen cartridges and a powderflask, useless in front of an enemy."

"Well," rejoined Athos, "did you not hear what D'Artagnan said?"

"And what did D'Artagnan say?" asked Porthos.

"D'Artagnan says that in last night's attack as many as eight or ten French were killed, and as many of the enemy."

"Well?"

"There has not been time to strip them, has there, seeing there was something more urgent to attend to?"

"Well?"

"Well, we shall find their muskets, powderflasks, and cartridges, and, instead of four muskets and a dozen balls, we shall have about fifteen muskets and a hundred rounds of ammunition to fire."

"Oh, Athos!" said Aramis, "you are indeed a great man!"

Porthos bowed his head in token of acquiescence.

D'Artagnan alone did not appear quite convinced.

Grimaud unquestionably partook of the young man's incredulity; for, seeing that they continued to march toward the bastion, of which he had before had some suspicion, he plucked his master by the skirt of his coat.

"Where are you going?" he inquired by a sign.

Athos pointed to the bastion.

"But," said the silent Grimaud, still in the same dialect, "we shall leave our skins there."

Athos raised his eyes and his hands to heaven.

Grimaud set down his basket on the ground, and seated himself upon it, shaking his head.

Athos took a pistol from his belt, looked at the priming, cocked it, and leveled it at Grimaud's ear.

Grimaud found himself lifted up and on his legs, as if by magic.

Athos then beckoned to him to take up the basket, and to march in front.

Grimaud obeyed; so that all the poor fellow had gained by this momentary pantomime was that he had been transformed from the rear guard to the van.

Having reached the bastion, the four friends looked behind them. More than three hundred soldiers, of every kind, had assembled at the entrance of the camp; and, in a separate group, they saw M. de Busigny, the dragoon, the Swiss, and the fourth wagerer.

Athos took off his hat, raised it on the end of his sword, and waved it in the air.

All the spectators returned his salutation, accompanying this act of politeness with a loud hurrah, which reached their ears.

After this occurrence they all four disappeared in the bastion, where Grimaud had already preceded them.

The Council of the Musketeers.

As Athos had foreseen, the bastion was tenanted alone by about a dozen dead — French and Rochellais.

"Gentlemen," said Athos, who had taken command of the expedition, "whilst Grimaud sets the table, let us begin by collecting muskets and ammunition. We can, moreover, converse whilst we are doing it. These gentlemen," added he, pointing to the dead bodies, "do not hear us."

"But we may, nevertheless, throw them into the ditches," said Porthos, "having first satisfied ourselves that they have nothing in their pockets."

"Yes," replied Athos, "but that is Grimaud's business."

"Well, then," said D'Artagnan, "let Grimaud search them, and throw them over the walls."

"Not upon any account," said Athos. "They may be of the utmost use to us."

"These dead of use to us!" exclaimed Porthos. "Ah, nonsense! you are surely going crazy, my dear friend."

"Do not judge rashly, advise both gospel and cardinal," replied Athos. "How many muskets are there, gentlemen?"

"Twelve."

"How much ammunition?"

"A hundred rounds."

"It is quite as many as we shall need: let us load our muskets."

The four companions set themselves to work: and just as they had loaded the last gun, Grimaud made a sign to them that breakfast was ready.

Athos indicated by a gesture that he was contented with what was done, and then pointed out to Grimaud a sort of sheltered box, where he was to place himself as sentinel. But, to mitigate the annoyance of his guard, Athos allowed him to take with him a loaf, a couple of cutlets, and a bottle of wine.

"And now, to breakfast!" said Athos.

The four friends seated themselves on the ground, with their legs crossed, like Turks or tailors.

"And now," said D'Artagnan, "as you are no longer afraid of being heard, I hope you are going to let us have the secret."

"I hope I am providing you at the same time with both amusement and glory, gentlemen!" said Athos. "I have induced you to take a charming little excursion: here is an admirable breakfast; and away over yonder, are five hundred persons, as you may perceive through the embrasures, who take us for madmen or heroes — two classes of fools that very much resemble each other."

" But this secret?"

"I saw My Lady last night," said Athos.

D'Artagnan was carrying his glass to his lips; but at the sound of her ladyship's name, his hand trembled so that he placed his glass on the ground, in order that he might not spill its contents.

" You have seen your wi—— "

"Hush, then!" interrupted Athos; "you forget, my dear fellow, that these gentlemen are not, like you, initiated in my family affairs. I have seen her ladyship."

"And where happened that?" demanded D'Artagnan.

"About two leagues from hence, at the Red Dovecote."

"In that case, I am a lost man," said D'Artagnan.

"Not just yet," replied Athos; "for, by this time, she must have quitted the shores of France."

D'Artagnan breathed again.

"But, after all," inquired Porthos, "who is this lady?"

"A charming woman!" said Athos, tasting a glass of sparkling wine. "Scamp of a landlord!" exclaimed he, "who gives us Anjou for champagne, and who thinks we shall be deceived by the substitution! Yes!" continued he, "a charming woman, to whom our friend D'Artagnan has done something unpardonable, for which she is seeking every human means to avenge herself — a month ago, by trying to get him shot; a week ago, by sending him poison; and yesterday, by demanding his head of the cardinal."

"What! demanding my head of the cardinal?" cried D'Artagnan, pale with terror.

"Yes," said Porthos, "it is as true as gospel; for I heard her with my own ears."

"And I also," said Aramis.

"Then," said D'Artagnan, letting his arm fall in a desponding manner, "it is useless to struggle longer: I may as well blow out my brains at once, and have done with it."

"That is the *last* folly a man should perpetrate," said Athos, "seeing it is the only one which will admit of no remedy."

"But with such enemies I shall never escape," said D'Artagnan. "First, my unknown antagonist of Meung; then, De Wardes, on whom I inflicted four wounds; next, this lady whose secret I found out; and, lastly, the cardinal, whose vengeance I intercepted."

"Well!" said Athos, "and all this makes only four, and we are four — one against one. Egad! if we may trust to Grimaud's signs, we are now about to engage with a far greater number of foes. What's the matter, Grimaud? Considering the seriousness of the circumstance, I permit you to speak, my friend; but be laconic, I beseech you. What do you see?"

"A troop."

"How many persons?"

"Twenty men."

"What sort of men?"

"Sixteen sappers and four dragoons."

"How far are they off?"

"Five hundred paces."

"Good! We have still time to finish our fowl, and to drink a glass of wine. To your health, D'Artagnan!"

"Your health!" repeated Aramis and Porthos.

"Well, then, to my health; although I do not imagine that your good wishes will be of much benefit to me."

"Bah!" said Athos. "God is great, as the Mohammedans say, and the future is in His hands."

Then, having swallowed his wine and put the glass down, Athos carelessly arose, took the first musket that came to hand, and strolled toward an embrasure.

The three others did the same. As for Grimaud, he had orders to place himself behind them and to reload their muskets.

An instant afterward they saw the troop appearing. It came along a kind of branch trench, which formed a communication between the bastion and the town.

"Zounds!" said Athos, "it is scarcely worth while to disturb ourselves for a score of fellows armed with pickaxes, mattocks, and spades! Grimaud ought to have quietly beckoned to them to go about their business, and I am quite convinced that they would have left us to ourselves."

"I must doubt it," said D'Artagnan, "for they come forward with great resolution. Besides, in addition to the workmen, there are four soldiers, and a brigadier, armed with muskets."

"That is because they have not seen us," replied Athos.

"Faith," said Aramis, "I confess that I am reluctant to fire upon these poor devils of citizens."

"He is a bad priest," said Porthos, "who pities heretics."

"Upon my word," said Athos, "Aramis is right. I will give them a preliminary talking to."

"What the plague are you doing?" cried D'Artagnan; "you will get yourself shot, my dear fellow."

But Athos paid no attention to this warning, and mounting on the breach, his fusee in one hand and his hat in the other:—

"Gentlemen," said he, bowing courteously, and addressing himself to the soldiers and pioneers, who, astonished by this apparition, halted at about fifty paces from the bastion; "gentlemen, we are, some of my friends and myself, engaged at breakfast in the bastion. Now you know that nothing is more disagreeable than to be disturbed at breakfast; so we entreat you, if you really have business here, to wait till we have finished our repast, or to come back in a little while: unless, indeed, you experience the salutary desire of forsaking the ranks of rebellion, and coming to drink with us to the health of the king of France."

"Take care, Athos," said D'Artagnan; "don't you see that they are taking aim at you."

"Yes, yes," said Athos; "but these are citizens, who are shocking bad marksmen, and will take particular care to shoot wide of the mark."

In fact, at that moment four shots were fired, and the bullets whistled around Athos, but without one touching him.

Four shots were instantaneously returned, but with a far better aim than that of the aggressors; three soldiers fell dead, and one of the pioneers was wounded.

"Grimaud," said Athos, from the breach, "another musket."

Grimaud obeyed instantly.

The three friends had also reloaded their arms. A second discharge soon followed the first, and the brigadier and two pioneers fell dead. The rest of the troop took to flight.

"Come, gentlemen, a sortie!" said Athos.

The four friends rushed out of the fort; reached the field of battle; picked up the muskets of the soldiers, and the half-pike of the brigadier; and, satisfied that the fugitives would never stop till they reached the town, they returned to the bastion, bearing with them the trophies of their victory.

"Reload, Grimaud," said Athos, "and let us, gentlemen, continue our breakfast and conversation. Where were we?"

"I recollect," said D'Artagnan; "you were saying that, after having demanded my head of the cardinal, her ladyship had left the shores of France. And where is she going?" added D'Artagnan, who was painfully anxious about the lady's itinerary.

"She is going to England," replied Athos.

"And with what object?"

"To assassinate the Duke of Buckingham, or to get him assassinated."

D'Artagnan uttered an exclamation of surprise and indignation.

"It is infamous!" exclaimed he.

"Oh, as to that," said Athos, "I beg you to believe that I concern myself very little about it. Now that you have finished, Grimaud," continued he, "take the half-pike of our brigadier, fasten a napkin to it, and fix it on the end of our bastion, that those rebellious Rochellais may see that they are opposed to brave and loyal subjects of the king."

Grimaud obeyed without reply: and an instant afterward the white flag floated over the heads of the four friends. A cry of joy, a thunder of applause, saluted its appearance. Half the camp was at the barriers.

"What?" said D'Artagnan, "you concern yourself but little about her killing Buckingham, or causing him to be killed? The duke is our friend."

"The duke is an Englishman: the duke fights against us: let her do therefore as she likes with the duke. I care as little about him as an empty bottle."

As Athos said this, he threw, some fifteen yards before him, a bottle which he held in his hand, and from which he had just emptied the last drop into his own glass.

"Wait an instant," said D'Artagnan, "I will not abandon Buckingham in that manner; he gave us some very beautiful horses."

"And especially some very beautiful saddles," added Porthos, who was then wearing the gold lace of one of them upon his cloak.

"Besides," said Aramis, "God seeks for the conversion, not the death, of a sinner."

"Amen!" said Athos, "and we will return to that by and

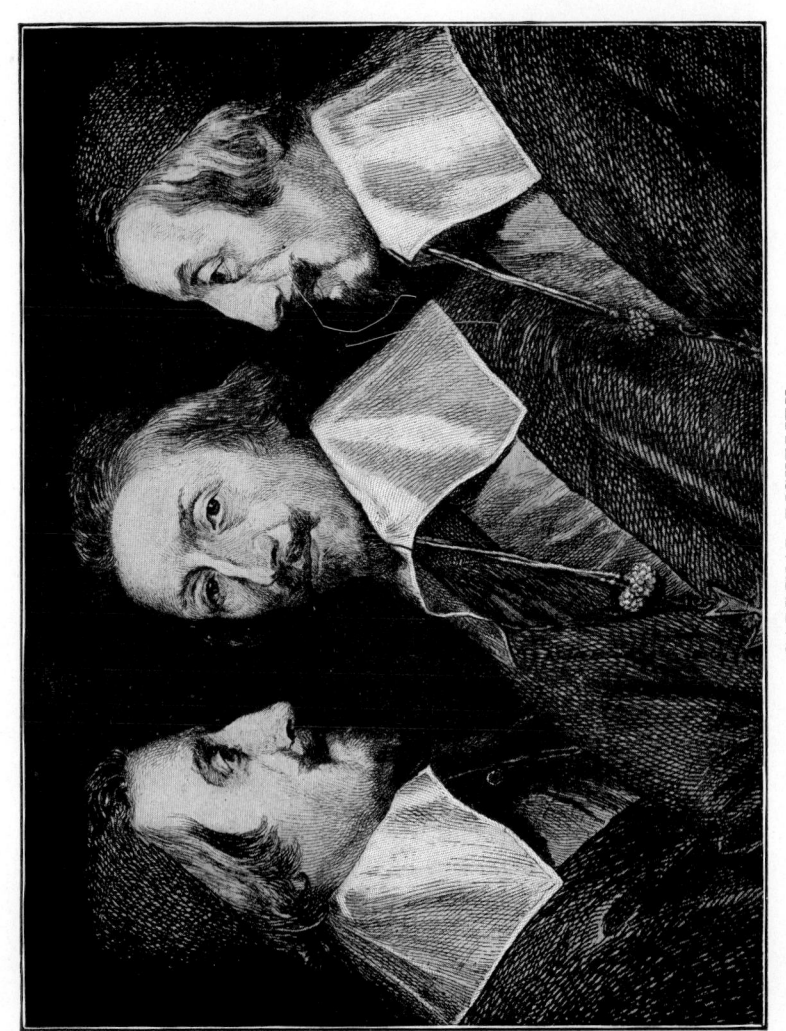

CARDINAL RICHELIEU.

by, if such is your pleasure; but that which most engaged my attention at the time, and I am sure you will understand why, D'Artagnan, was how to get from this woman a *carte blanche*, which she had extorted from the cardinal, and by means of which she might get rid of you, and perhaps the whole of us, with impunity."

"This creature is a very demon," said Porthos, holding his plate to Aramis, who was cutting up a fowl.

"And this document," said D'Artagnan, "did it remain in her hands?"

"No, it passed into mine. I cannot say without some trouble; for, if I did, I should tell a lie."

"My dear Athos," said D'Artagnan, "I can no longer count the times I owe my life to you."

"Then it was to visit her that you quitted us?" said Aramis.

"Exactly so."

"And you have got the cardinal's letter?" inquired D'Artagnan.

"Here it is," replied Athos.

He took the precious paper from the pocket of his coat. D'Artagnan unfolded it with a hand, of which he did not attempt to hide the trembling, and read: —

It is by my order, and for the good of the state, that the bearer of this did that which he has now done.
RICHELIEU.

"It is, in fact, a regular absolution," said Aramis.

"We must destroy this paper," said D'Artagnan, who seemed to read in it his own sentence of death.

"On the contrary," said Athos, "it must be most scrupulously preserved; and I would not give it up for the golden louis that would cover it."

"And what will she do now?" inquired D'Artagnan.

"Why," said Athos, carelessly, "she will write to the cardinal that a cursed musketeer named Athos took her safeguard from her by force; and she will, at the same time, advise his eminence to get rid of him, and also of his two friends, Porthos and Aramis. The cardinal will recollect that these are the very men that are always in his way. Then, some fine morning, he will have D'Artagnan arrested, and, that he may not be bored to death by solitude, will send us to keep him company in the Bastile."

"Ah!" said Porthos, "I think that you are making some rather dismal jokes."

"I am not joking," replied Athos.

"Do you know," said Porthos, "that I fancy it would be a more venial crime to twist this cursed lady's neck than those of these poor devils of Huguenots, who have never committed any greater crime than singing in French the very same psalms we sing in Latin."

"What does the abbé say to that?" quietly asked Athos.

"In that I am quite of Porthos' opinion."

"And I also," said D'Artagnan.

"Happily, she is far away," added Porthos; "for I confess she would much annoy me here."

"She annoys me in England, as well as in France," said Athos.

"She annoys me everywhere," said D'Artagnan.

"But, when you had her in your power," said Porthos, "why did you not drown, strangle, or hang her? It is only the dead who never return."

"Do you think so, Porthos?" said Athos, with a dark smile, which D'Artagnan alone could understand.

"I have an idea," said D'Artagnan.

"Let us hear it," cried the musketeers.

"*To arms!*" exclaimed Grimaud.

The young men arose hastily, and ran to their muskets.

This time there was a small band advancing, composed of twenty or five and twenty men, no longer pioneers, but soldiers of the garrison.

"Suppose we now return to the camp," said Porthos; "it seems to me that the match is not equal."

"Impossible, for three reasons," answered Athos. "The first is, because we have not finished our breakfast. The second, because we have still some important affairs to talk about; and the third, it will be still ten minutes before the hour elapses."

"But, nevertheless," said Aramis, "we must arrange a plan of battle."

"It is vastly simple," replied Athos. "As soon as the enemy is within musket shot, we must fire; if he continues to advance, we must fire again; in fact, we must fire away as long as we have guns loaded. If the remnant of the band should then wish to mount to the assault, we must let the besiegers descend as far as the ditch, and then we must heave on their heads a large mass of the wall, which only keeps up now by a miracle of equilibrium."

"Bravo!" exclaimed Porthos. "Athos, you are undoubtedly a born generalissimo, and the cardinal, who thinks himself a great warrior, is a mere corporal to you."

"Gentlemen," said Athos, "do not waste your ammunition, I beseech you; let each pick out his man."

"I have got mine," said D'Artagnan.

"And I mine," said Porthos.

"And I the same," said Aramis.

"Fire!" cried Athos.

The four guns made but one report, and four men fell.

The drum then beat, and the little band advanced to the charge.

The shots of the four friends were then fired without regularity, but invariably with the same deadly effect. Yet, as though they had known the numerical weakness of their opponents, the Rochellais continued to advance at a quick pace.

At three other shots, two men fell: yet the march of those who remained unwounded did not slacken.

Having reached the foot of the bastion, there were still twelve or fifteen of the enemy. A last discharge staggered, but did not arrest, them. They leaped into the ditch, and prepared to scale the breach.

"Now, my friends," said Athos, "let us finish them at one blow. To the wall! to the wall!"

And the four friends, assisted by Grimaud, set themselves to topple over, with the barrels of their muskets, an enormous mass of wall, which bowed as though the wind waved it, and loosening itself from its foundation, now fell with a tremendous crash into the ditch. A fearful cry was heard: a cloud of dust ascended toward the skies, and — all was over.

"Can we have crushed them all from the first to the last?" said Athos.

"Faith, it looks very like it," replied D'Artagnan.

"No," said Porthos; "there are two or three of them escaping, quite crippled."

In fact, three or four of these unfortunate beings, covered with mire and blood, fled along the hollow way and regained the town. They were all that had not perished of the little band.

Athos looked at his watch.

"Gentlemen," said he, "we have been here an hour, and now the wager is gained; but we will play our game triumphantly; besides, D'Artagnan has not yet told us his idea."

And the musketeer, with his habitual coolness, seated himself beside the remains of the breakfast.

"Would you like to hear my plan?" said D'Artagnan to his three companions, when, after the alarm which had had so fearful a termination for the little troop of Rochellais, they had resumed their places before the remnants of their meal.

"Yes," replied Athos; "you said that you had an idea."

"Ah! I have it," exclaimed D'Artagnan. "I will go to England for the second time, will find His Grace of Buckingham, and warn him of the plot which has been formed against his life."

"You will do no such thing, D'Artagnan," said Athos, coldly.

"Why not? Did I not go before?"

"Yes, but at that time we were not at war; at that time the Duke of Buckingham was an ally, and not an enemy; what you now suggest would be denominated treason."

"But," said Porthos, "I fancy that I, in my turn, have also got an idea."

"Silence for M. Porthos' idea," cried Aramis.

"I will ask leave of absence of M. de Tréville, on any pretext whatsoever that you can suggest; I am not very clever at excuses myself. The lady does not know me; I will get near her without exciting her alarm; and, when I have found beauty, I will wring her neck."

"Ah," said Athos, "I really am somewhat disposed to suggest that we second Porthos' idea."

"Fie, fie!" exclaimed Aramis; "kill a woman! No! Listen, *I* have the right idea."

"Let us have your idea, Aramis," said Athos, who had much deference for the young musketeer.

"Let us tell all to the queen."

"Ah, faith, yes!" said D'Artagnan and Porthos together; "I believe that we have found the true course at last."

"Announce it to the queen?" said Athos, "and how can we do that? Have we any connections at court? Can we send any one to Paris, without its becoming known all over the camp? There are a hundred and forty leagues between us and

Paris, and our letter will hardly have reached Angers before we ourselves shall be in a dungeon."

"As for getting a letter safely delivered to the queen," said Aramis, blushing, "I myself will undertake it. I know a very skillful person at Tours —— "

Aramis stopped — seeing Athos smile.

"Well! will you not adopt this plan, Athos?" inquired D'Artagnan.

"I do not entirely reject it," replied Athos, "but I would merely observe to Aramis that he cannot himself leave the camp; and that, with anybody but one of ourselves, there will be not the slightest security that, two hours after the messenger has started, all the capuchins, all the alguazils, all the black bonnets of the cardinal, will not know your letter by heart; and your very skillful person immediately arrested."

"Without calculating," added Porthos, "that the queen would try to save the Duke of Buckingham, but would leave *us* to our fate."

"Gentlemen," said D'Artagnan, "Porthos' objection is full of sense!"

"Ah, ha! what is going on in the town?" said Athos. "They are beating to arms."

The four friends listened, and the sound of the drum reached their ears.

"You will see," continued Athos, "that they will send an entire regiment against us."

"You do not expect us to stand our ground against an entire regiment?" said Porthos.

"Why not?" replied the musketeer. "I am just in the humor, and would hold it against an army, if we had only had the precaution to bring another dozen of wine!"

"Upon my word, the drum sounds nearer," said D'Artagnan.

"Let them come," replied Athos; "there is a quarter of an hour's march between the town and this place. It is more time than we shall require to arrange our plans. If we go away from here, we shall never again find such a convenient spot. And listen, gentlemen: the most appropriate idea in the world has come into my mind."

"Let us hear it."

Athos made a sign for his valet to come to him.

"Grimaud," said Athos, pointing to the dead bodies which lay in the bastion, "you will take these gentlemen, fix them upright against the wall, put their hats on their heads, and place their muskets in their hands."

"Oh, great man!" cried D'Artagnan, "I understand you."

"You understand?" said Porthos.

"And you, Grimaud, do you understand?" inquired Aramis. Grimaud gave a sign in the affirmative.

"It is all that is necessary," said Athos: "now let us return to my idea."

"I should like, however, to understand——" said Porthos.

"It is of no use."

"Yes, yes, Athos' idea!" cried D'Artagnan and Aramis at the same time.

"This lady, this woman, this creature, this viper, this demon, has a brother-in-law, I think you told me?"

"Yes; I even know him, and I believe that he has no great sympathy with his sister-in-law."

"There is no harm in that," replied Athos: "and if he detested her, even, it would be so much the more a virtue."

"In that case we are fitted to a nicety."

"Nevertheless," said Porthos, "I should like to understand what Grimaud is about."

"Silence, Porthos!" cried Aramis.

"What is the name of this brother-in-law?"

"Lord de Winter."

"Where is he at present?"

"He returned to London on the first report of the war."

"Well, he is precisely the man we want," said Athos. "It is to him that we must give information; we must let him know that his sister-in-law is going to assassinate some one, and entreat him not to lose sight of her. There must be in London, I should hope, some establishment like the Madelonnettes, or the Magdalen: he must place his sister-in-law there, and we shall then be at peace."

"Yes," said D'Artagnan, "until she gets out again."

"Ah, faith," said Athos, "you ask too much, D'Artagnan. I have given you all that I have, and I tell you now my budget is exhausted."

"I think it is the best plan we can devise," observed Aramis: "we will inform the queen and Lord de Winter at the same time."

"But by whom shall we convey the one letter to London and the other to Tours?"

"I answer for Bazin," replied Aramis.

"And I for Planchet," added D'Artagnan.

"In fact," said Porthos, "if we cannot leave the camp, our servants can."

"Certainly," added Aramis; "so we will write the letters this very day, give them sufficient money, and send them on the journey."

"We will give them sufficient money?" said Athos: "then you have got money, have you?"

The four friends looked at each other, and a cloud passed over the brows which had been for an instant brightened.

"Attention," cried D'Artagnan; "I see black and red points in movement below there. What were you saying about a regiment, Athos? It is a regular army."

"Faith, yes," replied Athos, "there they are. Do you see the crafty fellows, who are advancing without drum or trumpet! Ah, ah! Have you finished, Grimaud?"

Grimaud gave a sign in the affirmative, and pointed to a dozen dead bodies, which he had placed in the most picturesque attitudes — some carrying arms, others seeming to take aim, others sword in hand.

"Bravo!" cried Athos, "that does credit to your imagination."

"It is all the same," said Porthos; "and yet I should like to understand it."

"Let us decamp first," said D'Artagnan; "you will understand afterward."

"One moment, gentlemen — wait one moment; let us give Grimaud time to take away the breakfast things."

"Ah!" said Aramis, "here are the black and red points becoming visibly larger, and I am of D'Artagnan's opinion: I believe that we have no time to lose in regaining the camp."

"Faith," said Athos, "I have nothing more to say against a retreat: we bet for one hour, and we have remained an hour and a half. There is nothing more to argue or communicate: so let us be off, gentlemen, let us be off."

Grimaud had already commenced his retreat, with the basket and the fragments. The four friends followed behind him, and took about a dozen steps.

"Ah! What the plague are we about, gentlemen?" exclaimed Athos.

"Have you forgotten anything?" inquired Aramis.

"The flag: zounds! we must not leave a flag in the hands of the enemy, even when that flag is only a tablecloth."

And Athos rushed back into the bastion, mounted the platform, and took down the flag.

But, as the Rochellais had come within musket shot, they opened a sharp fire upon this man who thus exposed himself, as if for amusement, to their discharge. It might have been fancied, however, that Athos bore a charmed life, the bullets whizzed around him, yet he stood unharmed.

Athos waved his standard, as he turned his back on the town, and bowed toward the camp. Loud shouts resounded on both sides — shouts of anger from the one, and, from the other, of enthusiasm.

A second discharge soon followed the first, and three balls, by passing through it, made a regular standard of the tablecloth.

They heard the whole camp exclaiming — "Come down! come down!"

Athos slowly descended. His companions, who waited for him with anxiety, welcomed his reappearance with joy.

"Come along, Athos, come along," said D'Artagnan; "let us make haste. Now that we have found everything except money, it would be absurd to get killed."

But Athos persisted in his majestic walk; and his companions, finding all remonstrance useless, regulated their pace by his.

Grimaud and his basket formed the advance guard, and were both soon out of range.

After a minute or two they heard the sound of furious firing.

"What is that?" asked Porthos: "at what are they firing? I do not hear the bullets whistle, nor do I see anybody."

"They are firing at our *dead men!*" replied Athos.

"But our dead men will not return their fire."

"Exactly so. They will then believe that there is an ambuscade; they will deliberate, and will afterward reconnoiter; and by the time they discover the trick, we shall be beyond the reach of their fire. Thus, you see, it is unnecessary to give ourselves a fit of the pleurisy by overhaste."

"Oh! I understand now!" said the admiring Porthos.

"That's very fortunate," replied Athos, shrugging his shoulders.

THE THREE MUSKETEERS

The French on their side, perceiving their adventurous comrades returning, uttered cries of frantic enthusiasm.

At length, a fresh firing was heard, and this time the bullets were actually flattened on the stones around the four friends, and whistled mournfully about their ears. The Rochellais had at last taken possession of the bastion.

"They are a set of awkward fellows," remarked Athos: "how many of them have we killed? A dozen?"

"Or fifteen."

"How many did we make jelly of?"

"Eight or ten."

"And, in exchange for this, we have not got a scratch. Ah! yes, though! What is the matter there with your hand, D'Artagnan? It is bleeding."

"It is nothing," replied D'Artagnan.

"Was it a spent ball?"

"No."

"What then?"

We have said that Athos loved D'Artagnan as his own son, and though of a gloomy and inflexible character, he sometimes manifested toward the young man a solicitude truly paternal.

"Merely a scratch," replied D'Artagnan. "I caught my fingers between two stones — that of the wall and that of my ring — and the skin is cut."

"See what it is to wear diamonds, my master," said Athos, contemptuously.

"Ah!" exclaimed Porthos, "there is a diamond, in fact; and why the plague, then, as there is a diamond, do we battle about having no money?"

"See, there, now," said Aramis.

"Well done, Porthos; this time you really have an idea."

"Certainly," continued Porthos, bridling up at Athos' compliment; "and since there is a diamond, let us sell it."

"But," said D'Artagnan, "it is the queen's diamond."

"One reason more," said Athos — "the queen saving the Duke of Buckingham, her lover; nothing can be more just — the queen saving us, her friends: nothing can be more moral. Let us sell the diamond. What does the abbé say? I do not ask Porthos' opinion — it is already given."

"Why, I think," said Aramis, blushing, "that as the ring does not come from a mistress, and, consequently, is not a love token, D'Artagnan may sell it."

"My dear fellow, you speak like theology personified. So your advice is——"

"To sell the diamond," replied Aramis.

"Well," said D'Artagnan, gayly, "let us sell the diamond, and say no more about it."

The fusillade still continued, but the friends were beyond its reach, and the Rochellais seemed to be firing only for the satisfaction of their own pugnacity.

"Faith," said Athos, "it was quite time for this idea of Porthos' to present itself; for here we are at the camp. So now, gentlemen, not another word about this business. We are observed. They are coming to meet us, and we shall be carried home in triumph."

In fact, as we have already said, the whole camp was in commotion. More than two thousand soldiers had witnessed, as at a theater, the fortune-favored bravado of the four friends—a bravado of which they had been far from suspecting the true motive. Nothing could be heard but cries of "Long live the guards! Long live the musketeers!" M. de Busigny was the first who came to press the hand of Athos, and to confess that he had lost his bet. The dragoon and the Swiss followed him; and all their comrades followed the dragoon and the Swiss. There was no end to the congratulations, shaking of hands, embraces, and inextinguishable laughter at the Rochellais; and, last, the tumult was so great that the cardinal supposed there was a mutiny, and sent La Houdinière, the captain of his guards, to ascertain the cause of the disturbance. The incident was related to his messenger with all the warmth of enthusiasm.

"Well?" demanded the cardinal, on seeing La Houdinière return.

"Well, my lord," replied the latter, "it is three musketeers and a guardsman, who laid a bet with M. de Busigny to go and breakfast in the bastion of St. Gervais; and who, whilst at breakfast, maintained their ground for two hours against the Rochellais, and killed I know not how many of the enemy."

"Did you learn the names of these musketeers?"

"Yes, my lord."

"What are they?"

"Messrs. Athos, Porthos, and Aramis."

"Always my three brave fellows!" muttered the cardinal. "And the guard?"

"M. d'Artagnan."

"My young madcap again! Decidedly these four men must be mine."

On the same evening, the cardinal spoke to M. de Tréville of the exploit, which formed the subject of conversation throughout the whole camp. M. de Tréville, who had heard the recital of the adventure from the lips of those who were its heroes, recounted it in all its particulars to his eminence, without forgetting the episode of the tablecloth flag.

"Very good, M. de Tréville," said the cardinal; "give me this glorious standard, I entreat you. I will get three fleurs-de-lis embroidered on it in gold, and will give it to you as the battle flag of your company."

"My lord," said M. de Tréville, "that would be unjust towards the guards. M. d'Artagnan does not belong to me, but to M. des Essarts."

"Well, then, take him yourself," said the cardinal; "it is hardly fair that these four brave soldiers, who love each other so well, should not serve in the same company."

On the same evening, M. de Tréville announced this good news to the three musketeers, and to D'Artagnan, inviting them all four to breakfast with him on the following day.

D'Artagnan could not contain himself for joy. We know that the dream of his life had been to be a musketeer.

The three friends were also profoundly delighted.

"Faith," said D'Artagnan to Athos, "yours was a triumphant idea; and as you said, we have gained glory by it, besides being able to hold a conversation of the greatest importance."

"Which we may henceforth renew without suspicion; for, with God's help, we shall henceforth be looked upon as cardinalists."

On the same evening D'Artagnan went to pay his respects to M. des Essarts, and to inform him of his promotion.

M. des Essarts, who had great affection for D'Artagnan, offered him any assistance that he might require, as this change of regiment brought with it the expense of a new equipment.

D'Artagnan declined this aid; but thinking the opportunity a good one, he requested him to ascertain the value of the diamond, which he placed in his hands, stating that he wished him to turn it into money.

At eight o'clock the next morning, M. des Essarts' valet

came to D'Artagnan and handed to him a bag, containing seven thousand livres in gold. It was the price of the queen's diamond.

THE FATE OF MORDAUNT.

By ALEXANDRE DUMAS, Père.

(From "Twenty Years After.")

The Skiff "Lightning."

Mordaunt glided through the subterranean passage, and, gaining the neighboring house, stopped to take breath.

"Good," said he, "a mere nothing. Scratches, that is all. Now to my work."

He walked on at a quick pace, till he reached a neighboring cavalry barrack, where he happened to be known. Here he borrowed a horse, the best in the stables, and in a quarter of an hour was at Greenwich.

"'Tis well," said he, as he reached the river bank. "I am half an hour before them. Now," he added, rising in the stirrups, and looking about him, "which, I wonder, is the 'Lightning'?"

At this moment, as if in reply to his words, a man lying on a coil of cables rose and advanced a few steps toward him. Mordaunt drew a handkerchief from his pocket, and tying a knot at each corner — the signal agreed upon — waved it in the air, and the man came up to him. He was wrapped in a large rough cape, which concealed his form and partly his face.

"Do you wish to go on the water, sir?" said the sailor.

"Yes, just so. Along the Isle of Dogs."

"And perhaps you have a preference for one boat more than another. You would like one that sails as rapidly ——"

"As lightning," interrupted Mordaunt.

"Then mine is the boat you want, sir. I'm your man."

"I begin to think so, particularly if you had not forgotten a certain signal."

"Here it is, sir," and the sailor took from his coat a handkerchief, tied at each corner.

"Good, quite right!" cried Mordaunt, springing off his

horse. "There's not a moment to lose; now take my horse to the nearest inn, and conduct me to your vessel."

"But," asked the sailor, "where are your companions? I thought there were four of you."

"Listen to me, sir; I'm not the man you take me for; you are in Captain Rogers' post, are you not, under orders from General Cromwell? Mine, also, are from him!"

"Indeed, sir, I recognize you; you are Captain Mordaunt. Don't be afraid; you are with a friend. I am Captain Groslow. The general remembered that I had formerly been a naval officer, and he gave me the command of this expedition. Is there anything new in the wind?"

"Nothing."

"I thought, perhaps, that the king's death ——"

"Has only hastened their flight; in ten minutes they will, perhaps, be here. I am going to embark with you. I wish to aid in the deed of vengeance. All is ready, I suppose?"

"Yes."

"The cargo on board?"

"Yes — and we are sailing from Oporto to Antwerp, remember."

"'Tis well."

They then went down to the Thames. A boat was fastened to the shore by a chain fixed to a stake. Groslow jumped in, followed by Mordaunt, and in five minutes they were quite away from that world of houses which then crowded the outskirts of London; and Mordaunt could discern the little vessel riding at anchor near the Isle of Dogs. When they reached the side of this felucca, Mordaunt, dexterous in his eagerness for vengeance, seized a rope and climbed up the side of the vessel with a coolness and agility very rare among landsmen. He went with Groslow to the captain's berth — a sort of temporary cabin of planks — for the chief apartment had been given up by Captain Rogers to the passengers, who were to be accommodated at the other extremity of the boat.

"They will have nothing to do with this side of the ship, then," said Mordaunt.

"Nothing at all."

"That's a capital arrangement. Return to Greenwich, and bring them here. I shall hide myself in your cabin. You have a longboat?"

"That in which we came."

"It appeared light and well constructed."

"Quite a canoe."

"Fasten it to the poop with ropes — put the oars into it, so that it may follow in the track, and there will be nothing to do except to cut the cords away. Put a good supply of rum and biscuit in it for the seamen; should the night happen to be stormy, they will not be sorry to find something to console themselves with."

"Consider all this done. Do you wish to see the powder room?"

"No. When you return, I will set the fuse myself, but be careful to conceal your face, so that you cannot be recognized by them."

"Never fear."

"There's ten o'clock striking at Greenwich."

Groslow then, having given the sailor on duty an order to be on the watch with more than usual vigilance, went down into the longboat, and soon reached Greenwich. The wind was chilly, and the jetty was deserted, as he approached it; but he had no sooner landed than he heard a noise of horses galloping upon the paved road.

These horsemen were our friends, or rather, an *avant-garde*, composed of D'Artagnan and Athos. As soon as they arrived at the spot where Groslow stood, they stopped, as if guessing that he was the man they wanted. Athos alighted, and calmly opened the handkerchief tied at each corner, whilst D'Artagnan, ever cautious, remained on horseback, one hand upon his pistol, leaning forward watchfully.

On seeing the appointed signal, Groslow, who had at first crept behind one of the cannon planted on that spot, walked straight up to the gentlemen. He was so well wrapped up in his cloak, that it would have been impossible to have seen his face even if the night had not been so dark as to render precaution superfluous; nevertheless, the keen glance of Athos perceived at once it was not Rogers who stood before them.

"What do you want with us?" he asked of Groslow.

"I wish to inform you, my lord," replied Groslow, with an Irish accent, feigned of course, "that if you are looking for Captain Rogers you will not find him. He fell down this morning and broke his leg; but I'm his cousin; he told me everything, and desired me to look out for and conduct you to any place named by the four gentlemen who should bring me a handkerchief tied at each corner, like that one which you hold and one which I have in my pocket."

And he drew out the handkerchief.

"Was that all he said?" inquired Athos.

"No, my lord; he said you had engaged to pay seventy pounds if I landed you safe and sound at Boulogne, or any other port you chose in France."

"What do you think of all this?" said Athos, in a low tone, to D'Artagnan, after explaining to him in French what the sailor had said in English.

"It seems a likely story — to *me*."

"And to me, too."

"Besides, we can but blow out his brains if he proves false," said the Gascon; "and you, Athos, you know something of everything, and can be our captain. I dare say you know how to navigate, should he fail us."

"My dear friend, you guess well. My father meant me for the navy, and I have some vague notions about navigation."

"You see!" cried D'Artagnan.

They then summoned their friends, who, with Blaisois, Musqueton, and Grimaud, promptly joined them — leaving Parry behind them, who was to take their horses back to London; and they all proceeded instantly to the shore, and placed themselves in the boat, which, rowed by Groslow, began rapidly to clear the coast.

"At last," exclaimed Porthos, "we are afloat."

"Alas," said Athos, "we depart alone."

"Yes; but all four together, and without a scratch; which is a consolation."

"We are not yet at our destination," observed the prudent D'Artagnan; "beware of misadventure."

"Ah! my friend," cried Porthos, "like the crows, you always bring bad omens. Who could intercept us in such a night as this — pitch dark — when one does not see more than twenty yards before one?"

"Yes — but to-morrow morning ——"

"To-morrow we shall be at Boulogne. But it is refreshing to hear Monsieur d'Artagnan confess that he's afraid."

"I not only confess it, but am proud of it," returned the Gascon; "I'm not such a rhinoceros as you are. Oho! what's that?"

"The 'Lightning,'" answered the captain, "our felucca."

"So far, so good," laughed Athos.

They went on board, and the captain instantly conducted them to the berth prepared for them — a cabin which was to serve for all purposes, and for the whole party; he then tried to slip away under pretext of giving orders to some one.

"Stop a moment," cried D'Artagnan; "pray how many men have you on board, captain?"

"I don't understand," was the reply.

"Explain it, Athos."

Groslow, on the question being interpreted, answered, "Three, without counting myself."

"Oh!" exclaimed D'Artagnan. "I begin to be more at my ease; however, whilst you settle yourselves, I shall make the round of the boat."

"As for me," said Porthos, "I will see to the supper."

"A very good idea, Porthos," said the Gascon. "Athos, lend me Grimaud, who, in the society of his friend Parry, has, perhaps, picked up a little English, and can act as my interpreter."

"Go, Grimaud," said Athos.

D'Artagnan, finding a lantern on the deck, took it up, and with a pistol in his hand he said to the captain, in English, "Come" (being, with the classic English oath, the only English words he knew), and so saying, he descended to the lower deck.

This was divided into three compartments: one which was covered by the floor of that room in which Athos, Porthos, and Aramis were to pass the night; the second was to serve as the sleeping room for the servants; the third, under the prow of the ship, was under the temporary cabin in which Mordaunt was concealed.

"Oho!" cried D'Artagnan, as he went down the steps of the hatchway, preceded by the lantern; "what a number of barrels! one would think one was in the cave of Ali Baba. What is there in them?" he added, putting his lantern on one of the bins.

The captain seemed inclined to go upon deck again, but, controlling himself, he answered: —

"Port wine."

"Ah! port wine! 'tis a comfort," said the Gascon, "since we shall not die of thirst. Are they all full?"

Grimaud translated the question, and Groslow, who was wiping the perspiration from off his forehead, answered: —

"Some full, others empty."

D'Artagnan struck the barrels with his hand, and having ascertained that he spoke the truth, pushed his lantern, greatly to the captain's alarm, into the interstices between the barrels, and finding that there was nothing concealed in them: —

"Come along," he said; and he went toward the door of the second compartment.

"Stop!" said the Englishman. "I have the key of that door;" and he opened the door, with a trembling hand, into the second compartment, where Musqueton and Blaisois were preparing supper.

Here there was evidently nothing to seek, or to apprehend, and they passed rapidly to examine the third compartment.

This was the room appropriated to the sailors. Two or three hammocks hung upon the ceiling, a table and two benches composed the entire furniture. D'Artagnan picked up two or three old sails, hung on the walls, and meeting nothing to suspect, regained, by the hatchway, the deck of the vessel.

"And this room?" he asked, pointing to the captain's cabin.

"That's my room," replied Groslow.

"Open the door."

The captain obeyed. D'Artagnan stretched out his arm, in which he held the lantern, put his head in at the half-opened door, and seeing that the cabin was nothing better than a shed:

"Good," he said. "If there is an army on board it is not here that it is hidden. Let us see what Porthos has found for supper." And thanking the captain, he regained the state cabin, where his friends were.

Porthos had found nothing; and with him fatigue had prevailed over hunger. He had fallen asleep, and was in a profound slumber when D'Artagnan returned. Athos and Aramis were beginning to close their eyes, which they half opened when their companion came in again.

"Well?" said Aramis.

"All is well; we may sleep tranquilly."

On this assurance the two friends fell asleep; and D'Artagnan, who was very weary, bade good night to Grimaud, and laid himself down in his cloak, with naked sword at his side, in such a manner that his body barricaded the passage, and that it should be impossible to enter the room without upsetting him.

PORT WINE.

In ten minutes the masters slept; not so the servants — hungry and uncomfortable.

"Grimaud," said Musqueton to his companion, who had just come in after his round with D'Artagnan, "art thou thirsty?"

"As thirsty as a Scotchman!" was Grimaud's laconic reply.

And he sat down and began to cast up the accounts of his party, whose money he managed.

"Oh, lackadaisy! I'm beginning to feel queer!" cried Blaisois.

"If that's the case," said Musqueton, with a learned air, "take some nourishment."

"Do you call that nourishment?" said Blaisois, pointing to the barley bread and pot of beer upon the table.

"Blaisois," replied Musqueton, "remember that bread is the true nourishment of a Frenchman, who is not always able to get bread: ask Grimaud."

"Yes, but beer!" asked Blaisois, sharply, "is that their true drink?"

"As to that," answered Musqueton, puzzled how to get out of the difficulty, "I must confess that to me beer is as disagreeable as wine is to the English."

"What! Monsieur Musqueton! The English — do they dislike wine?"

"They hate it."

"But I have seen them drink it."

"As a punishment. For example, an English prince was plumped into a butt of Malmsey. I heard the Chevalier d'Herblay say so. It *settled* him."

"The fool!" cried Blaisois. "I wish I had been in his place."

"Thou canst be," said Grimaud, writing down his figures.

"How?" asked Blaisois, "I can? Explain yourself."

Grimaud went on with his sum, and cast up the whole.

"Port," he said, extending his hand in the direction of the first compartment examined by D'Artagnan and himself.

"Eh? eh? ah? — those barrels I saw through the door?"

"Port!" replied Grimaud, beginning a fresh sum.

"I have heard," said Blaisois, "that port is a very good wine."

THE FATE OF MORDAUNT.

"Excellent!" cried Musqueton, smacking his lips. "Excellent!"

"Supposing these Englishmen would sell us a bottle," said the honest Blaisois.

"Sell!" cried Musqueton, about whom there was a remnant of his ancient marauding character left. "One may well perceive, young man, that you are inexperienced. Why buy what one can take?"

"Take?" answered Blaisois. "To covet one's neighbor's chattels is forbidden, I believe."

"What a childish reason!" said Musqueton, condescendingly; "yes, childish; I repeat the word. Where did you learn, pray, to consider the English neighbors?"

"The saying's true, dear Mouston; but I don't remember where."

"Childish — still more childish," replied Musqueton. "Hadst thou been ten years engaged in war as Grimaud and I have been, my dear Blaisois, you would know the difference there is between the goods of others and the goods of enemies. Now an Englishman is an enemy; this port wine belongs to the English, therefore it belongs to us."

"And our masters?" asked Blaisois, stupefied by this harangue, delivered with an air of profound sagacity, "will they be of your opinion?"

Musqueton smiled disdainfully.

"I suppose that you think it necessary that I should disturb the repose of these illustrious lords to say, 'Gentlemen, your servant, Musqueton, is thirsty.' What does Monsieur Bracieux care, think you, whether I am thirsty or not?"

"'Tis a very expensive wine," said Blaisois, shaking his head.

"Were it liquid gold, Monsieur Blaisois, our masters would not deny themselves this wine. Know that Monsieur de Bracieux is rich enough to drink a tun of port wine, even if obliged to pay a pistole for every drop;" his manner became more and more lofty every instant: then he arose, and after finishing off the beer at one draught, he advanced majestically to the door of the compartment where the wine was. "Ah! locked!" he exclaimed; "these devils of English, how suspicious they are!"

"Shut!" said Blaisois; "ah! the deuce it is; unlucky, for I feel the sickness coming on squimier and squimier."

"Shut!" repeated Musqueton.

"But," Blaisois ventured to say, "I have heard you relate, Monsieur Musqueton, that once on a time, at Chantilly, you fed your master and yourself with partridges which were snared, carps caught by a line, and wine drawn with a cork-screw."

"Perfectly true; but there was an air hole in the cellar, and the wine was in bottles. I cannot throw the loop through this partition, nor move with a pack thread a cask of wine which may, perhaps, weigh two hundred pounds."

"No, but you can take out two or three boards of the partition," answered Blaisois, "and make a hole in the cask with a gimlet."

Musqueton opened his great round eyes to the utmost, astonished to find in Blaisois qualities for which he did not give him credit.

"'Tis true," he said; "but where can I get a chisel to take the planks out — a gimlet, to pierce the cask?"

"Trousers," said Grimaud, still squaring his accounts.

"Ah, yes!" said Musqueton.

Grimaud, in fact, was not only the accountant, but the armorer of the party; and as he was a man full of forethought, these trousers, carefully rolled up in his valise, contained every sort of tool for immediate use.

Musqueton, therefore, was soon provided with tools, and he began his task. In a few minutes he had extracted three boards. He tried to pass his body through the aperture; but not being like the frog in the fable, who thought he was larger than he really was, he found he must take out three or four more before he could get through.

He sighed and set to work again.

Grimaud had now finished his accounts. He arose, and stood near Musqueton.

"I," he said.

"What?" said Musqueton.

"I can pass ——"

"True — you" — answered Musqueton, casting a glance at the long thin form of his friend; "you can pass, and easily — go in then."

"Rinse the glasses," said Grimaud.

"Now," said Musqueton, addressing Blaisois; "now you shall see how we old soldiers drink when we are thirsty."

"My cloak," said Grimaud, from the bottom of the hold.

"What do you want?" asked Blaisois.

"My cloak — stop up the aperture with it."

"Why?" asked Blaisois.

"Simpleton!" exclaimed Musqueton; "suppose any one came into the room."

"Ah, true," cried Blaisois, with evident admiration; "but it will be dark in the cellar."

"Grimaud always sees, dark or light — night as well as day," answered Musqueton.

"Silence," cried Grimaud, "some one is coming."

In fact, the door of their cabin was opened. Two men, wrapped in their cloaks, appeared.

"Oh, ho!" said they, "not in bed at a quarter past eleven? That's against all rules. In a quarter of an hour let every one be in bed, and snoring."

These two men then went toward the compartment in which Grimaud was secreted; opened the door, entered and shut it after them.

"Ah!" cried Blaisois; "he's lost!"

"Grimaud's a cunning fellow," murmured Musqueton.

They waited for ten minutes, during which time no noise was heard which might indicate that Grimaud was discovered; and at the expiration of that anxious interval the two men returned, closed the door after them, and repeating their orders that the servants should go to bed, and extinguish their lights, disappeared.

At that very moment Grimaud drew back the cloak which hid the aperture, and came in with his face livid, his eyes staring wide open with terror, so that the pupils were contracted almost to nothing, with a large circle of white around them. He held in his hand a tankard full of some dark substance or another; and approaching the gleam of light shed by the lamp he uttered this single monosyllable — "Oh!" with such an expression of extreme terror that Musqueton started, alarmed, and Blaisois was near fainting from fright.

Both, however, cast an inquisitive glance into the tankard — it was full of gunpowder.

Convinced that the ship was full of powder instead of having a cargo of wine, Grimaud hastened to awake D'Artagnan, who had no sooner beheld him than he perceived that something extraordinary had taken place. Imposing silence, Grimaud put out the little night lamp, then knelt down, and poured into the lieutenant's ear a recital melodramatic enough not to require play of feature to give it pith.

This was the gist of his strange story:—

The first barrel that Grimaud had found on passing into the compartment he struck — it was empty. He passed on to another — it also was empty; but the third which he tried was, from the dull sound it gave out, evidently full. At this point Grimaud stopped, and was preparing to make a hole with his gimlet, when he found a spigot; he therefore placed his tankard under it, and turned the spout; something, whatever it was the cask contained, fell silently into the tankard.

Whilst he was thinking that he should first taste the liquor which the tankard contained, before taking it to his companions, the door of the cellar opened, and a man with a lantern in his hands, and enveloped in a cloak, came and stood just before the hogshead, behind which Grimaud, on hearing him come in, instantly crept. This was Groslow. He was accompanied by another man who carried in his hand something long and flexible, rolled up, resembling a washing line.

"Have you the wick?" asked the one who carried the lantern.

"Here it is," answered the other.

At the voice of this last speaker, Grimaud started, and felt a shudder creeping through his very marrow. He rose gently, so that his head was just above the round of the barrel; and, under the large hat, he recognized the pale face of Mordaunt.

"How long will this fuse burn?" asked this person.

"Nearly five minutes," replied the captain.

"Then tell the men to be in readiness — don't tell them why now; when the clock strikes a quarter after midnight collect your men. Get down into the longboat."

"That is when I have lighted the match?"

"I will undertake that. I wish to be sure of my revenge — are the oars in the boat?"

"Everything is ready."

"'Tis well."

Mordaunt knelt down and fastened one end of the train to the spigot, in order that he might have nothing to do but to set it on fire at the opposite end with the match.

He then arose.

"You hear me — at a quarter past midnight — in fact, in twenty minutes."

"I understand all perfectly, sir," replied Groslow; "but allow me to say, there is great danger in what you undertake — would it not be better to intrust one of the men to set fire to the train?"

"My dear Groslow," answered Mordaunt, "you know the French proverb, 'Nothing one does not do one's self is ever well done.' I shall abide by that rule."

Grimaud had heard all this — had seen the two mortal enemies of the musketeers — had seen Mordaunt adjust the fuse; then he felt, and felt again, the contents of the tankard that he held in his hand; and, instead of the lively liquor expected by Blaisois and Musqueton, he found beneath his fingers the grains of some coarse powder.

Mordaunt went away with the captain. At the door he stopped to listen.

"Do you hear how they sleep?" he said.

In fact, Porthos could be heard snoring through the partition.

"'Tis God who gives them into our hands," answered Groslow.

"This time the devil himself shall not save them," rejoined Mordaunt.

And they went out together.

End of the Port-Wine Mystery.

D'Artagnan, as one may suppose, listened to all these details with a growing interest. He awoke Aramis, Athos, and Porthos; and then, stretching out his arms, and closing them again, the Gascon collected in one small circle the three heads of his friends, so near as almost to touch each other.

He then told them under whose command the vessel was in which they were sailing that night; that they had Groslow for their captain, and Mordaunt acting under him as his lieutenant. Something more deathlike than a shudder, at this moment, shook the brave musketeers. The name of Mordaunt seemed to exercise over them a mysterious and fatal influence — to summons ghastly terror with its very sound.

"What is to be done?" asked Athos.

"You have some plan?"

D'Artagnan replied by going toward a very small, low

window, just large enough to let a man through. He turned it gently on its hinges.

"There," he said, "is our road."

"The deuce — it is a very cold one, my dear friend," said Aramis.

"Stay here, if you like, but I warn you, 'twill be rather too warm presently."

"But we cannot swim to the shore."

"The longboat is yonder, lashed to the felucca. We will take possession of it, and cut the cable. Come, my friends."

"A moment's delay," said Athos; "our servants?"

"Here we are," they cried.

Meantime the three friends were standing motionless before the awful sight which D'Artagnan, in raising the shutters, had disclosed to them through the narrow opening of the window.

Those who have once beheld such a spectacle know that there is nothing more solemn, more striking, than the raging sea, rolling, with its deafening roar, its dark billows beneath the pale light of a wintry moon.

"Gracious heaven! we are hesitating," cried D'Artagnan; "if we hesitate, what will the servants do?"

"I do not hesitate, you know," said Grimaud.

"Sir," interposed Blaisois, "I warn you that I can only swim in rivers."

"And I not at all," said Musqueton.

But D'Artagnan had now slipped through the window.

"You have decided, friend?" said Athos.

"Yes," the Gascon answered; "Athos! you, who are a perfect being, bid spirit triumph over body."

"Do you, Aramis, order the servants — Porthos, kill every one who stands in your way."

And, after pressing the hand of Athos, D'Artagnan chose a moment when the ship rolled backward, so that he had only to plunge into the water up to his waist.

Athos followed him before the felucca rose again on the waves: the cable which tied the boat to the vessel was then seen plainly rising out of the sea.

D'Artagnan swam to it, and held it, suspending himself by this rope, his head alone out of water.

In one second Athos joined him.

Then they saw, as the felucca turned, two other heads peeping — those of Aramis and Grimaud.

THE FATE OF MORDAUNT.

"I am uneasy about Blaisois," said Athos: "he can, he says, only swim in rivers."

"When people can swim at all they can swim anywhere. To the bark! to the bark!"

"But Porthos, I do not see him."

"Porthos is coming — he swims like Leviathan."

Porthos, in fact, did not appear. Musqueton and Blaisois had been appalled by the sight of the black gulf below them, and had shrunk back.

"Come along! I shall strangle you both if you don't get out," said Porthos at last, seizing Musqueton by the throat. "Forward! Blaisois."

A groan, stifled by the grasp of Porthos, was all the reply of poor Blaisois, for the giant, taking him neck and heels, plunged him into the water headforemost, pushing him out of the window as if he had been a plank.

"Now, Musqueton," he said, "I hope you don't mean to desert your master?"

"Ah, sir," replied Musqueton, his eyes filling with tears, "why did you reënter the army? We were all so happy in the Château de Pierrefonds!"

And, without any other complaint, passive and obedient, either from true devotion to his master, or from the example set by Blaisois, Musqueton leapt into the sea headforemost. A sublime action, at all events, for Musqueton looked upon himself as dead. But Porthos was not a man to abandon an old servant; and when Musqueton rose above the water, blind as a newborn puppy, he found he was supported by the large hand of Porthos, and that he was thus enabled, without having occasion even to move, to advance toward the cable with the dignity of a very triton.

In a few minutes, Porthos had rejoined his companions, who were already in the boat; but when, after they had all got in, it came to his turn, there was great danger that in putting his huge leg over the edge of the boat he would upset the little vessel. Athos was the last to enter.

"Are you all here?" he asked.

"Ah! have you your sword, Athos?" cried D'Artagnan.

"Yes."

"Cut the cable, then."

Athos drew a sharp poniard from his belt and cut the cord.

The felucca went on; the boat continued stationary, rocked only by the swashing waves.

"Come, Athos!" said D'Artagnan, giving his hand to the count; "you are going to see something curious," added the Gascon.

FATALITY.

Scarcely had D'Artagnan uttered these words than a ringing and sudden noise was heard resounding through the felucca, which now became dim in the obscurity of the night.

"That, you may be sure," said the Gascon, "means something."

They then, at the same instant, perceived a large lantern carried on a pole appear on the deck, defining the forms of shadows behind it.

Suddenly a terrible cry, a cry of despair, was wafted through space, and as if the shrieks of anguish had driven away the clouds, the veil which hid the moon was cleared away, and the gray sails and dark shrouds of the felucca were plainly visible beneath the silvery light.

Shadows ran, as if bewildered, to and fro on the vessel, and mournful cries accompanied these delirious walkers. In the midst of these screams they saw Mordaunt upon the poop, with a torch in hand.

The agitated figures, apparently wild with terror, consisted of Groslow, who, at the hour fixed by Mordaunt, had collected his men, and the sailors. Groslow, after having listened at the door of the cabin to hear if the musketeers were still asleep, had gone down into the cellar, convinced by their silence that they were all in a deep slumber. Then Mordaunt had run to the train — impetuous as a man who is excited by revenge and full of confidence — as are those whom God blinds — he had set fire to the wick of niter.

All this while, Groslow and his men were assembled on deck.

"Haul up the cable, and draw the boat to us," said Groslow.

One of the sailors got down the side of the ship, seized the cable, and drew it — it came without the least resistance.

"The cable is cut!" he cried, "no boat!"

"How! no boat!" exclaimed Groslow; "it is impossible."

"'Tis true, however," answered the sailor; "there's nothing in the wake of the ship, besides here's the end of the cable."

THE FATE OF MORDAUNT.

"What's the matter?" cried Mordaunt, who, coming up out of the hatchway, rushed to the stern, waving his torch.

"Only that our enemies have escaped — they have cut the cord, and gone off with the boat."

Mordaunt bounded with one step to the cabin, and kicked open the door.

"Empty!" he exclaimed; "the infernal demons!"

"We must pursue them," said Groslow; "they can't be gone far, and we will sink them, passing over them."

"Yes, but the fire," ejaculated Mordaunt; "I have lighted it."

"Ten thousand devils!" cried Groslow, rushing to the hatchway; "perhaps there is still time to save us."

Mordaunt answered only by a terrible laugh, threw his torch into the sea, and plunged in after it. The instant Groslow put his foot upon the hatchway steps, the ship opened like the crater of a volcano. A burst of flame arose toward the skies with an explosion like that of a hundred cannon; the air burned, ignited by flaming embers, then the frightful lightning disappeared, the brands sank, one after another, into the abyss, where they were extinguished, and, save for a slight vibration in the air, after a few minutes had lapsed, one would have thought that nothing had happened.

Only — the felucca had disappeared from the surface of the sea, and Groslow and his three sailors were consumed.

The four friends saw all this — not a single detail of this fearful scene escaped them. At one moment, bathed as they were in a flood of brilliant light, which illumined the sea for the space of a league, they might each be seen — each by his own peculiar attitude and manner expressing the awe which, even in their hearts of bronze, they could not help experiencing. Soon a torrent of vivid sparks fell round them — then, at last, the volcano was extinguished — then all was dark and still — the floating bark and heaving ocean.

They sat silent and dejected.

"By heaven!" at last said Athos, the first to speak, "by this time, I think, all must be over."

"Here, my lords! save me! help!" cried a voice, whose mournful accents reaching the four friends, seemed to proceed from some phantom of the ocean.

All looked around — Athos himself started.

"'Tis he! it is his voice!"

All still remained silent — the eyes of all were turned in the direction where the vessel had disappeared — endeavoring in vain to penetrate the darkness. After a minute or two they were able to distinguish a man, who approached them, swimming vigorously.

Athos extended his arm toward him — "Yes, yes, I know him well," he said.

"He — again!" cried Porthos, who was breathing like a blacksmith's bellows, "why, he is made of iron."

"Oh, my God!" muttered Athos.

Aramis and D'Artagnan whispered to each other.

Mordaunt made several strokes more, and raising his arm in sign of distress above the waves — "Pity, pity on me! gentlemen — in Heaven's name — my strength is failing me; I am dying."

The voice that implored aid was so piteous that it awakened pity in the heart of Athos.

"Miserable wretch," he exclaimed.

"Indeed!" said D'Artagnan, "monsters have only to complain to gain your sympathy. I believe he's swimming toward us. Does he think we are going to take him in? Row, Porthos, row." And setting the example, he plowed his oar into the sea — two strokes took the bark on twenty fathoms further.

"Ah! ah!" said Porthos to Mordaunt, "I think we have you now, my hero!"

"Oh! Porthos!" murmured the Comte de la Fère.

"Oh pray! for mercy's sake, don't fly from me. For pity's sake!" cried the young man, whose agony-drawn breath at times, when his head went under water, under the wave, exhaled and made the icy waters bubble.

D'Artagnan, however, who had consulted with Aramis, spoke to the poor wretch. "Go away," he said, "your repentance is too recent to inspire confidence. See! the vessel in which you wished to fry us is still smoking; and the situation in which you are is a bed of roses compared to that in which you wished to place us, and in which you have placed Monsieur Groslow and his companions."

"Sir!" replied Mordaunt, in a tongue of deep despair, "my penitence is sincere. Gentlemen, I am young, scarcely twenty-three years old. I was drawn on by a very natural resentment to avenge my mother. You would have done what I did."

Mordaunt wanted now only two or three fathoms to reach

THE FATE OF MORDAUNT.

the boat — for the approach of death seemed to give him supernatural strength.

"Alas!" he said, "I am then to die? you are going to kill the son, as you killed the mother! Surely, if I am culpable, and if I ask for pardon, I ought to be forgiven."

Then — as if his strength failed him — he seemed unable to sustain himself above the water, and a wave passed over his head, which drowned his voice.

"Oh! this is torture to me!" cried Athos.

Mordaunt reappeared.

"For my part," said D'Artagnan, "I say, this must come to an end; murderer, as you were, of your uncle! executioner, as you were, of King Charles! incendiary! I recommend you to sink forthwith to the bottom of the sea; and if you come another fathom nearer, I'll stave your wicked head in with this oar."

"D'Artagnan! D'Artagnan!" cried Athos, "my son, I entreat you; the wretch is dying: and it is horrible to let a man die without extending a hand to save him. I cannot resist doing so; he must live."

"Zounds!" replied D'Artagnan, "why don't you give yourself up directly, feet and hands bound, to that wretch? Ah! Comte de la Fère, you wish to perish by his hands! I, your son, as you call me, I will not let you!"

'Twas the first time D'Artagnan had ever refused a request from Athos.

Aramis calmly drew his sword, which he had carried between his teeth as he swam.

"If he lays his hand on the boat's edge, I will cut it off — regicide that he is."

"And I," said Porthos. "Wait."

"What are you going to do?" asked Aramis.

"Throw myself in the water, and strangle him."

"Oh, gentlemen!" cried Athos, "be men! be Christians! See! death is depicted on his face! Ah! do not bring on me the horrors of remorse! Grant me this poor wretch's life. I will bless you. I ——"

"I am dying!" cried Mordaunt, "come to me! come to me!"

D'Artagnan began to be touched. The boat at this moment turned round; and the dying man was by that turn brought nearer Athos.

"Monsieur the Comte de la Fère," he cried, "I supplicate

you! pity me! I call on you! where are you? **I see you no longer** — I am dying — help me! help me!"

"Here I am, sir!" said Athos, leaning, and stretching out his arm to Mordaunt with that air of dignity and nobility of soul habitual to him, "here I am, take my hand and jump into our boat."

Mordaunt made a last effort — rose — seized the hand thus extended to him, and grasped it with the vehemence of despair.

"That's right," said Athos, "put your other hand here." And he offered him his shoulder as another stay and support, so that his head almost touched that of Mordaunt; and these two mortal enemies were in as close an embrace as if they had been brothers.

"Now, sir," said the count, "you are safe — calm yourself."

"Ah! my mother," cried Mordaunt, with eyes on fire with a look of hate impossible to paint. "I can only offer thee one victim, but it shall, at any rate, be the one thou wouldst thyself have chosen!"

And whilst D'Artagnan uttered a cry, Porthos raised the oar, and Aramis sought a place to strike, a frightful shake given to the boat precipitated Athos into the sea; whilst Mordaunt, with a shout of triumph, grasped the neck of his victim, and, in order to paralyze his movements, twined arms and legs around the musketeer. For an instant, without an exclamation, without a cry for help, Athos tried to sustain himself on the surface of the waters, but the weight dragged him down; he disappeared by degrees; soon, nothing was to be seen except his long floating hair; then both men disappeared, and the bubbling of the water, which, in its turn, was soon effaced, alone indicated the spot where these two had sunk.

Mute with horror, the three friends had remained open-mouthed, their eyes dilated, their arms extended like statues, and, motionless as they were, the beating of their hearts was audible. Porthos was the first who came to himself — he tore his hair.

"Oh!" he cried, "Athos! Athos! thou man of noble heart; woe is me! I have let thee perish!"

At this instant, in the midst of the silver circle, illumined by the light of the moon, the same whirlpool which had been made by the sinking men was again obvious, and first were seen, rising above the waves, a wisp of hair — then a pale face with open eyes, yet, nevertheless, the eyes of death; then a

THE FATE OF MORDAUNT.

body which, after rising of itself even to the waist above the sea, turned gently on its back, according to the caprice of the waves, and floated.

In the bosom of this corpse was plunged a poniard, the gold hilt of which shone in the moonbeams.

"Mordaunt! Mordaunt!" cried the three friends, "'tis Mordaunt!"

"But Athos!" exclaimed D'Artagnan.

Suddenly the boat leaned on one side beneath a new and unexpected weight, and Grimaud uttered a shout of joy; every one turned round, and beheld Athos, livid, his eyes dim, and his hands trembling, supporting himself on the edge of the boat. Eight vigorous arms lifted him up immediately, and laid him in the boat, where, directly, Athos was warmed and reanimated, reviving with the caresses and cares of his friends, who were intoxicated with joy.

"You are not hurt?" asked D'Artagnan.

"No," replied Athos, "and he ——"

"Oh, he! now we may say at last, thank heaven! he is really dead. Look!"— and D'Artagnan, obliging Athos to look in the direction that he pointed, showed him the body of Mordaunt floating on its back, which, sometimes submerged, sometimes rising, seemed still to pursue the four friends with looks of insult and of mortal hatred.

At last he sank. Athos had followed him with a glance in which the deepest melancholy and pity were expressed.

"Bravo, Athos!" cried Aramis, with an emotion very rare in him.

"A capital blow you gave!" cried Porthos.

"I have a *son*. I wished to live," said Athos.

"In short," said D'Artagnan, "this has been the will of God."

"It was not I who killed him," sighed Athos, in a soft, low tone, "'twas destiny."

THE MAN IN THE IRON MASK.

By ALEXANDRE DUMAS, Père.

(From "The Viscount of Bragelonne.")

HIGH TREASON.

THE ungovernable fury which took possession of the king at the sight and at the perusal of Fouquet's letter to La Vallière by degrees subsided into a feeling of pain and extreme weariness. Youth, invigorated by health and lightness of spirits, requiring soon that what it loses should be immediately restored — youth knows not those endless, sleepless nights which enable us to realize the fable of the vulture unceasingly feeding on Prometheus. In cases where the man of middle life, in his acquired strength of will and purpose, and the old, in their state of natural exhaustion, find incessant augmentation of their bitter sorrow, a young man, surprised by the sudden appearance of misfortune, weakens himself in sighs, and groans, and tears, directly struggling with his grief, and is thereby far sooner overthrown by the inflexible enemy with whom he is engaged. Once overthrown, his struggles cease. Louis could not hold out more than a few minutes, at the end of which he had ceased to clench his hands, and scorch in fancy with his looks the invisible objects of his hatred; he soon ceased to attack with his violent imprecations not M. Fouquet alone, but even La Vallière herself; from fury he subsided into despair, and from despair to prostration. After he had thrown himself for a few minutes to and fro convulsively on his bed, his nerveless arms fell quietly down; his head lay languidly on his pillow; his limbs, exhausted with excessive emotion, still trembled occasionally, agitated by muscular contractions; while from his breast faint and infrequent sighs still issued. Morpheus, the tutelary deity of the apartment, towards whom Louis raised his eyes, wearied by his anger and reconciled by his tears, showered down upon him the sleep-inducing poppies with which his hands are ever filled; so presently the monarch closed his eyes and fell asleep. Then it seemed to him, as it often happens in that first sleep, so light and gentle, which raises the body above the couch, and the soul above the earth — it seemed to him, we say, as if the god Morpheus, painted

THE MAN IN THE IRON MASK.

on the ceiling, looked at him with eyes resembling human eyes; that something shone brightly, and moved to and fro in the dome above the sleeper; that the crowd of terrible dreams which thronged together in his brain, and which were interrupted for a moment, half revealed a human face, with a hand resting against the mouth, and in an attitude of deep and absorbed meditation. And strange enough, too, this man bore so wonderful a resemblance to the king himself, that Louis fancied he was looking at his own face reflected in a mirror; with the exception, however, that the face was saddened by a feeling of the profoundest pity. Then it seemed to him as if the dome gradually retired, escaping from his gaze, and that the figures and attributes painted by Lebrun became darker and darker as the distance became more and more remote. A gentle, easy movement, as regular as that by which a vessel plunges beneath the waves, had succeeded to the immovableness of the bed. Doubtless the king was dreaming, and in this dream the crown of gold, which fastened the curtains together, seemed to recede from his vision, just as the dome, to which it remained suspended, had done, so that the winged genius which, with both its hands, supported the crown, seemed, though vainly so, to call upon the king, who was fast disappearing from it. The bed still sank. Louis, with his eyes open, could not resist the deception of this cruel hallucination. At last, as the light of the royal chamber faded away into darkness and gloom, something cold, gloomy, and inexplicable in its nature seemed to infect the air. No paintings, nor gold, nor velvet hangings, were visible any longer, nothing but walls of a dull gray color, which the increasing gloom made darker every moment. And yet the bed still continued to descend, and after a minute, which seemed in its duration almost an age to the king, it reached a stratum of air black and chill as death, and then it stopped. The king could no longer see the light in his room, except as from the bottom of a well we can see the light of day. "I am under the influence of some atrocious dream," he thought. "It is time to awaken from it. Come! let me wake."

Every one has experienced the sensation the above remark conveys; there is hardly a person who, in the midst of a nightmare, whose influence is suffocating, has not said to himself, by the help of that light which still burns in the brain when every human light is extinguished, "It is nothing but a dream, after all." This was precisely what Louis XIV. said to himself; but when he said, "Come, come! wake up," he perceived that not only was he already awake, but still more, that he had his eyes open also. And then he looked all round him. On his right hand and on his left two armed men stood in stolid silence, each wrapped in a huge cloak, and the face covered with a mask; one of them held a small lamp in his hand, whose glimmering light revealed the saddest picture a king could look upon. Louis could not help saying to himself that his dream still lasted, and that all he had to do to cause it to disappear was to move his arms or to say something aloud; he darted from his bed, and found himself upon the damp, moist ground. Then, addressing himself to the man who held the lamp in his hand, he said: —

"What is this, monsieur, and what is the meaning of this jest?"

"It is no jest," replied in a deep voice the masked figure that held the lantern.

"Do you belong to M. Fouquet?" inquired the king, greatly astonished at his situation.

"It matters very little to whom we belong," said the phantom; "we are your masters now, that is sufficient."

The king, more impatient than intimidated, turned to the other masked figure. "If this is a comedy," he said, "you will tell M. Fouquet that I find it unseemly and improper, and that I command it should cease."

The second masked person to whom the king had addressed himself was a man of huge stature and vast circumference. He held himself erect and motionless as any block of marble. "Well!" added the king, stamping his foot, "you do not answer!"

"We do not answer you, my good monsieur," said the giant, in a stentorian voice, "because there is nothing to say."

"At least, tell me what you want?" exclaimed Louis, folding his arms with a passionate gesture.

"You will know by and by," replied the man who held the lamp.

"In the mean time tell me where I am."

"Look."

Louis looked all round him; but by the light of the lamp which the masked figure raised for the purpose, he could perceive nothing but the damp walls, which glistened here and there with the slimy traces of the snail. "Oh—oh!—a dungeon," cried the king.

"No, a subterranean passage."

"Which leads——"

"Will you be good enough to follow us?"

"I shall not stir from hence!" cried the king.

"If you are obstinate, my dear young friend," replied the taller of the two, "I will lift you up in my arms, and roll you up in your own cloak, and if you should happen to be stifled, why — so much the worse for you."

As he said this, he disengaged from beneath his cloak a hand of which Milo of Crotona would have envied him the possession, on the day when he had that unhappy idea of rending his last oak. The king dreaded violence, for he could well believe that the two men into whose power he had fallen had not gone so far with any idea of drawing back, and that they would consequently be ready to proceed to extremities, if necessary. He shook his head and said: "It seems I have fallen into the hands of a couple of assassins. Move on, then."

Neither of the men answered a word to this remark. The one who carried the lantern walked first, the king followed him, while the second masked figure closed the procession. In this manner they passed along a winding gallery of some length, with as many staircases leading out of it as are to be found in the mysterious and gloomy palaces of Ann Radcliffe's creation. All these windings and turnings, during which the king heard the sound of running water *over his head*, ended at last in a long corridor closed by an iron door. The figure with the lamp opened the door with one of the keys he wore suspended at his girdle, where, during the whole of the brief journey the king had heard them rattle. As soon as the door was opened and admitted the air, Louis recognized the balmy odors that trees exhale in balmy summer nights. He paused, hesitatingly, for a moment or two; but the huge sentinel who followed him thrust him out of the subterranean passage.

"Another blow," said the king, turning towards the one who had just had the audacity to touch his sovereign; "what do you intend to do with the King of France?"

"Try to forget that word," replied the man with the lamp, in a tone which as little admitted of a reply as one of the famous decrees of Minos.

"You deserve to be broken on the wheel for the words that

you have just made use of," said the giant, as he extinguished the lamp his companion handed to him; "but the king is too kind-hearted."

Louis, at that threat, made so sudden a movement that it seemed as if he meditated flight; but the giant's hand was in a moment placed on his shoulder, and fixed him motionless where he stood. "But tell me, at least, where we are going," said the king.

"Come," replied the former of the two men, with a kind of respect in his manner, and leading his prisoner towards a carriage which seemed to be in waiting.

The carriage was completely concealed amid the trees. Two horses, with their feet fettered, were fastened by a halter to the lower branches of a large oak.

"Get in," said the same man, opening the carriage door and letting down the step. The king obeyed, seated himself at the back of the carriage, the padded door of which was shut and locked immediately upon him and his guide. As for the giant, he cut the fastenings by which the horses were bound, harnessed them himself, and mounted on the box of the carriage, which was unoccupied. The carriage set off immediately at a quick trot, turned into the road to Paris, and in the forest of Senart found a relay of horses fastened to the trees in the same manner the first horses had been, and without a postilion. The man on the box changed the horses, and continued to follow the road towards Paris with the same rapidity; so that they entered the city about three o'clock in the morning. The carriage proceeded along the Faubourg Saint-Antoine, and, after having called out to the sentinel, "by the king's order," the driver conducted the horses into the circular inclosure of the Bastile, looking out upon the courtyard, called La Cour du Gouvernement. There the horses drew up, reeking with sweat, at the flight of steps, and a sergeant of the guard ran forward. "Go and wake the governor," said the coachman, in a voice of thunder.

With the exception of this voice, which might have been heard at the entrance of the Faubourg Saint-Antoine, everything remained as calm in the carriage as in the prison. Ten minutes afterwards, M. de Baisemeaux appeared in his dressing gown on the threshold of the door. "What is the matter now?" he asked; "and whom have you brought me there?"

The man with the lantern opened the carriage door, and

said two or three words to the one who acted as driver, who immediately got down from his seat, took up a short musket which he kept under his feet, and placed its muzzle on his prisoner's chest.

"And fire at once if he speaks!" added aloud the man who alighted from the carriage.

"Very good," replied his companion, without another remark.

With this recommendation, the person who had accompanied the king in the carriage ascended the flight of steps, at the top of which the governor was awaiting him. "M. d'Herblay!" said the latter.

"Hush!" said Aramis. "Let us go into your room."

"Good heavens! what brings you here at this hour?"

"A mistake, my dear M. de Baisemeaux," Aramis replied quietly. "It appears that you were quite right the other day."

"What about?" inquired the governor.

"About the order of release, my dear friend."

"Tell me what you mean, monsieur — no, monseigneur," said the governor, almost suffocated by surprise and terror.

"It is a very simple affair: you remember, dear M. de Baisemeaux, that an order of release was sent to you."

"Yes, for Marchiali."

"Very good! we both thought that it was for Marchiali?"

"Certainly; you will recollect, however, that I would not credit it, but that you compelled me to believe it?"

"Oh! Baisemeaux, my good fellow, what a word to make use of! — strongly recommended, that was all."

"Strongly recommended, yes; strongly recommended to give him up to you: and that you carried him off with you in your carriage."

"Well, my dear M. de Baisemeaux, it was a mistake; it was discovered at the ministry, so that I now bring you an order from the king to set at liberty — Seldon, that poor Scotch fellow, you know."

"Seldon! are you sure this time?"

"Well, read it yourself," added Aramis, handing him the order.

"Why," said Baisemeaux, "this order is the very same that has already passed through my hands."

"Indeed?"

"It is the very one I assured you I saw the other evening. *Parbleu!* I recognize it by the blot of ink."

"I do not know whether it is that; but all I know is that I bring it for you."

"But then, about the other?"

"What other?"

"Marchiali?"

"I have got him here with me."

"But that is not enough for me. I require a new order to take him back again."

"Don't talk such nonsense, my dear Baisemeaux; you talk like a child! Where is the order you received respecting Marchiali?"

Baisemeaux ran to his iron chest and took it out. Aramis seized hold of it, coolly tore it in four pieces, held them to the lamp, and burnt them. "Good heavens! what are you doing?" exclaimed Baisemeaux, in an extremity of terror.

"Look at your position quietly, my good governor," said Aramis, with imperturbable self-possession, "and you will see how very simple the whole affair is. You no longer possess any order justifying Marchiali's release."

"I am a lost man!"

"Far from it, my good fellow, since I have brought Marchiali back to you, and all accordingly is just the same as if he had never left."

"Ah!" said the governor, completely overcome by terror.

"Plain enough, you see; and you will go and shut him up immediately."

"I should think so, indeed."

"And you will hand over this Seldon to me, whose liberation is authorized by this order. Do you understand?"

"I — I ——"

"You do understand, I see," said Aramis. "Very good." Baisemeaux clasped his hands together.

"But why, at all events, after having taken Marchiali away from me, do you bring him back again?" cried the unhappy governor, in a paroxysm of terror, and completely dumfounded.

"For a friend such as you are," said Aramis — "for so devoted a servant, I have no secrets;" and he put his mouth close to Baisemeaux's ear, as he said in a low tone of voice, "You know the resemblance between that unfortunate fellow and ——"

"And the king? — yes!"

"Very good; the very first use that Marchiali made of his liberty was to persist —— Can you guess what?"

"How is it likely I should guess?"

"To persist in saying that he was king of France; to dress himself up in clothes like those of the king; and then pretend to assume that he was the king himself."

"Gracious Heavens!"

"That is the reason why I have brought him back again, my dear friend. He is mad and lets every one see how mad he is."

"What is to be done, then?"

"That is very simple; let no one hold any communication with him. You understand that when his peculiar style of madness came to the king's ears, the king, who had pitied his terrible affliction, and saw that all his kindness had been repaid by black ingratitude, became perfectly furious; so that, now — and remember this very distinctly, dear M. de Baisemeaux, for it concerns you most closely — so that there is now, I repeat, sentence of death pronounced against all those who may allow him to communicate with any one else but me or the king himself. You understand, Baisemeaux, sentence of death!"

"You need not ask me whether I understand."

"And now, let us go down, and conduct this poor devil back to his dungeon again, unless you prefer he should come up here."

"What would be the good of that?"

"It would be better, perhaps, to enter his name in the prison book at once!"

"Of course, certainly; not a doubt of it."

"In that case, have him up."

Baisemeaux ordered the drums to be beaten and the bell to be rung, as a warning to every one to retire, in order to avoid meeting a prisoner about whom it was desired to observe a certain mystery. Then, when the passages were free, he went to take the prisoner from the carriage, at whose breast Porthos, faithful to the directions which had been given him, still kept his musket leveled. "Ah! is that you, miserable wretch?" cried the governor, as soon as he perceived the king. "Very good, very good." And immediately, making the king get out of the carriage, he led him, still accompanied by Porthos, who had not taken off his mask, and Aramis, who again resumed his, up the stairs, to the second Bertaudière, and opened the door of the room in which Philippe for six long years had bemoaned his existence. The king entered the cell without pronouncing a single word : he faltered in as limp and haggard as a rain-struck lily. Baisemeaux shut the door upon him, turned the key twice in the lock, and then returned to Aramis. "It is quite true," he said in a low tone, "that he bears a striking resemblance to the king; but less so than you said."

"So that," said Aramis, "you would not have been deceived by the substitution of the one for the other."

"What a question!"

"You are a most valuable fellow, Baisemeaux," said Aramis; "and now, set Seldon free."

"Oh, yes. I was going to forget that. I will go and give orders at once."

"Bah! to-morrow will be time enough."

"To-morrow! — oh, no. This very minute."

"Well; go off to your affairs, I will away to mine. But it is quite understood, is it not?"

"What 'is quite understood'?"

"That no one is to enter the prisoner's cell, except with an order from the king; an order which I will myself bring."

"Quite so. Adieu, monseigneur."

Aramis returned to his companion. "Now, Porthos, my good fellow, back again to Vaux, and as fast as possible."

"A man is light and easy enough, when he has faithfully served his king; and, in serving him, saved his country," said Porthos. "The horses will be as light as if our tissues were constructed of the wind of heaven. So let us be off." And the carriage, lightened of a prisoner who might well be — as he in fact was — very heavy in the sight of Aramis, passed across the drawbridge of the Bastile, which was raised again immediately behind it.

The Morning.

In vivid contrast to the sad and terrible destiny of the king imprisoned in the Bastile, and tearing, in sheer despair, the bolts and bars of his dungeon, the rhetoric of the chroniclers of old would not fail to present, as a complete antithesis, the picture of Philippe lying asleep beneath the royal canopy. We do not pretend to say that such rhetoric is always bad, and always scatters, in places where they have no right to grow, the flowers with which it embellishes and enlivens history. But we shall, on the present occasion, carefully avoid polishing the antithesis in question, but shall proceed to draw another picture as minutely as possible, to serve as foil and counterfoil to the one in the preceding chapter. The young prince alighted from Aramis' room, in the same way the king had descended from the apartment dedicated to Morpheus. The dome gradually and slowly sank down under Aramis' pressure, and Philippe stood beside the royal bed, which had ascended again after having deposited its prisoner in the secret depths of the subterranean passage. Alone, in the presence of all the luxury which surrounded him; alone, in the presence of his power; alone, with the part he was about to be forced to act, Philippe for the first time felt his heart, and mind, and soul expand beneath the influence of a thousand mutable emotions, which are the vital throbs of a king's heart. He could not help changing color when he looked upon the empty bed, still tumbled by his brother's body. This mute accomplice had returned, after having completed the work it had been destined to perform; it returned with the traces of the crime; it spoke to the guilty author of that crime, with the frank and unreserved language which an accomplice never fears to use in the company of his companion in guilt; for it spoke the truth. Philippe bent over the bed, and perceived a pocket handkerchief lying on it, which was still damp from the cold sweat which had poured from Louis XIV.'s face. This sweat-bestained handkerchief terrified Philippe, as the gore of Abel frightened Cain.

"I am face to face with my destiny," said Philippe, his eyes on fire, and his face a livid white. "Is it likely to be more terrifying than my captivity has been sad and gloomy? Though I am compelled to follow out, at every moment, the sovereign power and authority I have usurped, shall I cease to listen to the scruples of my heart? Yes! the king has lain on this bed; it is indeed his head that has left its impression on this pillow; his bitter tears that have stained this handkerchief: and yet, I hesitate to throw myself on the bed, or to press in my hand the handkerchief which is embroidered with my brother's arms. Away with such weakness; let me imitate M. d'Herblay, who asserts that a man's action should be always one degree above his thoughts; let me imitate M. d'Herblay, whose thoughts are of and for himself alone, who regards himself as a man of honor, so long as he injures or betrays his enemies only. I, I alone, should have occupied this bed, if Louis XIV. had not, owing to my mother's criminal abandonment, stood in my way; and this handkerchief, embroidered with the arms of France, would in right and justice belong to me alone, if, as M. d'Herblay observes, I had been left my royal cradle. Philippe, son of France, take your place on that bed; Philippe, sole king of France, resume the blazonry that is yours! Philippe, sole heir presumptive to Louis XIII., your father, show yourself without pity or mercy for the usurper who, at this moment, has not even to suffer the agony of the remorse of all that you have had to submit to."

With these words, Philippe, notwithstanding an instinctive repugnance of feeling, and in spite of the shudder of terror which mastered his will, threw himself on the royal bed, and forced his muscles to press the still warm place where Louis XIV. had lain, while he buried his burning face in the handkerchief still moistened by his brother's tears. With his head thrown back and buried in the soft down of his pillow, Philippe perceived above him the crown of France, suspended, as we have stated, by angels with outspread golden wings.

A man may be ambitious of lying in a lion's den, but can hardly hope to sleep there quietly. Philippe listened attentively to every sound; his heart panted and throbbed at the very suspicion of approaching terror and misfortune; but confident in his own strength, which was confirmed by the force of an overpoweringly resolute determination, he waited until some decisive circumstance should permit him to judge for himself. He hoped that imminent danger might be revealed to him, like those phosphoric lights of the tempest which show the sailors the altitude of the waves against which they have to struggle. But nothing approached. Silence, that mortal enemy of restless hearts, and of ambitious minds, shrouded in the thickness of its gloom during the remainder of the night the future king of France, who lay there sheltered beneath his stolen crown. Towards the morning a shadow, rather than a body, glided into the royal chamber; Philippe expected his approach, and neither expressed nor exhibited any surprise.

"Well, M. d'Herblay?" he said

" Well, sire, all is accomplished."

" How ? "

" Exactly as we expected."

" Did he resist ? "

" Terribly ! tears and entreaties."

" And then ? "

" A perfect stupor."

" But at last ? "

" Oh ! at last, a complete victory, and absolute silence."

" Did the governor of the Bastile suspect anything ? "

" Nothing."

" The resemblance, however ———— "

" Was the cause of the success."

" But the prisoner cannot fail to explain himself. Think well of that. I have myself been able to do as much as that, on a former occasion."

" I have already provided for every chance. In a few days, sooner if necessary, we will take the captive out of his prison, and will send him out of the country, to a place of exile so remote ———— "

" People can return from their exile, M. d'Herblay."

" To a place of exile so distant, I was going to say, that human strength and the duration of human life would not be enough for his return."

Once more a cold look of intelligence passed between Aramis and the young king.

" And M. du Vallon ? " asked Philippe, in order to change the conversation.

" He will be presented to you to-day, and confidentially will congratulate you on the danger which that conspirator has made you run."

" What is to be done with him ? "

" With M. du Vallon ? "

" Yes ; confer a dukedom on him, I suppose."

" A dukedom," replied Aramis, smiling in a significant manner.

" Why do you laugh, M. d'Herblay ? "

" I laugh at the extreme caution of your idea."

" Cautious ; why so ? "

" Your majesty is doubtless afraid that that poor Porthos may probably become a troublesome witness, and you wish to get rid of him."

"What! in making him a duke?"

"Certainly; you would assuredly kill him, for he would die from joy, and the secret would die with him."

"Good heavens!"

"Yes," said Aramis, phlegmatically; "I should lose a very good friend."

At this moment, and in the middle of this idle conversation, under the light tone of which the two conspirators concealed their joy and pride at their mutual success, Aramis heard something which made him prick up his ears.

"What is that?" said Philippe.

"The dawn, sire."

"Well?"

"Well, before you retired to bed last night, you probably decided to do something this morning at break of day."

"Yes, I told my captain of the musketeers," replied the young man, hurriedly, "that I should expect him."

"If you told him that, he will certainly be here, for he is a most punctual man."

"I hear a step in the vestibule."

"It must be he."

"Come, let us begin the attack," said the young king, resolutely.

"Be cautious, for heaven's sake. To begin the attack, and with D'Artagnan, would be madness. D'Artagnan knows nothing, he has seen nothing; he is a hundred miles from suspecting our mystery in the slightest degree; but if he comes into this room the first this morning, he will be sure to detect something of what has taken place, and which he would imagine it his business to occupy himself about. Before we allow D'Artagnan to penetrate into this room, we must air the room thoroughly, or introduce so many people into it that the keenest scent in the whole kingdom may be deceived by the traces of twenty different persons."

"But how can I send him away, since I have given him a rendezvous?" observed the prince, impatient to measure swords with so redoubtable an antagonist.

"I will take care of that," replied the bishop, "and in order to begin, I am going to strike a blow which will completely stupefy our man."

"He too is striking a blow, for I hear him at the door," added the prince, hurriedly.

And in fact, a knock at the door was heard at that moment. Aramis was not mistaken; for it was indeed D'Artagnan who adopted that mode of announcing himself.

We have seen how he passed the night in philosophizing with M. Fouquet, but the musketeer was very weary even of feigning to fall asleep, and as soon as earliest dawn illumined with its gloomy gleams of light the sumptuous cornices of the superintendent's room, D'Artagnan rose from his armchair, arranged his sword, brushed his coat and hat with his sleeve, like a private soldier getting ready for inspection.

"Are you going out?" said Fouquet.

"Yes, monseigneur. And you?"

"I shall remain."

"You pledge your word?"

"Certainly."

"Very good. Besides, my only reason for going out is to try and get that reply, — you know what I mean?"

"That sentence, you mean ——"

"Stay, I have something of the old Roman in me. This morning, when I got up, I remarked that my sword had not caught in one of the *aiguillettes*, and that my shoulder belt had slipped quite off. That is an infallible sign."

"Of prosperity?"

"Yes, be sure of it; for every time that that confounded belt of mine sticks fast to my back, it always signified a punishment from M. de Tréville, or a refusal of money by M. de Mazarin. Every time my sword hung fast to my shoulder belt, it always predicted some disagreeable commission or another for me to execute, and I have had showers of them all my life through. Every time, too, my sword danced about in its sheath, a duel, fortunate in its result, was sure to follow: whenever it dangled about the calves of my legs, it signified a slight wound; every time it fell completely out of the scabbard, I was booked, and made up my mind that I should have to remain on the field of battle, with two or three months under surgical bandages into the bargain."

"I did not know your sword kept you so well informed," said Fouquet, with a faint smile, which showed how he was struggling against his own weakness. "Is your sword bewitched, or under the influence of some imperial charm?"

"Why, you must know that my sword may almost be regarded as part of my own body. I have heard that certain men seem to have warnings given them by feeling something the matter with their legs, or a throbbing of their temples. With me, it is my sword that warns me. Well, it told me of nothing this morning. But, stay a moment — look here, it has just fallen of its own accord into the last hole of the belt. Do you know what that is a warning of?"

"No."

"Well, that tells me of an arrest that will have to be made this very day."

"Well," said the superintendent, more astonished than annoyed by this frankness, "if there is nothing disagreeable predicted to you by your sword, I am to conclude that it is not disagreeable for you to arrest me."

"You! arrest *you!*"

"Of course. The warning ——"

"Does not concern you, since you have been arrested ever since yesterday. It is not you I shall have to arrest, be assured of that. That is the reason why I am delighted, and also the reason why I said that my day will be a happy one."

And with these words, pronounced with the most affectionate graciousness of manner, the captain took leave of Fouquet in order to wait upon the king. He was on the point of leaving the room, when Fouquet said to him, "One last mark of kindness."

"What is it, monseigneur?"

"M. d'Herblay; let me see M. d'Herblay."

"I am going to try and get him to come to you."

D'Artagnan did not think himself so good a prophet. It was written that the day would pass away and realize all the predictions that had been made in the morning. He had accordingly knocked, as we have seen, at the king's door. The door opened. The captain thought that it was the king who had just opened it himself; and this supposition was not altogether inadmissible, considering the state of agitation in which he had left Louis XIV. the previous evening; but instead of his royal master, whom he was on the point of saluting with the greatest respect, he perceived the long, calm features of Aramis. So extreme was his surprise that he could hardly refrain from uttering a loud exclamation. "Aramis!" he said.

"Good morning, dear D'Artagnan," replied the prelate, coldly.

"You here!" stammered out the musketeer.

"His majesty desires you to report that he is still sleeping, after having been greatly fatigued during the whole night."

"Ah!" said D'Artagnan, who could not understand how the bishop of Vannes, who had been so indifferent a favorite the previous evening, had become in half a dozen hours the most magnificent mushroom of fortune that had ever sprung up in a sovereign's bedroom. In fact, to transmit the orders of the king even to the mere threshold of that monarch's room, to serve as an intermediary of Louis XIV. so as to be able to give a single order in his name at a couple of paces from him, he must have become more than Richelieu had ever been to Louis XIII. D'Artagnan's expressive eye, half-opened lips, his curling mustache, said as much indeed in the plainest language to the chief favorite, who remained calm and perfectly unmoved.

"Moreover," continued the bishop, "you will be good enough, monsieur le capitaine des mousquetaires, to allow those only to pass into the king's room this morning who have special permission. His majesty does not wish to be disturbed just yet."

"But," objected D'Artagnan, almost on the point of refusing to obey this order, and particularly of giving unrestrained passage to the suspicions which the king's silence had aroused — "but, monsieur l'évêque, his majesty gave me a rendezvous for this morning."

"Later, later," said the king's voice, from the bottom of the alcove; a voice which made a cold shudder pass through the musketeer's veins. He bowed, amazed, confused, and stupefied by the smile with which Aramis seemed to overwhelm him, as soon as those words had been pronounced.

"And then," continued the bishop, "as an answer to what you were coming to ask the king, my dear D'Artagnan, here is an order of his majesty, which you will be good enough to attend to forthwith, for it concerns M Fouquet."

D'Artagnan took the order which was held out to him. "To be set at liberty!" he murmured. "Ah!" and he uttered a second "ah!" still more full of intelligence than the former; for this order explained Aramis' presence with the king, and that Aramis, in order to have obtained Fouquet's pardon, must have made considerable progress in the royal favor, and that this favor explained, in its tenor, the hardly conceivable assurance with which M. d'Herblay issued the order in the king's name. For D'Artagnan it was quite sufficient to have understood something of the matter in hand in order to understand the rest. He bowed and withdrew a couple of paces, as though he were about to leave.

"I am going with you," said the bishop.

"Where to?"

"To M. Fouquet; I wish to be a witness of his delight."

"Ah! Aramis, how you puzzled me just now!" said D'Artagnan again.

"But you understand *now*, I suppose?"

"Of course I understand," he said aloud; but then added in a low tone to himself, almost hissing the words between his teeth, "No, no, I do not understand yet. But it is all the same, for here is the order for it." And then he added, "I will lead the way, monseigneur," and he conducted Aramis to Fouquet's apartments.

The False King.

In the mean time, usurped royalty was playing out its part bravely at Vaux. Philippe gave orders that for his *petit lever*, the *grandes entrées*, already prepared to appear before the king, should be introduced. He determined to give this order notwithstanding the absence of M. d'Herblay, who did not return — our readers know the reason. But the prince, not believing that absence could be prolonged, wished, as all rash spirits do, to try his valor and his fortune far from all protection and instruction. Another reason urged him to this — Anne of Austria was about to appear; the guilty mother was about to stand in the presence of her sacrificed son. Philippe was not willing, if he had a weakness, to render the man a witness of it before whom he was bound thenceforth to display so much strength. Philippe opened his folding doors, and several persons entered silently. Philippe did not stir whilst his *valets de chambre* dressed him. He had watched, the evening before, all the habits of his brother, and played the king in such a manner as to awaken no suspicion. He was thus completely dressed in hunting costume when he received his visitors. His own memory and the notes of Aramis announced everybody to him, first of all Anne of Austria, to whom Monsieur gave his hand, and then Madame with M. de Saint-Aignan. He smiled at seeing these countenances, but trembled on recognizing his mother. That still so noble and imposing figure, ravaged by pain, pleaded in his heart the cause of the famous queen who had immolated a child to reasons of state. He found his mother still handsome. He knew that Louis XIV. loved her, and he promised himself to love her likewise, and not to prove a scourge to her old age. He contemplated his brother with a tenderness easily to be understood. The latter had usurped nothing, had cast no shades athwart his life. A separate tree, he allowed the stem to rise without heeding its elevation or majestic life. Philippe promised himself to be a kind brother to this prince, who required nothing but gold to minister to his pleasures. He bowed with a friendly air to Saint-Aignan, who was all reverences and smiles, and tremblingly held out his hand to Henrietta, his sister-in-law, whose beauty struck him; but he saw in the eyes of that princess an expression of coldness which would facilitate, as he thought, their future relations.

"How much more easy," thought he, "it will be to be the brother of that woman than her gallant, if she evinces toward me a coldness that my brother could not have for her, but which is imposed upon me as a duty." The only visit he dreaded at this moment was that of the queen; his heart — his mind — had just been shaken by so violent a trial, that, in spite of their firm temperament, they would not, perhaps, support another shock. Happily the queen did not come. Then commenced, on the part of Anne of Austria, a political dissertation upon the welcome M. Fouquet had given to the house of France. She mixed up hostilities with compliments addressed to the king, and questions as to his health, with little maternal flatteries and diplomatic artifices.

"Well, my son," said she, "are you convinced with regard to M. Fouquet?"

"Saint-Aignan," said Philippe, "have the goodness to go and inquire after the queen."

At these words, the first Philippe had pronounced aloud, the slight difference that there was between his voice and that of the king was sensible to maternal ears, and Anne of Austria looked earnestly at her son. Saint-Aignan left the room, and Philippe continued : —

"Madame, I do not like to hear M. Fouquet ill-spoken of, you know I do not — and you have even spoken well of him yourself."

"That is true; therefore I only question you on the state of your sentiments with respect to him."

"Sire," said Henrietta, "I, on my part, have always liked M. Fouquet. He is a man of good taste, — a superior man."

"A superintendent who is never sordid or niggardly," added Monsieur; "and who pays in gold all the orders I have on him."

"Every one in this thinks too much of himself, and nobody for the state," said the old queen. "M. Fouquet, it is a fact, M. Fouquet is ruining the state."

"Well, mother!" replied Philippe, in rather a lower key, "do you likewise constitute yourself the buckler of M. Colbert?"

"How is that?" replied the old queen, rather surprised.

"Why, in truth," replied Philippe, "you speak that just as your old friend Madame de Chevreuse would speak."

"Why do you mention Madame de Chevreuse to me?" said she, "and what sort of humor are you in to-day towards me?"

Philippe continued: "Is not Madame de Chevreuse always in league against somebody? Has not Madame de Chevreuse been to pay you a visit, mother?"

"Monsieur, you speak to me now in such a manner that I can almost fancy I am listening to your father."

"My father did not like Madame de Chevreuse, and had good reason for not liking her," said the prince. "For my part, I like her no better than *he* did; and if she thinks proper to come here as she formerly did, to sow divisions and hatreds under the pretext of begging money — why ——"

"Well! what?" said Anne of Austria, proudly, herself provoking the storm.

"Well!" replied the young man, firmly, "I will drive Madame de Chevreuse out of my kingdom — and with her all who meddle with its secrets and mysteries."

He had not calculated the effect of this terrible speech, or perhaps he wished to judge of the effect of it, like those who, suffering from a chronic pain, and seeking to break the monotony of that suffering, touch their wound to procure a sharper pang. Anne of Austria was nearly fainting; her eyes, open but meaningless, ceased to see for several seconds; she stretched out her arms towards her other son, who supported and embraced her without fear of irritating the king.

"Sire," murmured she, "you are treating your mother very cruelly."

"In what respect, madame?" replied he. "I am only speaking of Madame de Chevreuse; does my mother prefer Madame de Chevreuse to the security of the state and of my person? Well, then, madame, I tell you Madame de Chevreuse has returned to France to borrow money, and that she addressed herself to M. Fouquet to sell him a certain secret."

"A certain secret!" cried Anne of Austria.

"Concerning pretended robberies that monsieur le surintendant had committed, which is false," added Philippe. "M. Fouquet rejected her offers with indignation, preferring the esteem of the king to complicity with such intriguers. Then Madame de Chevreuse sold the secret to M. Colbert, and as she is insatiable, and was not satisfied with having extorted a hundred thousand crowns from a servant of the State, she has taken a still bolder flight, in search of surer sources of supply. Is that true, madame?"

"You know all, sire," said the queen, more uneasy than irritated.

"Now," continued Philippe, "I have good reason to dislike this fury, who comes to my court to plan the shame of some and the ruin of others. If Heaven has suffered certain crimes to be committed, and has concealed them in the shadow of its clemency, I will not permit Madame de Chevreuse to counteract the just designs of fate."

The latter part of this speech had so agitated the queen mother, that her son had pity on her. He took her hand and kissed it tenderly; she did not feel that in that kiss, given in spite of repulsion and bitterness of the heart, there was a pardon for eight years of suffering. Philippe allowed the silence of a moment to swallow the emotions that had just developed themselves. Then, with a cheerful smile: —

"We will not go to-day," said he, "I have a plan." And, turning towards the door, he hoped to see Aramis, whose absence began to alarm him. The queen mother wished to leave the room.

"Remain where you are, mother," said he, "I wish you to make your peace with M. Fouquet."

"I bear M. Fouquet no ill will; I only dreaded his prodigalities."

"We will put that to rights, and will take nothing of the superintendent but his good qualities."

"What is your majesty looking for?" said Henrietta, seeing the king's eyes constantly turned towards the door, and wishing to let fly a little poisoned arrow at his heart, supposing he was so anxiously expecting either La Vallière or a letter from her.

"My sister," said the young man, who had divined her thought, thanks to that marvelous perspicuity of which fortune was from that time about to allow him the exercise, "my sister, I am expecting a most distinguished man, a most able counselor, whom I wish to present to you all, recommending him to your good graces. Ah! come in, then, D'Artagnan."

"What does your majesty wish?" said D'Artagnan, appearing.

"Where is monsieur the bishop of Vannes, your friend?"

"Why, sire ——"

"I am waiting for him, and he does not come. Let him be sought for."

D'Artagnan remained for an instant stupefied; but soon, reflecting that Aramis had left Vaux privately on a mission from the king, he concluded that the king wished to preserve the secret. "Sire," replied he, "does your majesty absolutely require M. d'Herblay to be brought to you?"

"Absolutely is not the word," said Philippe; "I do not want him so particularly as that; but if he can be found ——"

"I thought so," said D'Artagnan to himself.

"Is this M. d'Herblay bishop of Vannes?"

"Yes, madame."

"A friend of M. Fouquet?"

"Yes, madame; an old musketeer."

Anne of Austria blushed.

"One of the four braves who formerly performed such prodigies."

The old queen repented of having wished to bite; she broke off the conversation, in order to preserve the rest of her teeth. "Whatever may be your choice, sire," said she, "I have no doubt it will be excellent."

All bowed in support of that sentiment.

"You will find in him," continued Philippe, "the depth and penetration of M. de Richelieu, without the avarice of M. de Mazarin!"

"A prime minister, sire?" said Monsieur, in a fright.

"I will tell you all about that, brother; but it is strange that M. d'Herblay is not here!"

He called out: —

"Let M. Fouquet be informed that I wish to speak to him — oh! before you, before you; do not retire!"

M. de Saint-Aignan returned, bringing satisfactory news of the queen, who only kept her bed from precaution, and to have strength to carry out all the king's wishes. Whilst everybody was seeking M. Fouquet and Aramis, the new king quietly continued his experiments, and everybody, family, officers, servants, had not the least suspicion of his identity, his air, voice, and manners were so like the king's. On his side, Philippe, applying to all countenances the accurate descriptions and key-notes of character supplied by his accomplice Aramis, conducted himself so as not to give birth to a doubt in the minds of those who surrounded him. Nothing from that time could disturb the usurper. With what strange facility had Providence just reversed the loftiest fortune of the world to substitute the lowliest in its stead! Philippe admired the goodness of God with regard to himself, and seconded it with all the resources of his admirable nature. But he felt, at times, something like a specter gliding between him and the rays of his new glory. Aramis did not appear. The conversation had languished in the royal family; Philippe, preoccupied, forgot to dismiss his brother and Madame Henrietta. The latter were astonished, and began, by degrees, to lose all patience. Anne of Austria stooped towards her son's ear, and addressed some words to him in Spanish. Philippe was completely ignorant of that language, and grew pale at this unexpected obstacle. But, as if the spirit of the imperturbable Aramis had covered him with his infallibility, instead of appearing disconcerted, Philippe rose. "Well! what?" said Anne of Austria.

"What is all that noise?" said Philippe, turning round towards the door of the second staircase.

And a voice was heard saying, "This way, this way! A few steps more, sire!"

"The voice of M. Fouquet," said D'Artagnan, who was standing close to the queen mother.

"Then M. d'Herblay cannot be far off," added Philippe.

But he then saw what he little thought to have beheld so near to him. All eyes were turned towards the door at which

M. Fouquet was expected to enter; but it was not M. Fouquet who entered. A terrible cry resounded from all corners of the chamber, a painful cry uttered by the king and all present. It is given to but few men, even to those whose destiny contains the strangest elements, and accidents the most wonderful, to contemplate a spectacle similar to that which presented itself in the royal chamber at that moment. The half-closed shutters only admitted the entrance of an uncertain light passing through thick violet velvet curtains lined with silk. In this soft shade, the eyes were by degrees dilated, and every one present saw others rather with imagination than with actual sight. There could not, however, escape, in these circumstances, one of the surrounding details; and the new object which presented itself appeared as luminous as though it shone out in full sunlight. So it happened with Louis XIV., when he showed himself, pale and frowning, in the doorway of the secret stairs. The face of Fouquet appeared behind him, stamped with sorrow and determination. The queen mother, who perceived Louis XIV., and who held the hand of Philippe, uttered the cry of which we have spoken, as if she had beheld a phantom. Monsieur was bewildered, and kept turning his head in astonishment, from one to the other. Madame made a step forward, thinking she was looking at the form of her brother-in-law reflected in a mirror. And, in fact, the illusion was possible. The two princes, both pale as death — for we renounce the hope of being able to describe the fearful state of Philippe — trembling, clenching their hands convulsively, measured each other with looks, and darted their glances, sharp as poniards, at each other. Silent, panting, bending forward, they appeared as if about to spring upon an enemy. The unheard-of resemblance of countenance, gesture, shape, height, even to the resemblance of costume, produced by chance — for Louis XIV. had been to the Louvre and put on a violet-colored dress — the perfect analogy of the two princes, completed the consternation of Anne of Austria. And yet she did not at once guess the truth. There are misfortunes in life so truly dreadful that no one will at first accept them; people rather believe in the supernatural and the impossible. Louis had not reckoned on these obstacles. He expected he had only to appear to be acknowledged. A living sun, he could not endure the suspicion of equality with any one. He did not admit that every torch should not become darkness at

THE MAN IN THE IRON MASK.

the instant he shone out with his conquering ray. At the aspect of Philippe, then, he was perhaps more terrified than any one round him, and his silence, his immobility, were, this time, a concentration and a calm which precede the violent explosions of concentrated passion.

But Fouquet! who shall paint his emotion and stupor in presence of this living portrait of his master! Fouquet thought Aramis was right, that this newly-arrived was a king as pure in his race as the other, and that, for having repudiated all participation in this *coup d'état*, so skillfully got up by the General of the Jesuits, he must be a mad enthusiast, unworthy of ever again dipping his hands in political grand strategy work. And then it was the blood of Louis XIII. which Fouquet was sacrificing to the blood of Louis XIII.; it was to a selfish ambition he was sacrificing a noble ambition; to the right of keeping he sacrificed the right of having. The whole extent of his fault was revealed to him at simple sight of the pretender. All that passed in the mind of Fouquet was lost upon the persons present. He had five minutes to focus meditation on this point of conscience; five minutes, that is to say five ages, during which the two kings and their family scarcely found energy to breathe after so terrible a shock. D'Artagnan, leaning against the wall in front of Fouquet, with his hand to his brow, asked himself the cause of such a wonderful prodigy. He could not have said at once why he doubted, but he knew assuredly that he had reason to doubt, and that in this meeting of the two Louis XIV.'s lay all the doubt and difficulty that during late days had rendered the conduct of Aramis so suspicious to the musketeer. These ideas were, however, enveloped in a haze, a veil of mystery. The actors in this assembly seemed to swim in the vapors of a confused waking. Suddenly Louis XIV., more impatient and more accustomed to command, ran to one of the shutters, which he opened, tearing the curtains in his eagerness. A flood of living light entered the chamber, and made Philippe draw back to the alcove. Louis seized upon this movement with eagerness, and addressing himself to the queen: —

"My mother," said he, "do you not acknowledge your son, since every one here has forgotten his king?" Anne of Austria started, and raised her arms towards heaven, without being able to articulate a single word.

"My mother," said Philippe, with a calm voice, "do you not

acknowledge your son?" And this time, in his turn, Louis drew back.

As to Anne of Austria, struck suddenly in head and heart with fell remorse, she lost her equilibrium. No one aiding her, for all were petrified, she sank back in her *fauteuil*, breathing a weak, trembling sigh. Louis could not endure the spectacle and the affront. He bounded towards D'Artagnan, over whose brain a vertigo was stealing, and who staggered as he caught at the door for support.

"*À moi! mousquetaire!*" said he. "Look us in the face and say which is the paler, he or I!"

This cry roused D'Artagnan, and stirred in his heart the fibers of obedience. He shook his head, and, without more hesitation, he walked straight up to Philippe, on whose shoulder he laid his hand, saying, "Monsieur, you are my prisoner!"

Philippe did not raise his eyes towards heaven, not stir from the spot, where he seemed nailed to the floor, his eye intently fixed upon the king his brother. He reproached him with a sublime silence for all misfortunes past, all tortures to come. Against this language of the soul the king felt he had no power; he cast down his eyes, dragging away precipitately his brother and sister, forgetting his mother sitting motionless within three paces of the son whom she left a second time to be condemned to death. Philippe approached Anne of Austria, and said to her, in a soft and nobly agitated voice: —

"If I were not your son, I should curse you, my mother, for having rendered me so unhappy."

D'Artagnan felt a shudder pass through the marrow of his bones. He bowed respectfully to the young prince, and said, as he bent, "Excuse me, monseigneur, I am but a soldier, and my oaths are his who has just left the chamber."

"Thank you, M. d'Artagnan. . . . What has become of M. d'Herblay?"

"M. d'Herblay is in safety, monseigneur," said a voice behind them; "and no one, while I live and am free, shall cause a hair to fall from his head."

"Monsieur Fouquet!" said the prince, smiling sadly.

"Pardon me, monseigneur," said Fouquet, kneeling, "but he who is just gone out from hence was my guest."

"Here are," murmured Philippe, with a sigh, "brave friends and good hearts. They make me regret the world. Oh, M. d'Artagnan, I follow you."

RACINE

At the moment the captain of the musketeers was about to leave the room with his prisoner, Colbert appeared, and, after remitting an order from the king to D'Artagnan, retired. D'Artagnan read the paper, and then crushed it in his hand with rage.

"What is it?" asked the prince.

"Read, monseigneur," replied the musketeer.

Philippe read the following words, hastily traced by the hand of the king: —

"M. d'Artagnan will conduct the prisoner to the Île Sainte-Marguerite. He will cover his face with an iron visor, which the prisoner shall never raise except at peril of his life."

"That is just," said Philippe, with resignation; "I am ready."

"Aramis was right," said Fouquet, in a low voice, to the musketeer, "this one is every whit as much a king as the other."

"More so!" replied D'Artagnan. "He only wanted you and me."

SCENES FROM "ATHALIAH."[1]

By RACINE.

[JEAN BAPTISTE RACINE, French dramatist, was born at La Ferté-Milon (dep. Aisne), December 21, 1639; studied the classics with the Jansenists at Port Royal; and finished his education at the Collège d'Harcourt. After composing an ode, entitled "Nymphes de la Seine," in honor of Louis XIV.'s marriage, he made the acquaintance of Boileau, Molière, and La Fontaine, and began to write for the stage. His first play, "La Thébaïde," was produced by Molière's troupe; "Andromaque" (1667) established his reputation; and then followed a brilliant series of tragedies: "Britannicus," "Bérénice," "Bajazet," "Mithridate," "Iphigénie," and "Phèdre." His only comedy, "Les Plaideurs," appeared in 1668. Racine withdrew from the theater after the production of "Phèdre," partly on account of envious intrigues and malicious criticisms, and settled down to a peaceful married life. After a silence of twelve years he wrote, at the solicitation of Madame de Maintenon, "Esther" and "Athalie," biblical tragedies. His death (in 1699) is said to have been hastened by grief at losing the king's favor.]

ATHALIAH, ABNER, MATTAN, ATTENDANTS OF ATHALIAH.

Mattan — Great Queen, is this a place for thee?
What trouble stirs, what terror chills thine heart?
What dost thou in the midst of enemies?
Darest thou this unhallowed fane approach?
Hast thou that bitter hatred cast away ——

[1] From Racine's Dramatic Works. By permission of Geo. Bell & Sons. 2 vols., price 3s. 6d. each.

Athaliah—
    Both of you lend me an attentive ear.
    I do not wish now to recall the past,
    Nor give account to you for blood I shed:
    A sense of duty prompted all my acts.
    Nor will I take for judge a hasty crowd;
    Whate'er they may presume to spread abroad,
    My vindication Heaven has made its care.
    My power, established on renowned success,
    Has magnified my name from sea to sea;
    Jerusalem enjoys profoundest peace;
    The wandering Arab Jordan sees no more
    Ravage his borders with continual raids;
    Nor boasts Philistia over Judah now,
    And Syria owns me for a sister Queen.
        Lastly the traitor who destroyed my House,
    And e'en to me thought to extend his rage,
    Jehu, fierce Jehu, in Samaria quails
    Before a mighty rival's rapid strokes,
    Whom I incited to attack my foe;
    And thus th' assassin leaves me mistress here,
    To reap the fruits of policy in peace.
        But for some days a gnawing care has come,
    To check the flood of my prosperity.
    A dream (why should a dream disquiet me?)
    Preys on my heart, and keeps it ill at ease;
    I try to banish it; it haunts me still.
        'Twas deepest night, when horror falls on man,
    My mother Jezebel before me stood,
    Richly attired as on the day she died,
    Her pride undaunted by misfortune's touch.
    That borrowed brightness still her features wore,
    Which she would paint upon her withered face,
    To hide the ravages of ruthless age:
    "Tremble," she said, "child worthy of myself;
    O'er thee too triumphs Judah's cruel god,
    And thou must fall into his dreadful hands,
    Whereat I grieve." With these alarming words,
    Her specter o'er my bed appeared to bend;
    I stretched my hands to clasp her; but I found
    Only a hideous mass of flesh and bones,
    Horribly bruised and mangled, dragged thro' mire,
    Bleeding and torn, whose limbs the dogs of prey
    Were growling over with devouring greed.

Abner—
    Great God!

ATHALIAH.

Athaliah— While thus disturbed, before me rose
The vision of a boy in shining robe,
Such as the Hebrew priests are wont to wear.
My drooping spirits at his sight revived:
But while my troubled eyes, to peace restored,
Admired his noble air and modest grace,
I felt the sudden stroke of murderous steel
Plunged deeply by the traitor in my breast.
Perhaps to you this dream, so strangely mixed,
May seem a work of chance, and I myself,
For long ashamed to let my fears prevail,
Referred it to a melancholy mood;
But while its memory lingered in my soul,
Twice in my sleep I saw that form again,
Twice the same child before my eyes appeared,
Always about to stab me to the heart.
    Worn out at last by horror's close pursuit,
I went to claim Baal's protecting care,
And, kneeling at his altars, find repose.
How strangely fear may sway our mortal minds!
And instinct seemed to drive me to these courts,
To pacify the god whom Jews adore;
I thought that offerings might appease his wrath
That this their god might grow more merciful.
Baal's High Priest, my feebleness forgive!
I entered; and the sacrifice was stayed,
The people fled, Jehoiada in wrath
Advanced to meet me. As he spake, I saw
With terror and surprise that selfsame boy
Who haunts me in my dreams. I saw him there;
His mien the same, the same his linen stole,
His gait, his eyes, each feature of his face;
It was himself; beside th' High Priest he walked
Till quickly they removed him from my sight.
    That is the trouble which detains me here,
And thereon would I fain consult you both.
Mattan, what means this omen marvelous?

Mattan—
Coincidence so strange fills me with dread.

Athaliah—
But, Abner, hast thou seen this fatal child?
Who is he? What his family, his tribe?

Abner—
Two children at the altar lend their aid,
One is the High Priest's son, the other is
To me unknown.

Mattan — Why hesitate to act?
Your Majesty must needs secure them both.
'Tis known how I regard Jehoiada,
Seeking no vengeance for my private wrongs,
In all my warnings studying to be fair;
But, after all, were this indeed his son,
Would he one moment let the guilty live?
Abner —
Of what crime can a child be capable?
Mattan —
Heaven showed him with a dagger in his hand;
And Heaven is just and wise, nor works in vain.
What more dost want?
Abner — But, trusting to a dream,
Say, wouldst thou have us bathe in infant blood?
Ye know not yet his father nor his name.
Mattan —
Enough for fear! I have considered all.
If from illustrious parentage he springs,
His ruin should be hastened by his rank;
If fate has placed him in a lot obscure,
What matters it if worthless blood be spilt?
Must kings keep pace when justice lags behind?
On promptitude their safety oft depends;
No irksome scruples need their freedom check;
To be suspected is all one with guilt.
Abner —
Mattan! Is this the language of a priest?
Nursed in the lap of war, in carnage reared,
Stern agent of the vengeful wrath of Kings,
'Tis I who now must urge misfortune's plea!
And thou, who owest him a father's love,
A minister of peace in times of wrath,
Cloaking resentment with pretended zeal
Dost chafe that blood should flow so tardily!
Thou badest me, Madam, speak my honest thought:
What, then, is this that moves thy fear so much?
A dream, a feeble child, whom, it may be
Too readily thy fancy recognized.
Athaliah —
Abner, I will admit I may be wrong,
Heeding too much, perchance, an idle dream.
More closely then must I behold that child,
And at my leisure scan his features well.
Let both the boys be brought before me now.

ATHALIAH.

Abner —
 I fear ——
Athaliah — What! Can they fail to grant me this?
 What reason could they have to say me no?
 'Twould rouse suspicion. Bid Jehosheba,
 Or else her husband, bring the children here;
 I can at pleasure use a monarch's tone.
 Abner, I tell thee candidly, your priests
 Have cause to bless my kindness hitherto;
 I know how far they freely have discussed
 My conduct, and abused my sovereign power;
 And yet they live, and yet their temple stands.
 But soon, I feel, the limit may be passed;
 Jehoiada must curb his savage zeal,
 And not provoke my wrath a second time.
 Go. [*Exit* ABNER.
Mattan — I may now at last in freedom speak,
 And clearly set the truth before thine eyes.
 A growing monster in this temple lurks;
 A tempest threatens, wait not till it breaks.
 Ere daylight Abner with th' High Priest conferred;
 Thou knowest well his love for David's line.
 What if Jehoiada should in their ranks
 Foist this young child with whom Heaven threatens thee,
 His son or not ——
Athaliah — Thou hast unsealed mine eyes,
 And Heaven's warning vision grows distinct.
 But I would fain be free from every doubt:
 Children will readily betray their thoughts,
 One word will oft disclose some deep design.
 Let me, dear Mattan, see him, question him.
 Go thou, meanwhile, and secret orders give
 That all my Tyrians quickly arm themselves.

JOASH, ATHALIAH, JEHOSHEBA, ZACHARIAH, ABNER, SALOME, TWO
 LEVITES, CHORUS, ATTENDANTS OF ATHALIAH.

Jehosheba [*to the* TWO LEVITES] —
 Keep constant watch, ye servants of the Lord,
 Over these children, precious and beloved.
Abner [*to* JEHOSHEBA] —
 Take courage, Princess; they shall be my charge.
Athaliah —
 Heavens! the more closely I examine him, —
 'Tis he! And horror seizes me again.
  [*Pointing to* JOASH.
 Wife of Jehoiada, is this thy son?

Jehosheba —
   He, Madam?
Athaliah —   **He.**
Jehosheba —   His mother? No, not I.
                            [*Pointing to* ZACHARIAH.
   There is my son.
Athaliah [*to* JOASH] — Who is thy father, child?
   Answer, thyself.
Jehosheba —   Heaven till this very day——
Athaliah —
   Why in such haste to answer for the boy?
   It is for him to speak.
Jehosheba —   From one so young
   What revelation canst thou hope to gain?
Athaliah —
   The young are innocent; and simple truth
   Their honest frankness knows not to disguise:
   Let him explain all that concerns himself.
Jehosheba [*aside*] —
   Great God, put now Thy wisdom in his mouth!
Athaliah —
   What is thy name?
Joash —   My name's Eliakim.
Athaliah —
   Thy father?
Joash —   Fatherless, they say, I am,
   Cast since my birth upon the arms of God;
   I never knew my parents, who they were.
Athaliah —
   Hast thou no parents?
Joash —   They abandoned me.
Athaliah —
   How? and how long ago?
Joash —   When I was born.
Athaliah —
   Where is thy home? This can at least be told.
Joash —
   This Temple is my home; none else I know.
Athaliah —
   Where wast thou found? Hast thou been **told of that?**
Joash —
   'Midst cruel wolves, ready to eat me up.
Athaliah —
   Who placed thee in this temple?
Joash —   One **unknown,**
   She gave **no** name, nor was she seen **again.**

ATHALIAH.

Athaliah —
 Whose guardian hands preserved thine **infant years**?
Joash —
 When did God e'er neglect His children's needs?
 The feathered nestlings He provides with food,
 And o'er all nature spreads His bounty wide.
 Daily I pray; and with a Father's care
 He feeds me from the sacred offerings.
Athaliah —
 New wonder comes to trouble and perplex!
 The sweetness of his voice, his infant grace
 Unconsciously make enmity give way
 To — can it be compassion that I feel!
Abner —
 Madam, is this thy dreaded enemy?
 'Tis evident thy dreams have played thee **false**;
 Unless thy pity, which now seems to vex,
 Should be the fatal blow that terrified.
Athaliah [*to* JOASH *and* JEHOSHEBA] —
 Why are ye leaving?
Jehosheba —   Thou hast heard his tale:
 His presence longer might be troublesome.
Athaliah [*to* JOASH] —
 Nay, child, come back.   What dost thou all the **day**?
Joash —
 I worship God, and hear His Law explained;
 His holy volume I am taught to read,
 And now to write it has my hand begun.
Athaliah —
 What says that Law?
Joash —   That God requires our **love**,
 Avenges, soon or late, His Name blasphemed,
 Is the protector of the fatherless,
 Resists the proud, the murderer punishes.
Athaliah —
 I understand.   But all within these walls,
 How are they occupied?
Joash —   In praising God.
Athaliah —
 Does God claim constant service here and **prayer**?
Joash —
 All else is banished from His holy courts.
Athaliah —
 What pleasures hast thou?
Joash —   Where God's altar **stands**,
 I sometimes help th' High Priest to offer salt

      Or incense, hear His lofty praises sung,
      And see His stately ritual performed.
Athaliah —
      What! Hast thou pastime none more sweet than that?
      Sad lot for one so young; but come with me,
      And see my palace and my splendor there.
Joash —
      God's goodness then would from my memory fade.
Athaliah —
      I would not force thee to forget Him, child.
Joash —
      Thou dost not pray to Him.
Athaliah —   But thou shalt pray.
Joash —
      There I should hear another's name invoked.
Athaliah —
      I serve my god: and thou shalt worship thine.
      There are two powerful gods.
Joash —   Thou must fear mine;
      He only is the Lord, and thine is naught.
Athaliah —
      Pleasures untold will I provide for thee.
Joash —
      The happiness of sinners melts away.
Athaliah —
      Of sinners, who are they?
Jehosheba —   Madam, excuse
      A child——
Athaliah —   I like to see how ye have taught him;
      And thou hast pleased me well, Eliakim,
      Being, and that past doubt, no common child.
      See thou, I am a queen, and have no heir;
      Forsake this humble service, doff this garb,
      And I will let thee share in all my wealth;
      Make trial of my promise from this day;
      Beside me at my table, everywhere,
      Thou shalt receive the treatment of a son.
Joash —
      A son!
Athaliah —   Yes, speak.
Joash —   And such a Father leave
      For——
Athaliah —   Well, what?
Joash —   Such a mother as thyself!
Athaliah [*to* Jehosheba]—
      His memory is good; in all he says

ATHALIAH.

I recognize the lessons ye have given.
Yes, this is how, corrupting guileless youth,
Ye both improve the freedom ye enjoy,
Inciting them to hatred and wild rage,
Until they shudder but to hear my name.

Jehosheba —

Can our misfortunes be concealed from them?
All the world knows them; are they not thy boast?

Athaliah —

Yea; with just wrath, that I am proud to own,
My parents on my offspring I avenged.
Could I see sire and brother massacred,
My mother from the palace roof cast down,
And the same day beheaded all at once
(Oh, horror!) fourscore princes of the blood;
And all to avenge a pack of prophets slain,
Whose dangerous frenzies Jezebel had curbed?
Have queens no heart, daughters no filial love,
That I should act the coward and the slave,
Too pitiful to cope with savages,
By rendering death for death, and blow for blow?
David's posterity from me received
Treatment no worse than had my father's sons!
Where should I be to-day, had I not quelled
All weakness and a mother's tenderness,
Had not this hand of mine like water shed
My own heart's blood, and boldly checked your plots?
Your god has vowed implacable revenge;
Snapt is the link between thine house and mine,
David and all his offspring I abhor,
Tho' born of mine own blood I own them not.

Jehosheba —

Thy plans have prospered.   Let God see, and judge!

Athaliah —

Your god, forsooth, your only refuge left,
What will become of his predictions now?
Let him present you with that promised King,
That Son of David, waited for so long, —
We meet again.   Farewell.   I go content:
I wished to see, and I have seen.   [*Exit.*

Abner [to JEHOSHEBA] —   The trust
I undertook to keep, I thus resign.

Jehosheba [to JEHOIADA] —

My lord, didst hear the Queen's presumptuous words?

Jehoiada —

I heard them all, and felt for thee the while.

These Levites were with me ready to aid
Or perish with you, such was our resolve.
                    [*To* JOASH, *embracing him.*
May God watch o'er thee, child, whose courage bore,
Just now, such noble witness to His Name.
Thy service, Abner, has been well discharged:
I shall expect thee at th' appointed hour.
I must return, this impious murderess
Has stained my vision, and disturbed my prayers;
The very pavement that her feet have trod
My hands shall sprinkle o'er with cleansing blood.

SIGISMUND.[1]

BY CALDERON.

(From "Life is a Dream": translated by Denis Florence MacCarthy.)

[PEDRO CALDERON DE LA BARCA, one of the chief poets of Spain, was born in Madrid, January 17, 1600; died there May 25, 1681. He received his schooling at a Jesuits' college in Madrid; studied history, philosophy, and law at Salamanca; and served ten years in the army in Milan and the Netherlands. He was then summoned to Madrid by Philip IV., a prince fond of theatrical amusements, and was appointed director of the court theater. In 1651 he entered the priesthood, but notwithstanding his religious duties continued to write for the stage, besides which he composed many "autos sacramentales," or the Corpus Christi plays, performed annually in the cathedrals of Toledo, Seville, and Granada. According to his own account he wrote one hundred and eleven plays, among which are: "The Fairy Lady," "'Tis Better than it Was," "The Mock Astrologer," "The Wonder-working Magician," "The Devotion of the Cross," "The Constant Prince," "Life is a Dream," "No Magic like Love."]

SIGISMUND, *Prince of Poland, has from his childhood been held in prison, it having been foretold that he would dethrone his father* BASILIUS. *To try his temper, he is taken asleep to the palace, and awakes to find himself no longer a captive but acknowledged Prince of Poland. His violent conduct justifies the former precautions, and after a day of royalty he is carried back to prison, again asleep.*

Scene : *The Prison.* — SIGISMUND, *as at first, clothed in skins, chained, and lying on the ground;* CLOTALDO, *his guardian;* CLARIN *(who has accidentally learned his story);* and Servants.

Clotaldo — Leave him here on the ground,
           Where his day — its pride being o'er,
           Finds its end too.

[1] By permission of Kegan Paul, Trench, Trübner & Co.

Servant —   As before
             With the chain his feet are bound.
Clarin — Never from that sleep profound
             Wake, O Sigismund! or rise
             To behold with wondering eyes
             All thy glorious life o'erthrown,
             Like a shadow that hath flown,
             Like a bright brief flame that dies!
Clotaldo —
             One who can so wisely make
             Such reflections on this case
             Should have ample time and space,
             Even for the Solon's sake,
             To discuss it. [*To the* Servants.] Him you'll take
             To this cell here, and keep bound!
                       [*He points to another room.*
Clarin — But why me?
Clotaldo —   Because 'tis found
             Safe, when clarions secrets know,
             Clarions to lock up, that so
             They may not have power to sound.
Clarin — Did I, since you treat me thus,
             Try to kill my father? No!
             Did I from the window throw
             That unlucky Icarus? [*Acts of Sigismund.*]
             Is *my* drink somniferous?
             Do I dream? Then why be pent?
Clotaldo —
             'Tis a clarion's punishment.
Clarin — Then a horn of low degree,
             Yea! a cornet I will be,
             A safe silent instrument.
                [*They take him away.* King BASILIUS *enters.*
                   SIGISMUND *still asleep.*
Basilius —
             Hark, Clotaldo!
Clotaldo —   My Lord here?
             Thus disguised, your Majesty!
Basilius —
             Foolish curiosity
             Leads me in this lowly gear
             To find out — ah me! with fear —
             How the sudden change he bore.
Clotaldo —
             There behold him as before
             In his miserable state!

Basilius — Wretched prince! unhappy fate!
Birth by baneful stars watched o'er! —
Go and wake him cautiously!
Now that strength and force lie chained
By the opiate he hath drained.
Clotaldo — Muttering something restlessly,
See, he lies!
Basilius — Let's listen! he
May some few clear words repeat.
Sigismund [*speaking in his sleep*] —
Perfect Prince is he whose heat
Smites the tyrant where he stands!
Yea! Clotaldo by my hands
Dies; my sire shall kiss my feet.
Clotaldo — Death he threatens in his rage.
Basilius — Outrage vile he doth intend.
Clotaldo — He my life hath sworn to end.
Basilius — He has vowed to insult my age.
Sigismund —
On the mighty world's great stage,
'Mid the admiring nations' cheer,
Valor mine! that has no peer,
Enter thou: the slave so shunned
Now shall reign Prince Sigismund,
And his sire his wrath shall fear — [*He wakes.*
But, ah me! where am I? O!
Basilius [*to* CLOTALDO] —
Me I must not let him see.
Listening I close by will be;
What you have to do you know. [*He retires.*
Sigismund —
Can it possibly be so?
Is the truth not what it seemed?
Am I chained and unredeemed?
Art not thou my lifelong tomb?
Dark old tower! Yes! what a doom!
God! what wondrous things I've dreamed.
Clotaldo — Now in this delusive play
Must my special part be taken. —
Is it not full time to waken?
Sigismund —
Yes! to waken well it may.
Clotaldo — Wilt thou sleep the livelong day?
Since we gazing from below
Saw the eagle sailing slow,

Soaring through the azure sphere,
All the time thou waited here
Didst thou never waken?

Sigismund — No!
Nor even now am I awake:
Since such thoughts my memory fill,
That it seems I'm dreaming still.
Nor is this a great mistake:
Since, if dreams could phantoms make
Things of actual substance seem,
I things seen may phantoms deem.
Thus, a double harvest reaping,
I can see when I am sleeping,
And when waking I can dream.

Clotaldo — What you may have dreamed of, say!
Sigismund — If I thought it only seemed,
I would tell not what I dreamed;
But what I beheld I may.
I awoke, and lo! I lay
(Cruel and delusive thing!)
In a bed whose covering,
Bright with blooms from rosy bowers,
Seemed a tapestry of flowers
Woven by the hand of Spring.
Then a crowd of nobles came,
Who addressed me by the name
Of their Prince, presenting me
Gems and robes, on bended knee.
Calm soon left me; and my frame
Thrilled with joy to hear thee tell
Of the fate that me befell,
For, though now in this dark den
I was Prince of Poland then.

Clotaldo — Doubtless you repaid me well?
Sigismund — No! not well: for, calling thee
Traitor vile, in furious strife
Twice I strove to take thy life.

Clotaldo — But why all this rage 'gainst me?
Sigismund — I was master, and would be
Well revenged on foe and friend.
Love one woman could defend ——
[*A woman had checked his waking savageness.*]
That at least for truth I deem.
All else ended like a dream;
That alone can never end.

Clotaldo [*aside*] —
    From his place the King hath gone,
    Touched by his pathetic words.
    [*Aloud.*] Speaking of the king of birds
    Soaring to ascend his throne,
    Thou didst fancy one thine own;
    But in dreams, however bright,
    Thou shouldst still have kept in sight
    How for years I tended thee, —
    For 'twere well, whoe'er we be,
    Even in dreams to do what's right.   [*Exit.*

Sigismund [*alone*] —
    That is true: then let's restrain
    This wild rage, this fierce condition
    Of the mind, this proud ambition,
    Should we ever dream again!
    And we'll do so: since 'tis plain,
    In this world's uncertain gleam,
    That to live is but to dream.
    Man dreams what he is, and wakes
    Only when upon him breaks
    Death's mysterious morning beam.
    The king dreams he is a king,
    And in this delusive way
    Lives and rules with sovereign sway;
    All the cheers that round him ring,
    Born of air, on air take wing;
    And in ashes — mournful fate! —
    Death dissolves his pride and state.
    Who would wish a crown to take,
    Seeing that he must awake
    In the dream beyond death's gate?
    And the rich man dreams of gold,
    Gilding cares it scarce conceals;
    And the poor man dreams he feels
    Want and misery and cold.
    Dreams he too who rank would hold;
    Dreams who bears toil's rough-ribbed hands;
    Dreams who wrong for wrong demands;
    And in fine, throughout the earth
    All men dream, whate'er their birth, —
    And yet no one understands.
    'Tis a dream that I in sadness
    Here am bound, the scorn of fate;
    'Twas a dream that once a state

I enjoyed of light and gladness.
What is life? 'Tis but a madness.
What is life? A thing that seems,
A mirage that falsely gleams,
Phantom joy, delusive rest:
Since is life a dream at best,
And even dreams themselves are dreams.

JUSTINA'S TEMPTATION.

By CALDERON.

The DEMON *tempts* JUSTINA.

Demon —
Abyss of Hell! I call on thee,
Thou wild misrule of thine own anarchy!
From the prison house set free
The spirits of voluptuous death,
That with their mighty breath
They may destroy a world of virgin thoughts!
Let her chaste mind with fancies thick as motes
Be peopled from thy shadowy deep,
Till her guiltless phantasy
Full to overflowing be!
And with sweetest harmony,
Let birds, and flowers, and leaves, and all things move
    To love, only to love!
Let nothing meet her eyes
But signs of Love's soft victories!
Let nothing meet her ear
But sounds of Love's sweet sorrow!
So that from faith no succor she may borrow,
But, guided by my spirit blind,
And in a magic snare entwined,
She may now seek Cyprian.
Begin! while I in silence bind
My voice, when thy sweet song thou hast begun.

A Voice [*within*] —
What is the glory far above
All else in human life?

All —   Love! love!

The First Voice —
There is no form in which the fire

    Of love its traces has impressed not.
    Man lives far more in love's desire
    Than by life's breath, soon possessed not.
    If all that lives must love or die,
    All shapes on earth or sea or sky
    With one consent to Heaven cry
    That the glory far above
    All else in life is ——

All —   Love! O love!
Justina — Thou melancholy thought which art
    So fluttering and so sweet! to thee
    When did I give the liberty
    Thus to afflict my heart?
    What is the cause of this new power
    Which doth my fevered being move,
    Momently raging more and more?
    What subtle pain is kindled now
    Which from my heart doth overflow
    Into my senses?

All —   Love! O love!
Justina — 'Tis that enamored nightingale
    Who gives me the reply;
    He ever tells the same soft tale
    Of passion and of constancy
    To his mate, who rapt and fond
    Listening sits, a bough beyond.
    Be silent, Nightingale! no more
    Make me think, in hearing thee
    Thus tenderly thy love deplore,
    If a bird can feel his so,
    What a man would feel for me.
    And, voluptuous vine! O thou
    Who seekest most when least pursuing,-
    To the trunk thou interlacest
    Art the verdure which embracest,
    And the weight which is its ruin, —
    No more, with green embraces, vine!
    Make me think on what thou lovest, —
    For whilst thou thus thy boughs entwine,
    I fear lest thou shouldst teach me, sophist!
    How arms might be entangled too.
    Light-enchanted sunflower! thou
    Who gazest ever true and tender
    On the sun's revolving splendor!
    Follow not his faithless glance
    With thy faded countenance;

Nor teach my beating heart to fear,
If leaves can mourn without a tear,
How eyes must weep! O Nightingale!
Cease from thy enamored tale;
Leafy vine! unwreathe thy bower;
Restless sunflower! cease to move;
Or tell me all, what poisonous power
Ye use against me!

All — Love! love! love!
Justina — It cannot be! — Whom have I ever loved?
Trophies of my oblivion and disdain,
Floro and Lelio did I not reject?
And Cyprian? ——

THE MIGHTY MAGICIAN.

(From Calderon's "Magico Prodigioso": Shelley's translation.)

Scene I.: CYPRIAN *as a student;* CLARIN *and* MOSCON *as poor scholars with books.*

Cyprian —
In the sweet solitude of this calm place,
This intricate wild wilderness of trees
And flowers and undergrowth of odorous plants,
Leave me: the books you brought out of the house
To me are ever best society,
And whilst with glorious festival and song
Antioch now celebrates the consecration
Of a proud temple to great Jupiter,
And bears his image in loud jubilee
To its new shrine, I would consume what still
Lives of the dying day, in studious thought,
Far from the throng and turmoil.
You, my friends,
Go and enjoy the festival, — it will
Be worth the labor, and return for me
When the sun seeks its grave among the billows,
Which among dim gray clouds on the horizon,
Dance like white plumes upon a hearse; — and here
I shall expect you.

Moscon — I cannot bring my mind,
Great as my haste to see the festival

Certainly is, to leave you, sir, without
Just saying some three or four thousand words.
How is it possible that on a day
Of such festivity, you can be content
To come forth to a solitary country
With three or four old books, and turn your back
On all this mirth?

Clarin — My master's in the right;
There is not anything more tiresome
Than a procession day, with troops, and priests,
And dances, and all that.

Moscon — From first to last,
Clarin, you are a temporizing flatterer:
You praise not what you feel but what he does; —
Toadeater!

Clarin — You lie — under a mistake —
For this is the most civil sort of lie
That can be given to a man's race. I now
Say what I think.

Cyprian — Enough, you foolish fellows!
Pufft up with your own doting ignorance,
You always take the two sides of one question.
Now go; and as I said, return for me
When night falls, veiling in its shadows wide
This glorious fabric of the universe.

Moscon —
How happens it, altho' you can maintain
The folly of enjoying festivals,
That yet you go there?

Clarin — Nay, the consequence
Is clear: — who ever did what he advises
Others to do? —

Moscon — Would that my feet were wings,
So would I fly to Livia. [*Exit.*

Clarin — To speak truth,
Livia is she who has surprised my heart;
But he is more than halfway there. — Soho!
Livia, I come; good sport, Livia, soho! [*Exit.*

Cyprian —
Now, since I am alone, let me examine
The question which has long disturbed my mind
With doubt, since first I read in Plinius
The words of mystic import and deep sense
In which he defines God. My intellect
Can find no God with whom these marks and signs

THE MIGHTY MAGICIAN.

   Fitly agree. It is a hidden truth
   Which I must fathom.
    [CYPRIAN *reads; the* DEMON, *dressed in a Court
     dress, enters.*

Demon —   Search even as thou wilt,
   But thou shalt never find what I can hide.

Cyprian —
   What noise is that among the boughs? Who **moves**?
   What art thou? —

Demon —   'Tis a foreign gentleman.
   Even from this morning I have lost my way
   In this wild place; and my poor horse at last,
   Quite overcome, has stretcht himself upon
   The enameled tapestry of this mossy mountain,
   And feeds and rests at the same time. I was
   Upon my way to Antioch upon business
   Of some importance, but wrapt up in cares
   (Who is exempt from this inheritance?)
   I parted from my company, and lost
   My way, and lost my servants and my comrades.

Cyprian —
   'Tis singular that even within the sight
   Of the high towers of Antioch you could lose
   Your way. Of all the avenues and green paths
   Of this wild wood there is not one but leads,
   As to its center, to the walls of Antioch;
   Take which you will you cannot miss your road.

Demon —
   And such is ignorance! Even in the sight
   Of knowledge, it can draw no profit from it;
   But as it still is early, and as I
   Have no acquaintances in Antioch,
   Being a stranger there, I will even wait
   The few surviving hours of the day,
   Until the night shall conquer it. I see
   Both by your dress and by the books in which
   You find delight and company, that you
   Are a great student; — for my part, I feel
   Much sympathy in such pursuits.

Cyprian —   Have you
   Studied much?

Demon —   No, — and yet I know enough
   Not to be wholly ignorant.

Cyprian —   Pray, sir,
   What science may you know? —

Demon — Many.
Cyprian — Alas!
Much pains must we expend on one alone,
And even then attain it not; — but you
Have the presumption to assert that you
Know many without study.
Demon — And with truth.
For in the country whence I come the sciences
Require no learning, — they are known.
Cyprian — Oh would
I were of that bright country! for in this
The more we study, we the more discover
Our ignorance.
Demon — It is so true, that I
Had so much arrogance as to oppose
The chair of the most high Professorship,
And obtained many votes, and tho' I lost,
The attempt was still more glorious, than the failure
Could be dishonorable. If you believe not,
Let us refer it to dispute respecting
That which you know the best, and altho' I
Know not the opinion you maintain, and tho'
It be the true one, I will take the contrary.
Cyprian —
The offer gives me pleasure. I am now
Debating with myself upon a passage
Of Plinius, and my mind is rackt with doubt
To understand and know who is the God
Of whom he speaks.
Demon — It is a passage, if
I recollect it right, couched in these words:
"God is one supreme goodness, one pure essence,
One substance, and one sense, all sight, all hands.
Cyprian —
'Tis true.
Demon — What difficulty find you here?
Cyprian —
I do not recognize among the Gods
The God defined by Plinius; if he must
Be supreme goodness, even Jupiter
Is not supremely good; because we see
His deeds are evil, and his attributes
Tainted with mortal weakness; in what manner
Can supreme goodness be consistent with
The passions of humanity?

Demon —   The wisdom
    Of the old world maskt with the names of Gods
    The attributes of Nature and of Man;
    A sort of popular philosophy.

Cyprian —
    This reply will not satisfy me, for
    Such awe is due to the high name of God
    That ill should never be imputed.   Then
    Examining the question with more care,
    It follows that the Gods would always will
    That which is best, were they supremely good.
    How then does one will one thing, one another?
    And that you may not say that I allege
    Poetical or philosophic learning:—
    Consider the ambiguous responses
    Of their oracular statues; from two shrines
    Two armies shall obtain the assurance of
    One victory.   Is it not indisputable
    That two contending wills can never lead
    To the same end?   And being opposite,
    If one be good is not the other evil?
    Evil in God is inconceivable;
    But supreme goodness fails among the Gods
    Without their union.

Demon —   I deny your major.
    These responses are means towards some end
    Unfathomed by our intellectual beam.
    They are the work of providence, and more
    The battle's loss may profit those who lose,
    Than victory advantage those who win.

Cyprian —
    That I admit; and yet that God should not
    (Falsehood is incompatible with deity)
    Assure the victory; it would be enough
    To have permitted the defeat.   If God
    Be all sight,— God, who had beheld the truth,
    Would not have given assurance of an end
    Never to be accomplisht: thus, altho'
    The Deity may according to his attributes
    Be well distinguisht into persons, yet
    Even in the minutest circumstance
    His essence must be one.

Demon —   To attain the end
    The affections of the actors in the scene
    Must have been thus influenced by his voice.

Cyprian —
  But for a purpose thus subordinate
  He might have employed Genii, good or evil,—
  A sort of spirits called so by the learned,
  Who roam about inspiring good or evil,
  And from whose influence and existence we
  May well infer our immortality.
  Thus God might easily, without descent
  To a gross falsehood in his proper person,
  Have moved the affections by this mediation
  To the just point.
Demon —   These trifling contradictions
  Do not suffice to impugn the unity
  Of the high Gods; in things of great importance
  They still appear unanimous; consider
  That glorious fabric man, — his workmanship
  Is stampt with one conception.
Cyprian —   Who made man
  Must have, methinks, the advantage of the others.
  If they are equal, might they not have risen
  In opposition to the work, and being
  All hands, according to our author here,
  Have still destroyed even as the other made?
  If equal in their power, unequal only
  In opportunity, which of the two
  Will remain conqueror?
Demon —   On impossible
  And false hypothesis there can be built
  No argument. Say, what do you infer
  From this?
Cyprian — That there must be a mighty God
  Of supreme goodness and of highest grace,
  All sight, all hands, all truth, infallible,
  Without an equal and without a rival,
  The cause of all things and the effect of nothing,
  One power, one will, one substance, and one essence.
  And in whatever persons, one or two,
  His attributes may be distinguisht, one
  Sovereign power, one solitary essence,
  One cause of all cause. *[They rise.*
Demon — How can I impugn
  So clear a consequence?
Cyprian —   Do you regret
  My victory?
Demon — Who but regrets a check

THE MIGHTY MAGICIAN.

In rivalry of wit? I could reply
And urge new difficulties, but will now
Depart, for I hear steps of men approaching,
And it is time that I should now pursue
My journey to the city.

Cyprian — Go in peace!

Demon —
Remain in peace! — Since thus it profits him
To study, I will wrap his senses up
In sweet oblivion of all thought, but of
A piece of excellent beauty; and as I
Have power given me to wage enmity
Against Justina's soul, I will extract
From one effect two vengeances. *[Aside and exit.*

Cyprian — I never
Met a more learned person. Let me now
Revolve this doubt again with careful mind.
[He reads.

FLORO *and* LELIO *enter.*

Lelio —
Here stop. These toppling rocks and tangled boughs
Impenetrable by the noonday beam,
Shall be sole witnesses of what we——

Floro — Draw!
If there were words, here is the place for deeds.

Lelio —
Thou needest not instruct me; well I know
That in the field, the silent tongue of steel
Speaks thus, — *[They fight.*

Cyprian — Ha! what is this? Lelio, — Floro,
Be it enough that Cyprian stands between you,
Altho' unarmed.

Lelio — Whence comest thou, to stand
Between me and my vengeance!

Floro — From what rocks
And desert cells?

Enter MOSCON *and* CLARIN.

Moscon — Run! run! for where we left
My master, I now hear the clash of swords.

Clarin —
I never run to approach things of this sort,
But only to avoid them. Sir! Cyprian! sir!

Cyprian —
    Be silent, fellows! What! two friends who are
    In blood and fame the eyes and hope of Antioch,
    One of the noble race of the Colalti,
    The other son o' the Governor, adventure
    And cast away, on some slight cause no doubt,
    Two lives, the honor of their country?
Lelio —   Cyprian!
    Altho' my high respect towards your person
    Holds now my sword suspended, thou canst not
    Restore it to the slumber of the scabbard:
    Thou knowest more of science than the duel;
    For when two men of honor take the field,
    No counsel nor respect can make them friends
    But one must die in the dispute.
Floro —   I pray
    That you depart hence with your people, and
    Leave us to finish what we have begun
    Without advantage. —
Cyprian —   Tho' you may imagine
    That I know little of the laws of duel,
    Which vanity and valor instituted,
    You are in error. By my birth I am
    Held no less than yourselves to know the limits
    Of honor and of infamy, nor has study
    Quencht the free spirit which first ordered them
    And thus to me, as one well experienced
    In the false quicksands of the sea of honor,
    You may refer the merits of the case;
    And if I should perceive in your relation
    That either has the right to satisfaction
    From the other, I give you my word of honor
    To leave you.
Lelio —   Under this condition then
    I will relate the cause, and you will cede
    And must confess the impossibility
    Of compromise; for the same lady is
    Beloved by Floro and myself.
Floro —   It seems
    Much to me that the light of day should look
    Upon that idol of my heart — but he —
    Leave us to fight, according to thy word.
Cyprian —
    Permit one question further: is the lady
    Impossible to hope or not?

THE MIGHTY MAGICIAN.

Lelio —   She is
So excellent, that if the light of day
Should excite Floro's jealousy, it were
Without just cause, for even the light of day
Trembles to gaze on her.
Cyprian —   Would you for your
Part, marry her?
Floro —   Such is my confidence.
Cyprian —
And you?
Lelio —   Oh! would that I could lift my hope
So high, for tho' she is extremely poor,
Her virtue is her dowry.
Cyprian —   And if you both
Would marry her, is it not weak and vain,
Culpable and unworthy, thus beforehand
To slur her honor? What would the world say
If one should slay the other, and if she
Should afterwards espouse the murderer?

[*The rivals agree to refer their quarrel to* CYPRIAN, *who in consequence visits* JUSTINA *and becomes enamored of her; she disdains him, and he retires to a solitary seashore.*

Scene II.

Cyprian — O memory! permit it not
That the tyrant of my thought
Be another soul that still
Holds dominion o'er the will,
That would refuse, but can no more,
To bend, to tremble, and adore.
Vain idolatry! — I saw,
    And gazing, became blind with error;
Weak ambition, which the awe
    Of her presence bound to terror!
So beautiful she was — and I,
Between my love and jealousy,
Am so convulst with hope and fear,
Unworthy as it may appear; —
So bitter is the life I live,
That, hear me, Hell! I now would give
To thy most detested spirit
My soul, forever to inherit,
To suffer punishment and pine,
So this woman may be mine.
Hear'st thou, Hell! dost thou reject it?
My soul is offered!

Demon [unseen] — I accept it.
[*Tempest, with thunder and lightning.*

Cyprian —
What is this? ye heavens forever pure,
At once intensely radiant and obscure!
Athwart the ethereal halls
The lightning's arrow and the thunder balls
The day affright.
As from the horizon round,
Burst with earthquake sound,
In mighty torrents the electric fountains; —
Clouds quench the sun, and thunder smoke
Strangles the air, and fire eclipses heaven.
Philosophy, thou canst not even
Compel their causes underneath thy yoke;
From yonder clouds even to the waves below
The fragments of a single ruin choke
Imagination's flight;
For, on flakes of surge, like feathers light,
The ashes of the desolation cast
Upon the gloomy blast,
Tell of the footsteps of the storm.
And nearer see the melancholy form
Of a great ship, the outcast of the sea,
Drives miserably!
And it must fly the pity of the port,
Or perish, and its last and sole resort
Is its own raging enemy.
The terror of the thrilling cry
Was a fatal prophecy
Of coming death, who hovers now
Upon that shattered prow,
That they who die not may be dying still.
And not alone the insane elements
Are populous with wild portents,
But that sad ship is as a miracle
Of sudden ruin, for it drives so fast
It seems as if it had arrayed its form
With the headlong storm.
It strikes — I almost feel the shock, —
It stumbles on a jagged rock, —
Sparkles of blood on the white foam are cast.
[*A tempest.*

All exclaim within —
We are all lost.

THE MIGHTY MAGICIAN.

Demon [*within*] —
    Now from this plank will I
Pass to the land and thus fulfill my scheme.
Cyprian —
  As in contempt of the elemental rage
   A man comes forth in safety, while the ship's
   Great form is in a watery eclipse
  Obliterated from the Ocean's page,
  And round its wreck the huge sea monsters sit,
  A horrid conclave, and the whistling wave
  Is heapt over its carcass, like a grave.

  The DEMON *enters, as escaped from the sea.*

Demon [*aside*] —
  It was essential to my purposes
  To wake a tumult on the sapphire ocean,
  That in this unknown form I might at length
  Wipe out the blot of the discomfiture
  Sustained upon the mountain, and assail
  With a new war the soul of Cyprian,
  Forging the instruments of his destruction
  Even from his love and from his wisdom. — Oh!
  Beloved earth, dear mother, in thy bosom
  I seek a refuge from the monster who
  Precipitates itself upon me.
Cyprian —   Friend,
  Collect thyself; and be the memory
  Of thy late suffering, and thy greatest sorrow
  But as a shadow of the past, — for nothing
  Beneath the circle of the moon, but flows
  And changes, and can never know repose.
Demon —
  And who art thou, before whose feet my fate
  Has prostrated me?
Cyprian —   One who, moved with pity,
  Would soothe its stings.
Demon —   Oh, that can never be!
  No solace can my lasting sorrow find.
Cyprian —
  Wherefore?
Demon —   Because my happiness is lost.
  Yet I lament what long has ceast to be
  The object of desire or memory,
  And my life is not life.

Cyprian —   Now, since the fury
    Of this earthquaking hurricane is still,
    And the crystalline heaven has reassumed
    Its windless calm so quickly, that it seems
    As if its heavy wrath had been awakened
    Only to overwhelm that vessel, — speak,
    Who art thou, and whence comest thou?
Demon —   Far more
    My coming hither cost, than thou hast seen
    Or I can tell. Among my misadventures
    This shipwreck is the least. Wilt thou hear?
Cyprian —   Speak.
Demon —
    Since thou desirest, I will then unveil
    Myself to thee; — for in myself I am
    A world of happiness and misery;
    This I have lost, and that I must lament
    Forever. In my attributes I stood
    So high and so heroically great,
    In lineage so supreme, and with a genius
    Which penetrated with a glance the world
    Beneath my feet, that won by my high merit
    A king — whom I may call the king of kings,
    Because all others tremble in their pride
    Before the terrors of his countenance,
    In his high palace rooft with brightest gems
    Of living light — call them the stars of Heaven —
    Named me his counselor. But the high praise
    Stung me with pride and envy, and I rose
    In mighty competition, to ascend
    His seat and place my foot triumphantly
    Upon his subject thrones. Chastised, I know
    The depth to which ambition falls; too mad
    Was the attempt, and yet more mad were now
    Repentance of the irrevocable deed: —
    Therefore I chose this ruin with the glory
    Of not to be subdued, before the shame
    Of reconciling me with him who reigns
    By coward cession. — Nor was I alone,
    Nor am I now, nor shall I be alone;
    And there was hope, and there may still be hope,
    For many suffrages among his vassals
    Hailed me their lord and king, and many still
    Are mine, and many more perchance shall be.
    Thus vanquisht, tho' in fact victorious,

I left his seat of empire, from mine eye
Shooting forth poisonous lightning, while my words
With inauspicious thunderings shook Heaven,
Proclaiming vengeance, public as my wrong,
And imprecating on his prostrate slaves
Rapine, and death, and outrage. Then I sailed
Over the mighty fabric of the world,
A pirate ambusht in its pathless sands,
A lynx croucht watchfully among its caves
And craggy shores; and I have wandered over
The expanse of these wild wildernesses
In this great ship, whose bulk is now dissolved
In the light breathings of the invisible wind,
And which the sea has made a dustless ruin,
Seeking ever a mountain, thro' whose forests
I seek a man whom I must now compel
To keep his word with me. I came arrayed
In tempest, and altho' my power could well
Bridle the forest winds in their career,
For other causes I forbore to soothe
Their fury to Favonian gentleness;
I could and would not; (thus I wake in him   [*Aside.*
A love of magic art). Let not this tempest,
Nor the succeeding calm excite thy wonder;
For by my art the sun would turn as pale
As his weak sister with unwonted fear.
And in my wisdom are the orbs of Heaven
Written as in a record; I have pierced
The flaming circles of their wondrous spheres
And know them as thou knowest every corner
Of this dim spot. Let it not seem to thee
That I boast vainly; wouldst thou that I work
A charm over this waste and savage wood,
This Babylon of crags and aged trees,
Filling its leafy coverts with a horror
Thrilling and strange? I am the friendless guest
Of these wild oaks and pines — and as from thee
I have received the hospitality
Of this rude place, I offer thee the fruit
Of years of toil in recompense; whate'er
Thy wildest dream presented to thy thought
As object of desire, that shall be thine.
     *   *   *   *   *   *
And thenceforth shall so firm an amity
'Twixt thee and me be, that neither fortune,

The monstrous phantom which pursues success,
That careful miser, that free prodigal,
Who ever alternates with changeful hand,
Evil and good, reproach and fame; nor Time,
That lodestar of the ages, to whose beam
The wingèd years speed o'er the intervals
Of their unequal revolutions; nor
Heaven itself, whose beautiful bright stars
Rule and adorn the world, can ever make
The least division between thee and me,
Since now I find a refuge in thy favor.

Scene III: *The* DEMON *tempts* JUSTINA, *who is a Christian.*

Demon —
    Abyss of Hell! I call on thee,
Thou wild misrule of thine own anarchy!
    From thy prison house set free
    The spirits of voluptuous death,
      That with their mighty breath
They may destroy a world of virgin thoughts;
Let her chaste mind with fancies thick as motes
    Be peopled from thy shadowy deep,
    Till her guiltless fantasy
    Full to overflowing be!
    And with sweetest harmony
Let birds, and flowers, and leaves, and all things move
    To love, only to love.
      Let nothing meet her eyes
    But signs of Love's soft victories;
      Let nothing meet her ear
    But sounds of Love's sweet sorrow,
So that from faith no succor she may borrow,
    But, guided by my spirit blind
    And in a magic snare entwined,
    She may now seek Cyprian.
    Begin, while I in silence bind
    My voice, when thy sweet song thou hast began.
A Voice [*within*] —
    What is the glory far above
    All else in human life!
All —   Love! love!
[*While these words are sung the* DEMON *goes out at one door and* JUSTINA *enters at another.*

THE MIGHTY MAGICIAN.

The First Voice —
    There is no form in which the fire
      Of love its traces has imprest not.
    Man lives far more in love's desire
      Than by life's breath, soon possest not.
    If all that lives must love or die,
    All shapes on earth, or sea, or sky,
    With one consent to Heaven cry
    That the glory far above
    All else in life is ——
All —   Love! oh love!
Justina — Thou melancholy thought which art
    So flattering and so sweet, to thee
    When did I give the liberty
      Thus to afflict my heart?
    What is the cause of this new power
      Which doth my fevered being move,
    Momently raging more and more?
    What subtle pain is kindled now
    Which from my heart doth overflow
      Into my senses? ——
All —   Love! oh love!
Justina —
    'Tis that enamored nightingale
      Who gives me the reply;
    He ever tells the same soft tale
      Of passion and of constancy
    To his mate who rapt and fond
    Listening sits a bough beyond.

    Be silent, Nightingale — no more
      Make me think, in hearing thee
    Thus tenderly thy love deplore,
      If a bird can feel his so,
    What a man would feel for me.
      And, voluptuous Vine, O thou
    Who seekest most when least pursuing, —
      To the trunk thou interlacest
      Art the verdure which embracest,
    And the weight which is its ruin, —
    No more with green embraces, Vine,
      Make me think on what thou lovest, —
    For whilst thus thy boughs entwine,
      I fear lest thou shouldst teach me, **sophist,**
    How arms might be entangled too.

Light-enchanted Sunflower, thou
Who gazest ever true and tender
On the sun's revolving splendor!
Follow not his faithless glance
With thy faded countenance,
Nor teach my beating heart to fear,
If leaves can mourn without a tear,
How must eyes weep! O Nightingale,
Cease from thy enamored tale,—
Leafy Vine, unwreathe thy bower,
  Restless Sunflower, cease to move,—
Or tell me all, what poisonous power
  Ye use against me——

All—   Love! love! love!
Justina—
It cannot be!—Whom have I ever loved?
Trophies of my oblivion and disdain,
Floro and Lelio did I not reject?
And Cyprian?
    [*She becomes troubled at the name of Cyprian.*
        Did I not requite him
With such severity, that he has fled
Where none has ever heard of him again?—
Alas! I now begin to fear that this
May be the occasion whence desire grows bold,
As if there were no danger. From the moment
That I pronounced to my own listening heart,
Cyprian is absent, O me miserable!
I know not what I feel! [*More calmly.*] It must be pity
To think that such a man, whom all the world
Admired, should be forgot by all the world,
And I the cause.   [*She again becomes troubled.*
        And yet if it were pity,
Floro and Lelio might have equal share,
For they are both imprisoned for my sake.
[*Calmly.*] Alas! what reasonings are these? it is
Enough I pity him, and that, in vain,
Without this ceremonious subtlety.
And woe is me! I know not where to find him now,
Even should I seek him thro' this wide world.

                Enter DEMON.
Demon—
Follow, and I will lead thee where he is.

THE MIGHTY MAGICIAN.

Justina —
 And who art thou, who hast found entrance hither,
 Into my chamber thro' the doors and locks?
 Art thou a monstrous shadow which my madness
 Has formed in the idle air?
Demon —   No. I am one
 Called by the thought which tyrannizes thee
 From his eternal dwelling; who this day
 Is pledged to bear thee unto Cyprian.
Justina —
 So shall thy promise fail. This agony
 Of passion which afflicts my heart and soul
 May sweep imagination in its storm;
 The will is firm.
Demon —   Already half is done
 In the imagination of an act.
 The sin incurred, the pleasure then remains;
 Let not the will stop halfway on the road.
Justina —
 I will not be discouraged, nor despair,
 Altho' I thought it, and altho' 'tis true
 That thought is but a prelude to the deed: —
 Thought is not in my power, but action is:
 I will not move my foot to follow thee.
Demon —
 But a far mightier wisdom than thine own
 Exerts itself within thee, with such power
 Compelling thee to that which it inclines
 That it shall force thy step; how wilt thou then
 Resist, Justina?
Justina —   By my free will.
Demon —   I
 Must force thy will.
Justina —   It is invincible;
 It were not free if thou hadst power upon it.
     [*He draws but cannot move her.*
Demon —
 Come, where a pleasure waits thee.
Justina —   It were bought
 Too dear.
Demon —
 'Twill soothe thy heart to softest peace.
Justina —
 'Tis dread captivity.
Demon —   'Tis joy, 'tis glory.

Justina —
    'Tis shame, 'tis torment, 'tis despair.
Demon —   But **how**
    Canst thou defend thyself from that or me,
    If my power drags thee onward?
Justina —   My defense
    Consists in God.
    [*He vainly endeavors to force her, and at last releases her.*
Demon —
                     Woman, thou hast subdued me,
    Only by not owning thyself subdued.
    But since thou thus findest defense in God,
    I will assume a feigned form, and thus
    Make thee a victim of my baffled rage.
    For I will mask a spirit in thy form
    Who will betray thy name to infamy,
    And doubly shall I triumph in thy loss,
    First by dishonoring thee, and then by turning
    False pleasure to true ignominy.   [*Exit.*
Justina —   I
    Appeal to Heaven against thee; so that Heaven
    May scatter thy delusions, and the blot
    Upon my fame vanish in idle thought,
    Even as flame dies in the envious air,
    And as the floweret wanes at morning frost,
    And thou shouldst never —   But, alas! to whom
    Do I still speak? — Did not a man but now
    Stand here before me? — No, I am alone,
    And yet I saw him.   Is he gone so quickly?
    Or can the heated mind engender shapes
    From its own fear?   Some terrible and strange
    Peril is near.   Lisander! father! lord!
    Livia! —

                    Enter LISANDER *and* LIVIA.

Lisander —   Oh, my daughter!   What?
Livia —   What?
Justina —   Saw you
    A man go forth from my apartment now? —
    I scarce contain myself!
Lisander —   A man here!
Justina —
    Have you not seen him?
Livia —   No, lady.

Justina —
    I saw him.
Lisander —
              'Tis impossible; the doors
    Which led to this apartment were all lockt.
Livia [*aside*] —
    I dare say it was Moscon whom she saw,
    For he was lockt up in my room.
Lisander —   It must
    Have been some image of thy fantasy.
    Such melancholy as thou feedest is
    Skillful in forming such in the vain air
    Out of the motes and atoms of the day.
Livia —
    My master's in the right.
Justina —   Oh would it were
    Delusion; but I fear some greater ill.
    I feel as if out of my bleeding bosom
    My heart was torn in fragments; ay,
    Some mortal spell is wrought against my frame
    So potent was the charm, that had not God
    Shielded my humble innocence from wrong,
    I should have sought my sorrow and my shame
    With willing steps. — Livia, quick, bring my cloak,
    For I must seek refuge from these extremes
    Even in the temple of the highest God
    Where secretly the faithful worship.
Livia —   Here.
Justina [*putting on her cloak*] —
    In this, as in a shroud of snow, may I
    Quench the consuming fire in which I burn,
    Wasting away!
Lisander —   And I will go with thee.
Livia —
    When once I see them safe out of the house
    I shall breathe freely.
Justina —   So do I confide
    In thy just favor, Heaven!
Lisander —   Let us go.
Justina —
    Thine is the cause, great God! turn for my sake,
    And for thine own, mercifully to me!

THE TIMES OF GUSTAVUS ADOLPHUS.

By ZACHRIS TOPELIUS.

[ZACHRIS TOPELIUS : Swedish poet, novelist, and historian ; born at Kuddnäs, near Nykarleby, Finland, January 14, 1818 ; died March, 1898. Educated at Helsingfors. From 1841 till 1860 editor of the Helsingfors *Tidningar* (Times), in which many of his poems and novels were originally published. From 1854 till 1874 he filled various chairs in the university. His songs and lyrics have been collected in several volumes. His best-known dramas are: "Efter femtio år" (After Fifty Years), 1851, and "Regina von Emmeritz," 1854. His "Faltskärns Berättelser," 1853–1867, have been translated into English under the title "The Surgeon's Stories." His children's tales, "Läsning för Barn," have also been successful in English.]

NUREMBERG AND LÜTZEN.

WALLENSTEIN the Terrible had become reconciled with the emperor, collected a formidable army, and turned like a dark thundercloud toward the wealthy city of Nuremberg. Gustaf Adolf broke off his victorious career in Bavaria, to hurry to meet him; and there, in two strongly fortified encampments, both armies stood motionless, opposite each other, for eleven weeks — the panther and the lion, crouching ready for a spring, and watching sharply each other's slightest movement. The whole region was drained for the subsistence of these armies, and provisions were constantly brought in from a distance by foraging parties. Among the Imperialists, Isolani's Croats distinguished themselves in this work; among the Swedes, Taupadel's dragoons and Stålhandske's Finnish cavalry.

Famine, the heat of summer, disease, and the depredations of the German soldiers spread want and misery everywhere. Gustaf Adolf, who, after joining Oxenstjerna's and Banér's combined armies, had a force of fifty thousand men, marched, on the 24th of August, 1632, against Wallenstein, who, with sixty thousand men, stood behind impregnable fortifications. Long before day, Torstenson's artillery commenced to thunder against Alte Veste. In the darkness of night, five hundred German musketeers of the White Brigade climbed up the steep heights, and, in spite of the terrible shower of balls, mounted the ramparts. For a moment victory seemed to reward their contempt of death; the drowsy foes' bewilderment, the shrieks of the women, and the Swedish balls, which threw

ESCORT OF THE CORPSE OF GUSTAVUS ADOLPHUS
From a painting by Werner Schuch

down tents and people, favored the attack. But Wallenstein maintained sense and composure, sent away the women, and turned mass upon mass against the besiegers. The gallant brigade was driven back with loss. The king did not give way; once more the White Brigade stormed — in vain. Then Gustaf Adolf called his Finns, "in order," as Schiller says, "to put the German cowards to the blush with their northern courage."

These were the East Bothnians, in the ranks of the Swedish brigade. They saw death before their eyes in the shape of a hundred fiery mouths; but resolutely, with unshaken courage, they clambered up the precipice, slippery with rain and blood. But against these solid ramparts, against this murderous shower of balls, all their valor rebounded; in the midst of fire and death, they tried once more to gain a foothold on the rampart, but in vain; the few who had escaped the bullets and pikes were hurled violently back. For the first time, Gustaf Adolf's Finns were seen to retreat; and equally futile were all attempts of succeeding troops. The Imperialists hastened out in pursuit, but were driven back. With great loss of life, the strife waged all day; many of the bravest leaders fell; and the death angel again aimed a bullet at the king, but without harming more than the sole of his boot.

On the left wing, the Imperial cavalry came in collision with the Swedes. Cronenberg, with his cuirassiers, clad in mail from head to foot, and widely celebrated as the "Invincibles," bore the Hessians to the ground. The Landgrave of Hesse remarked, resentfully, that the king wished to spare his own troops at the expense of the Germans. "Well, then," said Gustaf Adolf, "I will send my Finns; and I hope that the change of men will give a change of luck." Stålhandske, with the Finns, were now sent against Cronenberg and the "Invincibles." Between these superb troops ensued a proud, a glorious struggle, of imperishable memory. On the shore of the Regnitz River, thickly overgrown with bushes, the two detachments encountered each other, man to man, horse to horse; sword blades were dulled against helmets, long pistols flashed, and many valiant horsemen were driven down in the whirl of the river. It is probable that the Finnish horses here also held out better than the beautiful and swift Hungarian chargers; and this contributed to the victory. The brave Cronenberg fell; his "Invincibles" fled before the Finns. In his place,

Fugger, with a formidable force, charged the Finns, and drove them, under constant fighting, with breast toward the enemy, slowly to the underbrush. But here the Imperialists were met by the fire of the Swedish infantry. Fugger fell, and his cavalry were again repulsed by the fatigued Finns.

At nightfall, more than three thousand dead covered the heights and plain. "In the battle of Alte Veste," says Schiller, "Gustaf Adolf was considered conquered because he did not himself conquer." The next day he withdrew to Bavaria. Forty-four thousand persons — friends and enemies — had pest and war swallowed up during these fatal weeks in and around Nuremberg.

The darkness of autumn increased; its fogs covered Germany's blood-stained soil; and yet there seemed to be no end to the struggle. But a great spirit was destined here, after many storms, to find a peaceful haven, and to go from life's autumnal evening to the eternal light. Nearer and nearer hovered the death angel over Gustaf Adolf's noble head, shedding upon it the halo of a higher world, which is often seen to beam around the noble of earth in their last moments. The multitude about them misunderstand it, but the departing ones divine the meaning. Two days before his death, the people of Naumburg paid homage to Gustaf Adolf as to a god; but through his soul flew a presentiment of the end of his career, and he said to the court minister, Fabricius: —

"Perhaps God will soon punish both their idolatrous folly, and me, who am the object of it, and show that I also am a weak and mortal person."

The king had gone up to Saxony, to follow in the track of the ravaging Wallenstein. At Arnstadt he took farewell of Axel Oxenstjerna; at Erfurt, of Queen Maria Eleonora. There and at Nuremberg it was perceived, from many of his arrangements, that he was prepared for what was coming. Wallenstein, who believed that the king had gone into winter quarters, sent Pappenheim, with twelve thousand men, to Halle; he remained at Lützen, with twenty-eight thousand men, and the king in Naumburg with twenty thousand.

But on the 4th of November, when Gustaf Adolf learned of Pappenheim's departure, he hastily broke camp to surprise his weakened enemy, and would have succeeded had he come to the attack on the 5th. But Providence threw in his triumphant path a slight obstacle — the little stream Rippach, which, together with freshly plowed fields, hindered his progress. Not until late on the afternoon of the 5th did the king approach Lützen. Wallenstein had gained time, and knew how to use it. Along the highroad to Leipzig he had had ditches dug and breastworks thrown up on both sides of the way, and filled them with his best sharpshooters, intending to destroy with their cross fire the advancing Swedes. The king's council of war dissuaded from the attack. Only Duke Bernhard advised it, and the king was of the same opinion: "For," said he, "it is best to wash one's self thoroughly clean when one is once in the bath."

The night was dark and dreary. The king spent it in an old carriage, together with Kniephausen and Duke Bernhard. His restless soul had time to think of everything; and then, says the tradition, he drew from his right forefinger a little ring of copper, and handed it to Duke Bernhard, with instruction that, if anything should happen to him, he should deliver it to a young officer of the Finnish cavalry.

Early in the morning, Gustaf Adolf rode out to inspect the order of battle. He was clad in a jacket of elk skin, with a gray cloak. When exhorted to wear armor on such a day, he answered: —

"God is my armor."

A thick mist delayed the attack. At dawn the whole army joined in singing, "A mighty fortress is our God;" and as the fog continued, the king began, with his own voice, "God, be to us gracious and kind," as well as, "Be not dismayed, thou little flock," which latter he had shortly before composed. Then he rode along the ranks, crying: —

"To-day, boys, we will put an end to all our troubles;" and his horse stumbled twice.

It was eleven o'clock in the forenoon before the mist was dispelled by a slight gust of wind. The Swedish army immediately advanced to the assault. On the right wing, which was commanded by the king, again stood Stålhandske with the Finns, and behind them the Swedish troops; in the center, the Swedish Yellow and Green Brigades, under Nils Brahe; on the left wing, the German cavalry, under Duke Bernhard. Opposite the duke stood Colloredo, with the flower of the cavalry; in the center, Wallenstein himself, with close masses of infantry in four large tertiers, and seven cannon in their front; opposite Stålhandske stood Isolani, with his ferocious but brave Croats. The battle cry was on both sides the same as at Breitenfeld. When the king gave the order to attack, he clasped his hands and exclaimed : —

"Jesu, Jesu, help me to fight to-day for the glory of Thy holy name!"

Lützen was now set on fire by the Imperialists; the artillery began to thunder, and the Swedish army advanced, but suffered great losses at the very outset. At last the Swedish center crossed the trenches, took the seven cannon, and routed the enemy's first two brigades. The third had already turned to flee, when Wallenstein succeeded in rallying them; the Swedes were taken in the flank by the cavalry, and the Finns, who had put the Croats and Polanders to flight, had not yet crossed the trenches. Then the king rushed forward at the head of the Smålanders, only a few of whom had sufficiently good horses to follow him. It is said that an Imperial musketeer aimed at the king with a silver bullet; the certainty is that his left arm was crushed, and that he endeavored to conceal his wound, but soon, weakened by the loss of blood, begged the Duke of Lauenburg, who rode at his side, to lead him, unobserved, from the strife. But in the midst of the tumult, Götz's cuirassiers came up, led by Moritz von Falkenberg, who recognized the king, and shot him through the body, with the exclamation : —

"Thee have I long sought!" and directly afterwards Falkenberg himself fell, struck by a ball.

Now the king has reeled in his saddle, and entreated the duke to save his own life; the duke has seized him around the waist to support him, but at that instant a whole swarm of enemies have rushed upon them and separated them. A pistol shot has singed the duke's hair; the king's horse has been shot through the neck, and has reared; Gustaf Adolf has sunk from the saddle, has been dragged a little way by the stirrups, and then left on the ground. The young page, Leubelfingen, from Nuremberg, has offered him his horse, but has not been able to lift up the fallen man. Some Imperial cavalrymen have come to the spot, and asked who the wounded person was; and when Leubelfingen has not been willing to answer, one of them has run a sword through his body, another has shot the king through the head; after this, others have discharged several shots at them, and the two have been left under a pile of corpses. But Leubelfingen lived a few days after, to relate to after times the sad and never-to-be-forgotten story of Gustaf Adolf's heroic death.

In the mean time, the Swedish center had been compelled to retire, a thousand mutilated corpses covered the battlefield, and yet not a foot of soil had been gained. Both armies occupied nearly the same position as at the beginning of the battle.

Then the king's wounded horse, with the empty saddle covered with blood, galloped in among the ranks. "The king has fallen!" And, as Schiller beautifully says, "Life fell in value when the most sacred of all lives was no more; death had no longer any terror for the humblest, since it had not spared the crowned head."

Duke Bernhard galloped from rank to rank:—

"Ye Swedes, Finns, and Germans," said he, "liberty's defender, your defender, and ours, has fallen! Every man who holds the king dear will hasten forward to avenge his death!"

The first to respond to this appeal was Stålhandske and the Finns. With incredible exertion they leaped the trenches, and drove before them swarms of scattered enemies; all fell before their blows. Isolani, put to flight, wheeled round and attacked the Swedish wagon trains, but was again repulsed. With like fury, Brahe, with the center, pressed across the trenches; while Duke Bernhard, without heeding the ball which had crushed his arm, took one of the enemy's batteries. The whole Imperial army faltered, staggered, and broke before this fearful assault; their powder carts were blown into the air. Wallenstein's word of command and Piccolomini's brilliant valor were no longer able to stay the reckless flight.

But at that instant there resounded far over the plain the jubilant cry, "Pappenheim is here!" And Pappenheim, the bravest of the brave, was there with his cavalry, and his first question was:—

"Where is the King of Sweden?"

They pointed to Stålhandske's lines, and he started there. The hottest, the most infuriate contest now took place. The Imperialists, regaining courage, turned back and attacked from three sides at once. No one yielded ground. Brahe, and with him the Yellow Brigade, fell almost to the last man. Winckel, with the Blue, fell in like beautiful order, man by man, just as they stood in the ranks. The rest of the Swedish foot soldiers drew slowly back, and victory seemed to smile upon the all-powerful Pappenheim.

But he, the Ajax of his time, the man with a hundred scars, was not destined to see the day of triumph. Already, in the first attack against the Finns, a falconet ball had struck his hip; two musket balls had pierced his scarred breast; it is said that Stålhandske's own hand had reached him. He fell, even in his last moments rejoicing over Gustaf Adolf's death; and the news of his fall spread terror through the Imperial ranks. "Pappenheim is dead; all is lost!" Once more the Swedes advanced. Duke Bernhard, Kniephausen, Stålhandske, performed miracles; but Piccolomini also, who, with six wounds, mounted his seventh horse, fought with more than mortal courage. The Imperial center stood firm, and only darkness suspended the conflict. Wallenstein withdrew, and the exhausted Swedish army encamped on the battlefield. Nine thousand dead covered the plain of Lützen.

The results of this battle were severely felt by the Imperialists. They had lost all their artillery — Pappenheim's and Wallenstein's reputation for invincibility. The great Friedlander raged with fury; his hard hand dispensed the gallows to the cowardly as liberally as ducats to the brave. Sick and gloomy, he retired with the remainder of his army, about ten thousand men, back to Bohemia, where the stars became his nightly companions, treasonable plans his daily relaxation, and death, by Butler's hand, the end of his brilliant career.

But over the whole Catholic world went a great jubilee of victory, for Lutherism and the Swedes had lost infinitely more than their foes. Paralyzed was the arm that had so powerfully wielded the victorious sword of light and liberty. The grief of the Protestants was general and deep, mingled with fear for the future. Not without ground was the *Te Deum* sung in the cathedrals of Vienna, Brussels, and Madrid; twelve days' brilliant bullfights celebrated in Madrid the fall of the dreaded hero; but Emperor Ferdinand, greater than his contemporaries, is said to have shed tears at the sight of his slain enemy's bloody jacket.

Many stories were circulated about the great Gustaf Adolf's death; now it was the Duke Franz Albert of Lauenburg, now Richelieu, now Duke Bernhard, whom popular belief accused of participation in the king's fall; but none of these suspicions have been confirmed by the impartial historian. A recent German author communicates the following popular version: "Gustaf Adolf, King of Sweden, received, while he was yet very young, from a lady whom he much loved, a ring of iron, which he never afterwards allowed to be taken from his hand. The ring consisted of seven circles, which formed the letters of both his names. Seven days before his death, this ring was taken from him without his being aware, at the time, of the singular theft."

The reader knows that our story joins its thread to the same ring; but several reasons entitle us to the supposition that the ring was of copper.

The evening after the battle, Duke Bernhard sent his soldiers with lighted torches to look for the king's dead body; and they found it, plundered, disfigured, under a heap of corpses. Brought to the village of Meuchen, it was there embalmed, and the soldiers received permission to behold the remains of their king and hero. Bitter tears were there shed, but tears full of pride; for even the most humble considered himself great through the honor of having fought by the side of so heroic a king.

"See," said a veteran of Stålhandske's Finns, sobbing aloud, "they have robbed him of his gold chain and his copper ring. I still see the white mark left by the ring on his right forefinger."

"What would they care for a ring of copper?" asked a Scot, who had just come to the army, and knew nothing of the story which circulated among the people.

"His ring!" exclaimed a Pomeranian, mysteriously. "You may rely upon it that the Jesuits knew what it was good for. The ring was enchanted by a Finnish witch, and, as long as the king wore it, neither iron nor lead had any effect upon him."

"But, you see, to-day he lost it," joined in a third; "and therefore . . . do you comprehend?"

"What is that the Pomeranian pear eater says?" burst out the Finn, bitterly. "God's power, and no other, has protected our great king; but the ring was given him, a long while ago, by a Finnish girl whom he held very dear in his youth. I know something more about it than you, apple muncher!"

Duke Bernhard, who, somber and thoughtful, contemplated the king's pale features, looked around at these words, put his unhurt hand within his unbuttoned jacket, and turned to the Finn, saying: —

"Comrade, do you know one of Stålhandske's officers named Bertel?"

"Yes, certainly, your highness."

"Is he alive?"

"No, your highness."

The duke turned abstractedly to another, and gave orders right and left. In a few moments he again seemed, at the sight of the king, to be reminded of something.

"Was he a brave man?" asked he.

"He was one of Stålhandske's cavalry!" said the Finn, with emphasis, and with a pride which did not ill become him.

"When did he fall, and where?"

"In the last skirmish with the Pappenheimers."

"Search for him!"

The duke's command was executed without grumbling by these overwearied soldiers, who, with good reason, wondered why it was that one of the youngest officers should be searched for that very night, when Nils Brahe, Winckel, and so many other gray-haired generals were still lying in their blood on the battlefield. Not until early morning did those sent out return with the intelligence that Bertel's dead body was nowhere to be found.

"Hum!" said the duke, displeased; "great men have sometimes their little whims; what shall I now do with the king's ring?"

And the November sun rose blood-red over the field of Lützen. A new epoch dawned; the master was gone, and the pupils had now to see how they could carry out his work.

After Lützen.

It was a glorious but terrible sight when the Pappenheimers made their charge upon the Finns on the east side of the river Rippach. Mail-clad, irresistible, the cuirassiers descended upon Stålhandske, whose Finnish troopers reeled under this crushing attack: their horses, weary from the long conflict, recoiled, fell backwards, and for a time gave way. But Stålhandske rallied them again, man against man, horse against horse; they fought with their last strength, indifferent to death; and friends and enemies were mixed together in bloody confusion. Here fell Pappenheim; here fell his bravest men; half of

Stålhandske's cavalry were trampled under the horses' hoofs, and yet the strife raged without interruption until twilight.

At Stålhandske's side rode Bertel; and so it happened that he met Pappenheim. The youth of twenty was not able to cope with this arm of steel; a blow of the brave general's long sword struck Bertel across the helmet with such crushing force that his eyes were blinded and he became insensible. But in falling he unconsciously grasped his faithful horse, Lappen, by the mane, and Lappen, confused by the tumult, galloped away; while his master, with one foot in the stirrup and his hands convulsively twisted in the mane, was dragged with him.

When Bertel opened his eyes, he was in dense darkness. He remembered vaguely the adventures of the hot struggle; the last thing he there saw was Pappenheim's lifted sword. The thought entered his mind that he was now dead and lying in his grave. He put his hand to his heart, it beat; he bit his finger, it pained him. He realized that he was still living, but how and where it was impossible to guess. He stretched out his hand and picked up some straw. Under him he felt the damp ground, above him the empty air. He tried to raise himself up, but his head was as heavy as lead. It still felt the weight of Pappenheim's sword.

Then he heard not far from him a voice, which, half complaining, half mocking, uttered the following words in Swedish: —

"Ghosts and grenades! Not a drop of wine! Those scoundrelly Wallachians have stolen my flask; the miserable hen thieves! Holloa, Turk or Jew — it is all the same — bring here a drop of wine!"

"Is that you, Larsson?" said Bertel, in a faint voice; for his tongue was half paralyzed by a burning thirst.

"What sort of a marmot is it that whispers my name?" responded his neighbor, in the darkness. "Hurrah, boys! loose reins and a brisk gallop! When you have emptied your pistols, fling them to the devil, and slash away with swords! Cleave their skulls, the brutes; peel them like turnips. Beat them, grind them to powder! The king has fallen. . . . Devils and heroes, what a king! . . . To-day we shall bleed; to-day we shall die, but first we must be revenged. That's the way, boys! Hurrah! . . . Pitch in, East Bothnians!"

"Larsson," repeated Bertel; but his comrade did not hear

him. He continued in his delirium to lead his Finnish boys in the conflict.

After a while a streak of the late autumn morning dawned in through the window of the miserable hut where Bertel lay. He could now distinguish the straw which was strewn over the bare ground; and on the straw he saw two men asleep.

The door opened; a couple of wild bearded men entered, and pushed the slumberers rudely with the butts of their guns.

"*Raus!*" cried they, in Low Dutch; "reveille has sounded!"

And outside the hut was heard the well-known trumpet blast, which at that time was the usual signal to break camp.

"They may spear me like a frog," muttered one of the men, sulkily, "if I know what our reverend father intends to do with these unbelieving dogs. He might as well give them a passport to the archfiend, their lord and master."

"Blockhead!" retorted the other; "do you not know that the heretic king's death is to be celebrated with great pomp and state at Ingolstadt? The reverend father intends to hold a grand *auto-da-fé* in honor of the solemn occasion."

The two sleepers rose, half awake; and Bertel recognized, by the faint morning light, the little thick-set Larsson, of the East Bothnians, and his own faithful Pekka. But there was no time for explanations. All three were led out, bound, and packed into a cart; after which the train, consisting of a long line of wounded men and baggage wagons, under guard of the Croats, set itself slowly in motion.

Bertel now realized that he and his countrymen were prisoners of the Imperialists. His memory soon cleared, and he learned from his companions in misfortune how it had all happened. When the faithful Lappen felt the reins loose, he galloped with his unconscious rider back to the camp. But a swarm of the rapacious Croats were here, committing their depredations, and when they saw a Swedish officer dragged half dead after the horse, they took him with them in the hope of a good ransom. Pekka, who would not desert his master, was taken prisoner at the same time. Larsson, for his part, had, at the Pappenheimers' attack, ventured too far among the enemy, received a pike thrust in the shoulder and a wound in the arm, and being unable to cut his way through, had been borne along by the stream. Who had conquered, Larsson did not know with certainty.

It was now the third day after the battle; they had marched in a southerly direction a day and a night without stopping, and then rested a few hours in a deserted and plundered village.

"Cursed pack!" exclaimed the little captain, whose jovial disposition did not abandon him even in the jolting peasant cart; "if only they hadn't stolen my flask, so that we might have drunk Finland's health together! But these Croats are a thieving set, compared to which our gypsies at home are innocent angels. I wish I had a couple of hundred of them to hang on the ramparts of Korsholm, as they hang petticoats on the walls of a Finnish garret."

In the mean time the march continued, with brief halts, for three or four days, not without great suffering and discomfort for the wounded, who, badly bandaged, were hindered by their fetters from assisting each other. In the beginning they traveled through a plundered region, where with difficulty they obtained the slightest refreshment, and where the population everywhere took to flight before the dreaded Croats. But they soon came to richer sections, where the Catholic inhabitants showed themselves only to curse the heretics and exult over their king's fall. The whole Catholic world shared this rejoicing. It is stated that in Madrid brilliant spectacles were performed, in which Gustaf Adolf, another dragon, was conquered by Wallenstein, another St. George.

After seven days' tiresome journey, the cart with the captive Finns drove, late one evening, over a clattering drawbridge, and stopped in a narrow castle yard. The prisoners, still disabled from their wounds, were led out and taken up two crumbling flights of stairs into a turret room in the form of a half-circle. It seemed to Bertel as if he had seen this place before; but darkness and fatigue did not allow him clearly to distinguish objects. The stars shone in through the grated windows. The prisoners were refreshed with a cup of wine, and Larsson exclaimed joyously:—

"I wager that the thieves have stolen their wine from our cellars, while we lay in Würtzburg; for better stuff I never drank!"

"Würtzburg!" exclaimed Bertel, thoughtfully. "Regina!" added he, almost unconsciously.

"And the wine cellar!" sighed Larsson, mimicking him. "I will tell you something, my dear boy:—

"The biggest fool in the world
Is he who believes a girl;
When love, the heart thief, comes to harry,
Espouse the girl, but the wine cup marry.

As far as Regina is concerned, the black-eyed maiden sits and knits stockings at Korsholm. Yes, yes, Lady Märtha is not one of those who sigh in the moonlight. Since we last met I have had news from Wasa through that jolly sergeant, Bengt Kristerson. He had fought with your father, he said. There is no nonsense about the old man; he carried Bengt out at arms' length, and threw him down the steps there at your home in Storkyro. Bengt swore he would stuff the old man and twelve of his men into the windmill, and grind them to groats; but Meri begged them off. Brave fellow, Bengt Kristerson!— fights like a dragon and lies like a skipper. Your health!"

"What else did you hear from East Bothnia?" asked Bertel, who, with a youth's bashfulness, colored at the thought of revealing to the prosaic friend his life's secret, his love for the dark-eyed, beautiful, and unhappy Regina von Emmeritz.

"Not much news, except scant harvests, heavy war taxes, and conscriptions. The old men on the farm, your father and mine, squabble as usual, and make up again. Meri pines for you, and sings sorrowful songs. Do you remember Katri?— splendid girl; round as a turnip, red as mountain-ash berries, and soft about the chin as a lump of butter. Your health, my boy!— she has run away with a soldier!"

"Nothing else?" said Bertel, abstractedly.

"Nothing else! What the d——l do you want to know, when you don't care for the most buxom girl in all Storkyro? '*Ja, noch etwas,*' says the German. There has been a great fray at Korsholm. The recruits got it into their heads that Lady Regina had tried to kill the king with witchcraft, so they stormed Korsholm, and burned the girl alive. Cursedly jolly! —here's to the heretics! We also know how to get up *autos-da-fé*."

Bertel started up, forgetting his wounds; but pain overpowered him. Without a sound, he sank fainting in Larsson's arms.

The honest captain became both angry and troubled. While

he bathed Bertel's temples with the wine left in the tankard, and finally brought him to life again, he gave vent to his feelings in the following words—crescendo from piano to forte, from minor to major:—

"There, there, Bertel . . . what ails you? Does the devil ride you, boy? Are you in love with the girl? Well, well, calm yourself. Faint like a lady's maid? Courage!—did I say they had burned her? No, my boy, she was only roasted a little, according to what Bengt Kristerson says, and afterward she scratched both eyes out of Lady Märtha and climbed like a squirrel up on top of the castle. Such things happen every day in war. . . . Well, you have got your eyes open at last. So you are still alive, you milk-baked wheat cake! Are you not ashamed, boy, to be like a piece of china? You a soldier? A pretty soldier you are! *Blitzdonnerwetterkreutspappenheim!* you are a pomade pot, and no soldier! Curse it! now the tankard is empty!"

The little round warrior would undoubtedly have continued to give free reins to his bad humor, especially as he had no longer any consolation in the tankard, had not the door opened and a female form stepped in among the prisoners. At this sight, the captain's puffy although now somewhat pale face brightened perceptibly. Bertel was pushed aside, and Larsson leaned forward, so as to see better; for the light of the single lamp was quite dim. But the result of his survey did not seem especially satisfactory.

"A nun! Ah, by Heaven . . . to convert us!"

"Peace be with you," sounded a youthful voice, of fresh and agreeable tone, from under the veil. "I am sent here by the reverend prioress of the convent of Our Lady, to bind your wounds and, if it is the will of the saints, to heal them."

"Upon my honor, beautiful friend, I am very much obliged; let us then become a little better acquainted," replied the captain, somewhat more mildly disposed, and stretched out his hand with the intention of raising the nun's veil. Instantly the latter drew back a few steps; and just then two soldiers, of forbidding aspect, appeared at the door.

"Ah, I understand!" exclaimed Larsson, startled. "The devil! what proud nuns they have here! When I was in Franconia, at Würtzburg, I used to get at least half a dozen kisses a day from the young sisters in the convent; for such sins are never refused absolution. Well," continued the brave captain, when the nun still lingered, hesitating, at the door, "your reverence must not take offense at a soldier's freedom of speech. *Nunquam nemo nasitur caballerus*, says the Spaniard; an honest soldier is born a gallant. Your reverence sees that I, although an unbelieving heretic, can talk Latin like a true monk. When we were at Munich I lived in intimate friendship with a genuine Bavarian nun, twenty-seven years old, brown eyes, Roman nose . . ."

"Hold your tongue!" whispered Bertel, impatiently. "You will drive the nun away."

"I haven't said a word. Walk in, your reverence; don't be frightened. I wager it is a good while since your reverence was twenty-seven. *Posito*, as the Frenchman says, that your reverence is an old granny."

The nun returned in silence, accompanied by two sisters in waiting, and began to examine the wound on Bertel's head, which had been badly dressed. A delicate white hand drew out a pair of scissors and cut off the youth's hair at each side of the broad mark left by Pappenheim's sword. Within twenty minutes Bertel's wounds were dressed by a skillful hand. The youth, touched by this compassion, raised the nun's hand to his lips and kissed it.

"Upon my honor, beautiful matron," cried the voluble captain, "I feel half inclined to be jealous of my friend, who is fifteen years younger than I. Now deign to stretch out your gentle hand and plaster this brave arm, which has conquered the piety of so many pious sisters."

The nun, still without speaking, began to undo the ragged scarf which covered Larsson's wounds. Her hand, in doing this, happened to touch his.

"*Potz donnerwetter!*" burst out the captain, with a connoisseur's surprise. "What a fine, soft little hand! I beg your pardon, amiable lady doctor; *ex ungua leonem*, says Saint Homer, one of the fathers of the church . . . for I also have studied the fathers of the church . . . that is to say, in good Swedish, by the paw one knows the lion. I wager ten bottles of old Rhine wine against a cast-off stirrup, that this little white hand is much better fitted to caress a cavalier's cheek than to finger rosaries night and day."

The nun drew her hand away for an instant, and seemed to hesitate. The gallant captain began to fear the consequences of his gallantry. "I will say nothing more; I am as silent as a Carthusian monk. But I do say that one who dares to presume that such a soft hand belongs to an old granny ... well, well, your lovely reverence hears that I am silent."

"*Tempus est consummatum, itur in missam,*" said a sepulchral voice at the door, and the nun hastened to finish dressing the wound. In a few moments the two prisoners were again alone.

"I have heard that voice before," remarked Bertel, thoughtfully. "Are we then surrounded by nothing but mysteries?"

"Bah!" replied the captain, "it was a bald-headed, jealous monk. Bless me, what a sweet little hand!"

Two Old Acquaintances.

The following morning, as the late autumn sun sent its first rays into the turret room, Bertel arose and went to take a look out of the narrow grated window. It was a glorious prospect. Below him wound a magnificent stream, on whose further shore lay a town with thirty spires, and beyond were seen a number of still verdant vineyards.

At the first glance, Bertel recognized Würtzburg. Castle Marienburg, where the prisoners were confined, had, at the Swedes' retreat, fallen again into the bishop's hands; but on account of the insecurity of the times, his princely grace had not returned there himself, but remained most of the time in Vienna. The castle had suffered much from the last conquest and the attendant plundering; one tower had been destroyed, and the moat was filled up in several places. At present there were only fifty men in the garrison, but there were sick and wounded, nursed by the sisters of charity from the convent in the town. When Bertel inspected his prison more closely, he thought he recognized Regina's chamber, the same one where the beautiful lady with her maid contemplated the strife, and where the Swedish cannon ball shattered the image of the saint in the window. This discovery seemed beyond value to the romantic youth. Here had she stood, the wondrously beautiful unhappy daughter of the prince; here had she slumbered the last night before the assault. It was in Bertel's eyes a sacred place; when he pressed his lips to the cold walls, he fancied that he kissed the traces of Regina's tears.

Like a flash, a strange thought ran through his mind. If

the nun who visited them yesterday could have been a disguised princess! . . . if the delicate white hand belonged to — Regina! That would be a miracle, but . . . love believes in miracles. Bertel's heart beat violently. The gentle nurse's care had already greatly improved his neglected wounds. He felt twice as strong already.

His companions in misfortune, tired from the journey, were still asleep. Then the door opened softly, and with noiseless step the nun entered, to bring the wounded men a healing draught. Bertel felt his head swim. Overcome by his violent emotion, he fell on his knees before her.

"Your name, you angel of mercy, who remember the imprisoned!" exclaimed he. "Tell me your name, reveal your face! . . . Ah, I should recognize you among a thousand. . . . You are Regina herself!"

"You are mistaken," said the same fresh voice which Bertel had heard yesterday. It was not Regina's voice, and yet it was a very familiar one; but whose?

Bertel sprang up, and snatched the veil from the nun's head. Before him stood the pretty and gentle Kätchen, with a smiling face. Bertel stepped back, bewildered.

"Impudent one!" said Kätchen, and hastily covered her face. "I had desired to have you under my charge, and you force me to leave my place to another."

Kätchen disappeared. That same day, in the afternoon, a nun again entered the room. Larsson delivered an eloquent harangue, raised her hand to his lips, and pressed upon it a resounding kiss. Then he swore by a million devils; he had kissed an old withered hand, whose surface was like hundred-year-old parchment.

"Verily, my dear Bertel," said the deceived captain, with philosophic resignation, "there are things in nature which must eternally remain an enigma to human sagacity. This hand, for example . . . *manus, mana, manum,* hand, as the old Roman so truly expressed himself . . . this hand, my friend, would undoubtedly occupy a conspicuous place in the Greek poet Ovid's 'Metamorphoses,' which we formerly studied in the cathedral school at Åbo, the time my father wanted to make me a priest. Yesterday I could have pledged my soul that it was a delicate lady's hand; and to-day I will let them shave me into a monk if this hand does not belong to a seventy-year-old washerwoman. *Sic unde ubi apud unquam post,* as they expressed themselves in olden times. That is to say: so can a pretty girl become a witch before any one knows it."

The prisoners' wounds healed rapidly under the careful nursing of the nuns. The dark autumn storm roared around the castle turrets, and the heavy rains beat against the small windows. The vineyards withered; a thick and chilling mist arose from the Main, and obscured the view of the town.

"I can't stand it any longer," grumbled Larsson. "These wretches give us neither wine nor dice. And may Saint Brita forgive me, but the devil may kiss their nuns; I will neither kiss hand nor mouth, for *habeo multum respectum pro matronibus*, — I have much respect for old women. No, I can't stand it, I will jump out of the window. . . ."

"Do it," said Bertel, provoked.

"No, I will not jump out of the window," rejoined the captain. "No, my friend, *micus ameus*, as we used to express ourselves. . . . I shall instead honor this fellow-prisoner of ours with a game of pitch and toss."

And the captain, fertile in resources, was pleased to honor Pekka for the thirtieth time with the monotonous game which constituted his diversion, and which was played with a six-öre piece of Charles X.

"Tell me, rather," resumed Bertel, "what they are building there on the square in Würtzburg opposite us?"

"A tavern," answered Larsson. "Heads!"

"It seems to me to look more like a pyre."

"Tails!" repeated Larsson, mechanically. "Plague on it, what ill luck I have! That cursed Limingo peasant wins from me horse, saddle, and stirrups."

"The first morning of our imprisonment," continued Bertel, "I heard them say something about an *auto-da-fé*, in celebration of the battle of Lützen. What do you think of it?"

"I? What should I have against burning a dozen witches, much to our amusement?"

"But if it now concern us? If they were only waiting for the bishop's arrival?"

Larsson opened his small gray eyes, and stroked his goatee. "*Blitzdonnerkreutz!* . . . the miserable Jesuits! They would roast us like turkeys — us, the conquerors of the holy Roman empire! . . . It seems to me, friend Bertel, that in such desperate circumstances, *in rebus desperatus*, an honest soldier could not be blamed if he should quietly steal away — for example, through the window. . . ."

"It is seventy feet above the Main, and the flood is straight beneath."

"The door?" . . . continued the captain, inquiringly.

"It is guarded night and day by two armed men."

The honest captain sank into melancholy reflections. Time passed; it became afternoon; it became night. The nun with the evening repast was not heard from.

"Festivities begin with fasting," muttered the captain, gruffly. "May I turn into a fish if I don't wring the neck of our neglectful nun the first time she shows herself."

At that instant the door opened and the nun entered, but this time without attendants. Larsson exchanged an expressive glance with his comrades, approached the nun hastily, seized her by the neck, and held her fast against the wall.

"Keep still, like a good child, most reverend abbess," mocked the captain. "If you make a sound, it is all over with you. I ought really to throw you out of the window to swim in the Main, so as to teach you *punctum preciosum*, that is to say, a precise punctuality in your attendance upon us. But I will let grace prevail instead of justice. Tell me only, you most miserable of all meal bringers, *miserabile pecorale*, what is the meaning of that fire they are preparing on the square, and who is going to be roasted there?"

"For the sake of all the saints, speak low!" whispered the nun, in a scarcely audible voice. "I am Kätchen, and have come to save you. A great danger threatens you. The prince bishop is expected to-morrow, and Father Hieronymus, the implacable enemy of you and all other Finns, has sworn to burn you alive in honor of the saints."

"The little, delicate, soft hand!" exclaimed Larsson, in delight. "Upon my honor, if I was not a booby not to recognize it immediately. Well, then, my charming friend, to Saint Brita's honor I will take a kiss on the spot. . . ."

And the captain kept his word. But Kätchen tore herself from him, and said rapidly: —

"If you do not behave yourself, young man, you will furnish fuel to the flame, that is certain. Quick, bind me fast to the bedpost and tie a handkerchief over my mouth."

"Bind you fast . . ." replied the captain, roguishly.

"Quick! The guards have had wine and are asleep, but in

twenty minutes they will be visited by the father himself. Take their cloaks and hasten out. The watchword is 'Peter and Paul.'"

"And you, yourself?" demurred the captain.

"They will find me bound; I have been overpowered and gagged."

"Noble girl! Crown among all Franconia's sisters of charity! Had I not sworn never to marry . . . Well, hurry up, Bertel! Hurry, Pekka, you lazy dog! Farewell, little rogue! One more kiss . . . good-by!"

And the three prisoners hastened out.

But scarcely were they outside the door, on the dark spiral staircase, before they felt themselves seized by iron hands, thrown down and bound.

"Take the dogs down to the treasure room!" said a well-known voice.

It was the voice of the Jesuit Hieronymus.

The Treasure Room.

Overpowered and bound hand and foot, the prisoners soon found themselves in the dark, damp dungeon, hewn deep in the rock, where the bishop of Würtzburg had kept his treasure before the Swedes saved him the trouble. No ray of light penetrated into this musty vault, and the moisture from the rocks trickled through the crevices and dripped monotonously on the ground.

"Lightning and Croats! may all demons take you, cursed earless monk!" yelled the captain, when he again felt the firm ground under his feet. "To shut us up, the officers of his royal majesty and the crown, in such a rat trap! *Diabolus infernalis multum plus plurimum!* . . . Are you alive, Bertel?"

"Yes. In order to be burned alive to-morrow."

"Do you think so, Bertel?" asked the captain, almost sadly.

"I know this treasure room. On three sides is the rock, on the fourth a door of iron, and the man who guards us is harder than rock and iron. Never shall we see Finland again. Never shall I see *her* more. . . ."

"Listen to me, Bertel; you are a sensible fellow, but that does not hinder you from sometimes talking like a milksop. You are in love with the black-haired Regina; well, well, I will say nothing about that; *Amor est valde lurifaxius,* — love is a bandit, — as Ovid so truly expresses himself. But I cannot stand whimpering. If we live, there are enough other girls to kiss; if we die, then we will say good riddance to them. So you really think that they intend to roast us like plucked woodcocks?"

"That depends upon yourselves!" answered a voice from the darkness. All three prisoners started with affright.

"The evil one is amongst us!" exclaimed Larsson.

Pekka began to say his prayers. Then the clear rays of a dark lantern pierced the gloom, and all perceived the Jesuit Hieronymus standing alone near the captives.

"It depends upon you," repeated he. "To fly is impossible. Your king is dead, your army is beaten, the whole world acknowledges the power of the church and the emperor. The pile is ready for your bodies to be burned in honor of the saints. But the holy church, in its clemency, has thought of a way of still sparing you, and has sent me here to offer you mercy."

"Indeed!" exclaimed Larsson, mockingly. "Come, reverend father, loose my bonds and let me embrace you. I offer you my friendship, and of course you believe me. How says Seneca? — *homo homini lupus, wir Wölfe sind alle Brüder.*"

"I offer you mercy," continued the Jesuit, coldly, "on three conditions, which you certainly will not refuse. The first is that you abjure your heretic faith and publicly join the only saving church."

"Never!" exclaimed Bertel, fiercely.

"Be still!" said the captain. "Well, *posito* that we abjure the Lutheran faith?"

"Then," continued the Jesuit, "you shall, as prisoners of war, be exchanged for the highborn lady and princess Regina von Emmeritz, whom your king tyrannically sent in captivity to the North."

"It shall be done!" answered Bertel, eagerly.

"Be still!" cried Larsson. "Well, go on; *posito* that we accomplish the highborn lady's deliverance?"

"Then there remains but a trifle. I demand of Lieutenant Bertel King Gustaf Adolf's ring."

"Your purse or your life, in highwayman fashion!" said Larsson, derisively.

"You ask what I do not possess," answered Bertel.

The Jesuit looked at him distrustfully.

"The king commanded Duke Bernhard to give you the ring, and you must have received it."

"All this is entirely unknown to me," said Bertel, with perfect truth, but feeling surprised and overjoyed at the unexpected intelligence.

The Jesuit resumed his smiling composure.

"If that is the way the case stands, my dear sons," said he, "let us talk no more about the ring. As far as your conversion to the true church is concerned . . ."

Bertel was about to answer, but was interrupted by the captain, who for some moments had been engaged in a certain rubbing motion with that part of his body not reached by the light of the lantern.

"Yes, so far as that matter is concerned," Larsson hastened to interpose, "you know, reverend father, that there are two sides to it: *questio an* and *questio quomodo*. Now to speak first of *questio an*, my late rector Vincentius Flachsenius used to say, in his time, always place *negare* as *prima regula juris*. Your reverence will undoubtedly find it unexpected and pleasant to hear a royal captain talk Latin like a cardinal. Your reverence ought, therefore, to know that we, in Åbo Cathedral school, studied both Cicero, Seneca, and Ovid, also called Naso. For my part, I have always considered Cicero a great talker, and Seneca a blockhead; but as for Ovid . . ."

The Jesuit moved toward the door, and said dryly:—

"Thus you choose the stake?"

"Rather that than the disgrace of an apostasy!" exclaimed Bertel, who had not noticed Larsson's hints and signs.

"My friend," the captain hastened to add, "my friend thinks, quite sensibly and naturally, that the ugly part of the matter would be the public scandal. Thus, reverend father, let us confer about *questio quomodo*. *Posito* that we become good Catholics, and enter into the emperor's service . . . But deign to come a little nearer; my friend Bertel is rather hard of hearing ever since he had the pleasure of making the acquaintance of the great Pappenheim."

The Jesuit cautiously advanced a few steps closer, yet not without convincing himself by a glance that retreat stood open.

"It is I who decide the manner," said he, haughtily. "Yes or no?"

"Yes, yes, of course," replied Larsson, quickly, as he continued to rub himself. "Consequently we are in clear waters both with *questio an* and *questio quomodo*. Your reverence has a most persuasive eloquence. We now come to *questio ubi* and *questio quando*, for according to *logicam* and *metaphysicam* . . . Pardon me, worthy father, I don't have a word of objection; I consent to it all. But," continued the captain, as he lowered his voice, "deign to cast a glance at my friend Bertel's right forefinger. I will tell your reverence, my friend is a great rogue; I am very much mistaken if he does not have the king's ring on at this very moment."

The Jesuit, carried away by his curiosity, came a few steps nearer. Swift as an eel, Larsson, unable to rise on account of his bonds, rolled himself between the Jesuit and the door, and when the monk wished to retreat, he found that the captain had scraped against a sharp stone the ligatures which held his right arm, with which he suddenly embraced the Jesuit's legs, and drew him down over him. Father Hieronymus made desperate efforts to free himself; the lantern was broken into fragments, the light extinguished, and a thick darkness enveloped the wrestlers. Bertel and Pekka, both unable to get up and help, rolled themselves toward the spot, but without reaching it. Then the brave captain felt a sharp pain in his shoulder, and directly afterwards a warm stream of blood. With a *Blitzdonnerkreutz!* he wrenched the dagger from his enemy's hand and returned the stab. The Jesuit now sued for mercy in his turn.

"With the greatest pleasure, my son!" answered the captain, mockingly. "But only on three conditions: the first is that you abjure Loyola, your lord and master, and declare him a great milksop. Do you agree to it?"

"I agree to everything," sighed the father.

"The second is that you start off and hang yourself to the first hook you find in the ceiling."

"Yes, yes, only let go of me."

"The third is that you travel to Beelzebub, your patron saint," . . . and with these words, Larsson flung his enemy violently against the rocky wall, after which the place became quite silent. The dagger was now used hastily to cut the prisoners' bonds, and then it only remained to find the door.

When the three fugitives, after having bolted the door of the treasure room from without, reached the dark narrow staircase which led to the upper regions of the castle, they stopped a moment to consult together. Their situation was anything but enviable, for they knew of old that the stairs led to the bishop's former bedchamber, from whence two or three parlors had to be crossed before they came to the large armory, and through that to the castle yard, after which they still had to pass the closed drawbridge and the guard. All the rooms except the bedchamber, which the Jesuit himself seemed to have taken possession of, had only two hours before, when the prisoners were brought down, been filled partly with soldiers, partly with the sick and their nurses.

"One thing grieves me," whispered Larsson, "and that is that I did not draw the fur off the fox when I held him by the ears. In the garments of piety I could have gone scot-free through purgatory, like another *Saulus inter prophetas*. But as it is, my friend Bertel, I ask, in my simplicity: how shall we get away from here?"

"We will fight our way through. The garrison are asleep; the darkness of night favors us."

"I confess, my friend, that if anybody, even were it I, Larsson himself, should call you a coward, I would call that fellow a liar. It is true that you once, as good as *solo*, alone, *alienus*, all by yourself, took this castle; but you had then at least a sword in your hand and a few thousand brave boys in the rear. . . . Hush! I hear a tread on the stairs; — no, it was nothing. Let us push on cautiously. Here it stands one in need to tread like a maiden: that stupid Limingo peasant tramps as if we had a squadron of cavalry at our heels."

The fugitives had ascended about thirty or forty steps, and the way still led upward, when a faint ray of light glimmered at the top of the passage. They came to a door, which stood ajar. They stopped and held their breath; not a sound was heard. The brave captain now ventured to push in his head, then his foot, and finally his whole stout person.

"We are on the right track," whispered he; "boots off! the whole company must march in stockings — *posito* that the company has stockings. March!"

The bishop's bedchamber, which the three now entered on tiptoe, was a large and once magnificent room. A flickering lamp dimly illumined the precious Gobelin tapestry, the gilded images of the saints, and the ebony bedstead, inlaid with pearl, where the rich prelate used to fall asleep with his goblet of Rhine wine beside him. No living creature was to be seen; but from one of the windows which overlooked the courtyard they could see the castle chapel opposite brilliantly lighted, and filled with people. Even the castle yard, which was lighted by the reflection from the windows, was thronged with people, many of whom carried candles in their hands.

"I will let them salt and pickle me like cucumbers in a jar, if I understand what all those people are doing here in the middle of the night," muttered the captain, testily. "Perhaps they have come to see three honest Finnish soldiers roasted by a slow fire like Åland herrings!"

"We must look for weapons, and die like men," said Bertel, as he searched through the room. "Hurrah!" exclaimed he, "here are three swords, just what we need."

"And three daggers," added Larsson, who, in a large niche behind the image of a saint, had found a small arsenal of all sorts of weapons. "The reverend fathers have a weakness for daggers, as the East Bothnians have for their sheath knives."

"I think," joined in the close-mouthed Pekka, as he caught sight of a good-sized flask in a corner, "I think that as it is Christmas night . . ."

"Brave boy!" interrupted the captain, inspired by this prospect; "you have a remarkable scent when it is a question of something to drink. Pious Jesuit! you have accomplished some good in the world! Christmas night, did you say? Blockhead! why didn't you tell us at once? It is as clear as day, that half Würtzburg is streaming to the castle to hear Father Hieronymus say mass. By my honor, I am afraid he will make them wait some time, the good pater. Here goes, my friend; I drink to you; an officer ought always to set his troops a good example. Your health, my boys. . . . Damnation! . . . the miserable monk has cheated us; I have swallowed poison; I am a dead man!" And the honest captain became pale as a corpse.

But both Bertel and Pekka had hard work to restrain their laughter, notwithstanding their dangerous situation, when they saw Larsson at once white from fright and black from the fluid he had drunk and spilled over himself.

"Be more moderate another time," said Bertel, "and you will avoid drinking ink."

"Ink! I might have known that the earless scrawler would be up to some deviltry. Two things trouble me to-night more than all *autos-da-fé:* that the sweet Kätchen, with the soft hand, deceived us, and that I have swallowed the most useless stuff in the world — ink. Bah!"

"If we had nothing else to do, I could show you something that ink has done," rejoined Bertel, as he hastily turned over a pile of papers on the writing table. "Here is a letter from the princely bishop . . . he is coming to-morrow . . . we are to be solemnly burned . . . they will tempt us to abjure our faith, and promise us grace . . . but burn us, nevertheless! Infamous!"

"Roman fashion!" observed the captain, phlegmatically.

In the mean time Larsson had drawn out three monks' cloaks; they put them on, and now ventured to proceed farther in the dangerous regions.

The next two rooms were empty. Two rude beds gave evidence that some serving brothers had their abode here, and were now gone to mass.

"Bravo!" whispered Larsson, "they will take us for sheep in wolves' clothing, and believe that we also are going to attend mass. . . . Hark! didn't you hear something? — a woman's voice? Be quiet!"

They stopped, and heard in the darkness a young female voice, praying : —

"Holy Virgin, forgive me this time, and save me from death; I will to-morrow take the veil, and serve you all my life!"

"It is Kätchen's voice!" said the captain. "Can it be that she is innocent, poor child? Upon my honor, it would be base of a cavalier not to rescue a sweet girl with such a soft hand!"

"Let us be off!" whispered Bertel, in vexation. But the captain had already found a little door, bolted on the outside; beyond the door was a cell, and in that cell was a trembling girl. Her eyes, accustomed to the darkness, distinguished the monk's garb; she threw herself at the captain's feet, and exclaimed : —

"Grace, my father, grace! I will confess all; I have favored the prisoners' flight, I have given wine to the guard. But spare my life, have mercy upon me for the saints' sake! I am so young. I do not wish to die yet!"

"Who the devil has said that you shall die, my brave girl?" interrupted the captain. "No, you shall live, with your soft hand and your warm lips, as true as I am not a Jesuit, but Lars Larsson, captain in the service of his royal majesty and the crown, and herewith take you . . . as my wedded wife, for better or for worse," continued the captain, undoubtedly because he considered that the well-known formula must be said to an end when he once began it.

"Away, away! with or without the girl, but away! — they are coming, and we still have to pass the large armory!"

"Allow me to tell you, my friend, Bertel, that you are the greatest fiddle-faddle I know; *maximus fiescus*, as the ancients so truly expressed themselves. How is it, my girl, you are not a nun, but only a novice? Well, it is all the same to me. You shall be my wedded wife, in case I ever marry. Here is a cloak; there now, put that on and look bold."

"It is no cloak, it is a mass robe," whispered Kätchen, who had scarcely time to recover from her amazement.

"The deuce! a mass robe! Wait; you take my cloak and I will take the robe. I will chant *dies iræ* in their ears, so that they all will be astonished."

The sound of several voices in the armory outside interrupted the captain in his priestly meditations.

"They have missed the Jesuit; they are looking for him, and we are lost through your silly nonsense," whispered Bertel, in exasperation. "We must now be careful not to betray ourselves. Come along, all of you."

"And the Latinist first!" exclaimed the captain.

All four went out. In the armory were some thirty sick beds, but only two sisters in attendance. This sight was reassuring, but all the more dangerous was the meeting with the two monks, who stood in excited altercation close by the door. When they saw Larsson in the mass robe, and behind him three figures in cloaks, the pious fathers were greatly startled. The captain raised his arms to bless them, uttered a solemn *pax vobiscum*, and was about to steal by with a grave step, when he was checked by the foremost monk.

"Reverend father," said the latter, as he closely eyed the unknown prelate from head to foot, "what procures our castle this honor at so unusual a time?"

"*Pax vobiscum!*" repeated the captain, devoutly. "The pious Father Hieronymus commands you to say mass the best you know how. ... His reverence is sick ... he has toothache."

"Let us seek his reverence," said one of the monks, entering the smaller room. But the other seized Larsson by the robe, and looked at him in a way which did not at all please the brave captain.

"*Quis vus e, quid eltis!*" repeated the captain, nonplussed. "*Qui quoe quod, meus tuus suus* . . . go to the devil, you bald-headed baboons!" roared Larsson, unable to restrain himself longer, and pushed the resisting monks into the chamber and bolted the door. Then all four hastened down to the courtyard. Behind them rose a great outcry; the monks shouted with all their might, the nuns joined in, and soon the attention of the crowd of people who thronged the courtyard began to be attracted.

"We are lost," whispered Kätchen, "unless we can reach the drawbridge by the back way."

They hastened there. The tumult increased. They passed the guard at the large sally port.

"Halt! Who goes there?"

"*Peter and Paul*," answered Bertel, promptly.

They passed out. Fortunately the drawbridge was down. But the whole castle was now in alarm.

"Let us jump into the river; the night is dark; they will not find us!" cried Bertel.

"No," said Larsson, "I will not leave my girl, if it should cost me my neck."

"Here stand three saddled horses! Be quick!"

"Up, you sweetest of all the nuns in Franconia! up in the saddle!" and the agile captain swung the trembling Kätchen before him on the horse's back. They all galloped away in the darkness. But behind them was tumult and uproar; the alarm bells sounded in all the turrets, and the whole of Würtzburg wondered what could have happened on this Christmas night.

FROM THE KALEVALA.

(Translated by John M. Crawford. Used by permission of Robert Clarke & Co.)

[KALEVALA (signifying "abode of heroes"): The national epic of Finland, the elements of which are popular songs, legendary poems, etc. It owes its present form to Dr. Elias Lönnrott, a Finnish scholar (1802–1884), who spent many years in travel in Finland and the Finnish parts of Lapland and Russia, faithfully recording all the songs and stories that he heard from peasants, fishermen, etc. The first version (1835) contained twelve thousand verses, in thirty-two runes or cantos; the second version (1849), the present form of the poem, has twenty-three thousand verses, in fifty runes. Professor Max Müller said that the Kalevala possessed merits not dissimilar to those of the Iliad, and would claim its place as the fifth national epic of the world.]

RUNE XXIX: THE ISLE OF REFUGE.

LEMMINKAINEN, full of joyance,
Handsome hero, Kaukomieli,
Took provisions in abundance,
Fish and butter, bread and bacon,
Hastened to the Isle of Refuge,
Sailed away across the oceans,
Spake these measures on departing:—
"Fare thee well, mine island dwelling,
I must sail to other borders,
To an island more protective,
Till the second summer passes;
Let the serpents keep the island,
Lynxes rest within the glenwood,
Let the blue moose roam the mountains,
Let the wild geese eat the barley.
Fare thee well, my helpful mother!
When the warriors of the Northland,
From the dismal Sariola,
Come with swords, and spears, and crossbows,
Asking for my head in vengeance,
Say that I have long departed,
Left my mother's island dwelling,
When the barley had been garnered."

Then he launched his boat of copper,
Threw the vessel to the waters,
From the iron-banded rollers,
From the cylinders of oak wood,
On the masts the sails he hoisted,
Spread the magic sails of linen,
In the stern the hero settled
And prepared to sail his vessel,
One hand resting on the rudder.

Then the sailor spake as follows,
These the words of Lemminkainen:—
"Blow, ye winds, and drive me onward,
Blow ye steady, winds of heaven,
Toward the island in the ocean,
That my bark may fly in safety
To my father's place of refuge,
To the far and nameless island!"

Soon the winds arose as bidden,
Rocked the vessel o'er the billows,
O'er the blue back of the waters,
O'er the vast expanse of ocean;
Blew two months and blew unceasing,
Blew a third month toward the island,
Toward his father's Isle of Refuge.

Sat some maidens on the seaside,
On the sandy beach of ocean,
Turned about in all directions,
Looking out upon the billows;
One was waiting for her brother,
And a second for her father,
And a third one, anxious, waited
For the coming of her suitor;
There they spied young Lemminkainen
There perceived the hero's vessel
Sailing o'er the bounding billows;
It was like a hanging cloudlet,
Hanging 'twixt the earth and heaven.

Thus the island maidens wondered,
Thus they spake to one another:—
"What this stranger on the ocean,
What is this upon the waters?
Art thou one of our sea vessels?
Wert thou builded on this island?
Sail thou straightway to the harbor,
To the island point of landing,
That thy tribe may be discovered."

Onward did the waves propel it,
Rocked his vessel o'er the billows,
Drove it to the magic island,
Safely landed Lemminkainen
On the sandy shore and harbor.

Spake he thus when he had landed,
These the words that Ahti uttered:—
"Is there room upon this island,
Is there space within this harbor,
Where my bark may lie at anchor,
Where the sun may dry my vessel?"

This the answer of the virgins,
Dwellers on the Isle of Refuge:—
"There is room within this harbor,
On this island, space abundant,
Where thy bark may lie at anchor,

Where the sun may dry thy vessel;
Lying ready are the rollers,
Cylinders adorned with copper;
If thou hadst a hundred vessels,
Shouldst thou come with boats a thousand,
We would give them room in welcome."
　　Thereupon wild Lemminkainen
Rolled his vessel in the harbor,
On the cylinders of copper,
Spake these words when had ended: —
"Is there room upon this island,
Or a spot within these forests,
Where a hero may be hidden
From the coming din of battle,
From the play of spears and arrows?"
Thus replied the island maidens: —
"There are places on this island,
On these plains a spot befitting,
Where to hide thyself in safety,
Hero son of little valor.
Here are many, many castles,
Many courts upon this island;
Though there come a thousand heroes,
Though a thousand spearmen follow,
Thou canst hide thyself in safety."
Spake the hero, Lemminkainen: —
"Is there room upon this island,
Where the birch tree grows abundant,
Where this son may fell the forest,
And may cultivate the fallow?"
Answered thus the island maidens: —
"There is not a spot befitting,
Not a place upon the island,
Where to rest thy wearied members,
Not the smallest patch of birch wood,
Thou canst bring to cultivation.
All our fields have been divided,
All these woods have been apportioned,
Fields and forests have their owners."
　　Lemminkainen asked this question,
These the words of Kaukomieli: —
"Is there room upon this island,
Worthy spot in field or forest,
Where to sing my songs of magic,
Chant my gathered store of wisdom,

Sing mine ancient songs and legends?"
Answered thus the island maidens: —
"There is room upon this island,
Worthy place in these dominions,
Thou canst sing thy garnered wisdom,
Thou canst chant thine ancient legends,
Legends of the times primeval,
In the forest, in the castle,
On the island plains and pastures."
  Then began the reckless minstrel
To intone his wizard sayings;
Sang he alders to the waysides,
Sang the oaks upon the mountains,
On the oak trees sang he branches,
On each branch he sang an acorn,
On the acorns, golden rollers,
On each roller sang a cuckoo;
Then began the cuckoos, calling,
Gold from every throat came streaming,
Copper fell from every feather,
And each wing emitted silver,
Filled the isle with precious metals.
  Sang again young Lemminkainen,
Conjured on, and sang, and chanted,
Sang to precious stones the sea sands,
Sang the stones to pearls resplendent,
Robed the groves in iridescence,
Sang the island full of flowers,
Many-colored as the rainbow.
Sang again the magic minstrel,
In the court a well he conjured,
On the wall a golden cover,
On the lid a silver dipper,
That the boys might drink the water,
That the maids might lave their eyelids.
On the plains he conjured lakelets,
Sang the duck upon the waters,
Golden-cheeked and silver-headed,
Sang the feet from shining copper;
And the island maidens wondered,
Stood entranced at Ahti's wisdom,
At the songs of Lemminkainen,
At the hero's magic power.
  Spake the singer, Lemminkainen,
Handsome hero, Kaukomieli: —

"I would sing a wondrous legend,
Sing in miracles of sweetness,
If within some hall or chamber,
I were seated at the table.
If I sing not in the castle,
In some spot by walls surrounded,
Then I sing my songs to zephyrs,
Fling them to the fields and forests."
Answered thus the island maidens:—
"On this isle are castle chambers,
Halls for use of magic singers,
Courts complete for chanting legends,
Where thy singing will be welcome,
Where thy songs will not be scattered
To the forests of the island,
Nor thy wisdom lost in ether."
 Straightway Lemminkainen journeyed
With the maidens to the castle;
There he sang and conjured pitchers
On the borders of the tables,
Sang and conjured golden goblets
Foaming with the beer of barley;
Sang he many well-filled vessels,
Bowls of honey drink abundant,
Sweetest butter, toothsome biscuit,
Bacon, fish, and veal, and venison,
All the dainties of the Northland,
Wherewithal to still his hunger.
But the proud heart, Lemminkainen,
Was not ready for the banquet,
Did not yet begin his feasting,
Waited for a knife of silver,
For a knife of golden handle;
Quick he sang the precious metals,
Sang a blade from purest silver,
To the blade a golden handle,
Straightway then began his feasting,
Quenched his thirst and stilled his hunger,
Charmed the maidens on the island.
 Then the minstrel, Lemminkainen,
Roamed throughout the island hamlets,
To the joy of all the virgins,
All the maids of braided tresses;
Wheresoe'er he turned his footsteps,
There appeared a maid to greet him;

When his hand was kindly offered,
There his hand was kindly taken;
When he wandered out at evening,
Even in the darksome places,
There the maidens bade him welcome;
There was not an island village
Where there were not seven castles,
In each castle seven daughters,
And the daughters stood in waiting,
Gave the hero joyful greetings,
Only one of all the maidens
Whom he did not greet with pleasure.

Thus the merry Lemminkainen
Spent three summers in the ocean,
Spent a merry time in refuge,
In the hamlets on the island,
To the pleasure of the maidens,
To the joy of all the daughters;
Only one was left neglected,
She a poor and graceless spinster,
On the isle's remotest border,
In the smallest of the hamlets.

Then he thought about his journey
O'er the ocean to his mother,
To the cottage of his father.
There appeared the slighted spinster,
To the Northland son departing,
Spake these words to Lemminkainen: —
"O thou handsome Kaukomieli,
Wisdom bard, and magic singer,
Since this maiden thou hast slighted,
May the winds destroy thy vessel,
Dash thy bark to countless fragments
On the ocean rocks and ledges!"

Lemminkainen's thoughts were homeward,
Did not heed the maiden's murmurs,
Did not rise before the dawning
Of the morning on the island,
To the pleasure of the maiden
Of the much-neglected hamlet.
Finally at close of evening,
He resolved to leave the island,
He resolved to waken early,
Long before the dawn of morning;
Long before the time appointed,

He arose that he might wander
Through the hamlets of the island,
Bid adieu to all the maidens,
On the morn of his departure.
As he wandered hither, thither,
Walking through the village pathways
To the last of all the hamlets;
Saw he none of all the castles,
Where three dwellings were not standing;
Saw he none of all the dwellings
Where three heroes were not watching;
Saw he none of all the heroes,
Who was not engaged in grinding
Swords, and spears, and battle-axes,
For the death of Lemminkainen.
And these words the hero uttered:—
"Now alas! the Sun arises
From his couch within the ocean,
On the frailest of the heroes,
On the saddest child of Northland;
On my neck the cloak of Lempo
Might protect me from all evil,
Though a hundred foes assail me,
Though a thousand archers follow."
　　Then he left the maids ungreeted,
Left his longing for the daughters
Of the nameless Isle of Refuge,
With his farewell words unspoken,
Hastened toward the island harbor,
Toward his magic bark at anchor;
But he found it burned to ashes,
Sweet revenge had fired his vessel,
Lighted by the slighted spinster.
Then he saw the dawn of evil,
Saw misfortune hanging over,
Saw destruction round about him.
Straightway he began rebuilding
Him a magic sailing vessel,
New and wondrous, full of beauty;
But the hero needed timber,
Boards, and planks, and beams, and braces,
Found the smallest bit of lumber,
Found of boards but seven fragments,
Of a spool he found three pieces,
Found six pieces of the distaff;

With these fragments builds his vessel,
Builds a ship of magic virtue,
Builds the bark with secret knowledge,
Through the will of the magician;
Strikes one blow, and builds the first part,
Strikes a second, builds the center,
Strikes a third with wondrous power,
And the vessel is completed.

Thereupon the ship he launches,
Sings the vessel to the ocean,
And these words the hero utters:—
"Like a bubble swim these waters,
Like a flower ride the billows;
Loan me of thy magic feathers,
Three, O eagle, four, O raven,
For protection to my vessel,
Lest it flounder in the ocean!"

Now the sailor, Lemminkainen,
Seats himself upon the bottom
Of the vessel he has builded,
Hastens on his journey homeward,
Head depressed and evil-humored,
Cap awry upon his forehead,
Mind dejected, heavy-hearted,
That he could not dwell forever
In the castles of the daughters
Of the nameless Isle of Refuge.

Spake the minstrel, Lemminkainen,
Handsome hero, Kaukomieli:—
"Leave I must this merry island,
Leave her many joys and pleasures,
Leave her maids with braided tresses,
Leave her dances and her daughters,
To the joys of other heroes;
But I take this comfort with me:
All the maidens on the island,
Save the spinster who was slighted,
Will bemoan my loss for ages,
Will regret my quick departure;
They will miss me at the dances,
In the halls of mirth and joyance,
In the homes of merry maidens,
On my father's Isle of Refuge."

Wept the maidens on the island,
Long lamenting, loudly calling

To the hero sailing homeward: —
"Whither goest, Lemminkainen,
Why depart, thou best of heroes?
Dost thou leave from inattention,
Is there here a dearth of maidens,
Have our greetings been unworthy?"
　Sang the magic Lemminkainen
To the maids as he was sailing,
This in answer to their calling: —
"Leaving not for want of pleasure,
Do not go from dearth of women;
Beautiful the island maidens,
Countless as the sands their virtues.
This the reason of my going,
I am longing for my home land,
Longing for my mother's cabins,
For the strawberries of Northland,
For the raspberries of Kalew,
For the maidens of my childhood,
For the children of my mother."
　Then the merry Lemminkainen
Bade farewell to all the island;
Winds arose and drove his vessel
On the blue back of the ocean,
O'er the far extending waters,
Toward the island of his mother.
On the shore were grouped the daughters
Of the magic Isle of Refuge,
On the rocks sat the forsaken,
Weeping stood the island maidens,
Golden daughters, loud lamenting.
Weep the maidens of the island
While the sail yards greet their vision,
While the copper beltings glisten;
Do not weep to lose the sail yards,
Nor to lose the copper beltings;
Weep they for the loss of Ahti,
For the fleeing Kaukomieli
Guiding the departing vessel.
Also weeps young Lemminkainen,
Sorely weeps, and loud lamenting,
Weeps while he can see the island,
While the island hilltops glisten;
Does not mourn the island mountains,
Weeps he only for the maidens,
Left upon the Isle of Refuge.

KALEVALA.

Thereupon sailed Kaukomieli
On the blue back of the ocean;
Sailed one day, and then a second,
But, alas! upon the third day,
There arose a mighty stormwind,
And the sky was black with fury.
Blew the black winds from the northwest,
From the southeast came the whirlwind,
Tore away the ship's forecastle,
Tore away the vessel's rudder,
Dashed the wooden hull to pieces.
Thereupon wild Lemminkainen
Headlong fell upon the waters;
With his head he did the steering,
With his hands and feet, the rowing;
Swam whole days and nights unceasing,
Swam with hope and strength united,
Till at last appeared a cloudlet,
Growing cloudlet to the westward,
Changing to a promontory,
Into land within the ocean.

Swiftly to the shore swam **Ahti**,
Hastened to a magic castle,
Found therein a hostess baking,
And her daughters kneading barley,
And these words the hero uttered: —
"O thou hostess, filled with kindness,
Couldst thou know my pangs of hunger,
Couldst thou guess my name and station,
Thou wouldst hasten to the storehouse.
Bring me beer and foaming liquor,
Bring the best of thy provisions,
Bring me fish, and veal, and bacon,
Butter, bread, and honeyed biscuits,
Set for me a wholesome dinner,
Wherewithal to still my hunger,
Quench the thirst of Lemminkainen.
Days and nights have I been swimming,
Buffeting the waves of ocean,
Seemed as if the wind protected,
And the billows gave me shelter."

Then the hostess, filled with kindness,
Hastened to the mountain storehouse,
Cut some butter, veal, and bacon,
Bread, and fish, and honeyed biscuit,

Brought the best of her provisions,
Brought the mead and beer of barley,
Set for him a toothsome dinner,
Wherewithal to still his hunger,
Quench the thirst of Lemminkainen.

When the hero's feast had ended,
Straightway was a magic vessel
Given by the kindly hostess
To the weary Kaukomieli,
Bark of beauty, new and hardy,
Wherewithal to aid the stranger
In his journey to his home land,
To the cottage of his mother.

Quickly sailed wild Lemminkainen
On the blue back of the ocean;
Sailed he days and nights unceasing,
Till at last he reached the borders
Of his own loved home and country;
There beheld he scenes familiar,
Saw the islands, capes, and rivers,
Saw his former shipping stations,
Saw he many ancient landmarks,
Saw the mountains with their fir trees,
Saw the pine trees on the hilltops,
Saw the willows in the lowlands;
Did not see his father's cottage,
Nor the dwellings of his mother.
Where a mansion once had risen,
There the alder trees were growing,
Shrubs were growing on the homestead,
Junipers within the courtyard.
Spake the reckless Lemminkainen: —
"In this glen I played and wandered,
On these stones I rocked for ages,
On this lawn I rolled and tumbled,
Frolicked on these woodland borders,
When a child of little stature.
Where then is my mother's dwelling,
Where the castles of my father?
Fire, I fear, has found the hamlet,
And the winds dispersed the ashes."

Then he fell to bitter weeping,
Wept one day, and then a second,
Wept the third day without ceasing;
Did not mourn the ancient homestead,
Nor the dwellings of his father;

Wept he for his darling mother,
Wept he for the dear departed,
For the loved ones of the island.
    Then he saw the bird of heaven,
Saw an eagle flying near him,
And he asked the bird this question: —
"Mighty eagle, bird majestic,
Grant to me the information,
Where my mother may have wandered,
Whither I may go and find her!"
    But the eagle knew but little,
Only knew that Ahti's people
Long ago together perished;
And the raven also answered
That his people had been scattered
By the swords, and spears, and arrows,
Of his enemies from Pohya.
Spake the hero, Lemminkainen: —
"Faithful mother, dear departed,
Thou who nursed me in my childhood,
Art thou dead and turned to ashes,
Didst thou perish for my follies,
O'er thy head are willows weeping,
Junipers above thy body,
Alders watching o'er thy slumbers?
This my punishment for evil,
This the recompense of folly!
Fool was I, a son unworthy,
That I measured swords in Northland
With the landlord of Pohyola.
To my tribe came fell destruction,
And the death of my dear mother,
Through my crimes and misdemeanors.
    Then the minstrel looked about him,
Anxious, looked in all directions,
And beheld some gentle footprints,
Saw a pathway lightly trodden
Where the heather had been beaten.
Quick as thought the path he followed,
Through the meadows, through the brambles,
O'er the hills, and through the valleys,
To a forest, vast and cheerless;
Traveled far and traveled farther,
Still a greater distance traveled,
To a dense and hidden glenwood,

In the middle of the island;
Found therein a sheltered cabin,
Found a small and darksome dwelling
Built between the rocky ledges,
In the midst of triple pine trees;
And within he spied his mother,
Found his gray-haired mother weeping.
    Lemminkainen loud rejoices,
Cries in tones of joyful greetings,
These the words that Ahti utters:—
"Faithful mother, well-beloved,
Thou that gavest me existence,
Happy I, that thou art living,
That thou hast not yet departed
To the kingdom of Tuoni,
To the islands of the blessed.
I had thought that thou hadst perished,
Hadst been murdered by my foemen,
Hadst been slain with bows and arrows.
Heavy are mine eyes from weeping,
And my cheeks are white with sorrow,
Since I thought my mother slaughtered
For the sins I had committed!"
Lemminkainen's mother answered:—
"Long, indeed, hast thou been absent,
Long, my son, hast thou been living
In thy father's Isle of Refuge,
Roaming on the secret island,
Living at the doors of strangers,
Living in a nameless country,
Refuge from the Northland foeman."
Spake the hero, Lemminkainen:—
"Charming is that spot for living,
Beautiful the magic island,
Rainbow-colored was the forest,
Blue the glimmer of the meadows,
Silvered were the pine-tree branches,
Golden were the heather blossoms;
All the woodlands dripped with honey,
Eggs in every rock and crevice,
Honey flowed from birch and sorb tree,
Milk in streams from fir and aspen,
Beer foam dripping from the willows,
Charming there to live and linger,
All their edibles delicious.

PIERRE CORNEILLE.

This their only source of trouble:
Great the fear for all the maidens,
All the heroes filled with envy,
Feared the coming of the stranger;
Thought that all the island maidens,
Thought that all the wives and daughters,
All the good, and all the evil,
Gave thy son too much attention;
Thought the stranger, Lemminkainen,
Saw the island maids too often;
Yet the virgins I avoided,
Shunned the good and shunned the evil,
Shunned the host of charming daughters,
As the black wolf shuns the sheepfold,
As the hawk neglects the chickens."

THE CID.[1]

By CORNEILLE.

[PIERRE CORNEILLE, the great French dramatist, was born at Rouen, June 6, 1606. He practiced law for a time at Rouen, but the success of his first comedy, "Mélite," induced him to enter upon a literary career. After producing a series of comedies, he began writing tragedies, and brought out in rapid succession "Médée"; "Le Cid," which established his fame; "Horace"; "Cinna"; "Polyeucte," frequently regarded as his greatest work; "La Mort de Pompée" (Death of Pompey); "Théodore"; "Rodogune." "Le Menteur" (The Liar) entitles him to be called the father of French comedy as well as of tragedy. There was a distinct decline in the quality of Corneille's later works, and during the closing years of his life he was overshadowed by his younger contemporary, Racine. Corneille became a member of the French Academy in 1647. He died in Paris, October 1, 1684.]

Chimène — What! Rodrigo! In broad daylight! Whence comes this audacity? Go, thou art ruining my honor; retire, I beseech thee.

Don Rodrigo — I go to die, dear lady, and I come to bid you in this place, before the mortal blow, a last adieu. This unchangeable love, which binds me beneath your laws, dares not to accept my death without paying to you homage for it.

Chimène — Thou art going to death!

[1] Copyright, 1896, by Hinds and Noble, and used by their permission.

Don Rodrigo — I speed to those happy moments which will deliver my life from your resentment.

Chimène — Thou art going to death! Is Don Sancho, then, so formidable that he can inspire terror in this invincible heart? What has rendered thee so weak? or what renders him so strong? Does Rodrigo go to fight, and believe himself already slain? He who has not feared the Moors nor my father, goes to fight Don Sancho, and already despairs? Thus, then, thy courage lowers itself in the hour of need.

Don Rodrigo — I speed to my punishment, and not to the combat; and, since you seek my death, my faithful ardor will readily deprive me of the desire of defending my life. I have always the same courage, but I have not the arm, when it is needed, to preserve that which does not please you; and already this night would have been fatal to me, if I had fought for my own private wrong; but, defending my king, his people, and my country, by carelessly defending myself, I should have betrayed *them*. My highborn spirit does not hate life so much as to wish to depart from it by perfidy, now that it regards my interests only. You demand my death — I accept its decree. Your resentment chose the hand of another; I was unworthy to die by yours. They shall not see me repel its blows; I owe more respect to him who fights for you; and delighted to think that it is from you these blows proceed — since it is your honor that his arms sustain — I shall present to him my unprotected breast, worshiping through his hand thine that destroys me.

Chimène — If the just vehemence of a sad sense of duty, which causes me, in spite of myself, to follow after thy valiant life, prescribes to thy love a law so severe that it surrenders thee without defense to him who combats for me, in this infatuation, lose not the recollection that, with thy life, thine honor is tarnished, and that, in whatever renown Rodrigo may have lived, when men shall know him to be dead, they will believe him conquered. Thine honor is dearer to thee than I am dear, since it steeps thine hands in the blood of my father, and causes thee to renounce, in spite of thy love, the sweet hope of gaining me. I see thee, however, pay such little regard to it that, without fighting, thou wishest to be overcome. What inconsistency mars thy valor! Why hast thou it no more? or why didst thou possess it formerly? What! art thou valiant only to do me an injury? Unless it be to offend me, hast thou no courage at all? And dost thou treat my father with such rigor that, after having conquered him, thou wilt endure a conqueror? Go! without wishing to die, leave me to pursue thee, and defend thine honor, if thou wilt no longer live.

Don Rodrigo — After the death of the count and the defeat of the Moors, will my renown still require other achievements? That may scorn the care of defending myself; it is known that my courage dares to attempt all, that my valor can accomplish all, and that, here below, in comparison with mine honor, nothing is precious to me. No! no! in this combat, whatever thou mayest please to think, Rodrigo may die without risking his renown: without men daring to accuse him of having wanted spirit: without being considered as conquered, without enduring a conqueror. They will say only: "He adored Chimène; he would not live and merit her hatred; he yielded himself to the severity of his fate, which compelled his mistress to seek his death; she wished for his head, and his magnanimous heart, had that been refused to her, would have considered it a crime. To avenge his honor, he lost his love; to avenge his mistress, he forsook life, preferring (whatever hope may have enslaved his soul) his honor to Chimène, and Chimène to his existence." Thus, then, you will see that my death in this conflict, far from obscuring my glory, will increase its value; and this honor will follow my voluntary death, that no other than myself could have satisfied you.

Chimène — Since, to prevent thee from rushing to destruction, thy life and thine honor are feeble inducements, if ever I loved thee, dear Rodrigo, in return, defend thyself now, to rescue me from Don Sancho. Fight, to release me from a compact which delivers me to the object of my aversion. Shall I say more to thee? Go, think of thy defense, to overcome my sense of duty, to impose on me silence; and if thou feelest thine heart still enamored for me, come forth, as a conqueror, from a combat of which Chimène is the reward. Adieu; this thoughtlessly uttered word causes me to blush for shame!

[*Exit* CHIMÈNE.

Don Rodrigo — Where is the foe I could not now subdue? Come forth, warriors of Navarre, Morocco, and Castile! and all the heroes that Spain has produced; unite together and form an army, to contend against one hand thus nerved. Unite all your efforts against a hope so sweet — you have too little power to succeed in destroying it! . . .

The Infanta — Shall I listen to thee still, pride of my birth, that makest a crime out of my passions? Shall I listen to thee, love, whose delicious power causes my desires to rebel against this proud tyrant? Poor princess! to which of the two oughtest thou to yield obedience? Rodrigo, thy valor renders thee worthy of me; but although thou art valiant, thou art not the son of a king.

Pitiless fate, whose severity separates my glory and my desires! Is it decreed that the choice of such rare merit should cost my passion such great anguish? O heaven! for how many sighs must my heart prepare itself, if, after such a long, painful struggle, it never succeeds in either extinguishing the love, or accepting the lover!

But there are too many scruples, and my reason is alarmed at the contempt of a choice so worthy; although to monarchs only my birth may assign me, Rodrigo, with honor I shall live under thy laws. After having conquered two kings, couldst thou fail in obtaining a crown? And this great name of Cid, which thou hast just now won — does it not show too clearly over whom thou art destined to reign?

He is worthy of me, but he belongs to Chimène; the present which I made of him injures me. Between them, the death of a father has interposed so little hatred that the duty of blood with regret pursues him. Thus let us hope for no advantage, either from his transgression or from my grief, since, to punish me, destiny has allowed that love should continue even between two enemies.

Infanta — Why comest thou, Leonora?

Leonora — To congratulate you, dear lady, on the tranquillity which at last your soul has recovered.

Infanta — Whence should this tranquillity come, — in an accumulation of sorrow?

Leonora — If love lives on hope, and if it dies with it, Rodrigo can no more charm your heart; you know of the combat in which Chimène involves him; since he must die in it, or become her husband, your hope is dead and your spirit is healed.

Infanta — Ah! how far from it!

Leonora — What more can you expect?

Infanta — Nay, rather, what hope canst thou forbid me? If Rodrigo fights under these conditions, to counteract the effect of it I have too many resources. Love, this sweet author of my cruel punishments, teaches the minds of lovers too many stratagems.

Leonora — Can *you* accomplish anything, since a dead father has not been able to kindle discord in their minds. For Chimène clearly shows by her behavior that hatred to-day does not cause her pursuit. She obtains the combat, and for her champion, she accepts on the moment the first that offers. She has not recourse to those noble hands whom so many famous exploits render so glorious; Don Sancho suffices her, and merits her choice, because he is going to arm himself for the first time; she loves in this duel his want of experience; as he is without renown, so is she without apprehension; and her readiness ought to make you clearly see that she seeks for a combat which her duty demands, but which yields her Rodrigo an easy victory, and authorizes her at length to seem appeased.

Infanta — I observe it clearly; and nevertheless my heart, in rivalry with Chimène, adores this conqueror. On what shall I resolve, hopeless lover that I am?

Leonora — To remember better from whom you are sprung. Heaven owes you a king; you love a subject!

Infanta — The object of my attachment has completely changed: I no longer love Rodrigo as a mere nobleman. No; it is not thus that my love entitles him. If I love him, it is as the author of so many brilliant deeds, — as the valiant Cid, the master of two kings. I shall conquer myself, however; not from dread of any censure, but in order that I may not disturb so glorious a love; and even though, to favor me, they should crown him, I will not take back a gift which I have given. Since in such a combat his triumph is certain, let us go once more to give that gift to Chimène. And thou, who seest the love arrows with which my heart is pierced, come see me finish as I have begun.

Chimène — Elvira, how greatly I suffer; and how much I am to be pitied! I know not what to hope, and I see everything to be dreaded. No wish escapes me to which I dare consent. I desire nothing without a quick repentance. I have caused two rivals to take up arms for me: the most happy result will cause me tears; and though fate may decree in my favor, my father is without revenge, or my lover is dead.

Elvira — On the one side and the other I see you consoled: either you have Rodrigo, or you are avenged. And however fate may ordain for you, it maintains your honor and gives you a spouse.

Chimène — What! the object of my hatred or of such resentment! — the slayer of Rodrigo, or that of my father! In either case they give me a husband, still all stained with the blood that I cherished most; in either case my soul revolts, and I fear more than death the ending of my quarrel. Away! vengeance, love — which agitate my feelings. Ye have no gratifications for me at such a price; and Thou, Powerful Controller of the destiny which afflicts me, terminate this combat without any advantage, without rendering either of the two conquered or conqueror.

Elvira — This would be treating you with too much severity. This combat is a new punishment for your feelings, if it leaves you compelled to demand justice, to exhibit always this proud resentment, and continually to seek after the death of your lover. Dear lady, it is far better that his unequaled valor, crowning his brow, should impose silence upon you; that the conditions of the combat should extinguish your sighs; and that the King should compel you to follow your inclinations.

Chimène — If he be conqueror, dost thou believe that I shall surrender? My sense of duty is too strong and my loss too great; and this combat and the will of the King are not strong enough to dictate conditions to them. He may conquer Don Sancho with very little difficulty, but he shall not with him conquer the sense of duty of Chimène; and whatever reward a monarch may have promised to his victory, my self-respect will raise against him a thousand other enemies.

Elvira — Beware lest, to punish this strange pride, Heaven may at last permit you to revenge yourself. What! — you will still reject the happiness of being able now to be silent with honor? What means this duty, and what does it hope for? Will the death of your lover restore to you a father? Is one stroke of misfortune insufficient for you? Is there need of loss upon loss, and sorrow upon sorrow? Come, in the caprice in which your humor persists, you do not deserve the lover that is destined for you, and we may see the just wrath of Heaven, by his death, leaving you Don Sancho as a spouse.

Chimène — Elvira, the griefs which I endure are sufficient: do not redouble them by this fatal augury. I wish, if I can, to avoid both; but if not, in this conflict Rodrigo has all my prayers; not because a weak affection inclines me to his side,

but because, if he were conquered, I should become the bride of Don Sancho. This fear creates my desire——
[*Enter* DON SANCHO.
What do I see, unhappy I! Elvira, all is lost!

Don Sancho — Compelled to bring this sword to thy feet——
Chimène — What! still reeking with the blood of Rodrigo! Traitor, dost thou dare to show thyself before mine eyes, after having taken from me that which I love the best? Declare thyself my love, and thou hast no more to fear. My father is satisfied; cease to restrain thyself. The same stroke has placed my honor in safety, my soul in despair, and my passion at liberty!
Don Sancho — With a mind more calmly collected——
Chimène — Dost thou still speak to me, detestable assassin of a hero whom I adore? Go; you fell upon him treacherously. A warrior so valiant would never have sunk beneath such an assailant! Hope nothing from me. Thou hast not served me; and believing that thou wert avenging me, thou hast deprived me of life.
Don Sancho — Strange delusion, which, far from listening to me——
Chimène — Wilt thou that I should listen to thee while boasting of his death? — that I should patiently hear with what haughty pride thou wilt describe his misfortune, my own crime, and thy prowess?

Chimène — Sire, there is no further need to dissemble that which all my struggles have not been able to conceal from you. I loved, you knew it; but, to avenge my father, I even wished to sacrifice so dear a being. Sire, your majesty may have seen how I have made love yield to duty. At last, Rodrigo is dead; and his death has converted me from an unrelenting foe into an afflicted lover. I owed this revenge to him who gave me existence; and to my love I now owe these tears. Don Sancho has destroyed me in undertaking my defense; and I am the reward of the arm which destroys me. Sire, if compassion can influence a king, for mercy's sake revoke a law so severe. As the reward of a victory by which I lose that which I love, I leave him my possessions; let him leave me to myself, that in a sacred cloister I may weep continually, even to my last sigh, for my father and my lover.

Don Diego — In brief, she loves, sire, and no longer believes it a crime to acknowledge with her own lips a lawful affection.

Don Fernando — Chimène, be undeceived; thy lover is not dead, and the vanquished Don Sancho has given thee a false report.

Don Sancho — Sire, a little too much eagerness, in spite of me, has misled her; I came from the combat to tell her the result. This noble warrior of whom her heart is enamored, when he had disarmed me, spoke to me thus: "Fear nothing — I would rather leave the victory uncertain, than shed blood risked in defense of Chimène; but, since my duty calls me to the King, go, tell her of our combat; on the part of the conqueror, carry her thy sword." Sire, I came; this weapon deceived her; seeing me return, she believed me to be conqueror, and her resentment suddenly betrayed her love, with such excitement and so much impatience, that I could not obtain a moment's hearing. As for me, although conquered, I consider myself fortunate; and in spite of the interests of my enamored heart, though losing infinitely, I still love my defeat, which causes the triumph of a love so perfect.

Don Fernando — My daughter, there is no need to blush for a passion so glorious, nor to seek means of making a disavowal of it; a laudable shame in vain solicits thee; thy honor is redeemed, and thy duty performed; thy father is satisfied, and it was to avenge him that thou didst so often place thy Rodrigo in danger. Thou seest how Heaven otherwise ordains. Having done so much for him, do something for thyself; and be not rebellious against my command, which gives thee a spouse beloved so dearly.

Infanta — Dry thy tears, Chimène, and receive without sadness this noble conqueror from the hands of thy princess.

Don Rodrigo — Be not offended, sire, if in your presence an impassioned homage causes me to kneel before her. I come not here to ask for the reward of my victory; I come once more to offer you my head, dear lady. My love shall not employ in my own favor either the law of the combat or the will of the King. If all that has been done is too little for a father, say by what means you must be satisfied. Must I still contend against a thousand and a thousand rivals, and to the two ends of the earth extend my labors, myself alone storm a camp, put to flight an army, surpass the renown of fabulous heroes? If my deep offense can be by that means washed away, I dare undertake all, and can accomplish all. But if this proud honor, always inexorable, cannot be appeased without the death of the guilty, arm no more against me the power of mortals; mine head is at thy feet, avenge thyself by thine own hands; thine hands alone have the right to vanquish the invincible. Take thou a vengeance to all others impossible. But at least let my death suffice to punish me; banish me not from thy remembrance, and, since my doom preserves your honor, to recompense yourself for this, preserve my memory, and say sometimes, when deploring my fate: "Had he not loved me, he would not have died."

Chimène — Rise, Rodrigo. I must confess it, sire, I have said too much to be able to unsay it. Rodrigo has noble qualities which I cannot hate; and, when a king commands, he ought to be obeyed. But to whatever you may have already doomed me, can you, before your eyes, tolerate this union? And when you desire this effort from my feeling of duty, is it entirely in accord with your sense of justice? If Rodrigo becomes so indispensable to the state, of that which he has done for you ought I to be the reward, and surrender myself to the everlasting reproach of having imbrued my hands in the blood of a father?

Don Fernando — Time has often rendered lawful that which at first seemed impossible, without being a crime. Rodrigo has won thee, and thou art justly his. But, although his valor has by conquest obtained thee to-day, it would need that I should become the enemy of thy self-respect, to give him so soon the reward of his victory. This bridal deferred does not break a law which, without specifying the time, devotes thy faith to him. Take a year, if thou wilt, to dry thy tears; Rodrigo, in the mean time, must take up arms. After having vanquished the Moors on our borders, overthrown their plans. and repulsed their attacks, go, carry the war even into their country, command my army, and ravage their territory. At the mere name of Cid they will tremble with dismay. They have named thee lord! they will desire thee as their king! But, amidst thy high achievements, be thou to her always faithful; return, if it be possible, still more worthy of her, and by thy great exploits acquire such renown that it may be glorious for her to espouse thee then.

Don Rodrigo — To gain Chimène, and for your service, what command can be issued to me that mine arm cannot accomplish?

Yet, though absent from her eyes, I must suffer grief, sire, I have too much happiness in being able — to hope!

Don Fernando — Hope in thy manly resolution; hope in my promise, and already possessing the heart of thy mistress, let time, thy valor, and thy king exert themselves to overcome a scrupulous feeling of honor which is contending against thee.

THE STORY OF ALI-BEY, THE PERSIAN.

By FÉNELON.

[FRANÇOIS DE SALIGNAC DE LA MOTHE-FÉNELON, French divine and author, was born at the Château de Fénelon in Périgord, August 6, 1651. He received holy orders at the seminary of St. Sulpice in Paris, and on the revocation of the Edict of Nantes (1685) was sent on a mission for the conversion of Protestants in Saintonge and Poitou. He was later intrusted with the education of Louis XIV.'s grandson, the Duke of Burgundy, and received as a reward for his services the abbey of St. Valery and the archbishopric of Cambrai. For many years Fénelon was engaged in a theological dispute with Bossuet concerning the devotional mysticism of the celebrated Madame Guyon, whose opinions he defended in the "Maxims of the Saints." Fénelon's masterpiece, "The Adventures of Telemachus," was published in 1699. Intended by the author only for the amusement and instruction of the young Duke of Burgundy, it was regarded by the king as a satire on the court. In consequence the book was suppressed and Fénelon was restrained within his own diocese. Other works are: "Dialogues of the Dead," "Dialogues on Eloquence," "Letters on Religion," etc. Fénelon died at Cambrai in 1715.]

SHAH ABBAS, king of Persia, once when making a journey, withdrew from all his court, in order to travel through the country without being recognized, and to see the people in all their natural liberty; he therefore took with him only one of his courtiers. "I do not know at all," said the king to him, "the true manners of men; everything that we come in contact with is disguised. It is art, and not simple nature, that we see. I wish to study rustic life, and to see the class of men that is so scorned, although it is the true support of human society. I am tired of seeing courtiers who observe me in order to surprise me with flatteries, and I desire to visit laborers and shepherds who do not know me." He passed with his follower through several villages where the country people were dancing, and he was charmed to find far from courts these tranquil and inexpensive pleasures. He had a meal in

FÉNELON.

a hut, and as he was very hungry, having walked an unusual distance, the coarse food of the peasants seemed to him more agreeable than all the delicate dishes of his own table.

While passing through a meadow sown with flowers and bordering on a clear stream, he saw a young shepherd playing the flute under a great elm, among his sheep. He accosted him, and on questioning him found his expression pleasant and his manner simple and ingenuous, but noble and gracious. The rags in which he was clad did not lessen the effect of his beauty, and the king supposed at first that it was some person of illustrious birth tending sheep in disguise; but he learned from the shepherd that his father and mother were in a neighboring village, and that his name was Ali-bey. As the king questioned him, he admired his sensible answers. The lad's eyes were bright, but neither burning nor fierce, and his voice was gentle and sympathetic. His face was not in the least coarse, neither was it weak and effeminate. The shepherd boy, about seventeen years old, had no idea how he appeared to others, and supposed that he thought and spoke like all the other shepherds of his village; whereas he had learned, without education, all that reason can teach those who listen to her. The king, having conversed with him familiarly, was charmed by him. He found out from the boy about the state of the people, which kings never learn from the crowd of flatterers who surround them. From time to time he laughed at the innocence of this child, who made no effort to please by his answers. It was a great novelty for the king to hear any one speak so naturally. He made a sign to the courtier who accompanied him not to reveal that he was the king, for he feared that Ali-bey would lose in a moment all his naturalness if he should learn to whom he was speaking. "I see clearly," said the king to the courtier, "that nature is not less beautiful in the lowest ranks than in the highest. Never did a king's son appear better than this lad who keeps sheep. I should consider myself most happy to have a son as stalwart, as sensible, and as gentle. He seems to me fit for any career, and if any one would take the pains to educate him, he would surely be one day a great man."

So the king carried off Ali-bey, who was greatly surprised to know to whom he had made himself agreeable. He was taught to read, to write, to sing, and finally had masters for the ornamental arts and sciences. At first he was somewhat dazzled by the court, and his great change of fortune changed his heart a little. His youth and popularity together altered a little his wisdom and moderation. Instead of his crook, his flute, and shepherd's dress, he had a robe of purple embroidered with gold, and a turban covered with precious stones. His beauty surpassed all that was in the court before him; he made himself capable of dealing with serious affairs, and won the confidence of his master; who, knowing Ali-bey's exquisite taste in all the magnificent splendors of a palace, gave him finally an office, in Persia very important, involving the charge of all the king's jewels and most precious possessions.

During the life of the Shah Abbas, the favor of Ali-bey continued to increase. As he gradually grew to a mature age, he often thought of his former condition and often regretted it. "O beautiful days!" he used to say to himself, "innocent days when I enjoyed a pure and untroubled happiness; days since when I have seen nothing so sweet, shall I never see you again? He who has deprived me of you, though giving me so great riches, has deprived me of everything." He went back to see his village, and visited with sadness all the places where he had once danced, sung, and played the flute with his companions. He made presents to all his relatives and friends; but he wished them, as the greatest happiness, never to leave their country life, never to experience the sorrows of the court.

He himself experienced these sorrows after the death of his good master Shah Abbas. His son, Shah Sephi, succeeded him, and envious and treacherous courtiers found means of warning him against Ali-bey. "He has abused the confidence of the late king," they said; "he has amassed enormous treasures, and has appropriated several costly articles of which he was guardian." Shah Sephi was at the same time young and a prince, which was enough to render him credulous, neglectful, and reckless. He had the vanity to wish to seem to reform what his father had done, and to judge better than he. In order to have a pretext for removing Ali-bey from his office, he followed the advice of the envious courtiers, and ordered him to produce a scimiter ornamented with diamonds of enormous price, which the king's grandfather had been accustomed to carry in battle. Shah Abbas had long ago caused all the diamonds to be removed from the scimiter, and Ali-bey proved by trustworthy witnesses that the removal had taken place by the order of the late king, and before he had received his office.

When Ali-bey's enemies saw that they could not employ this pretext to destroy him, they advised Shah Sephi to command him to make within two weeks an exact inventory of all the precious objects in his charge. At the end of the two weeks the king desired to see all the things himself. Ali-bey opened all the doors, and showed the king all that he had in his care. Nothing was lacking, all was well cared for and in good order. The king, greatly astonished at finding everything so carefully kept, had almost decided to restore Ali-bey to favor, when he noticed, at the end of a long gallery full of sumptuous furnishings, an iron door with three large locks. "There is the place," whispered the jealous courtiers, "in which Ali-bey has hidden all the precious jewels that he has stolen from you." Immediately the king cried out angrily, "I wish to see what is the other side of that door. What have you put there? Show me." At these words Ali-bey threw himself on his knees, and begged the king not to deprive him of his most precious possessions on earth. "It is not just," said he, "that I should lose in one moment all that remains to me, and gives me repose, after having labored so many years for your royal father. Take from me, if you will, all the rest, but leave me this." The king did not doubt that it was some wrongfully acquired treasure that Ali-bey had hoarded, so he took a more imperative tone, and ordered absolutely that the door should be opened. Finally Ali-bey, who had the keys, opened it himself. But nothing was to be found there except the crook, flute, and shepherd's dress that Ali-bey had worn of old, which he often came to see, from fear of forgetting his early life. "Behold, great king," said he, "the precious relics of my former happiness; neither fortune nor your power have been able to deprive me of them. Here is my treasure, that I am keeping to enrich me when you have made me poor. Take back all the rest, but leave me these dear pledges of my early happiness. O, dear symbol of a quiet and happy life, it is with you that I would live and die!" The king, hearing these words, understood Ali-bey's innocence, and being indignant at the courtiers who had tried to ruin him, exiled them from the court. Ali-bey became his chief minister, and had charge of the most private affairs of state; but every day he went to see his crook, flute, and shepherd's dress, which he kept always ready in case a change of fortune should deprive him of the royal favor. He died in a ripe old age, without having wished either to punish his enemies, or to **accumulate** a treasure, and left to his heirs only enough to maintain them as shepherds, a condition of life which he thought the most secure and the most happy.

SONNETS OF LOPE DE VEGA.

Translated by LONGFELLOW.

[LOPE DE VEGA (Lope Felix de Vega Carpio), the famous Spanish dramatist and poet, was born at Madrid on the 25th of November, 1562. He went to the Jesuits' college of Madrid and the University of Alcalá, after which he was attached to the service of the Bishop of Avila and the Duke of Alva. In 1588 he joined the Armada and while at sea wrote the poem entitled "Angelica." He entered the Church about 1612, and took priest's orders (1614). He died at Madrid, August 27, 1635. Vega was the idol of his contemporaries, and his popularity outside of Spain was almost as remarkable. One of the most prolific authors in the history of literature, he wrote, according to a conservative estimate, eighteen hundred three-act plays, besides hundreds of "autos," several long epic poems, prose romances, religious pastorals, dramatic interludes, etc. Of his four hundred and fifty printed plays may be mentioned: "The Star of Seville," his chief work; "The Gardener's Dog"; "Love and Honor"; "Cavalier of Olmedo."]

THE GOOD SHEPHERD.

SHEPHERD! that with thine amorous, sylvan song
Hast broken the slumber which encompassed me,—
That mad'st thy crook from the accursed tree,
On which thy powerful arms were stretched so long!
Lead me to mercy's ever-flowing fountains;
For thou my shepherd, guard, and guide shalt be;
I will obey thy voice, and wait to see
Thy feet all beautiful upon the mountains.
Hear, Shepherd!—thou who for thy flock art dying,
O, wash away these scarlet sins, for thou
Rejoicest at the contrite sinner's vow.
O, wait!—to thee my weary soul is crying,—
Wait for me!—Yet why ask it, when I see,
With feet nailed to the cross, thou'rt waiting still for me!

TO-MORROW.

Lord, what am I, that, with unceasing care,
Thou didst seek after me,—that thou didst wait,
Wet with unhealthy dews, before my gate,
And pass the gloomy nights of winter there?

O strange delusion! — that I did not greet
Thy blest approach, and O, to Heaven how lost,
If my ingratitude's unkindly frost
Has chilled the bleeding wounds upon thy feet.
How oft my guardian angel gently cried,
"Soul, from thy casement look, and thou shalt see
How he persists to knock and wait for thee!"
And, O! how often to that voice of sorrow,
"To-morrow we will open," I replied,
And when the morrow came I answered still, "To-morrow."

FUNERAL ORATION ON HENRIETTA, DUCHESS OF ORLEANS.

By BOSSUET.

[JACQUES BÉNIGNE BOSSUET, French prelate, pulpit orator, and theologian, was born at Dijon, September 27, 1627. After studying at the Jesuits' college there and at the College of Navarre in Paris, he took priest's orders and became canon of Metz. His fame as a pulpit orator procured him the honor of preaching before Louis XIV., and in 1669 he was ordained Bishop of Condom. He resigned the see on being appointed preceptor to the Dauphin, for whom he is said to have written the "Discourse on Universal History." In 1681 he was raised to the bishopric of Meaux, and passed the remainder of his life in his diocese. He died at Paris, April 12, 1704. Bossuet was one of the ablest defenders of the doctrines of the Church of Rome, but took up a strong attitude in favor of the independence of the Gallican Church. In his old age he opposed Quietism and became involved in a controversy with Fénelon, Archbishop of Cambrai. In addition to his main work he published, "Funeral Orations," those on the Duchess of Orleans and the great Condé being masterpieces of eloquence; "History of the Variations of the Protestant Churches"; "Exposition of the Catholic Doctrine."]

PART THE FIRST.

AM I then called upon once more to pay the last honors to the dead? is she whom (a few months past) I beheld so attentive while I was discharging this mournful duty to the Queen, her mother, is she become the melancholy theme of this day's solemnity? Oh, vanity! oh, airy nothing! Little did she imagine, while the filial tear was stealing down her cheek, that in so short a space of time the same company should be assembled, to perform the same mournful honors to her own memory. Lamented princess! must England not only deplore thy absence, but also lament thy death? And has France no other pomp, no other triumph, no other trophies than these to celebrate thy return? — Vanity of vanities, and all is vanity! These are the only thoughts that occur, this the only reflection that clings to my soul in the present unforeseen and sudden calamity. This text, which comes home to every bosom, which regards every state, and accompanies all the events and vicissitudes of life, acquires a particular illustration from the object of our present concern. For never were the vanities of this world so strongly displayed, and so conspicuously degraded. The scene that now arrests and terrifies our attention, urges me to declare that health is but an empty name, life a troubled dream, and celebrity a fugitive meteor. Is then man (made after God's own image) a despicable being? is man, whom the Savior of the world, without debasement, redeemed with his precious blood; is man, thus honored, a mere shadow? This mournful exhibition of human vanity, this untimely death, which chills the public hope, misled my judgment. Man must not be allowed to entertain an unqualified idea of self-degradation. Solomon, who begins his divine work with the words of my text, concludes with revealing to man his dignity: "Fear God, and keep his commandments, for this is the whole duty of man: for God shall bring every work into judgment, with every secret thing, whether it be good, or whether it be evil!" So everything is vain and unimportant that relates to man, when we advert to the transitory course of his mortality: everything becomes dignified when we look to the goal to which he is hastening. Let us then, in the presence of that altar and of that tomb, meditate upon that passage of Ecclesiastes, where the first part discovers the nothingness of man, and the second establishes his greatness. Let yonder tomb convince us of our wretchedness, while yon altar (from whence our prayers ascend) informs us of our dignity. You are now apprised of the truths which I wish this day to inculcate, which are not unworthy of the notice of the great personage, and of the illustrious assembly, before whom I am now speaking.

As a stream glides rapidly along, thus flows the course of our existence, which, after having traversed, with more or less noise, a greater or less extent of country, disembogues at length into a dark gulf! where honors, distinctions, and worldly prerogatives are unacknowledged and unknown; like rivers which lose their name and their celebrity when they mingle with the ocean.

If human nature could receive any partial exaltation, if a

small portion of the dust of which we are all formed could admit of any solid and durable distinction, who had a greater title to such preëminence? Does not the person who now awfully enforces the vanity of human greatness, does not she trace her origin to the remotest antiquity? Wherever I cast my view I am surrounded and dazzled with the splendor which streams from the crowns of England and of Scotland.

The Princess Henrietta, born, as it were, on a throne, possessed a mind superior to her illustrious birth, a mind which the misfortunes of her family could not subdue. How frequently have we said that Providence had snatched her from the enemies of her august father to make a present of her to France? Precious and inestimable gift! if enduring possession had accompanied a present of such value. This melancholy recollection intrudes itself everywhere. No sooner do we cast our eyes on this illustrious personage, than the specter Death rushes on our thoughts. Let me, however, recall to your mind, how she grew up amidst the wishes, the applause, and affection of a whole kingdom: every year added to her personal attractions, and brought with it an accession of mental accomplishments. Her judgment in works of literature was clear and unerring; authors, when they met with her approbation, felicitated themselves on having attained that point of perfection to which they aspired. History, to which her attention was particularly directed, she used to call the counselor of kings. In the historic page the greatest monarchs assume no other rank than what they are entitled to by their virtues: degraded by the hand of Death, they enter, unattended by flatterers, this severe court of justice, to receive the awful judgment of posterity. Here the gaudy coloring, which the harlot pencil of sycophancy had applied, languishes and fades away. In this school our young disciple studied the duties of those persons whose life forms the groundwork of history. This knowledge matured her youthful mind, and fenced it with a circumspective prudence. "He that has no rule over his own spirit," says the Wise Man, "is like a city that is broken down and without walls." The object of our present admiration was exalted above this weakness; nor interest, nor vanity, nor the enchantment of flattery, nor the persuasive voice of friendship, could allure the confided secret from her bosom. This characteristic feature entitled her to a confidence of the highest nature. Without presuming to enter upon a subject which does not belong to this place, I may be allowed to say that, by the mediation of the sister, some controverted points which lately existed between two great monarchs were happily adjusted. No sooner had she erected this monument to her fame, than she was swept to the grave. Have I ventured amidst this triumph of death to pronounce again the word "fame"? Let me hence forbear all pomp and splendor of expression with which human arrogance dazzles and blinds herself for the purpose of not beholding her own nothingness! Let me rather entreat you to attend to the reflection of a profound reasoner, not to the words of a philosopher in the porch, or a monk in his cloister. I wish to humble the great by one whom the great revere; by one who was well acquainted with the vanity of greatness, and who uttered his observations from a throne. "Oh, God," says the Psalmist, "thou hast numbered my days!" Now, whatever is numbered is finite, and whatever is born to end cannot be said to be emancipated from that nothing to which it is destined so soon to return. While the hand of nature chains us to the ground, how can we hope to be exalted? Survey the various distinctions that elevate man, you will discover none so conspicuous, so effective, so glittering, as the glory which encircles the laurels of a conqueror; and yet this conqueror must, in his turn, fall beneath the stroke of Death. Then will the conquered invite the triumphant hero to their society; then from the tomb a voice will come to blast all human grandeur: "Art thou become weak as we? art thou become like unto us?"

Perhaps, as a supplement to the deficiency of power and fortune, the mental accomplishments, expansive thought, invention pregnant with great designs, may suffice to raise the possessor to eminence. Ah, trust not to this flattering suggestion: the thoughts which have not God for their object belong to the domain of Death. Solomon comprises amidst the illusions by which the human race are misled, even wisdom! because, inclosed within the pale of human wishes, she buries herself in the dust along with those perishable objects.

Have we not seen the great and exalted of this world fall frequent sacrifices at the altar of God's vengeance for our instruction? And surely, if we stand in need of the impressions of surprise and terror to disenchant us from our attachment to the world, the calamity with which we are now subdued is sufficiently awful! Oh ever-memorable, oh disastrous, oh terrific night! when consternation reigned throughout the palace!

when, like a burst of thunder, a desolating voice cried out, Henrietta is expiring, Henrietta is no more! The usual march of Death is by perceptible but slow advances; in the present instance it was rapid as it was alarming. Did we not behold her in the morning attired with every grace, embellished with every attraction, and in the evening did we not behold her as a faded flower! Let us then survey her as Death presents her to our view: yet even these mournful honors, with which she is now encircled, will soon disappear, she will be despoiled of this melancholy decoration, and be conveyed into the dread receptacle, the last sombrous habitation, to sleep in the dust with annihilated kings; among whom it will be difficult to place her, so closely do the ranks press upon each other! so prompt, so indefatigable, is death in crowding this dreary vault with departed greatness. Yet even here our imagination deludes us; for this form, destitute of life, which still retains the human resemblance! the faint similitude which still lingers on the countenance, must undergo a change, and be turned into a terrific something, for which no language has a name; so true it is that everything dies belonging to man; even (as Tertullian observes) those funereal expressions which designate his remains. On a life which inevitably ends in such a catastrophe, what splendid project can the fondest hope erect? Is then despair the lot of man? Amidst this universal wreck is there no plank to lay hold of? Here I behold another order of things arise; the cloud breaks, the gloom of death disappears, a new scene bursts upon me, to which I beg leave to direct your attention.

Part the Second.

Let us gratefully remember that God infuses into our perishable frame a spiritual power, which can acknowledge the truth of his existence, adore the redundant plenitude of his perfections, rely on his goodness, fear his justice, and aspire to his immortality. By the principle of analogy, as our material form shall return to its mother earth, so our spiritual part shall return unto its Creator. This, indeed, is a proud distinction which brings into contact and alliance the spiritual part of man with the supreme and primitive greatness, God! Let then the wise man speak with derision of every state and condition of life, since, wherever we cast our view, we behold the funereal gloom of death hovering over our brightest hours. Let the wise man equalize the fool and the sage; let him even confound the lord of the earth with the beast of the field: for if we look at man, but through the medium of a coarse corporeal eye, what do we behold in his fugitive existence but folly, solicitude, and disappointment? and what do we behold in his death but an expiring vapor, or a machine whose springs are deranged, and which lose the power of action? Do ye wish to save anything from this total ruin? cast your affection as an anchor on God! This our Christian heroine eminently manifested during the period that immediately preceded her dissolution. She beheld the approaches of Death with an undaunted eye. He came to demand of her youth, the residue of its years! of her beauty, the resignation of its charms! of her high rank, the dispossession of its advantages! of her richly cultivated mind, the spoliation of its acquirements! To all which she meekly submitted without a murmur. Far other reflections now possess her soul. She calls for the same crucifix which the Queen, her mother, in her last moments bathed with her tears. She calls for the same crucifix, as if she fondly hoped still to find upon it the effusion of her mother's piety: she applied this signal of our salvation to her expiring lips: then did I hear her utter these affecting words, "Oh my God, why did I not always place my confidence in thee?" Ah! let the proud conqueror no longer engross our admiration; our heroine illustrates the truth of these words, "He that ruleth his spirit is better than he that taketh a city." With a tranquillity almost amounting to satisfaction, she resigned herself to an unforeseen and untimely death. What an attention did she pay to the prayers that are offered up for the dying! which frequently (by some spiritual magic) suspend the agonizing pains, and, what I have been often a witness to, charm away the terrors of death.

Have we not lamented that the opening flower was suddenly blasted? that the picture whose first warm touches excited such expectation was suddenly effaced? But I will no longer speak this language; I will rather say that Death has put an end to those perils to which she was in this life eminently exposed. What dazzling attractions, what seductive flattery, would have assailed so elevated a situation? Would not success have pampered her expectations, and adulation outrun her desire? And, to use the forcible expression of an ancient his-

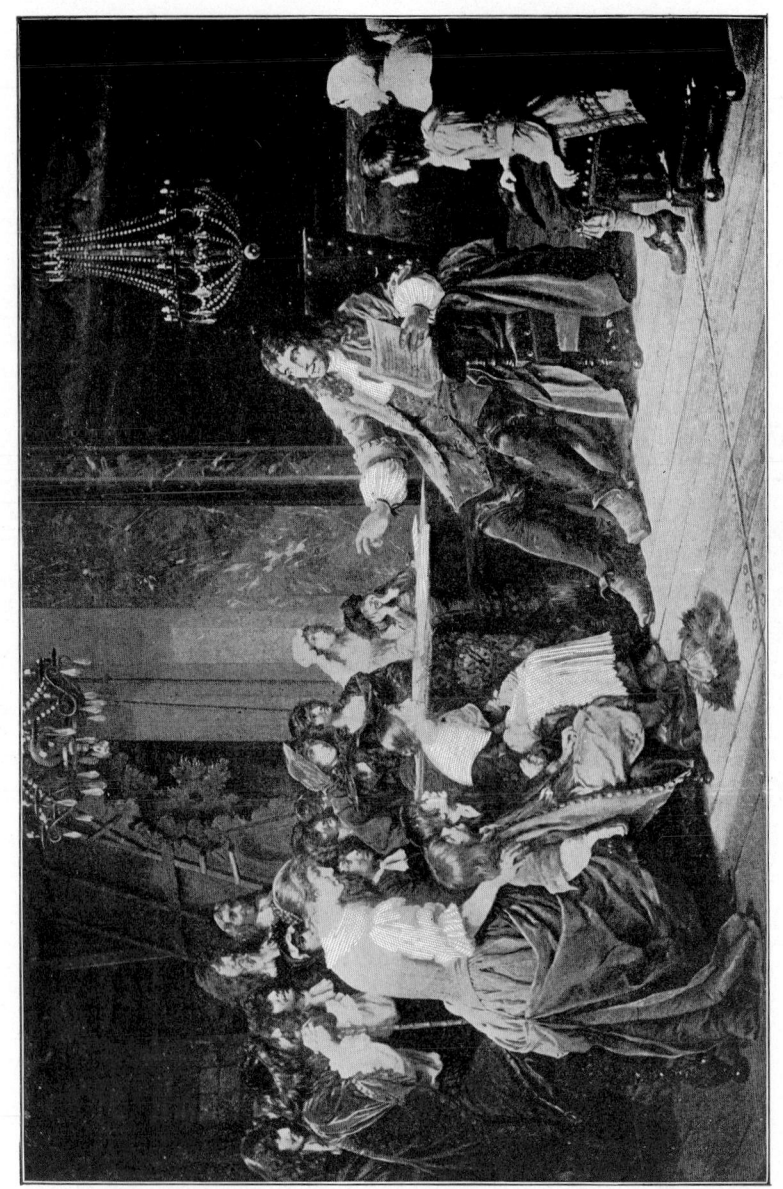

MOLIÈRE AND HIS TROUPE OF PLAYERS.

torian, "she would have been precipitated into the gulf of human grandeur."— *In ipsam gloriam præceps agebatur.* (Tacitus, "Vita Agricolæ.")

Let us draw some salutary reflection from the scene that is now before us. Shall we wait till the dead arise, before we open our bosom to one serious thought? What this day descends into the grave should be sufficient to awaken and alarm our lethargy. Could the Divine Providence bring nearer to our view, or more forcibly display, the vanity and emptiness of human greatness? How incurable must be our blindness, if, as every day we approach nearer and nearer to the grave (and rather dying than living), we wait till the last moment before we admit that serious and important reflection which ought to have accompanied us through the whole course of our lives! If persuasion hung upon my lips, how earnestly would I entreat you to begin from this hour to despise the smiles of fortune, and the favors of this transitory world! And whenever you shall enter those august habitations, those sumptuous palaces which received an additional luster from the personage we now lament; when you shall cast your eyes around those splendid apartments, and find their better wanting! then remember that the exalted station she held, that the accomplishments and attractions she was known to possess, augmented the dangers to which she was exposed in this world, and now form the subject of a rigorous investigation in the other.

THE AFFECTED LADIES.[1]

By MOLIÈRE.

(Translated by Charles Heron Wall.)

[MOLIÈRE (stage name of Jean Baptiste Poquelin), the greatest of French comedy writers, was the son of an upholsterer, and was born in Paris in 1622. He studied law for a time at Orleans, but, preferring the theatrical profession, at twenty-one joined a company styling themselves "Illustre Théâtre," and traveled in the provinces for many seasons. He was playing at Lyons in 1653, where his first piece, "L'Étourdi," a comedy of intrigue, was brought out. In 1658 Molière's company acted at Paris before Louis XIV., who was so highly pleased that he allowed them to establish themselves in the city under the title of the "Troupe de Monsieur" (later denominated "Troupe du Roi"). Molière continued his career as actor and dramatist, and produced in rapid succes-

[1] From "Moliere's Dramatic Works." By permission of Geo. Bell & Sons. 3 vols., price 1s. 6d. each.

sion "Les Précieuses Ridicules," "L'École des Femmes," "Le Misanthrope," "Le Médecin Malgré Lui," "Tartuffe," "L'Avare," "Le Bourgeois Gentilhomme," and "Le Malade Imaginaire." In 1662 he made an ill-assorted marriage with Armande Béjart, a young actress twenty years his junior, a union that embittered the latter part of his life. About 1667 he showed symptoms of lung disease, and on February 17, 1673, after a performance of "Le Malade Imaginaire," died of a hemorrhage. It was only through the intervention of the king that the Church allowed him burial. In the literature of comedy Molière bears the greatest name among the moderns after Shakespeare.]

Present: LA GRANGE, DU CROISY.

Du Croisy — I say, La Grange.

La Grange — What?

Du Croisy — Look at me a little without laughing.

La Grange — Well!

Du Croisy — What do you think of our visit; are you much pleased with it?

La Grange — Has either of us reason to be so, in your opinion?

Du Croisy — No great reason, if the truth be told.

La Grange — For my part I am dreadfully put out about it. Did ever anybody meet with a couple of silly country wenches giving themselves such airs as these? Did ever anybody see two men treated with more contempt than we were? It was as much as they could do to bring themselves to order chairs for us. I never saw such whispering, such yawning, such rubbing of eyes, such constant asking what o'clock it was. Why, they answered nothing but *yes* or *no* to all we said to them. Don't you think with me, that had we been the meanest persons in the world, they could hardly have behaved more rudely than they did?

Du Croisy — You seem to take it very much to heart.

La Grange — I should think I do. I feel it so much that I am determined to be revenged on them for their impertinence. I know well enough what made them look so coldly upon us: euphuism not only infects Paris, but has spread all over the country, and our absurd damsels have inhaled their good share of it. In a word, they are a compound of pedantry and affectation. I see pretty well what a man must be like to be well received by them; and if you take my advice, we will play them a trick which shall show them their folly, and teach them in future to judge people with more discernment.

Du Croisy — All right; but how will you manage it?

La Grange — I have a certain valet, named Mascarille, who in the opinion of many people passes for a kind of wit, — nothing is cheaper nowadays than wit, — an absurd fellow, who has taken into his head to ape the man of rank. He prides himself upon love intrigues and poetry, and despises those of his own condition so far as to call them vulgar wretches.

Du Croisy — And what use do you intend to make of him?

La Grange — I will tell you; he must — But let us first get away from here.

Enter GORGIBUS.

Gorgibus — Well, gentlemen, you have seen my daughter and my niece; did all run smoothly? what is the result of your visit?

La Grange — This you may better learn from them than from us; all we can say is that we thank you for the honor you have done us, and remain your most humble servants.

Du Croisy — And remain your most humble servants.

[*Exeunt.*

Gorgibus — Heyday! They seem to go away dissatisfied; what can have displeased them? I must know what's the matter. I say there!

Enter MAROTTE.

Marotte — Did you call, sir?

Gorgibus — Where are your mistresses?

Marotte — In their dressing room, sir.

Gorgibus — What are they doing?

Marotte — Making lip salve.

Gorgibus — They are always making salve. Tell them to come down. [*Exit* MAROTTE.

Gorgibus [*alone*] — I believe these foolish girls have determined to ruin me with their ointments. I see nothing about here but white of eggs, milk of roses, and a thousand fiddle-faddles that I know nothing about. Since we came here they have used the fat of a dozen hogs at least, and four servants might live on the sheep's trotters they daily require.

Enter MADELON *and* CATHOS.

Gorgibus — There is great need, surely, for you to spend so much money in greasing your nozzles! Tell me, please, what you can have done to those gentlemen, that I see them going away so coldly. Did I not ask you to receive them as persons whom I intended to give you for husbands?

Madelon — What! my father, could you expect us to have any regard for the unconventional proceedings of such people?

Cathos — What! my uncle, could you expect any girl, to the smallest extent in her senses, to reconcile herself to their persons?

Gorgibus — And what is there the matter with them?

Madelon — A fine way of making love to be sure, to begin at once with marriage!

Gorgibus — And what would you have them begin with — concubinage? Does not their conduct honor you as much as it does me? Can anything be more complimentary to you? and is not the sacred bond they propose a proof of the honesty of their intentions?

Madelon — Ah! father, how all you are saying betrays the vulgarity of your taste; I am ashamed to hear you speak as you do, and really you should make yourself acquainted with the fashionable air of things.

Gorgibus — I care neither for airs nor songs. I tell you that marriage is a holy and sacred thing, and that they acted like honorable men in speaking of it to you from the first.

Madelon — Really, if everybody was like you, how soon a love romance would be ended! What a fine thing it would have been if at starting Cyrus had married Mandane, and Aronce had been given straight off to Clélie! [In Mademoiselle de Scudéry's romances.]

Gorgibus — What in the world is the girl talking about!

Madelon — My cousin will tell you, as well as I, that marriage, my father, should never take place till after other adventures. A lover who wants to be attractive should know how to utter noble sentiments, to sigh delicate, tender, and rapturous vows. He should pay his addresses according to rules. In the first place, it should be either at church or in the promenade, or at some public ceremony, that he first sees the fair one with whom he falls in love; or else fate should will his introduction to her by a relation or a friend, and he should leave her house thoughtful and melancholy. For a while, he conceals his love from the object of his passion, but in the mean time pays her several visits, during which he never fails to start some subject of gallantry to exercise the thoughts of the assembled company. The day arrives for him to make his declaration. This should take place usually in some leafy garden walk, whilst everybody is out of hearing. The declaration is followed by our immediate displeasure, which shows itself by our blushing, and causes our lover to be banished for a time from our presence. He finds afterwards the means to appease us; to accustom us, by insensible degrees, to the rehearsal of his passion, and to obtain from us that confession which causes us so much pain. Then follow adventures: rivals who thwart our mutual inclination, persecution of fathers, jealousy based upon false appearances, reproaches, despair, elopement, and its consequences. It is thus things are carried on in high society, and in a well-regulated love affair these rules cannot be dispensed with. But to plunge headlong into a proposal of marriage, to make love and the marriage settlements go hand in hand, is to begin the romance at the wrong end. Once more, father, there is nothing more shopkeeper-like than such proceedings, and the bare mention of it makes me feel ill.

Gorgibus — What the devil is the meaning of all this jargon? Is that what you call "elevated style"?

Cathos — Indeed, uncle, my cousin states the case with all veracity. How can one be expected to receive with gratification persons whose addresses are altogether an impropriety? I feel certain that they have never seen the map of the "Country of Tenderness," and that "Billets-doux," "Trifling attentions," "Flattering letters," and "Sprightly verses," are regions unknown to them. [In Mademoiselle de Scudéry.] Was it not plainly marked in all their person? Are you not conscious that their external appearance was in no way calculated to give a good opinion of them at first sight? To come on a love visit with a leg lacking adornment, a hat destitute of feathers, a head unartistic as to its hair, and a coat that suffers from an indigence of ribbons! Heavens! what lovers! What frugality of dress! What barrenness of conversation! It is not to be endured. I also noticed that their bands were not made by the fashionable milliner, and that their hauts-de-chausses [breeches] were at least six inches too narrow.

Gorgibus — I believe they are both crazed; not a word can I understand of all this gibberish — Cathos, and you, Madelon ——

Madelon — Pray, father, give up those strange names, and call us otherwise.

Gorgibus — Strange names! what do you mean? are they not those which were given you at your baptism?

Madelon — Ah me! how vulgar you are! My constant wonder is that you could ever have such a soul of wit as I for a daughter. Did ever anybody in refined language speak of "Cathos" [Kitty] and "Madelon," and must you not admit that a name such as either of these would be quite sufficient to ruin the finest romance in the world?

Cathos — It is but too true, uncle, that it painfully shocks a delicate ear to hear those names pronounced; and the name of Polixène which my cousin has chosen, and that of Aminte which I have taken for myself, have a charm which you cannot deny.

Gorgibus — Listen to me; one word is as good as a hundred. I won't have you adopt any other names than those given to you by your godfathers and godmothers; and as for the gentlemen in question, I know their families and their fortune, and I have made up my mind that you shall take them for husbands. I am tired of having you upon my hands; it is too much for a man of my age to have to look after two young girls.

Cathos — Well, uncle, all I can say is that I think marriage is altogether a very shocking thing.

Madelon — Let us enjoy for a time the *beau monde* of Paris, where we are only just arrived. Let us leisurely weave our own romance, and do not, we beg, hasten so much its conclusion.

Gorgibus [*aside*] — They are far gone, there is no doubt about it. [*Aloud*] Once more, understand me, get rid of all this nonsense, for I mean to have my own way; to cut matters short, either you will both be married before long, or, upon my word, you shall both be shut up in a nunnery. I'll take my oath of it. [*Exit*.

Cathos — Ah! my dear, how deeply immersed in matter your father is, how dull is his understanding, and what darkness overcasts his soul.

Madelon — What can I say, my dear? I am thoroughly ashamed for him. I can scarcely persuade myself that I am really his daughter, and I feel sure that at some future time it will be discovered that I am of a more illustrious descent.

Cathos — I fully believe it; yes, it is **exceedingly probable.** And when I too consider myself ——

Enter MAROTTE.

Marotte — There is a footman below, inquiring if you are at home; he says that his master wants to see you.

Madelon — Learn, imbecile, to express yourself with less vulgarity. Say: Here is an indispensable, who is inquiring if it is convenient for you to be visible.

Marotte — Why! I don't understand Latin, and I haven't learned filsofy out of the "Grand Cyrus," as you have done.

Madelon — The wretched creature! what a trial it is to bear with it! And who is this footman's master?

Marotte — He told me it was the Marquis of Mascarille.

Madelon — Ah! my dear, a marquis! Go by all means, and say that we are visible. No doubt it is some wit who has heard us spoken of.

Cathos — It must be so, my dear.

Madelon — We must receive him in this parlor rather than in our own room. Let us at least arrange our hair a little and keep up our reputation. Quick, come along and hold before us, in here, the counselor of the graces.

Marotte — Goodness! I don't know what kind of an animal that is; you must speak like a Christian if you wish me to understand you.

Cathos — Bring us the looking-glass, ignorant girl that you are, and mind you do not defile its brightness by the communication of your image. [*Exeunt.*

Present: MASCARILLE *and two* CHAIRMEN.

Mascarille — Stop, chairmen, stop! Gently, gently, be careful I say! One would think these rascals intend to break me to pieces against the walls and pavement.

First Chairman — Well! you see, master, the door is narrow, and you wished us to bring you right in.

Mascarille — I should think so! Would you have me, jackanapes, risk the condition of my feathers to the inclemencies of the rainy season, and that I should give to the mud the impression of my shoes? Be off, take your chair away.

Second Chairman — Pay us, then, sir, if you please.

Mascarille — Ha! what's that you say?

Second Chairman — I say, sir, that we want our money, if you please.

Mascarille [*giving him a box on the ear*] — How, scoundrel, you ask money of a person of my rank!

Second Chairman — Are poor people to be paid in this fashion? and does your rank get us a dinner?

Mascarille — Ha! I will teach you to know your right place! Do you dare, you scoundrels, to set me at defiance?

First Chairman [*taking up one of the poles of the chair*] — Pay us at once; that's what I say.

Mascarille — What?

First Chairman — I must have the money this minute.

Mascarille — Now this is a sensible fellow.

First Chairman — Quick then.

Mascarille — Ay, you speak as you should do; but as for that other fellow, he doesn't know what he says. Here, are you satisfied?

First Chairman — No, you struck my companion, and I — [*holding up his pole*].

Mascarille — Gently, here's something for the blow. People can get everything out of me when they set about it in the right way; now go, but mind you come and fetch me by and by, to carry me to the Louvre for the *petit coucher*.

Enter MAROTTE

Marotte — Sir, my mistresses will be here directly.

Mascarille — Tell them not to hurry themselves; I am comfortably established here for waiting.

Marotte — Here they are. [*Exit*.

Enter MADELON *and* CATHOS *with* ALMANZOR.

Mascarille [*after having bowed to them*] — Ladies, you will be surprised, no doubt, at the boldness of my visit, but your reputation brings this troublesome incident upon you; merit has for me such powerful attractions, that I run after it wherever it is to be found.

Madelon — If you pursue merit, it is not in our grounds that you should hunt for it.

Cathos — If you find merit among us, you must have brought it here yourself.

Mascarille — I refuse to assent to such an assertion. Fame tells the truth in speaking of your worth; and you will pique, repique, and capot all the fashionable world of Paris.

Madelon — Your courtesy carries you somewhat too far in the liberality of your praises, and we must take care, my cousin and I, not to trust too much to the sweetness of your flattery.

Cathos — My dear, we should call for chairs.

Madelon — Almanzor!

Almanzor — Madam.

Madelon — Quick! convey us hither at once the appliances of conversation. [ALMANZOR *brings chairs.*

Mascarille — But stay, is there any security for me here?

Cathos — What can you fear?

Mascarille — Some robbery of my heart, some assassination of my freedom. I see before me two eyes which seem to me to be very dangerous fellows; they abuse liberty and give no quarter. The deuce! no sooner is any one near, but they are up in arms, and ready for their murderous attack! Ah! upon my word I mistrust them! I shall either run away or require good security that they will do me no harm.

Madelon — What playfulness, my dear.

Cathos — Yes, I see he is an Amilcar.

Madelon — Do not fear; our eyes have no evil intentions, your heart may sleep in peace and may rest assured of their innocence.

Cathos — But, for pity's sake, sir, do not be inexorable to that armchair which for the last quarter of an hour has stretched out its arms to you; satisfy the desire it has of embracing you.

Mascarille [*after having combed himself and adjusted his canions*] — Well, ladies, what is your opinion of Paris?

Madelon — Alas! can there be two opinions? It would be the antipodes of reason not to confess that Paris is the great museum of wonders, the center of good taste, of wit and gallantry.

Mascarille — I think for my part that out of Paris people of position cannot exist.

Cathos — That is a never-to-be-disputed truth.

Mascarille — It is somewhat muddy, but then we have sedan chairs.

Madelon — Yes, a chair is a wonderful safeguard against the insults of mud and bad weather.

Mascarille — You must have many visitors? What great wit belongs to your circle?

Madelon — Alas! we are not known yet; but we have every hope of being so before long, and a great friend of ours has promised to bring us all the gentlemen who have written in the "Elegant Extracts."

Cathos — As well as some others who, we are told, are the sovereign judges in matters of taste.

Mascarille — Leave that to me! I can manage that for you better than any one else. They all visit me, and I can truly say that I never get up in the morning without having half a dozen wits about me.

Madelon — Ah! we should feel under the greatest obligation to you if you would be so kind as to do this for us: for it is certain one must be acquainted with all those gentlemen in order to belong to society. By them reputations are made in Paris, and you know that it is quite sufficient to be seen with some of them to acquire the reputation of a connoisseur, even though there should be no other foundation for the distinction. But, for my part, what I value most is that in such society we learn a hundred things which it is one's duty to know and which are the quintessence of wit: the scandal of the day; the latest things out in prose or verse. We hear exactly and punctually that a Mr. A. has composed the most beautiful piece in the world on such and such a subject; that Mrs. B. has adapted words to such and such an air, that Mr. C. has composed a madrigal on the fidelity of his ladylove, and Mr. D. upon the faithlessness of his; that yesterday evening Mr. E. wrote a sixain to Miss F., to which she sent an answer this morning at eight o'clock; that Mr. G. has such and such a project in his head, that Mr. H. is occupied with the third volume of his romance, and that Mr. J. has his work in the press. By knowledge like this we acquire consideration in every society; whereas if we are left in ignorance of such matters, all the wit we may possess is a thing of naught and as dust in the balance.

Cathos — Indeed, I think it is carrying the ridiculous to the extreme, for any one who makes the least pretense to wit, not to know even the last little quatrain that has been written. For my part, I should feel greatly ashamed if some one were by chance to ask me if I had seen some new thing which I had not seen.

THE AFFECTED LADIES.

Mascarille — It is true that it is disgraceful not to be one of the very first to know what is going on. But do not make yourself anxious about it; I will establish an Academy of wits in your house, and I promise you that not a single line shall be written in all Paris which you shall not know by heart before anybody else. I, your humble servant, indulge a little in writing poetry when I feel in the vein; and you will find handed about in all the most fashionable drawing-rooms of Paris two hundred songs, as many sonnets, four hundred epigrams, and more than a thousand madrigals, without reckoning enigmas and portraits.

Madelon — I must acknowledge that I am madly fond of portraits; there is nothing more elegant according to my opinion.

Mascarille — Portraits are difficult, and require a deep insight into character: but you shall see some of mine which will please you.

Cathos — I must say that for my part I am appallingly fond of enigmas.

Mascarille — They form a good occupation for the mind, and I have already written four this morning, which I will give you to guess.

Madelon — Madrigals are charming when they are neatly turned.

Mascarille — I have a special gift that way, and I am engaged in turning the whole Roman History into madrigals.

Madelon — Ah! that will be exquisite. Pray let me have a copy, if you publish it.

Mascarille — I promise you each a copy beautifully bound. It is beneath my rank to occupy myself in that fashion, but I do it for the benefit of the publishers, who leave me no peace.

Madelon — I should think that it must be a most pleasant thing to see one's name in print.

Mascarille — Undoubtedly. By the bye, let me repeat to you some extempore verses I made yesterday at the house of a friend of mine, a duchess, whom I went to see. You must know that I am a wonderful hand at impromptus.

Cathos — An impromptu is the touchstone of genius.

Mascarille — Listen.

Madelon — We are all ears.

Mascarille —

>Oh! oh! I was not taking care.
>While thinking not of harm, I watch my fair.
>Your lurking eye my heart doth steal away.
>Stop thief! Stop thief! Stop thief! I say.

Cathos — Ah me! It is gallant to the last degree.

Mascarille — Yes, all I do has a certain easy air about it. There is a total absence of the pedant about all my writings.

Madelon — They are thousands and thousands of miles from that.

Mascarille — Did you notice the beginning? "Oh! oh!" There is something exceptional in that "Oh! oh!" like a man who bethinks himself all of a sudden — "Oh! oh!" Surprise is well depicted, is it not? "Oh! oh!"

Madelon — Yes, I think that "Oh! oh!" admirable.

Mascarille — At first sight it does not seem much.

Cathos — Ah! what do you say? these things cannot be too highly valued.

Madelon — Certainly, and I would rather have composed that "Oh! oh!" than an epic poem.

Mascarille — Upon my word now, you have good taste.

Madelon — Why, yes, perhaps it's not altogether bad.

Mascarille — But do you not admire also, "I was not taking care?" "I was not taking care:" I did not notice it, quite a natural way of speaking you know: "I was not taking care." "While thinking not of harm:" whilst innocently, without forethought, like a poor sheep, "I watch my fair:" that is to say, I amuse myself by considering, observing, contemplating you. "Your lurking eye"— what do you think of this word "lurking"? Do you not think it well chosen?

Cathos — Perfectly well.

Mascarille — "Lurking," hiding: you would say, a cat just going to catch a mouse: "lurking."

Madelon — Nothing could be better.

Mascarille — "My heart doth steal away:" snatch it away, carries it off from me. "Stop thief! Stop thief! Stop thief!" Would you not imagine it to be a man shouting and running after a robber? "Stop thief! Stop thief! Stop thief!"

Madelon — It must be acknowledged that it is witty and gallant.

Mascarille — I must sing you the tune I made to it.

Cathos — Ah! you have learnt music?

Mascarille — Not a bit of it!

Cathos — Then how can you have set it to music?

Mascarille — People of my position know everything without ever having learnt.

Madelon — Of course it is so, my dear.

Mascarille — Just listen, and see if the tune is to your taste; hem, hem, la, la, la, la, la. The brutality of the season has greatly injured the delicacy of my voice; but it is of no consequence; permit me, without ceremony : [*he sings*]

> Oh! oh! I was not taking care.
> While thinking not of harm, I watch my **fair**.
> Your lurking eye my heart doth steal away.
> Stop thief! Stop thief! Stop thief! I say.

Cathos — What soul-subduing music! One would willingly die while listening.

Madelon — What soft languor creeps over one's heart!

Mascarille — Do you not find the thought clearly expressed in the song? "*Stop thief*, stop *thief*." And then as if one suddenly cried out "*stop, stop, stop, stop,* stop thief." Then all at once, like a person out of breath — "*Stop* thief!"

Madelon — It shows a knowledge of perfect beauty; every part is inimitable, both the words and the air enchant me.

Cathos — I never yet met with anything worthy of being compared to it.

Mascarille — All I do comes naturally to me. I do it without study.

Madelon — Nature has treated you like a fond mother; you are her spoiled child.

Mascarille — How do you spend your time, ladies?

Cathos — Oh! in doing nothing at all.

Madelon — Until now, we have been in a dreadful dearth of amusements.

Mascarille — I should be happy to take you to the play one of these days, if you would permit me; the more so as there is a new piece going to be acted which I should be glad to see in your company.

Madelon — There is no refusing such an offer.

Mascarille — But I must beg of you to applaud it well when we are there, for I have promised my help to praise up the piece; and the author came to me again this morning to beg my assistance. It is the custom for authors to come and read their new plays to us people of rank, so that they may persuade us to approve their work, and to give them a reputation. I leave you to imagine if, when we say anything, the pit dare contradict us. As for me, I am most scrupulous, and when once I have promised my assistance to a poet I always call out "splendid! beautiful!" even before the candles are lighted.

Madelon — Do not speak of it; Paris is a most wonderful place; a hundred things happen every day there of which country people, however clever they may be, have no idea.

Cathos — It is sufficient; now we understand this, we shall consider ourselves under the obligation of praising all that is said.

Mascarille — I do not know whether I am mistaken; but you seem to me to have written some play yourselves.

Madelon — Ah! there may be some truth in what you say.

Mascarille — Upon my word, we must see it. Between ourselves, I have composed one which I intend shortly to bring out.

Cathos — Indeed; and to what actors do you mean to give it?

Mascarille — What a question! Why, to the actors of the Hôtel de Bourgogne [a rival company to Molière's], of course; they alone can give a proper value to a piece. The others are a pack of ignoramuses, who recite their parts just as one speaks every day of one's life; they have no idea of thundering out verses, or of pausing at a fine passage. How can one make out where the fine lines are if the actor does not stop at them, and thus tell you when you are to applaud?

Cathos — Certainly, there is always a way of making an audience feel the beauties of a play; and things are valued according to the way they are put before you.

Mascarille — How do you like my lace, feathers, and et-ceteras? Do you find any incongruity between them and my coat?

Cathos — Not the slightest.

Mascarille — The ribbon is well chosen, you think?

Madelon — Astonishingly well. It is real Perdrigeon.

Mascarille — What do you say of my canions?

Madelon — They look very fashionable.

Jodelet—And in places too where it was warm indeed.

Mascarille [*looking at* CATHOS *and* MADELON]—Ay, ay, but not so warm as it is here! Ha, ha, ha!

Jodelet—Our acquaintance began in the army; the first time we met he commanded a regiment of horse on board the galleys of Malta.

Mascarille—It is true; but you were in the service before me, and I remember that I was but a subaltern when you commanded two thousand horse.

Jodelet—War is a grand thing. But s'death! nowadays the court rewards very badly men of merit like us.

Mascarille—Yes, yes, there's no doubt about it; and I intend to let my sword rest in its scabbard.

Cathos—For my part I am unutterably fond of men of the army.

Madelon—And so am I, but I like to see wit season bravery.

Mascarille—Do you remember, Viscount, our carrying that half-moon at Arras?

Jodelet—What do you mean by "half-moon"? It was a complete full one.

Mascarille—Yes, I believe you are right.

Jodelet—I ought to remember it, I was wounded then in the leg by a hand grenade, and I still bear the scars. Just feel here, I pray: you can realize what a wound it was.

Cathos [*after having felt the place*]—It is true that the scar is very large.

Mascarille—Give me your hand, and feel this one, just here at the back of my head! Have you found it?

Madelon—Yes, I feel something.

Mascarille—It is a musket shot I received the last campaign I made.

Jodelet [*uncovering his breast*]—Here is another wound which went quite through me at the battle of Gravelines.

Mascarille [*about to unbutton*]—And I will show you a terrible scar which ——

Madelon—Pray do not; we believe you without seeing.

Mascarille—They are honorable marks, which tell the stuff a man is made of.

Cathos—We have no doubt whatever of your valor.

Mascarille—Viscount, is your carriage waiting?

Jodelet—Why?

Mascarille — Because we would have taken these ladies for a drive, and have given them a collation.

Madelon — Thank you, but we could not have gone out to-day.

Mascarille — Very well, then, let us send for musicians and have a dance.

Jodelet — A happy thought, upon my word.

Madelon — We can consent to that: but we must make some addition to our company.

Mascarille — Hallo there! Champagne, Picard, Bourguignon, Cascaret, Basque, La Verdure, Lorrain, Provençal, La Violette! Deuce take all the lackeys! I don't believe there is a man in all France worse served than I am. The villains are always out of the way when they are wanted.

Madelon — Almanzor, tell the servants of the Marquis to go and fetch some musicians, and then ask those gentlemen and ladies who live close by to come and people the solitude of our ball. [*Exit* ALMANZOR.

Mascarille — Viscount, what do you say of those eyes?

Jodelet — And you, Marquis, what do you think of them yourself?

Mascarille — I? I say that our liberty will have some trouble in coming off scathless. At least as far as I am concerned, I feel an unaccustomed agitation, and my heart hangs as by a single thread.

Madelon — How natural is all that he says! He gives to everything a most pleasing turn.

Cathos — His expenditure of wit is really tremendous.

Mascarille — To show you the truth of what I say, I will make some extempore verses upon the state of my feelings.

Cathos — Oh! I beseech you by all the devotion of my heart to let us hear something made expressly for us.

Jodelet — I should delight to do as much, but the quantity of blood I have lately lost has rather weakened my poetic vein.

Mascarille — Deuce take it all! I can always make the first verse to my satisfaction, but feel perplexed about the rest. After all, you know, this is being a little too much in a hurry. I will take my own time to make you some extempore verses, which you will find the most beautiful in the world.

Jodelet [*to* MADELON] — His wit is devilish fine!

Madelon — Gallant and neatly turned.

Mascarille — Viscount, tell me, have you seen the countess lately?

Jodelet — It is about three weeks since I paid her a visit.

Mascarille — Do you know that the duke came to see me this morning, and wanted to take me out into the country to hunt a stag with him?

Madelon — Here come our friends.

Enter LUCILE, CELIMÈNE, ALMANZOR, *and* Musicians.

Madelon — My dears, we beg you will excuse us. These gentlemen had a fancy for the soul of motion, and we sent for you to fill up the void of our assembly.

Lucile — You are very kind.

Mascarille — This is only a ball got up in haste, but one of these days we will have one in due form. Have the musicians come?

Almanzor — Yes, sir, here they are.

Cathos — Come then, my dears, take your places.

Mascarille [*dancing alone by way of prelude*] — La, la, la, la, la, la, la, la.

Madelon — He has a most elegant figure.

Cathos — And seems a proper dancer.

Mascarille [*taking out* MADELON *to dance*] — The liberty of my heart will dance a coranto as well as my feet. Play in time, musicians. Oh, what ignorant fellows! There is no possibility of dancing with them. Devil take you, can't you play in time? La, la, la, la, la, la, la, la. Steady, you village scrapers.

Jodelet [*dancing in his turn*] — Gently, don't play so fast, I have only just recovered from an illness.

Enter DU CROISY *and* LA GRANGE.

La Grange [*a stick in his hand*] — Ah! scoundrels, what are you doing here? We have been looking for you these three hours. [*He beats* MASCARILLE *and* JODELET.

Mascarille — Oh! oh! oh! You never said anything about blows.

Jodelet — Oh! oh! oh!

La Grange — It becomes you well, you rascal, to ape the man of rank.

Du Croisy — This will teach you to know your position.

[*Exeunt* Du Croisy *and* La Grange.

Madelon — What does this all mean?

Jodelet — It is a wager.

Cathos — What! to suffer yourselves to be beaten in that fashion!

Mascarille — Yes, I would not take any notice of it: I have a violent temper, and I should not have been able to command it.

Madelon — Such an insult in our presence!

Mascarille — Not worth mentioning, we have known each other for a long while now; and among friends we must not take offense at such trifles.

Reënter Du Croisy *and* La Grange.

La Grange — Ah! you rascals, you shall not laugh at us, I assure you. Come in, you there. [*Three or four ruffians enter.*

Madelon — What do you mean by coming to disturb us in our own house?

Du Croisy — What, ladies! shall we suffer our servants to be better received than we were? shall we allow them to come and make love to you at our expense, and to give you a ball?

Madelon — Your servants!

La Grange — Yes, our servants; and it is neither proper nor honest in you to entice them away from their duty as you have done.

Madelon — Heavens! What insolence!

La Grange — But they shall not have the advantage of wearing our clothes to dazzle your eyes, and if you wish to love them, it shall be for their good looks. Quick, you fellows, strip them at once.

Jodelet — Farewell our finery.

Mascarille — Farewell, marquisate; farewell, viscountship!

Du Croisy — Ah! ah! rascals, have you the impudence to wish to cut us out? You will have to find elsewhere, I can tell you, wherewith to make yourselves agreeable to your ladyloves.

La Grange — To supplant us; and that, too, in our own clothes. It is too much!

Mascarille — O Fortune, how inconstant thou art!

Du Croisy — Quick, I say, strip off everything that belongs to us.

La Grange — Take away all the clothes; quick! Now,

ladies, in their present condition, you may make love to them as much as you please. We leave you entirely free to act. This gentleman and I assure you that we shall be in no way jealous.

[*Exeunt all but* MADELON, CATHOS, JODELET, MASCARILLE, *and* Musicians.

Cathos — Ah! what humiliation.

Madelon — I am nearly dying with vexation.

First Musician [*to* MASCARILLE] — And what does all this mean? Who is to pay us?

Mascarille — Ask my lord the Viscount.

Second Musician [*to* JODELET] — Who is to give us our money?

Jodelet — Ask my lord the Marquis.

Enter GORGIBUS.

Gorgibus [*to* MADELON *and* CATHOS] — From all I hear and see, you have got us into a nice mess; the gentlemen and ladies who have just left have given me a fine account of your doings!

Madelon — Ah! my father, it is a most cruel trick they have played us.

Gorgibus — Yes, it is a cruel trick, no doubt, but one which results from your folly — miserable simpletons that you are. They felt insulted by your way of receiving them; and I, wretched man, must swallow the affront as best I may.

Madelon — Ah! I will be revenged or die in the attempt. And you, wretches! dare you stop here after all your insolence?

Mascarille — To treat a marquis in this manner! Yes, that's the way of the world; we are spurned by those who till lately cherished us. Come along, come along, my friend, let us go and seek our fortunes elsewhere; I see that nothing but outward show pleases here, and that they have no consideration for virtue unadorned. [*Exeunt* MASCARILLE *and* JODELET.

First Musician — Sir, we shall expect you to pay us, since they do not; for it was here we played.

Gorgibus [*beating them*] — Yes, yes, I will pay you, and here is the coin you shall receive. As for you, stupid, foolish girls, I don't know what keeps me from giving you as much. We shall become the laughingstock of the whole neighborhood; this is the result of all your ridiculous nonsense. Go, hide yourselves, idiots; hide yourselves forever [*exeunt* MADELON *and* CATHOS]; and you, the cause of all their folly, worthless trash, mischievous pastimes of vacant minds, romances, verses, songs, sonnets, lays and lies, may the devil take you all!

THE FABLES OF LA FONTAINE.

[JEAN DE LA FONTAINE, the noted French fabulist, was the son of a superintendent of woods and forests, and was born at Château-Thierry in Champagne, July 8, 1621. He left the College of Rheims at the age of nineteen to study for the ministry, but gave up that pursuit after two years. Invited to Paris by the Duchesse de Bouillon, he enjoyed the patronage of the Duchesse d'Orléans, Madame de Sablière, and Madame d'Hervart; and was on intimate terms with Molière, Boileau, Racine, and other contemporary celebrities. He became a member of the French Academy in 1683, but not without some opposition from Louis XIV., with whom he was never a favorite; and died at Paris, April 13, 1695. The "Fables," with which his name is chiefly associated, appeared between 1688 and 1694, the first six being inscribed to the Dauphin of France. His other writings consist of two volumes of "Contes" (Tales), "The Love of Psyche and Cupid," and some unimportant comedies.]

THE PEACOCK COMPLAINING TO JUNO.

THE peacock to the queen of heaven
  Complained in some such words:
" Great goddess, you have given
  To me, the laughingstock of birds,
A voice which fills, by taste quite just,
  All nature with disgust;
Whereas that little paltry thing,
  The nightingale, pours from her throat
  So sweet and ravishing a note,
She bears alone the honors of the spring."

  In anger Juno heard,
And cried, " Shame on you, jealous bird!
Grudge you the nightingale her voice,
Who in the rainbow neck rejoice,
Than costliest silks more richly tinted,
In charms of grace and form unstinted, —
  Who strut in kingly pride,
  Your glorious tail spread wide
With brilliants which in sheen do
Outshine the jeweler's bow window?

THE PEACOCK COMPLAINING TO JUNO

Is there a bird beneath the blue
   That has more charms than you?
No animal in everything can shine.
By just partition of our gifts divine,
Each has its full and proper share:
Among the birds that cleave the air,
The hawk's a swift, the eagle is a brave one,
For omens serves the hoarse old raven,
The rook's of coming ills the prophet;
   And if there's any discontent,
      I've heard not of it.
   Cease, then, your envious complaint;
   Or I, instead of making up your lack,
Will take your boasted plumage from your back."

The Lion going to War.

The lion had an enterprise in hand;
   Held a war council, sent his provost marshal,
   And gave the animals a call impartial, —
Each, in his way, to serve his high command.
The elephant should carry on his back
The tools of war, the mighty public pack,
And fight in elephantine way and form;
The bear should hold himself prepared to storm;
The fox all secret stratagems should fix;
The monkey should amuse the foe by tricks.
" Dismiss," said one, " the blockhead asses,
   And hares, too cowardly and fleet."
"No," said the king; "I use all classes;
   Without their aid my force were incomplete.
The ass shall be our trumpeter, to scare
Our enemy. And then the nimble hare
Our royal bulletins shall homeward bear."

A monarch provident and wise
Will hold his subjects all of consequence,
   And know in each what talent lies.
There's nothing useless to a man of sense.

The Stag seeing Himself in the Water.

   Beside a placid, crystal flood,
   A stag admired the branching wood
   That high upon his forehead stood,

But gave his Maker little thanks
For what he called his spindleshanks.
"What limbs are these for such a head!
So mean and slim!" with grief he said.
" My glorious head o'ertops
The branches of the copse;
My legs are my disgrace."
As thus he talked, a bloodhound gave him chase.
To save his life he flew
Where forests thickest grew.
His horns, — pernicious ornament! —
Arresting him where'er he went,
Did unavailing render
What else, in such a strife,
Had saved his precious life, —
His legs, as fleet as slender.
Obliged to yield, he cursed the gear
Which nature gave him every year.

Too much the beautiful we prize;
The useful, often, we despise:
Yet oft, as happened to the stag,
The former doth to ruin drag.

The Dog that dropped the Substance for the Shadow.

This world is full of shadow chasers,
Most easily deceived.
Should I enumerate these racers,
I should not be believed.
I send them all to Æsop's dog,
Which, crossing water on a log,
Espied the meat he bore, below;
To seize its image, let it go;
Plunged in; to reach the shore was glad,
With neither what he hoped, nor what he'd had.

The Carter in the Mire.

The Phaëton who drove a load of hay
Once found his cart bemired.
Poor man! the spot was far away
From human help — retired,
In some rude country place,
In Brittany, as near as I can trace,

Near Quimper Corentan, —
A town that poet never sang, —
Which Fate, they say, puts in the traveler's path,
When she would rouse the man to special wrath.
May Heaven preserve us from that route!
But to our carter, hale and stout:
Fast stuck his cart; he swore his worst,
And, filled with rage extreme,
The mudholes now he cursed,
And now he cursed his team,
And now his cart and load, —
Anon, the like upon himself bestowed.
Upon the god he called at length,
Most famous through the world for strength.
"Oh, help me, Hercules!" cried he;
"For if thy back of yore
This burly planet bore,
Thy arm can set me free."
This prayer gone up, from out a cloud there broke
A voice which thus in godlike accents spoke:
"The suppliant must himself bestir,
Ere Hercules will aid confer.
Look wisely in the proper quarter,
To see what hindrance can be found;
Remove the execrable mud and mortar
Which, axle deep, beset thy wheels around.
Thy sledge and crowbar take,
And pry me up that stone, or break;
Now fill that rut upon the other side.
Hast done it?" "Yes," the man replied.
"Well," said the voice, "I'll aid thee now;
Take up thy whip." "I have . . . but, how?
My cart glides on with ease!
I thank thee, Hercules."
"Thy team," rejoined the voice, "has light ado;
So help thyself, and Heaven will help thee too."

MADAME DE SÉVIGNÉ'S LETTERS.

[MARIE DE RABUTIN-CHANTAL, MARQUISE DE SÉVIGNÉ, French epistolary writer, was the daughter of the Baron de Chantal, representative of an ancient Burgundian family, and was born at Paris, February 6, 1626. She lost her parents in early childhood, and was brought up by her mother's brother, the Abbé de Coulanges. At eighteen she married the dissolute Marquis Henri de Sévigné, who was killed in a duel occasioned by one of his amours. The marquise for a time devoted herself to the education of her son and daughter, and then removed to Paris. Here she became a leader in the brilliant society of the French capital, and numbered among her admirers Prince Conti, Turenne, and Fouquet. In 1669 her daughter, to whom she was greatly attached, married the Comte de Grignan, governor of Provence, and the consequent separation occasioned the famous correspondence which still ranks as one of the finest monuments in the French language. The "Letters" cover a period of twenty-five years, and are a valuable source of information for the history and social condition of the time. Madame de Sévigné died at Grignan, April 18, 1696.]

The Drama of M. de Lauzun.

I.

TO HER COUSIN, M. DE COULANGES, MAÎTRE DES REQUÊTES.

PARIS, *Monday, Dec. 15, 1670.*

I AM going to tell you a thing the most astonishing, the most surprising, the most marvelous, the most miraculous, the most magnificent, the most confounding, the most unheard-of, the most singular, the most extraordinary, the most incredible, the most unforeseen, the greatest, the least, the rarest, the most common, the most public, the most private till to-day, the most brilliant, the most enviable, — in short, a thing of which there is but one example in past ages, and that not an exact one neither; a thing that we cannot believe at Paris, how then will it gain credit at Lyons? a thing which makes everybody cry, "Lord have mercy upon us!" a thing which causes the greatest joy to Madame de Rohan and Madame de Hauterive [because they married beneath their rank]; a thing, in fine, which is to happen on Sunday next, when those who are present will doubt the evidence of their senses; a thing which, though it is to be done on Sunday, yet perhaps will be unfinished on Monday. I cannot bring myself to tell it you: guess what it is. I give you three times to do it in. What, not a word to throw at a dog? Well, then, I find I must tell you. M. de Lauzun is to be married next Sunday at the Louvre to,—pray guess to whom! I give you four times to do it in, I give you six, I give you a hundred. Says Madame de Coulanges, "It is really very hard to guess; perhaps it is Madame de La Vallière."

Indeed, Madame, it is not.

"It is Mademoiselle de Retz, then."

No, nor she either; you are extremely provincial.

"Lord bless me," say you, "what stupid wretches we are! it is Mademoiselle de Colbert all the while."

Nay, now you are still farther from the mark.

"Why, then, it must certainly be Mademoiselle de Créqui."

You have it not yet. Well, I find I must tell you at last. He is to be married next Sunday, at the Louvre, with the king's leave, to Mademoiselle, Mademoiselle de — Mademoiselle — guess, pray guess her name; he is to be married to MADEMOISELLE, the great Mademoiselle; Mademoiselle, daughter to the late Monsieur [Gaston, Duc d'Orléans, brother of Louis XIII.]; Mademoiselle, granddaughter of Henry IV.; Mademoiselle d'Eu, Mademoiselle de Dombes, Mademoiselle de Montpensier, Mademoiselle d'Orléans, mademoiselle, the king's cousin-german, mademoiselle, destined to the throne, mademoiselle, the only match in France that was worthy of Monsieur [Philippe, Duc d'Orléans, brother of Louis XIV., and one of Mademoiselle's rejected suitors]. What glorious matter for talk! If you should burst forth like a bedlamite, say we have told you a lie, that it is false, that we are making a jest of you, and that a pretty jest it is without wit or invention, — in short, if you abuse us we shall think you quite in the right, for we have done just the same things ourselves. Farewell; you will find by the letters you receive this post whether we tell you truth or not.

II.

TO M. DE COULANGES.

PARIS, *Friday, Dec.* 19, 1670.

What is called falling from the clouds happened last night at the Tuileries; but I must go farther back. You have already shared in the joy, the transport, the ecstasies, of the princess and her happy lover. It was just as I told you; the affair was made public on Monday. Tuesday was passed in talking, astonishment, and compliments. Wednesday Mademoiselle made a deed of gift to M. de Lauzun, investing him with certain titles, names, and dignities necessary to be inserted in the marriage contract, which was drawn up that day. She gave him then, till she could give him something better, four duchies: the first was the county of Eu, which entitles him to rank as the first peer of France; the duchy of Montpensier, which title he bore all that day; the duchy of Saint Fargeau, and the duchy of Châtellerault, — the whole valued at twenty-two millions of livres. The contract was then drawn up, and he took the name of Montpensier. Thursday morning, which was yesterday, Mademoiselle was in expectation of the king's signing the contract, as he had said he would do; but about seven o'clock in the evening the queen, Monsieur, and several old dotards that were about him had so persuaded his Majesty that his reputation would suffer in the affair, that, sending for Mademoiselle and M. de Lauzun, he announced to them before the prince, that he forbade them to think any further of this marriage. M. de Lauzun received the prohibition with all the respect, submission, firmness, and, at the same time, despair that could be expected in so great a reverse of fortune. As for Mademoiselle, she gave loose to her feelings and burst into tears, cries, lamentations, and the most violent expressions of grief; she keeps her bed all day long and takes nothing within her lips but a little broth. What a fine dream is here! what a glorious subject for a tragedy or romance, but especially for talking and reasoning eternally! This is what we do day and night, morning and evening, without end and without intermission; we hope you will do likewise, *E fra tanto vi bacio le mani* ("and with this I kiss your hands").

III.

TO M. DE COULANGES.

Paris, *Wednesday, Dec.* 24, 1670.

You are now perfectly acquainted with the romantic story of Mademoiselle and of M. de Lauzun. It is a story well adapted for a tragedy, and in all the rules of the theater; we laid out the acts and scenes the other day. We took four days instead of four and twenty hours, and the piece was complete. Never was such a change seen in so short a time; never was there known so general an emotion. You certainly never received so extraordinary a piece of intelligence before. M. de Lauzun behaved admirably; he supported his misfortune with such courage and intrepidity, and at the same time showed so deep a sorrow, mixed with such profound respect, that he has gained the admiration of everybody. His loss is doubtless great, but then the king's favor, which he has by this means preserved, is likewise great, so that upon the whole his condition does not seem so very deplorable. Mademoiselle too has behaved extremely well on her side. She has wept much and bitterly; but yesterday, for the first time, she returned to pay her duty at the Louvre, after having received the visits of every one there. So the affair is all over. Adieu.

IV.

TO M. DE COULANGES.

PARIS, *Wednesday, Dec.* 31, 1670.

I have received your answers to my letters. I can easily conceive the astonishment you were in at what passed between the 15th and 20th of this month; the subject called for it all. I admire likewise your penetration and judgment in imagining so great a machine could never support itself from Monday to Sunday. Modesty prevents my launching out in your praise on this head, because I said and thought exactly as you did. I told my daughter on Monday, "This will never go on as it should do till Sunday; I will wager, notwithstanding this wedding seems to be sure, that it will never come to a conclusion." In effect, the sky was overcast on Thursday morning, and about ten o'clock, as I told you, the cloud burst. That very day I went about nine in the morning to pay my respects to Mademoiselle, having been informed that she was to go out of town to be married, and that the Coadjutor of Rheims was to perform the ceremony. These were the resolves on Wednesday night, but matters had been determined otherwise at the Louvre ever since Tuesday. Mademoiselle was writing; she had me shown in, finished her letter, and then, as she was in bed, made me place myself on my knees at her bedside; she told me to whom she was writing, and upon what subject, and also of the fine presents she had made the night before, and the titles she had conferred, and as there was no match in any of the courts of Europe for her, she was resolved, she said, to provide for herself. She related to me, word for word, a conversation she had had with the king, and appeared overcome with joy to think how happy she should make a man of merit. She mentioned with a great deal of tenderness the worth and gratitude of M.

de Lauzun. To all which I made her this answer, "Upon my word, Mademoiselle, you seem quite happy! but why was not this affair finished at once last Monday? Do you not perceive that the delay will give time and opportunity to the whole kingdom to talk, and that it is absolutely tempting God and the king, to protract an affair of so extraordinary a nature as this is to so distant a period?" She allowed me to be in the right, but was so sure of success that what I said made little or no impression on her at the time. She repeated the many amiable qualities of M. de Lauzun, and the noble house he was descended from. To which I replied in these lines of Sévère in "Polyeucte,"—

> Blame on her choice at least, I may not fling:
> Polyeucte can match, in name and blood, a king.

Upon which she embraced me tenderly. Our conversation lasted above an hour. It is impossible to repeat all that passed between us, but I may without vanity say that my company was agreeable to her, for her heart was so full that she was glad of any one to unburden it to. At ten o'clock she gave herself to the rest of France, who crowded to pay their compliments to her. She waited all the morning for news from court, but none came. All the afternoon she amused herself with putting M. de Montpensier's apartment in order. You know what happened at night. The next morning, which was Friday, I waited upon her, and found her in bed. Her grief redoubled at seeing me; she called me to her, embraced me, and whelmed me with her tears. "Ah!" said she, "you remember what you said to me yesterday. What foresight! what cruel foresight!" In short she made me weep, to see her weep so violently. I have seen her twice since; she still continues in great affliction but behaves to me as to a person that sympathized with her in her distress; in which she is not mistaken, for I really feel sentiments for her that are seldom felt for persons of such superior rank. This, however, between us two and Madame de Coulanges; for you are sensible that this chit-chat would appear ridiculous to others.

The Fire at M. Guitaud's.

TO MADAME DE GRIGNAN.

Friday, Feb. 20, 1671.

I cannot express how desirous I am to hear from you. Consider, my dear, I have not had a letter since that from La Palisse; I know nothing of the rest of your journey to Lyons, nor of your route to Provence. I am very certain that there are letters coming; but I await them, and I have them not. I have nothing left to comfort and amuse me but writing to you.

You must know that Wednesday night last, after I came from M. de Coulanges', where we had been making up our packets for the post, I began to think of going to bed. "That is nothing very extraordinary," you will say; but what follows is so. About three o'clock in the morning I was wakened with a cry of "Thieves! fire!" and it seemed so near, and grew so loud, that I had not the least doubt of its being in the house; I even fancied I heard them talking of my little granddaughter. I imagined she was burned to death, and in that apprehension got up without a light, trembling in such a manner that I could scarcely stand. I ran directly to her room, which is the room that was yours, and found everything quiet; but I saw Guitaud's house all in flames, and the fire spreading to Madame de Vauvineux's. The flames cast a light over our courtyard, and that of Guitaud, that made them look shocking. All was outcry, hurry, and confusion, and the beams and joists falling down made a dreadful noise. I immediately ordered our doors to be opened, and my people to give assistance. M. de Guitaud sent me a casket of valuables, which I secured in my cabinet, and then went into the street to gape like the rest. There I found Monsieur and Madame de Guitaud, Madame de Vauvineux, the Venetian ambassador, and all his people, with little Vauvineux, whom they were carrying fast asleep to the ambassador's house, with a great quantity of movables and plate. Madame de Vauvineux had removed all her goods. I knew our house was as safe as if it had been in an island, but I was greatly concerned for my poor neighbors. Madame Guêton and her brother gave some excellent directions, but we were all in consternation; the fire was so fierce that there was no approaching it, and no one supposed it would cease till it had burned poor Guitaud's house entirely down.

Guitaud himself was a melancholy object. He was for flying to save his mother, who was in the midst of the flames, as he supposed, in the upper part of the house; but his wife clung about him, and held him as tightly as she could. He was in the greatest distress. . . .

At last he begged me to lay hold of her, which I did, and he went in search of his mother, who, he found, had passed through the flames and was safe. He then endeavored to save some papers, but found it impossible to get near the place where they were. At length he came back to the spot where he had left us, and where I had prevailed on his wife to sit down. Some charitable Capuchins worked so well and so skillfully that they cut off the communication of the fire. Water was thrown upon the rest that was burning, and at last the battle ceased for want of combatants, but not till several of the best apartments were entirely consumed. It was looked upon as fortunate that any part of the house was saved, though as it is poor Guitaud will lose at least ten thousand crowns; for it is proposed to rebuild the room that was painted and gilded. There were lost several fine pictures of M. le Blanc's (whose house it was), besides tables, looking-glasses, tapestry, and other valuable pieces of furniture. They are greatly concerned about some letters, which I imagine to be those of the prince. By this it was near five o'clock in the morning, and time to think of getting Madame de Guitaud to rest. I offered her my bed; but Madame Guêton put her into hers, as she had several apartments in her house unoccupied. . . . She is still at Madame Guêton's, where everybody goes to see her.

You will naturally ask how the fire happened; but that no one can tell. There was not a spark in the room where it first broke out. Could any one have thought of diverting himself at so melancholy a time, what pictures might he not have drawn of us in the situation we were then in! Guitaud was naked, except his shirt and drawers; his wife was without stockings, and had lost one of her slippers; Madame de Vauvineux was in a short under petticoat, without a dressing gown; all the footmen and neighbors were in their nightcaps. The ambassador, in his dressing gown and long peruke, maintained very well the importance of a *serenissimo;* but his secretary was a most admirable figure. . . . So much for the melancholy news of our quarter. Let me beg of Deville that he will go his rounds every night after the family is in bed, to see that the fire is out everywhere, for we cannot be too careful to prevent accidents of this kind.

I hope the water was favorable to you in your passage; in a word, I wish you every happiness, and implore the God of heaven to preserve you from every evil. . . .

VATEL'S SUICIDE.

I.

TO HER DAUGHTER, MADAME DE GRIGNAN.

FRIDAY EVENING, *April* 24, 1671.
(From M. de La Rochefoucauld's.)

Here, then, I make up my packet. I had intended to tell you that the king arrived yesterday evening at Chantilly. He hunted a stag by moonlight; the lamps did wonders; the fireworks were a little eclipsed by the brightness of our serene friend, the moon; but the evening, the supper, and the entertainment went off admirably well. The weather we had yesterday gave us hopes of an end worthy of so fine a beginning. But what do you think I learned when I came here? I am not yet recovered and hardly know what I write. Vatel, the great Vatel, late *maître-d'hôtel* to M. Fouquet, and in that capacity with the prince [de Condé], a man so eminently distinguished for taste, and whose abilities were equal to the government of a State, — this man whom I knew so well, finding, at eight o'clock this morning, that the fish he had sent for did not come at the time he expected it, and unable to bear the disgrace that he thought would inevitably attach to him, ran himself through with his own sword. Guess what confusion so shocking an accident must have occasioned. Think too that perhaps the fish might come in just as he was expiring. I know no more of the affair at present; and I suppose you think this enough. I make no doubt the consternation was general; it must be very disagreeable to have so fatal an event break in upon an entertainment that cost fifty thousand crowns.

M. de Menars is to be married to Mademoiselle de La Grange-Neuville; but I do not know how I can have the heart to speak to you about anything but Vatel.

II.

TO MADAME DE GRIGNAN.

PARIS, *Sunday, April 26,* 1671.

This is Sunday, April 26, and this letter will not go out till Wednesday; but it is not so much a letter as a narrative that I have just learned from Moreuil of what passed at Chantilly with regard to poor Vatel. I wrote to you last Friday that he had stabbed himself. These are the particulars of the affair: The king arrived there on Thursday night; the walk and the collation, which was served in a place set apart for the purpose, and strewed with jonquilles, were just as they should be. Supper was served, but there was no roast meat at one or two of the tables on account of Vatel's having been obliged to provide several dinners more than were expected. This affected his spirits, and he was heard to say several times, —

"I have lost my fame! I cannot bear this disgrace!" "My head is quite bewildered," said he to Gourville. "I have not had a wink of sleep these twelve nights; I wish you would assist me in giving orders."

Gourville did all he could to comfort and assist him; but the failure of the roast meat (which, however, did not happen at the king's table, but at some of the other twenty-five) was always uppermost with him. Gourville mentioned it to the prince [Condé], who went directly to Vatel's room and said to him, "Everything is extremely well conducted, Vatel; nothing could be more admirable than his Majesty's supper." "Your Highness's goodness," replied he, "overwhelms me; I am aware that there was a deficiency of roast meat at two tables."

"Not at all," said the prince; "do not worry yourself, and all will go well."

Midnight came; the fireworks did not succeed, they were covered with a thick cloud; they cost sixteen thousand francs. At four o'clock in the morning Vatel went round, and found everybody asleep; he met one of the under purveyors, who had just come in with only two loads of fish.

"What!" said he, "is that all?"

"Yes, sir," said the man, not knowing that Vatel had dispatched other people to all the seaports round. Vatel waited for some time; the other purveyors did not arrive; his head grew distracted; he thought there was no more fish to be had; he flew to Gourville; "Sir," said he, "I cannot outlive this disgrace."

Gourville laughed at him. Vatel went up to his room, set the hilt of his sword against the door, and, after two ineffectual attempts, succeeded in the third in forcing the sword through his heart: he fell dead. At that instant the carriers arrived with the fish; Vatel was inquired after to distribute it. People went to his room, knocked at the door, broke it open, and found him weltering in his blood. They ran to acquaint the prince, who was in despair. The duke wept, for his Burgundy journey depended upon Vatel. The prince related the whole affair to his Majesty with an expression of great concern. It was considered as the consequence of too nice a sense of honor; some blamed, others praised him for his courage. The king said he had put off this excursion for more than five years, because he was aware that it would be attended with infinite trouble, and told the prince that he ought to have had but two tables, and not have been at the expense of so many, and declared he would never suffer him to do so again; but all this was too late for poor Vatel.

However, Gourville endeavored to supply the loss of Vatel, which he did in great measure. The dinner was elegant, the collation was the same. They supped, they walked, they hunted; all was perfumed with jonquilles, all was enchantment.

Yesterday, which was Saturday, the entertainments were renewed, and in the evening the king set out for Liancourt, where he had ordered a *media-noche* [a hearty meal of meat, eaten just after the stroke of midnight, when a feast day succeeds a fast day]; he is to stay there three days. This is what Moreuil has told me, hoping I should acquaint you with it. I wash my hands of the rest, for I know nothing about it. M. d'Hacqueville, who was present at the scene, will no doubt give you a faithful account of all that passed; but because his handwriting is not quite so legible as mine, I write too. If I am circumstantial, it is because on such an occasion I should like circumstantiality myself.

MEMOIRS OF THE DUKE OF SAINT-SIMON ON THE REIGN OF LOUIS XIV. AND THE REGENCY.[1]

[LOUIS DE ROUVROY, DUC DE SAINT-SIMON, a French writer of memoirs, was born at Paris, January 16, 1675, the son of a favorite nobleman of Louis XIII.'s court. He entered the army and fought at the siege of Namur, the battle of Neerwinden, etc., but in 1702 handed in his commission and turned his attention to court statesmanship. He was a member of the council of the regency under the Duke of Orleans, and in 1721 was sent to Spain as ambassador extraordinary to negotiate a marriage between the Infanta and the young king, Louis XV. His last years were clouded by domestic misfortunes and financial reverses, and he died a bankrupt on his estate at Laferté, March 2, 1755. His entertaining "Memoirs" throw a flood of light on court life under Louis XIV. and Louis XV.]

CHAPTER IV.

AFTER having paid the last duties to my father, I betook myself to Mons to join the Royal Roussillon cavalry regiment, in which I was captain. The King, after stopping eight or ten days with the ladies at Quesnoy, sent them to Namur, and put himself at the head of the army of M. de Boufflers, and camped at Gembloux, so that his left was only half a league distant from the right of M. de Luxembourg. The Prince of Orange was encamped at the Abbey of Pure, was unable to receive supplies, and could not leave his position without having the two armies of the King to grapple with: he entrenched himself in haste, bitterly repenting having allowed himself to be thus driven into a corner. We knew afterwards that he wrote several times to his intimate friend the Prince de Vaudemont, — saying that he was lost, and that nothing short of a miracle could save him.

We were in this position, with an army in every way infinitely superior to that of the Prince of Orange, and with four whole months before us to profit by our strength, when the King declared on the 8th of June that he should return to Versailles, and sent off a large detachment of the army into Germany. The surprise of the Maréchal de Luxembourg was without bounds. He represented the facility with which the Prince of Orange might now be beaten with one army and pursued by another, and how important it was to draw off detachments of the Imperial forces from Germany into Flanders, and how, by sending an army into Flanders instead of Germany, the

[1] By permission of Swan, Sonnenschein & Co., Ltd. (3 vols., 8vo., price 12s. net.)

whole of the Low Countries would be in our power. But the King would not change his plans, although M. de Luxembourg went down on his knees and begged him not to allow such a glorious opportunity to escape. Madame de Maintenon, by her tears when she parted from his Majesty, and by her letters since, had brought about this resolution.

The news had not spread on the morrow, June 9th. I chanced to go alone to the quarters of M. de Luxembourg, and was surprised to find not a soul there, every one having gone to the King's army. Pensively bringing my horse to a stand, I was ruminating on a fact so strange, and debating whether I should return to my tent or push on to the royal camp, when up came M. le Prince de Conti with a single page and a groom leading a horse. "What are you doing there?" cried he, laughing at my surprise. Thereupon he told me he was going to say adieu to the King, and advised me to do likewise. "What do you mean by 'saying adieu'?" answered I. He sent his servants to a little distance, and begged me to do the same, and with shouts of laughter told me about the King's retreat, making tremendous fun of him, despite my youth, for he had confidence in me. I was astonished. We soon after met the whole company coming back; and the great people went aside to talk and sneer. I then proceeded to pay my respects to the King, by whom I was honorably received. Surprise, however, was expressed by all faces, and indignation by some.

The effect of the King's retreat, indeed, was incredible, even amongst the soldiers and the people. The general officers could not keep silent upon it, and the inferior officers spoke loudly, with a license that could not be restrained. All through the army, in the towns, and even at Court, it was talked about openly. The courtiers, generally so glad to find themselves again at Versailles, now declared that they were ashamed to be there; as for the enemy, they could not contain their surprise and joy. The Prince of Orange said that the retreat was a miracle he could not have hoped for; that he could scarcely believe in it, but that it had saved his army, and the whole of the Low Countries. In the midst of all this excitement the King arrived with the ladies, on the 25th of June, at Versailles.

We gained some successes, however, this year. Maréchal de Villeroy took Huy in three days, losing only a sub-engineer and some soldiers. On the 29th of July we attacked at dawn the Prince of Orange at Neerwinden, and after twelve hours of hard fighting, under a blazing sun, entirely routed him. I was of the third squadron of the Royal Roussillon, and made five charges. One of the gold ornaments of my coat was torn away, but I received no wound. During the battle our brigadier, Quoadt, was killed before my eyes. The Duc de Feuillade became thus commander of the brigade. We missed him immediately, and for more than half an hour saw nothing of him; he had gone to make his toilette. When he returned he was powdered and decked out in a fine red surtout, embroidered with silver, and all his trappings and those of his horses were magnificent; he acquitted himself with distinction.

Our cavalry stood so well against the fire from the enemy's guns, that the Prince of Orange lost all patience, and turning away, exclaimed, "Oh, the insolent nation!" He fought until the last, and retired with the Elector of Hanover only when he saw there was no longer any hope. After the battle my people brought us a leg of mutton and a bottle of wine, which they had wisely saved from the previous evening, and we attacked them in good earnest, as may be believed. The enemy lost about twenty thousand men, including a large number of officers; our loss was not more than half that number. We took all their cannon, eight mortars, many artillery wagons, a quantity of standards, and some pairs of kettledrums. The victory was complete.

Meanwhile, the army which had been sent to Germany under the command of Monseigneur and of the Maréchal de Lorges, did little or nothing. The Maréchal wished to attack Heilbronn, but Monseigneur was opposed to it; and, to the great regret of the principal generals and of the troops, the attack was not made. Monseigneur returned early to Versailles.

At sea we were more active. The rich merchant fleet of Smyrna was attacked by Tourville; fifty vessels were burnt or sunk, and twenty-seven taken, all richly freighted. This campaign cost the English and Dutch dear. It is believed their loss was more than thirty millions of écus.

The season finished with the taking of Charleroy. On the 16th of September the Maréchal de Villeroy, supported by M. de Luxembourg, laid siege to it, and on the 11th of October, after a good defense, the place capitulated. Our loss was very slight. Charleroy taken, our troops went into winter quarters, and I returned to Court, like the rest. The roads and the posting service were in great disorder. Amongst other adventures I met with, I was driven by a deaf and dumb postilion, who stuck me fast in the mud when near Quesnoy. At Pont Saint-Maxence all the horses were retained by M. de Luxembourg. Fearing I might be left behind, I told the postmaster that I was a governor (which was true), and that I would put him in jail if he did not give me horses. I should have been sadly puzzled how to do it; but he was simple enough to believe me, and gave the horses. I arrived, however, at last in Paris, and found a change at the Court, which surprised me.

Daquin — first doctor of the King and creature of Madame de Montespan — had lost nothing of his credit by her removal, but had never been able to get on well with Madame de Maintenon, who looked coldly upon all the friends of her predecessor. Daquin had a son, an abbé, and wearied the King with solicitations on his behalf. Madame de Maintenon seized the opportunity, when the King was more than usually angry with Daquin, to obtain his dismissal; it came upon him like a thunderbolt. On the previous evening the King had spoken to him for a long time as usual, and had never treated him better. All the Court was astonished also. Fagon, a very skillful and learned man, was appointed in his place at the instance of Madame de Maintenon.

Another event excited less surprise than interest. On Sunday, the 29th of November, the King learned that La Vauguyon had killed himself in his bed, that morning, by firing twice into his throat. I must say a few words about this Vauguyon. He was one of the pettiest and poorest gentlemen of France; he was well made, but very swarthy, with Spanish features, had a charming voice, played the guitar and lute very well, and was skilled in the arts of gallantry. By these talents he had succeeded in finding favor with Madame de Beauvais, much regarded at the Court as having been the King's first mistress. I have seen her — old, blear-eyed, and half blind — at the toilette of the Dauphiness of Bavaria, where everybody courted her, because she was still much considered by the King. Under this protection La Vauguyon succeeded well; was several times sent as ambassador to foreign countries; was made councilor of state, and to the scandal of everybody, was raised to the Order in 1688. Of late years, having no appointments, he had scarcely the means of living, and endeavored, but without success, to improve his condition.

Poverty by degrees turned his brain; but a long time passed before it was perceived. The first proof that he gave of it was at the house of Madame Pelot, widow of the Chief President of the Rouen parliament. Playing at *brelan* one evening, she offered him a stake, and because he would not accept it bantered him, and playfully called him a poltroon. He said nothing, but waited until all the rest of the company had left the room; and when he found himself alone with Madame Pelot, he bolted the door, clapped his hat on his head, drove her up against the chimney, and holding her head between his two fists, said he knew no reason why he should not pound it into a jelly, in order to teach her to call him poltroon again. The poor woman was horribly frightened, and made perpendicular courtesies between his two fists, and all sorts of excuses. At last he let her go, more dead than alive. She had the generosity to say no syllable of this occurrence until after his death; she even allowed him to come to the house as usual, but took care never to be alone with him.

One day, a long time after this, meeting, in a gallery, at Fontainebleau, M. de Courtenay, La Vauguyon drew his sword, and compelled the other to draw also, although there had never been the slightest quarrel between them. They were soon separated and La Vauguyon immediately fled to the King, who was just then in his private closet, where nobody ever entered unless expressly summoned. But La Vauguyon turned the key, and, in spite of the usher on guard, forced his way in. The King in great emotion asked him what was the matter. La Vauguyon on his knees said he had been insulted by M. de Courtenay and demanded pardon for having drawn his sword in the palace. His Majesty, promising to examine the matter, with great trouble got rid of La Vauguyon. As nothing could be made of it, M. de Courtenay declaring he had been insulted by La Vauguyon and forced to draw his sword, and the other telling the same tale, both were sent to the Bastille. After a short imprisonment they were released, and appeared at the Court as usual.

Another adventure, which succeeded this, threw some light upon the state of affairs. Going to Versailles, one day, La Vauguyon met a groom of the Prince de Condé leading a saddled horse: he stopped the man, descended from his coach, asked whom the horse belonged to, said that the Prince would not object to his riding it, and leaping upon the animal's back, galloped off. The groom, all amazed, followed him. La Vauguyon rode on until he reached the Bastille, descended there, gave a gratuity to the man, and dismissed him: he then went straight to the governor of the prison, said he had had the misfortune to displease the King, and begged to be confined there. The governor, having no orders to do so, refused, and sent off an express for instructions how to act. In reply he was told not to receive La Vauguyon, whom at last, after great difficulty, he prevailed upon to go away. This occurrence made great noise. Yet even afterwards the King continued to receive La Vauguyon at the Court, and to affect to treat him well, although everybody else avoided him and was afraid of him. His poor wife became so affected by these public derangements, that she retired from Paris, and shortly afterwards died. This completed her husband's madness; he survived her only a month, dying by his own hand, as I have mentioned. During the last two years of his life he carried pistols in his carriage, and frequently pointed them at his coachman and postilion. It is certain that without the assistance of M. de Beauvais he would often have been brought to the last extremities. Beauvais frequently spoke of him to the King; and it is inconceivable that having raised this man to such a point, and having always shown him particular kindness, his Majesty should perseveringly have left him to die of hunger and become mad from misery.

Chapter XV.

On the 12th of August, Madame de Saint-Simon was happily delivered of a second son, who bore the name of Marquis de Ruffec. A singular event which happened soon after made all the world marvel.

There arrived at Versailles a farrier, from the little town of Salon, in Provence, who asked to see the King in private. In spite of the rebuffs he met with, he persisted in his request, so that at last it got to the ears of the King. The King sent word that he was not accustomed to grant such audiences to whoever liked to ask for them. Thereupon the farrier declared that if he was allowed to see the King he would tell him things so secret and so unknown to everybody else that he would be persuaded of their importance, demanding, if the King would not see him, to be sent to a minister of state. Upon this the King allowed him to have an interview with one of his secretaries, Barbezieux. But Barbezieux was not a minister of state, and to the great surprise of everybody, the farrier, who had only just arrived from the country, and who had never before left it or his trade, replied that not being a minister of state he would not speak with him. Upon this he was allowed to see Pomponne, and converse with him; and this is the story he told.

He said that, returning home late one evening, he found himself surrounded by a great light, close against a tree and near Salon. A woman clad in white — but altogether in a royal manner, and beautiful, fair, and very dazzling — called him by his name, commanded him to listen to her, and spake to him more than half an hour. She told him she was the Queen, who had been the wife of the King; to whom she ordered him to go and say what she had communicated, assuring him that God would assist him through all the journey, and that upon a secret thing he should say, the King, who alone knew that secret, would recognize the truth of all he uttered. She said that in case he could not see the King he was to speak with a minister of state, telling him certain things, but reserving certain others for the King alone. She told him, moreover, to set out at once, assuring him he would be punished with death if he neglected to acquit himself of his commission. The farrier promised to obey her in everything, and the Queen then disappeared. He found himself in darkness near the tree. He lay down and passed the night there, scarcely knowing whether he was awake or asleep. In the morning he went home, persuaded that what he had seen was a mere delusion and folly, and said nothing about it to a living soul.

Two days afterward he was passing by the same place, when the same vision appeared to him, and he was addressed in the same terms. Fresh threats of punishment were uttered if he did not comply, and he was ordered to go at once to the Intendant of the province, who would assuredly furnish him with money, after saying what he had seen. This time the farrier was convinced there was no delusion in the matter; but, halting between his fears and doubts, knew not what to do, told no one what had passed, and was in great perplexity. He remained thus eight days, and at last resolved not to make the journey; when, passing by the same spot, he saw and heard the same vision, which bestowed upon him so many dreadful menaces that he no longer thought of anything but setting out immediately. In two days from that time he presented himself at Aix, to the Intendant of the province, who without a moment's hesitation urged him to pursue his journey, and gave him sufficient money to travel by a public conveyance. Nothing more of the story was ever known.

The farrier had three interviews with M. de Pomponne, each of two hours' length. M. de Pomponne rendered, in private, an account of these to the King, who desired him to speak more fully upon the point in a council composed of the Ducs de Beauvilliers, Pontchartrain, Torcy, and Pomponne himself, — Monseigneur to be excluded. This council sat very long, perhaps because other things were spoken of. Be that as it may, the King after this wished to converse with the farrier, and did so in his cabinet. Two days afterwards he saw the man again, and each time was nearly an hour with him, and was careful that no one was within hearing.

The day after the first interview, as the King was descending the staircase, to go a hunting, M. de Duras, who was in waiting, and who was upon such a footing that he said almost what he liked, began to speak of this farrier with contempt, and, quoting the bad proverb, said, "The man was mad, or the King was not noble." At this the King stopped, and, turning round, a thing he scarcely ever did in walking, replied, "If that be so, I am not noble, for I have discoursed with him long, he has spoken to me with much good sense, and I assure you he is far from being mad."

These last words were pronounced with a sustained gravity which greatly surprised those near, and which in the midst of deep silence opened all eyes and ears. After the second interview the King felt persuaded that one circumstance had been related to him by the farrier, which he alone knew, and which had happened more than twenty years before. It was that he had seen a phantom in the forest of Saint Germain. Of this phantom he had never breathed a syllable to anybody.

The King on several other occasions spoke favorably of the farrier; moreover, he paid all the expenses the man had been put to, gave him a gratuity, sent him back free, and wrote to the Intendant of the province to take particular care of him, and never to let him want for anything all his life.

The most surprising thing of all this is that none of the

ministers could be induced to speak a word upon the occurrence. Their most intimate friends continually questioned them, but without being able to draw forth a syllable. The ministers either affected to laugh at the matter or answered evasively. This was the case whenever I questioned M. de Beauvilliers or M. de Pontchartrain, and I knew from their most intimate friends that nothing more could ever be obtained from M. de Pomponne or M. de Torcy. As for the farrier himself, he was equally reserved. He was a simple, honest, and modest man, about fifty years of age. Whenever addressed upon this subject, he cut short all discourse by saying, " I am not allowed to speak," and nothing more could be extracted from him. When he returned to his home he conducted himself just as before, gave himself no airs, and never boasted of the interview he had had with the King and his ministers. He went back to his trade, and worked at it as usual.

Such is the singular story which filled everybody with astonishment, but which nobody could understand. It is true that some people persuaded themselves, and tried to persuade others, that the whole affair was a clever trick, of which the simple farrier had been the dupe. They said that a certain Madame Arnoul, who passed for a witch, and who, having known Madame de Maintenon when she was Madame Scarron, still kept up a secret intimacy with her, had caused the three visions to appear to the farrier, in order to oblige the King to declare Madame de Maintenon queen. But the truth of the matter was never known.

The King bestowed at this time some more distinctions on his illegitimate children. M. de Maine, as grand master of the artillery, had to be received at the Chambre des Comptes; and his place ought to have been, according to custom, immediately above that of the senior member. But the King wished him to be put between the first and second president; and this was done. The King accorded also to the Princess de Conti that her two ladies of honor should be allowed to sit at the Duchess de Bourgogne's table. It was a privilege that no lady of honor to a Princess of the blood had ever been allowed. But the King gave these distinctions to the ladies of his illegitimate children, and refused it to those of the Princesses of the blood.

In thus according honors, the King seemed to merit some new ones himself. But nothing fresh could be thought of. What had been done, therefore, at his statue in the Place des

Victoires, was done over again at the Place Vendôme on the 13th of August, after midday. Another statue which had been erected there was uncovered. The Duc de Gesvres, Governor of Paris, was in attendance on horseback, at the head of the city troops, and made turns, and reverences, and other ceremonies, imitated from those in use at the consecration of the Roman Emperors. There were, it is true, no incense and no victims: something more in harmony with the title of Christian King was necessary. In the evening, there was upon the river a fine illumination, which Monsieur and Madame went to see.

A difficulty arose soon after this with Denmark. The Prince Royal had become King, and announced the circumstance to our King, but would not receive the reply sent him because he was not styled in it "Majesty." We had never accorded to the Kings of Denmark this title, and they had always been contented with that of "Serenity." The King in his turn would not wear mourning for the King of Denmark, just dead, although he always did so for any crowned head, whether related to him or not. This state of things lasted some months; until, in the end, the new King of Denmark gave way, received the reply as it had been first sent, and our King wore mourning as if the time for it had not long since passed.

Boucherat, chancellor and keeper of the seals, died on the 2d of September. Harlay, as I have previously said, had been promised this appointment when it became vacant. But the part he had taken in our case with M. de Luxembourg had made him so lose ground, that the appointment was not given to him. M. de La Rochefoucauld, above all, had undermined him in the favor of the King; and none of us had lost an opportunity of assisting in this work. Our joy, therefore, was extreme when we saw all Harlay's hopes frustrated, and we did not fail to let it burst forth. The vexation that Harlay conceived was so great, that he became absolutely intractable, and often cried out with a bitterness he could not contain, that he should be left to die in the dust of the palace. His weakness was such, that he could not prevent himself six weeks after from complaining to the King at Fontainebleau, where he was playing the valet with his accustomed suppleness and deceit. The King put him off with fine speeches, and by appointing him to take part in a commission then sitting for the purpose of bringing about a reduction in the price of corn in Paris and the suburbs, where it had become very dear. Harlay made a semblance of being contented, but remained not the less annoyed. His health and his head were at last so much attacked that he was forced to quit his post: he then fell into contempt after having excited so much hatred. The chancellorship was given to Pontchartrain, and the office of comptroller general, which became vacant at the same time, was given to Chamillart, a very honest man, who owed his first advancement to his skill at billiards, of which game the King was formerly very fond. It was while Chamillart was accustomed to play billiards with the King, at least three times a week, that an incident happened which ought not to be forgotten. Chamillart was Counselor of the Parliament at that time. He had just reported on a case that had been submitted to him. The losing party came to him, and complained that he had omitted to bring forward a document that had been given into his hands, and that would assuredly have turned the verdict. Chamillart searched for the document, found it, and saw that the complainer was right. He said so, and added, "I do not know how the document escaped me, but it decides in your favor. You claimed twenty thousand francs, and it is my fault you did not get them. Come to-morrow, and I will pay you." Chamillart, although then by no means rich, scraped together all the money he had, borrowing the rest, and paid the man as he had promised, only demanding that the matter should be kept a secret. But after this, feeling that billiards three times a week interfered with his legal duties, he surrendered part of them, and thus left himself more free for other charges he was obliged to attend to.

The Comtesse de Fiesque died very aged, while the Court was at Fontainebleau this year. She had passed her life with the most frivolous of the great world. Two incidents amongst a thousand will characterize her. She was very straitened in means, because she had frittered away all her substance, or allowed herself to be pillaged by her business people. When those beautiful mirrors were first introduced, she obtained one, although they were then very dear and very rare. "Ah, Countess!" said her friends, "where did you find that?"

"Oh!" replied she, "I had a miserable piece of land, which only yielded me corn; I have sold it, and I have this mirror instead. Is not this excellent? Who would hesitate between corn and this beautiful mirror?"

On another occasion she harangued with her son, who was as poor as a rat, for the purpose of persuading him to make a good match and thus enrich himself. Her son, who had no desire to marry, allowed her to talk on, and pretended to listen to her reasons. She was delighted — entered into a description of the wife she destined for him, painting her as young, rich, an only child, beautiful, well educated, and with parents who would be delighted to agree to the marriage. When she had finished, he pressed her for the name of this charming and desirable person. The Countess said she was the daughter of Jacquier, a man well known to everybody, and who had been a contractor of provisions to the armies of M. de Turenne. Upon this, her son burst into a hearty laugh, and she in anger demanded why he did so, and what he found so ridiculous in the match.

The truth was, Jacquier had no children, as the Comtesse soon remembered. At which she said it was a great pity, since no marriage would have better suited all parties. She was full of such oddities, which she persisted in for some time with anger, but at which she was the first to laugh. People said of her that she had never been more than eighteen years old. The memoirs of Mademoiselle paint her well. She lived with Mademoiselle, and passed all her life in quarrels about trifles.

It was immediately after leaving Fontainebleau that the marriage between the Duc and Duchesse de Bourgogne was consummated. It was upon this occasion that the King named four gentlemen to wait upon the Duc, — four who in truth could not have been more badly chosen. One of them, Gamaches, was a gossip, who never knew what he was doing or saying — who knew nothing of the world, or the court, or of war, although he had always been in the army. D'O was another; but of him I have spoken. Cheverny was the third, and Saumery the fourth. Saumery had been raised out of obscurity by M. de Beauvilliers. Never was man so intriguing, so truckling, so mean, so boastful, so ambitious, so intent upon fortune; and all this without disguise, without veil, without shame! Saumery had been wounded, and no man ever made so much of such a mishap. I used to say of him that he limped audaciously, and it was true. He would speak of personages the most distinguished, whose antechambers even he had scarcely seen, as though he spoke of his equals or of his particular friends. He related what he had heard, and was not ashamed to say before people who at least had common sense, "Poor *Mons.* Turenne said to me," M. de Turenne never having probably heard of his existence. With *Monsieur* in full he honored nobody. It was *Mons.* de Beauvilliers, *Mons.* de Chevreuse, and so on; except with those whose names he clipped off short, as he frequently would even with princes of the blood. I have heard him say many times, " the Princess de Conti," in speaking of the daughter of the king; and " the Prince de Conti," in speaking of Monsieur her brother-in-law ! As for the chief nobles of the Court, it was rare for him to give them the *Monsieur* or the *Mons.* It was Maréchal d'Humières, and so on with the others. Fatuity and insolence were united in him, and by dint of mounting a hundred staircases a day, and bowing and scraping everywhere, he had gained the ear of I know not how many people. His wife was a tall creature, as impertinent as he, who wore the breeches, and before whom he dared not breathe. Her effrontery blushed at nothing, and after many gallantries she had linked herself on to M. de Duras, whom she governed, and of whom she was publicly and absolutely the mistress, living at his expense. Children, friends, servants, all were at her mercy, — even Madame de Duras herself when she came, which was but seldom, from the country.

Such were the people whom the King placed near M. le Duc de Bourgogne.

The Duc de Gesvres, a malicious old man, a cruel husband, and an unnatural father, sadly annoyed Maréchal de Villeroy towards the end of this year, having previously treated me very scurvily for some advice that I gave him respecting the ceremonies to be observed at the reception by the King of M. de Lorraine as Duc de Bar. M. de Gesvres and M. de Villeroy had both had fathers who made large fortunes and who became secretaries of state. One morning M. de Gesvres was waiting for the King, with a number of other courtiers, when M. de Villeroy arrived, with all that noise and those airs he had long assumed, and which his favor and his appointments rendered more superb. I know not whether this annoyed De Gesvres more than usual, but as soon as the other had placed himself, he said, " Monsieur le Maréchal, it must be admitted that you and I are very lucky." The Maréchal, surprised at a remark which seemed to be suggested by nothing, assented with a modest air, and, shaking his head and his wig, began to talk to some one else. But M. de Gesvres had not commenced without a purpose. He went on, addressed M. de Villeroy point blank, admiring their mutual good fortune, but when he came to speak of the father of each, "Let us go no further," said he, "for what did our fathers spring from? From tradesmen; even tradesmen they were themselves. Yours was the son of a dealer in fresh fish at the markets, and mine of a peddler, or, perhaps, worse. Gentlemen," said he, addressing the company, "have we not reason to think our fortune prodigious — the Maréchal and I?" The Maréchal would have liked to strangle M. de Gesvres, or to see him dead — but what can be done with a man who, in order to say something cutting to you, says it to himself first? Everybody was silent, and all eyes were lowered. Many, however, were not sorry to see M. de Villeroy so pleasantly humiliated. The King came and put an end to the scene, which was the talk of the Court for several days.

Omissions must be repaired as soon as they are perceived. Other matters have carried me away. At the commencement of April, Ticquet, councilor at the parliament, was assassinated in his own house; and if he did not die, it was not the fault of his porter, or of the soldier who had attempted to kill him, and who left him for dead, disturbed by a noise they heard. This councilor, who was a very poor man, had complained to the King, the preceding year, of the conduct of his wife with Montgeorges, captain in the Guards, and much esteemed. The King prohibited Montgeorges from seeing the wife of the councilor again.

Such having been the case, when the crime was attempted, suspicion fell upon Montgeorges and the wife of Ticquet, a beautiful, gallant, and bold woman, who took a very high tone in the matter. She was advised to fly, maintaining that in all such cases it is safer to be far off than close at hand. The woman would listen to no such advice, and in a few days she was no longer able. The porter and the soldier were arrested and tortured, and Madame Ticquet, who was foolish enough to allow herself to be arrested, also underwent the same examination, and avowed all. She was condemned to lose her head, and her accomplice to be broken on the wheel. Montgeorges managed so well, that he was not legally criminated. When Ticquet heard the sentence, he came with all his family to the King, and sued for mercy. But the King would not listen to him, and the execution took place on Wednesday, the 17th of

June, after midday, at the Grève. All the windows of the Hôtel de Ville, and of the houses in the Place de Grève, in the streets that lead to it from the Conciergerie of the palace where Madame Ticquet was confined, were filled with spectators, men and women, many of title and distinction. There were even friends of both sexes of this unhappy woman, who felt no shame or horror in going there. In the streets the crowd was so great that it could not be passed through. In general, pity was felt for the culprit; people hoped that she would be pardoned, and it was because they hoped so, that they went to see her die. But such is the world; so unreasoning, and so little in accord with itself.

Chapter XXVI.

The Prince d'Harcourt at last obtained permission to wait on the King, after having never appeared at Court for seventeen years. He had followed the King in all his conquests in the Low Countries and Franche-Comté; but he had remained little at the Court since his voyage to Spain, whither he had accompanied the daughter of Monsieur to the King, Charles II., her husband. The Prince d'Harcourt took service with Venice, and fought in the Morea until the Republic made peace with the Turks. He was tall, well made; and, although he looked like a nobleman and had wit, reminded one at the same time of a country actor. He was a great liar, and a libertine in body and mind; a great spendthrift, a great and impudent swindler, with a tendency to low debauchery, that cursed him all his life. Having fluttered about a long time after his return, and found it impossible either to live with his wife — which is not surprising — or accommodate himself to the Court or to Paris, he set up his rest at Lyons, with wine, street walkers, a society to match, a pack of hounds, and a gaming table to support his extravagance and enable him to live at the expense of the dupes, the imbeciles, and the sons of fat tradesmen, whom he could lure into his nets. Thus he spent many years, and seemed to forget that there existed in the world another country besides Lyons. At last he got tired, and returned to Paris. The King, who despised him, let him alone, but would not see him; and it was only after two months of begging for him by the Lorraines, that he received permission to present himself. His wife, the

Princesse d'Harcourt, was a favorite of Madame de Maintenon. The origin of their friendship is traced to the fact that Brancas, the father of the Princesse, had been one of the lovers of Madame de Maintenon. No claim less powerful could have induced the latter to take into her favor a person who was so little worthy. Like all women who know nothing but what chance has taught them, and who have long languished in obscurity before arriving at splendor, Madame de Maintenon was dazzled by the very name of Princess, even if assumed; as to a real Princess, nothing equaled her in her opinion. The Princesse then tried hard to get the Prince invited to Marly, but without success. Upon this she pretended to sulk, in hopes that Madame de Maintenon would exert all her influence; but in this she was mistaken. The Prince accordingly by degrees got disgusted with the Court, and retired into the provinces for a time.

The Princesse d'Harcourt was a sort of personage whom it is good to make known, in order better to lay bare a Court which did not scruple to receive such as she. She had once been beautiful and gay; but though not old, all her grace and beauty had vanished. The rose had become an ugly thorn. At the time I speak of she was a tall, fat creature, mightily brisk in her movements, with a complexion like milk porridge; great, ugly, thick lips, and hair like tow, always sticking out and hanging down in disorder, like all the rest of her fittings out. Dirty, slatternly, always intriguing, pretending, enterprising, quarreling — always low as the grass or high as the rainbow, according to the person with whom she had to deal: she was a blonde Fury, nay more, a harpy; she had all the effrontery of one, and the deceit and violence; all the avarice and the audacity; moreover, all the gluttony, and all the promptitude to relieve herself from the effects thereof; so that she drove out of their wits those at whose house she dined; was often a victim of her confidence; and was many a time sent to the devil by the servants of M. du Maine and M. le Grand. She, however, was never in the least embarrassed, tucked up her petticoats and went her way; then returned, saying she had been unwell. People were accustomed to it.

Whenever money was to be made by scheming and bribery, she was there to make it. At play she always cheated, and if found out stormed and raged; but pocketed what she had won. People looked upon her as they would have looked upon a fish fag, and did not like to commit themselves by quarreling with her. At the end of every game she used to say that she gave whatever might have been unfairly gained to those who had gained it, and hoped that others would do likewise. For she was very devout by profession, and thought by so doing to put her conscience in safety; because, she used to add, in play there is always some mistake. She went to church always, and constantly took the Sacrament, very often after having played until four o'clock in the morning.

One day, when there was a grand fête at Fontainebleau, Madame la Maréchale de Villeroy persuaded her, out of malice, to sit down and play, instead of going to evening prayers. She resisted some time, saying that Madame de Maintenon was going; but the Maréchale laughed at her for believing that her patron could see who was and who was not at the chapel; so down they sat to play. When the prayers were over, Madame de Maintenon, by the merest accident — for she scarcely ever visited any one — went to the apartments of the Maréchale de Villeroy. The door was flung back, and she was announced. This was a thunderbolt for the Princesse d'Harcourt. "I am ruined," cried she, unable to restrain herself; "she will see me playing, and I ought to have been at chapel;" down fell the cards from her hands, and down fell she all abroad in her chair. The Maréchale laughed most heartily at so complete an adventure. Madame de Maintenon entered slowly, and found the Princesse in this state, with five or six persons. The Maréchale de Villeroy, who was full of wit, began to say that, whilst doing her a great honor, Madame was the cause of great disorder, and showed her the Princesse d'Harcourt in her state of discomfort. Madame de Maintenon smiled with majestic kindness, and addressing the Princesse d'Harcourt, "Is this the way," said she, "that you go to prayers?" Thereupon the Princesse flew out of her half faint into a sort of fury; said that this was the kind of trick that was played off upon her; that no doubt the Maréchale knew that Madame de Maintenon was coming, and for that reason had persecuted her to play. "Persecuted!" exclaimed the Maréchale, "I thought I could not receive you better than by proposing a game; it is true you were for a moment troubled at missing the chapel, but your tastes carried the day. This, Madame, is my whole crime," continued she, addressing Madame de Maintenon. Upon this everybody laughed louder than before. Madame de Maintenon, in order to stop the quarrel, commanded them both to continue their game; and they continued accordingly, the Princesse d'Harcourt, still grumbling, quite beside herself, blinded with fury, so as to commit fresh mistakes every minute. So ridiculous an adventure diverted the Court for several days; for this beautiful Princesse was equally feared, hated, and despised.

Monseigneur le Duc and Madame la Duchesse de Bourgogne continually played off pranks upon her. They put, one day, crackers all along the avenue of the Château at Marly, that led to the Perspective where she lodged. She was horribly afraid of everything. The Duc and Duchesse bribed two porters to be ready to take her into the mischief. When she was right in the middle of the avenue, the crackers began to go off, and she to cry aloud for mercy; the chairmen set her down and ran for it. There she was, then, struggling in her chair, furiously enough to upset it, and yelling like a demon. At this the company, which had gathered at the door of the château to see the fun, ran to her assistance, in order to have the pleasure of enjoying the scene more fully. Thereupon she set to abusing everybody right and left, commencing with Monseigneur and Madame la Duchesse de Bourgogne. At another time, M. de Bourgogne put a cracker under her chair in the salon, where she was playing at piquet. As he was about to set fire to this cracker, some charitable soul warned him that it would maim her, and he desisted.

Sometimes they used to send about twenty Swiss guards, with drums, into her chamber, who roused her from her first sleep by their horrid din. Another time — and these scenes were always at Marly — they waited until very late for her to go to bed and sleep. She lodged not far from the post of the captain of the Guards, who was at that time the Maréchal de Lorges. It snowed very hard, and had frozen. Madame la Duchesse de Bourgogne and her suite gathered snow from the terrace which is on a level with their lodgings; and in order to be better supplied, waked up, to assist them, the Maréchal's people, who did not let them want for ammunition. Then with a false key, and lights, they gently slipped into the chamber of the Princesse d'Harcourt; and suddenly drawing the curtains of her bed, pelted her amain with snowballs. The filthy creature, waking up with a start, bruised and stifled in snow, with which even her ears were filled, with disheveled hair, yelling at the top of her voice, and wriggling like an eel, without knowing where to hide, formed a spectacle that diverted people more than half an hour: so that at last the nymph swam in her bed, from which the water flowed everywhere, slushing all the chamber. It was enough to make one die of laughter. On the morrow she sulked, and was more than ever laughed at for her pains.

Her fits of sulkiness came over her either when the tricks played were too violent, or when M. le Grand abused her. He thought, very properly, that a person who bore the name of Lorraine should not put herself so much on the footing of a buffoon; and, as he was a rough speaker, he sometimes said the most abominable things to her at table; upon which the Princesse would burst out crying, and then, being enraged, would sulk. The Duchesse de Bourgogne used then to pretend to sulk, too; but the other did not hold out long, and came crawling back to her, crying, begging pardon for having sulked, and praying that she might not cease to be a source of amusement! After some time the Duchesse would allow herself to be melted, and the Princesse was more villainously treated than ever, for the Duchesse de Bourgogne had her own way in everything. Neither the King nor Madame de Maintenon found fault with what she did, so that the Princesse d'Harcourt had no resource; she did not even dare to complain of those who aided in tormenting her; yet it would not have been prudent in any one to make her an enemy.

The Princesse d'Harcourt paid her servants so badly, that they concocted a plan, and one fine day drew up on the Pont Neuf. The coachman and footmen got down, and came and spoke to her at the door, in language she was not used to hear. Her ladies and chambermaid got down, and went away, leaving her to shift as she might. Upon this she set herself to harangue the blackguards who collected, and was only too happy to find a man, who mounted upon the seat and drove her home. Another time, Madame de Saint-Simon, returning from Versailles, overtook her, walking in full dress in the street, and with her train under her arms. Madame de Saint-Simon stopped, offered her assistance, and found that she had been left by her servants, as on the Pont Neuf. It was volume the second of that story; and even when she came back she found her house deserted, every one having gone away at once by agreement. She was very violent with her servants, beat them, and changed them every day.

Upon one occasion, she took into her service a strong and robust chambermaid, to whom, from the first day of her arrival, she gave many slaps and boxes on the ear. The chambermaid said nothing, but after submitting to this treatment for five or six days, conferred with the other servants; and one morning, while in her mistress' room, locked the door without being perceived, said something to bring down punishment upon her, and, at the first box on the ear she received, flew upon the Princesse d'Harcourt, gave her no end of thumps and slaps, knocked her down, kicked her, mauled her from her head to her feet, and when she was tired of this exercise, left her on the ground, all torn and disheveled, howling like a devil. The chambermaid then quitted the room, double-locked the door on the outside, gained the staircase, and fled the house.

Every day the Princesse was fighting, or mixed up in some adventures. Her neighbors at Marly said they could not sleep for the riot she made at night; and I remember that, after one of these scenes, everybody went to see the room of the Duchesse de Villeroy and that of Madame d'Espinoy, who had put their bed in the middle of their room, and who related their night vigils to every one.

Such was this favorite of Madame de Maintenon; so insolent and so insupportable to every one, but who had favors and preferences for those who brought her over, and who had raised so many young men, amassed their wealth, and made herself feared even by the Prince and minister.

Chapter XXXIII.

Two very different persons died towards the latter part of this year. The first was Lamoignon, Chief President, the second Ninon, known by the name of Mademoiselle de l'Enclos. Of Lamoignon I will relate a single anecdote, curious and instructive, which will show the corruption of which he was capable.

One day — I am speaking of a time many years previous to the date of the occurrences just related — one day there was a great hunting party at Saint Germain. The chase was pursued so long, that the King gave up, and returned to Saint Germain. A number of courtiers, among whom was M. de Lauzun, who related this story to me, continued their sport, and just as darkness was coming on, discovered that they had lost their way. After a time they espied a light, by which they guided their steps, and at length reached the door of a kind of castle. They knocked, they called aloud, they named themselves, and asked for hospitality. It was then between ten and eleven at night, and towards the end of autumn. The door was opened to them. The master of the house came forth. He made them take their boots off, and warm themselves; he put their horses into his stables; and at the same time had a supper prepared for his guests, who stood much in need of it. They did not wait long for the meal; yet when served it proved excellent; the wines served with it, too, were of several kinds, and excellent likewise; as for the master of the house, he was so polite and respectful, yet without being ceremonious or eager, that it was evident he had frequented the best company. The courtiers soon learnt that his name was Fargues, that the place was called Courson, and that he had lived there in retirement several years. After having supped, Fargues showed each of them into separate bedrooms, where they were waited upon by his valets with every proper attention. In the morning, as soon as the courtiers had dressed themselves, they found an excellent breakfast awaiting them; and upon leaving the table they saw their horses ready for them, and as thoroughly attended to as they had been themselves. Charmed with the politeness and with the manners of Fargues, and touched by his hospitable reception of them, they made him many offers of service, and made their way back to Saint Germain. Their non-appearance on the previous night had been the common talk, their return and the adventure they had met with was no less so.

These gentlemen were then the very flower of the Court, and all of them very intimate with the King. They related to him, therefore, their story, the manner of their reception, and highly praised the master of the house and his good cheer. The King asked his name, and, as soon as he heard it, exclaimed: "What, Fargues! is he so near here, then?" The courtiers redoubled their praises, and the King said no more; but soon after he went to the Queen mother, and told her what had happened.

Fargues, indeed, was no stranger, either to her or to the King. He had taken a prominent part in the movements of Paris against the Court and Cardinal Mazarin. If he had not been hanged, it was because he was well supported by his party, who had him included in the amnesty granted to those who had been engaged in these troubles. Fearing, however, that the hatred of his enemies might place his life in danger if he remained in Paris, he retired from the capital to this country house which has just been mentioned, where he continued to live in strict privacy, even when the death of Cardinal Mazarin seemed to render such seclusion no longer necessary.

The King and the Queen mother, who had pardoned Fargues in spite of themselves, were much annoyed at finding that he was living in opulence and tranquillity so near the Court; thought him extremely bold to do so; and determined to punish him for this and for his former insolence. They directed Lamoignon, therefore, to find out something in the past life of Fargues for which punishment might be awarded; and Lamoignon, eager to please, and make a profit out of his eagerness, was not long in satisfying them. He made researches, and found means to complicate Fargues in a murder that had been committed in Paris at the height of the troubles. Officers were accordingly sent to Courson, and its owner was arrested.

Fargues was much astonished when he learnt of what he was accused. He exculpated himself, nevertheless, completely; alleging, moreover, that as the murder of which he was accused had been committed during the troubles, the amnesty in which he was included effaced all memory of the deed, according to law and usage, which had never been contested until this occasion. The courtiers who had been so well treated by the unhappy man did everything they could with the judges and the King to obtain the release of the accused. It was all in vain. Fargues was decapitated at once, and all his wealth was given by way of recompense to the Chief President Lamoignon, who had no scruple thus to enrich himself with the blood of the innocent.

The other person who died at the same time was, as I have said, Ninon, the famous courtesan, known, since age had compelled her to quit that trade, as Mademoiselle de l'Enclos. She was a new example of the triumph of vice carried on cleverly and repaired by some virtue. The stir that she made, and still more the disorder that she caused among the highest and most brilliant youth, overcame the extreme indulgence that, not without cause, the Queen mother entertained for persons whose conduct was gallant, and more than gallant, and made her send her an order to retire into a convent. But Ninon, observing that no special convent was named, said, with a great courtesy, to the officer who brought the order, that, as the option was left to her, she would choose "the convent of the Cordeliers at Paris"; which impudent joke so diverted the Queen that she left her alone for the future. Ninon never had but one lover at a time — but her admirers were numberless — so that when wearied of one incumbent, she told him so frankly, and took another. The abandoned one might groan and complain: her decree was without appeal; and this creature had acquired such an influence that the deserted lovers never dared to revenge on the favored one, and were too happy to remain on the footing of friend of the house. She sometimes kept faithful to one, when he pleased her very much, during an entire campaign.

Ninon had illustrious friends of all sorts, and had so much wit that she preserved them all and kept them on good terms with each other; or, at least, no quarrels ever came to light. There was an external respect and decency about everything that passed in her house, such as princesses of the highest rank have rarely been able to preserve in their intrigues.

In this way she had among her friends a selection of the best members of the Court; so that it became the fashion to be received by her, and it was useful to be so, on account of the connections that were thus formed. There was never any gambling there, nor loud laughing, nor disputes, nor talk about religion or politics; but much and elegant wit, ancient and modern stories, news of gallantries, yet without scandal. All was delicate, light, measured; and she herself maintained the conversation by her wit and her great knowledge of facts. The respect which, strange to say, she had acquired, and the number and distinction of her friends and acquaintances, continued when her charms ceased to attract, and when propriety and fashion compelled her to use only intellectual baits. She knew all the intrigues of the old and the new court, serious and otherwise; her conversation was charming; she was disinterested, faithful, secret, safe to the last degree; and, setting aside her frailty, virtuous and full of probity. She frequently succored her friends with money and influence, constantly did them the most important services, and very faithfully kept the secrets or the money deposits that were confided to her.

She had been intimate with Madame de Maintenon during the whole of her residence at Paris; but Madame de Maintenon, although not daring to disavow this friendship, did not like to hear her spoken about. She wrote to Ninon with amity from time to time, even until her death; and Ninon in like manner, when she wanted to serve any friend in whom she took great interest, wrote to Madame de Maintenon, who did her what service she required efficaciously and with promptness. But since Madame de Maintenon came to power, they had seen each other only two or three times, and then in secret.

Ninon was remarkable for her repartees. One that she made to the last Maréchal de Choiseul is worth repeating. The Maréchal was virtue itself, but not fond of company or blessed with much wit. One day, after a long visit he had paid her, Ninon gaped, looked at the Maréchal, and cried : —

"Oh, my lord! how many virtues you make me detest!"— a line from I know not what play. The laughter at this may be imagined. L'Enclos lived long beyond her eightieth year, always healthy, visited, respected. She gave her last years to God, and her death was the news of the day. The singularity of this personage has made me extend my observations upon her.

A short time after the death of Mademoiselle de l'Enclos, a terrible adventure happened to Courtenvaux, eldest son of M. de Louvois. Courtenvaux was commander of the Cent-Suisses, fond of obscure debauches, with a ridiculous voice, miserly, quarrelsome, though modest and respectful; and in fine a very stupid fellow. The King, more eager to know all that was passing than most people believed, although they gave him credit for not a little curiosity in this respect, had authorized Bontems to engage a number of Swiss in addition to those posted at the doors, and in the parks and gardens. These attendants had orders to stroll morning, noon, and night along the corridors, the passages, the staircases, even into the private places, and, when it was fine, in the courtyards and gardens; and in secret to watch people, to follow them, to notice where they went, to notice who was there, to listen to all the conversation they could hear, and to make reports of their discoveries. This was assiduously done at Versailles, at Marly, at Trianon, at Fontainebleau, and in all the places where the King was. These new attendants vexed Courtenvaux considerably, for over such newcomers he had no sort of authority. This season, at Fontainebleau, a room which had formerly been occupied by a party of the Cent-Suisses and of the bodyguard was given up entirely to the new corps. The room was in a public passage of communication indispensable to all in the chateau, and in consequence excellently well adapted for watching those who passed through it. Courtenvaux, more than ever vexed by this new arrangement, regarded it as a fresh encroachment upon his authority, and flew into a violent rage with the newcomers, and railed at them in good set terms. They allowed him to fume as he would; they had their orders, and were too wise to be disturbed by his rage. The King, who heard of all this, sent at once for Courtenvaux. As soon as he appeared in the cabinet, the King called to him from the other end of the room, without giving him time to approach, and in a rage so terrible, and for him so novel, that not only Courtenvaux, but princes, princesses, and everybody in the chamber, trembled. Menaces that his post should be taken away from him, terms the most severe and the most unusual, rained upon Courtenvaux, who, fainting with fright, and ready to sink under the ground, had neither the time nor the means to prefer a word. The reprimand finished by the King saying, "Get out." He had scarcely the strength to obey.

The cause of this strange scene was that Courtenvaux, by the fuss he had made, had drawn the attention of the whole Court to the change effected by the King, and that, when once seen, its object was clear to all eyes. The King, who hid his spy system with the greatest care, had counted upon this change passing unperceived, and was beside himself with anger when he found it made apparent to everybody by Courtenvaux's noise. He never regained the King's favor during the rest of his life; and but for his family he would certainly have been driven away, and his office taken from him.

BOILEAU'S ART OF POETRY.

Translated by SOAME.

[NICHOLAS BOILEAU-DESPRÉAUX, French critic and poet, was born at Paris, November 1, 1636. He studied law and theology at Beauvais, but appears to have devoted himself entirely to authorship. He began his literary career by composing a satire for recitation to his friends, among whom were Racine, Molière, and La Fontaine. This was the forerunner of a series of seven, composed between 1661 and 1665, and published in one volume in 1666. In 1677 he received a pension of two thousand livres and an appointment as joint historiographer to Louis XIV., with Racine; and in 1684 entered the French Academy at the expressed desire of the king. His last years were passed in retirement at Auteuil, where he died March 13, 1711. Besides the "Satires," Boileau wrote: "The Art of Poetry" (L'Art Poétique); "The Lecturn" (Le Lutrin), a mock-heroic poem; "Epistles"; a collection of epigrams, etc.]

Canto I.

Rash author, 'tis a vain presumptuous crime
To undertake the sacred art of rime;
If at thy birth the stars that ruled thy sense
Shone not with a poetic influence,
In thy strait genius thou wilt still be bound,
Find Phœbus deaf, and Pegasus unsound.
You, then, that burn with a desire to try
The dangerous course of charming poetry,
Forbear in fruitless verse to lose your time,
Or take for genius the desire of rime;
Fear the allurements of a specious bait,
And well consider your own force and weight.

Nature abounds in wits of every kind,
And for each author can a talent find:
One may in verse describe an amorous flame,
Another sharpen a short epigram;
Waller a hero's mighty acts extol,
Spenser sing Rosalind in pastoral.
But authors, that themselves too much esteem,
Lose their own genius, and mistake their theme:
Thus in times past Dubartas vainly writ,
Alloying sacred truth with trifling wit;
Impertinently, and without delight,
Described the Israelites' triumphant flight;
And, following Moses o'er the sandy plain,
Perished with Pharaoh in the Arabian main.

Whate'er you write of pleasant or sublime,
Always let sense accompany your rime;
Falsely they seem each other to oppose,—
Rime must be made with reason's laws to close;
And when to conquer her you bend your force,
The mind will triumph in the noble course;
To reason's yoke she quickly will incline,
Which, far from hurting, renders her divine;
But if neglected, will as easily stray,
And master reason, which she should obey.
Love reason then; and let whate'er you write
Borrow from her its beauty, force, and light.

Most writers mounted on a resty muse,
Extravagant and senseless objects choose;
They think they err, if in their verse they fall
On any thought that's plain or natural.
Fly this excess; and let Italians be
Vain authors of false glittering poetry.
All ought to aim at sense: but most in vain
Strive the hard pass and slippery path to gain;
You drown, if to the right or left you stray;
Reason to go has often but one way.

Sometimes an author, fond of his own thought,
Pursues its object till it's overwrought:
If he describes a house, he shows the face,
And after walks you round from place to place;
Here is a vista, there the doors unfold,
Balconies here are balustered with gold;
Then counts the rounds and ovals in the halls.
"The festoons, friezes, and the astragals."
Tired with his tedious pomp, away I run,
And skip o'er twenty pages, to be gone.
Of such descriptions the vain folly see,
And shun their barren superfluity.
All that is needless carefully avoid;
The mind once satisfied is quickly cloyed.
He cannot write who knows not to give o'er,
To mend one fault he makes a hundred more:
A verse was weak, you turn it much too strong,
And grow obscure for fear you should be long;
Some are not gaudy, but are flat and dry;
Not to be low, another soars too high.

Would you of every one deserve the praise?
In writing vary your discourse and phrase;
A frozen style, that neither ebbs nor flows,
Instead of pleasing, makes us gape and doze.
Those tedious authors are esteemed by none,
Who tire us, humming the same heavy tone.

Happy who in his verse can gently steer
From grave to light, from pleasant to severe!
His works will be admired wherever found,
And oft with buyers will be compassed round.

In all you write be neither low nor vile;
The meanest theme may have a proper style.
The dull burlesque appeared with impudence,
And pleased by novelty in spite of sense;
All, except trivial points, grew out of date;

Parnassus spoke the cant of Billingsgate;
Boundless and mad, disordered rime was seen;
Disguised Apollo changed to Harlequin.
This plague, which first in country towns began,
Cities and kingdoms quickly overran;
The dullest scribblers some admirers found,
And the Mock Tempest was awhile renowned.
But this low stuff the town at last despised,
And scorned the folly that they once had prized,
Distinguished dull from natural and plain,
And left the villages to Flecknoe's reign.
Let not so mean a style your muse debase,
But learn from Butler the buffooning grace,
And let burlesque in ballads be employed.
 Yet noisy bombast carefully avoid,
Nor think to raise, though on Pharsalia's plain,
"Millions of mourning mountains of the slain."
Nor, with Dubartas, "bridle up the floods,
And periwig with wool the baldpate woods."
Choose a just style. Be grave without constraint,
Great without pride, and lovely without paint.
 Write what your reader may be pleased to hear.
And for the measure have a careful ear;
On easy numbers fix your happy choice;
Of jarring sounds avoid the odious noise;
The fullest verse, and the most labored sense,
Displease us if the ear once take offense.
 Our ancient verse, as homely as the times,
Was rude, unmeasured, only tagged with rimes;
Number and cadence, that have since been shown,
To those unpolished writers were unknown.
Fairfax was he, who, in that darker age,
By his just rules restrained poetic rage;
Spenser did next in pastorals excel,
And taught the noble art of writing well,
To stricter rules the stanza did restrain,
And found for poetry a richer vein.
Then Davenant came, who, with a new-found art,
Changed all, spoiled all, and had his way apart;
His haughty muse all others did despise,
And thought in triumph to bear off the prize,
Till the sharp-sighted critics of the times
In their Mock Gondibert exposed his rimes,
The laurels he pretended did refuse,
And dashed the hopes of his aspiring muse.

This headstrong writer, falling from on high,
Made following authors take less liberty.
   Waller came last, but was the first whose **art**
Just weight and measure did to verse impart,
That of a well-placed word could teach the **force,**
And showed for poetry a nobler course.
His happy genius did our tongue refine,
And easy words with pleasing numbers join;
His verses to good method did apply,
And changed hard discord to soft harmony.
All owned his laws; which, long approved and **tried,**
To present authors now may be a guide;
Tread boldly in his steps, secure from fear,
And be, like him, in your expressions clear.
If in your verse you drag, and sense delay,
My patience tires, my fancy goes astray,
And from your vain discourse I turn my **mind,**
Nor search an author troublesome to find.
   There is a kind of writer pleased with sound,
Whose fustian head with clouds is compassed round—
No reason can disperse them with its light;
Learn then to think ere you pretend to write.
As your idea's clear, or else obscure,
The expression follows, perfect or impure;
What we conceive with ease we can express;
Words to the notions flow with readiness.
   Observe the language well in all you write,
And swerve not from it in your loftiest flight.
The smoothest verse and the exactest sense
Displease us, if ill English give offense;
A barbarous phrase no reader can approve,
Nor bombast, noise, or affectation love.
In short, without pure language, what you **write**
Can never yield us profit or delight.
   Take time for thinking; never work in **haste;**
And value not yourself for writing fast;
A rapid poem, with such fury writ,
Shows want of judgment, not abounding **wit.**
More pleased we are to see a river lead
His gentle streams along a flowery mead,
Than from high banks to hear loud torrents **roar,**
With foamy waters, on a muddy shore.
Gently make haste, of labor not afraid;
A hundred times consider what you've **said;**
Polish, repolish, every color lay,

And sometimes add, but oftener take away.
    'Tis not enough, when swarming faults are **writ,**
That here and there are scattered sparks of **wit;**
Each object must be fixed in the due place,
And differing parts have corresponding **grace;**
Till, by a curious art disposed, we find
One perfect whole of all the pieces joined.
Keep to your subject close in all you say,
Nor for a sounding sentence ever stray.
    The public censure for your writings **fear,**
And to yourself be critic most severe.
Fantastic wits their darling follies love;
But find you faithful friends that will **reprove,**
That on your works may look with careful **eyes,**
And of your faults be zealous enemies.
Lay by an author's pride and vanity,
And from a friend a flatterer descry,
Who seems to like but means not what he **says;**
Embrace true counsel, but suspect false praise.
    A sycophant will everything admire;
Each verse, each sentence, sets his soul on fire;
All is divine! there's not a word amiss!
He shakes with joy, and weeps with tenderness;
He overpowers you with his mighty praise.
Truth never moves in those impetuous ways.
    A faithful friend is careful of your fame,
And freely will your heedless errors blame;
He cannot pardon a neglected line,
But verse to rule and order will confine,
Reprove of words the too-affected sound, —
"Here the sense flags, and your expression's **round,**
Your fancy tires, and your discourse grows vain,
Your terms improper; make it just and plain."
Thus 'tis a faithful friend will freedom use.
    But authors partial to their darling muse
Think to protect it they have just pretense,
And at your friendly counsel take offense.
"Said you of this, that the expression's flat?
Your servant, sir, you must excuse me that,"
He answers you. — "This word has here no grace,
Pray leave it out." — "That, sir, 's the properest **place." —**
"This turn I like not." — "'Tis approved **by all."**
Thus, resolute not from one fault to **fall,**
If there's a symbol of which you **doubt,**
'Tis a sure reason not to blot it out.

Yet still he says you may his faults confute,
And over him your power is absolute.
But of his feigned humility take heed,
'Tis a bait laid to make you hear him read;
And, when he leaves you, happy in his Muse,
Restless he runs some other to abuse,
And often finds; for in our scribbling times
No fool can want a sot to praise his rimes;
The flattest work has ever in the court
Met with some zealous ass for its support;
And in all times a forward scribbling fop
Has found some greater fool to cry him up.

Canto II.

As a fair nymph, when rising from her bed,
With sparkling diamonds dresses not her head,
But without gold, or pearl, or costly scents,
Gathers from neighboring fields her ornaments;
Such, lovely in its dress, but plain withal,
Ought to appear a perfect Pastoral.
Its humble method nothing has of fierce,
But hates the rattling of a lofty verse;
There native beauty pleases and excites,
And never with harsh sounds the ear affrights.

But in this style a poet often spent,
In rage throws by his rural instrument,
And vainly, when disordered thoughts abound,
Amidst the eclogue makes the trumpet sound;
Pan flies alarmed into the neighboring woods,
And frighted nymphs dive down into the floods.

Opposed to this, another, low in style,
Makes shepherds speak a language low and vile;
His writings flat and heavy, without sound,
Kissing the earth and creeping on the ground;
You'd swear that Randal, in his rustic strains,
Again was quavering to the country swains,
And changing, without care of sound or dress,
Strephon and Phyllis into Tom and Bess.

'Twixt these extremes 'tis hard to keep the right;
For guides take Virgil and read Theocrite;
Be their just writings, by the gods inspired,
Your constant pattern, practiced and admired.
By them alone you'll easily comprehend
How poets without shame may condescend
To sing of gardens, fields, of flowers and fruit,

To stir up shepherds and to tune the flute;
Of love's rewards to tell the happy hour,
Daphne a tree, Narcissus make a flower,
And by what means the eclogue yet has power
To make the woods worthy a conqueror;
This of their writings is the grace and flight;
Their risings lofty, yet not out of sight.

    The Elegy, that loves a mournful style,
With unbound hair weeps at a funeral pile;
It paints the lover's torments and delights,
A mistress flatters, threatens, and invites;
But well these raptures if you'll make us see,
You must know love as well as poetry.

    I hate those lukewarm authors, whose forced fire
In a cold style describes a hot desire;
That sigh by rule, and, raging in cold blood,
Their sluggish muse whip to an amorous mood.
Their feigned transports appear but flat and vain;
They always sigh, and always hug their chain,
Adore their prisons and their sufferings bless,
Make sense and reason quarrel as they please.
'Twas not of old in this affected tone
That smooth Tibullus made his amorous moan.
Nor Ovid, when, instructed from above,
By nature's rule he taught the art of love.
The heart in elegies forms the discourse.

    The Ode is bolder and has greater force;
Mounting to heaven in her ambitious flight,
Amongst the gods and heroes takes delight;
Of Pisa's wrestlers tells the sinewy force,
And sings the dusty conqueror's glorious course;
To Simois' streams does fierce Achilles bring,
And makes the Ganges bow to Britain's king.
Sometimes she flies like an industrious bee,
And robs the flowers by nature's chemistry,
Describes the shepherd's dances, feasts, and bliss,
And boasts from Phyllis to surprise a kiss,
"When gently she resists with feigned remorse,
That what she grants may seem to be by force."
Her generous style at random oft will part,
And by a brave disorder shows her art.

    Unlike those fearful poets whose cold rime
In all their raptures keeps exactest time;
That sing the illustrious hero's mighty praise—
Lean writers!—by the terms of weeks and days,

And dare not from least circumstances part,
But take all towns by strictest rules of art.
Apollo drives those fops from his abode;
And some have said that once the humorous **god**,
Resolving all such scribblers to confound,
For the short Sonnet ordered this strict bound,
Set rules for the just measure and the time,
The easy running and alternate rime;
But, above all, those licenses denied
Which in these writings the lame sense **supplied**,
Forbade a useless line should find a place,
Or a repeated word appear with grace.
A faultless sonnet, finished thus, would be
Worth tedious volumes of loose poetry.
A hundred scribbling authors, without ground,
Believe they have this only phenix found,
When yet the exactest scarce have two or three,
Among whole tomes, from faults and censure **free;**
The rest, but little read, regarded less,
Are shoveled to the pastry from the press.
Closing the sense within the measured time,
'Tis hard to fit the reason to the rime.
    The Epigram, with little art composed,
Is one good sentence in a distich closed.
These points that by Italians first were prized,
Our ancient authors knew not, or despised;
The vulgar, dazzled with their glaring light,
To their false pleasures quickly they invite;
But public favor so increased their pride,
They overwhelmed Parnassus with their tide.
The Madrigal at first was overcome,
And the proud Sonnet fell by the same doom;
With these grave Tragedy adorned her flights,
And mournful Elegy her funeral rites;
A hero never failed them on the stage,
Without his point a lover durst not rage;
The amorous shepherds took more care to **prove**
True to his point, than faithful to their love.
Each word, like Janus, had a double face,
And prose, as well as verse, allowed it place;
But think not, when your verse and sense are **lame,**
With a dull point to tag your epigram.